## SUBSTANTIVE ACCOUNTABILITY IN EUROPE'S NEW ECONOMIC GOVERNANCE

The EU has become an increasingly powerful economic actor, but we lack research on how EU economic decision-makers can be held to account. This book argues that the EU suffers from important substantive accountability deficits; that is, while numerous procedures exist to hold institutions like the European Commission and European Central Bank (ECB) to account, there are few mechanisms to contest the merit and impact of economic decisions. The book combines detailed empirical research on how accountability practices are evolving across different fields of EU economic governance with a novel conceptual framework to assess where accountability deficits lie and how they might be addressed.

Combining leading research in law and political science, this book will be of interest to scholars with an interest in the questions of accountability and economic governance arising from the budgets, central banks and financial institutions of the EU. This title is also available as Open Access on Cambridge Core.

Mark Dawson is currently the co-editor of the series Cambridge Studies in European Law and Policy and a member of the Editorial Board of the *European Law Review*. He has published two monographs and a textbook with Cambridge University Press, as well as articles in leading journals in law and political science, such as the *Modern Law Review*, *Oxford Journal of Legal Studies*, *Journal of European Public Policy*, *Journal of Common Market Studies* and *Common Market Law Review*.

# Substantive Accountability in Europe's New Economic Governance

Edited by

**MARK DAWSON**
Hertie School

CAMBRIDGE
UNIVERSITY PRESS

CAMBRIDGE
UNIVERSITY PRESS

Shaftesbury Road, Cambridge CB2 8EA, United Kingdom

One Liberty Plaza, 20th Floor, New York, NY 10006, USA

477 Williamstown Road, Port Melbourne, VIC 3207, Australia

314–321, 3rd Floor, Plot 3, Splendor Forum, Jasola District Centre, New Delhi – 110025, India

103 Penang Road, #05–06/07, Visioncrest Commercial, Singapore 238467

Cambridge University Press is part of Cambridge University Press & Assessment, a department of the University of Cambridge.

We share the University's mission to contribute to society through the pursuit of education, learning and research at the highest international levels of excellence.

www.cambridge.org
Information on this title: www.cambridge.org/9781009228831

DOI: 10.1017/9781009228800



When citing this work, please include a reference to the DOI 10.1017/9781009228800

First published 2023

*A catalogue record for this publication is available from the British Library*

*Library of Congress Cataloging-in-Publication Data*
NAMES: Dawson, Mark, 1983– editor.
TITLE: Substantive accountability in Europe's new economic governance / edited by Mark Dawson, Hertie School.
DESCRIPTION: Cambridge, United Kingdom ; New York, NY : Cambridge University Press, 2023. | Includes bibliographical references and index.
IDENTIFIERS: LCCN 2023009632 (print) | LCCN 2023009633 (ebook) | ISBN 9781009228831 (hardback) | ISBN 9781009228800 (ebook)
SUBJECTS: LCSH: Finance, Public – Law and legislation – European Union countries. | Financial institutions – Law and legislation – European Union countries. | Government accountability – European Union countries.
CLASSIFICATION: LCC KJE7050 .S83 2023 (print) | LCC KJE7050 (ebook) | DDC 343.2407–dc23/eng/20230724
LC record available at https://lccn.loc.gov/2023009632
LC ebook record available at https://lccn.loc.gov/2023009633

ISBN 978-1-009-22883-1 Hardback

# Contents

# Contributors

**Adina Akbik** is Assistant Professor of European Politics at the University of Leiden and an affiliate research fellow at the Jacques Delors Centre, Berlin.

**Ana Bobić** is Référendaire to Advocate General Tamara Ćapeta at the Court of Justice of the European Union and an affiliate research fellow at the Jacques Delors Centre, Berlin.

**Mark Dawson** is Professor of European Law and Governance at the Hertie School, Berlin.

**Anuscheh Farahat** is Professor of Public Law, Migration Law and Human Rights at Friedrich-Alexander-University Erlangen-Nürnberg.

**Diane Fromage** is Professor of European Law at the University of Salzburg.

**Matthias Goldmann** is Professor of International Law at the EBS Law School.

**Roy L. Heidelberg** is Associate Professor and Department Chair at Louisiana State University.

**Menelaos Markakis** is Assistant Professor at the Erasmus School of Law. He is also Coordinator, Erasmus Center for Economic and Financial Governance.

**Joana Mendes** is Professor of Comparative Administrative Law at the University of Luxembourg.

**Anastasia Poulou** is a postdoctoral researcher at the Max Planck Institute for Social Law and Social Policy.

**Armin Steinbach** is Jean Monnet Professor of Law and Economics, European Law and International Law at HEC Paris.

**Teresa Violante** is a research fellow at Friedrich-Alexander-Universität Erlangen-Nürnberg and a visiting research fellow at the Max Planck Institute for Comparative Public Law and International Law.

**Tomasz P. Wozniakowski** is Assistant Professor (*adiunkt*) at the Institute of Political Science, University of Wrocław.

# Acknowledgements

This book and its associated research were generously supported by the European Research Council under the EU's Horizon 2020 research and innovation programme (grant agreement no. 716923). The research project upon which this volume was based was conducted at the Jacques Delors Centre of the Hertie School from 2017 to 2022. I am grateful to many people for providing the environment from which this book sprang. Foremost among them are the three wonderful postdoctoral researchers who spearheaded this project and whose work is showcased in this volume: Ana Bobić, Adina Akbik and Tomasz Wozniakowski. Working with these researchers has been one of the most rewarding phases of my academic career, and I am very grateful that they decided to take this important step on their academic journeys with me at Hertie. During the project, we were assisted by a number of research assistants, some of whom directly assisted with this volume. We would like, therefore, to thank Harry McNeill Adams, Elena Bertolini, Theresa Boesl, Evi Kroeker, Francesco Lanzone, Ronan Riordan and Rebecca Segall for their work at various stages of the project. I would like to thank Gabi Bruhl, Nina Shadrina, Markus Jachtenfuchs and the Jacques Delors Centre for providing the intellectual home in which this book was written. I would like to thank my authors for participating in the project and workshop, to begin with, and for their dedication and patience in seeing it to fruition, as well as Bitteschoen.tv for the cover art at the front of the book. Finally, I would like to thank Pierre, Lily and Tristan for their love and patience regarding the time this research project took from them. I hope our readers enjoy the volume.

# Introduction

## *The Accountability Impasse of the EU's New Economic Governance*

*Mark Dawson*[*]

### I.1 IS EMU ACCOUNTABILITY 'IMPOSSIBLE'?[1]

The development of the Economic and Monetary Union (EMU) from the early 1990s onwards has been a landmark change in the trajectory of EU integration. While the internal market has historically been seen as the 'core' of the European Union, EMU has increasingly been at the centre of crucial debates in EU law and politics. It is the area where the EU has built powerful new institutions, such as the Eurogroup and European Central Bank (ECB). It is also the area where core normative principles of the EU order – such as solidarity, equality between Member States and competence conferral – have been contested and fleshed out. It has witnessed enormous changes in the vertical balance of power between the Union and its Member States, in areas ranging from financial supervision to fiscal policy and financial assistance. Finally, it has recently become an area in which the EU may have experienced an important 'constitutional moment', namely the development of a genuine fiscal capacity, funded through debt rather than Member State contributions.[2] If the EU has taken a leap forward in the past three decades, this is where the leap is most apparent.

With greater power, authority and innovation, however, come ever more crucial questions about how this new authority ought to be controlled. Previous leaps forward in integration have generally been accompanied by the parallel development of accountability structures designed to keep newly held

[*] Hertie School, Berlin. This research was supported by the European Research Council under the European Union's Horizon 2020 research and innovation program (grant agreement no. 716923).

[1] Brandsma, Heidbreder and Mastenbroek, 'Accountability in the Post-Lisbon European Union', 82 *International Review of Administrative Sciences* 4 (2016), 621–637, at 624.

[2] Georgiou, 'Europe's "Hamiltonian Moment"? On the Political Uses and Explanatory Usefulness of a Recurrent Historical Comparison', 51 *Economy and Society* 1 (2022), 138–159.

EU powers in check. The early development of the Community was therefore quickly followed by a Court of Justice endowing itself with strong powers of judicial review; the development of the single market was accompanied by a simultaneous growth in the authority of the European Parliament; and the establishment in the 1990s of the EU's 'regulatory state' through agencies and Commission delegation equally saw new means of political control, such as comitology and other forms of regulatory oversight.

In the case of EMU, however, the EU has accrued powers without necessarily developing the parallel institutions needed to hold that power to account. To give one prominent example, while the ECB of the early 2020s has a radically different set of powers to that of the late 1990s – such as new unconventional monetary policy instruments and regulatory authority over all large Eurozone financial institutions – it still relies (with some tweaks) on the same set of basic accountability tools it carried from its inception (e.g. press conferences, limited access to documents and sporadic dialogues with the European Parliament).[3]

We therefore have two phenomena side by side. On the one hand, EMU is an increasingly powerful and important element both of EU and of national politics. EMU has prompted a significant politicization of EU integration, leading to greater contestation of its policies and institutions than ever before.[4] In the wake of the financial crisis, some protesters went so far as to attempt to burn down its central bank.[5] At the national level, numerous euro-sceptic political movements have leveraged dissatisfaction with EU economic policy to successfully challenge establishment parties.[6] On the other hand, EMU does not carry the obvious mechanisms of political responsiveness and accountability to temper or respond to this contestation.

This is so because EMU suffers from all of the classical problems of rendering accountability in an EU setting,[7] while adding a few more complications of its very own. Certainly, it is an example of multi-level governance, with a multitude of responsible actors. This creates enormous difficulties for voters, Courts and political bodies in disentangling who is responsible for what. To take the example of financial assistance, who ultimately determined the conditionality

3 For a (more optimistic) overview, see Fraccaroli, Giovannini and Jamet, 'The Evolution of the ECB's Accountability Practices During the Crisis', *Economic Bulletin Articles* 5 (European Central Bank, 2018).

4 Hutter and Kriesi, 'Politicizing Europe in Times of Crisis', 26 *Journal of European Public Policy* 7 (2019), 996–1017.

5 'Why Europeans are trying to burn down their central bank' (13.04.14), The World Post.

6 Kneuer, 'The Tandem of Populism and Euroscepticism: A Comparative Perspective in the Light of the European Crises', 14 *Contemporary Social Science* 1 (2019), 26–42.

7 Arnull and Wincott (eds.), *Accountability and Legitimacy in the European Union* (Oxford University Press, 2003).

measures responsible for the degradation of social rights in numerous 'bail-out' states in the mid-2010s: the Council, which adopted the measures; the Eurogroup, which determined them; the Member States that implemented them; or the 'expert' institutions, such as the ECB and International Monetary Fund (IMF), which monitored and enforced them?[8] This is but one of numerous problems in 'locating' accountability found across EU governance.

In the specific case of EMU, however, unique problems are thrown into the mix. One is the problem of independence. How can we ensure proper political accountability for institutions, such as the ECB and accompanying agencies, who are unaccountable as a matter of intentional institutional design?[9] A second is the problem of salience. Even if it were legally possible to render full political accountability for bodies like the ECB or European Banking Authority (EBA), do traditional political institutions like the European Parliament or national Parliaments have the ability and incentives to really scrutinize and contest economic decisions? While there may therefore be high political contestation of some EMU policies, many others (of equal long-term importance) carry significant complexity and low political salience, making serious scrutiny by media, politicians and citizens unlikely.[10] The problem of EMU accountability is not just, therefore one of institutional design but one of the correct political incentives.

## I.2 THE SCHOLARLY IMPASSE

How do we square these tensions? The starting point of this volume is that the seeming 'impasse' of EMU accountability is not simply a problem of everyday politics but also a conceptual problem. Scholarship on EMU accountability has also reached an impasse, as is further discussed in the first conceptual chapter of this volume (by Akbik and Dawson). The starting point of the impasse is the difficult question of how to approach accountability in EMU. Existing literature has tried a number of methods with two standing out. The first is a comparative method, for example, comparing the accountability regime of the ECB with other central banks.[11] While this literature has

8 See Violante and Poulou in this volume.

9 Dawson, Maricut-Akbik and Bobić, 'Reconciling Independence and Accountability at the European Central Bank: The False Promise of Proceduralism', 25 *European Law Journal* 1 (2019), 75–93.

10 See Goldmann, Fromage and Akbik in this volume.

11 See, for example, Amtenbrink, *The Democratic Accountability of Central Banks: A Comparative Study of the European Central Bank* (Hart Publishing, 1999); Chang, 'Sui Generis No More? The ECB's Second Decade', 42 *Journal of European Integration* 3 (2020), 311–325.

produced numerous insights – highlighting, for example, the narrowness of the ECB's mandate and its unique independence in comparison to others – it also carries limitations. In simple terms, like is not being compared with like: there is, for example, simply no other central bank operating in the absence of a state setting and with a mandate determined by an international Treaty.

To remedy this problem, a second set of literature tries to build accountability standards within the specific setting of the EU.[12] A logical starting point is the EU Treaties themselves, which carry both a number of general principles (such as those of Article 2) and a number of specific principles guiding the Treaties' economic chapter, for example, the need for the ECB to maintain price stability and for governments in delivering fiscal policies (under Article 119(3) TFEU). This approach also, however, carries severe limitations. One is a problem of clash and indeterminacy. What should we do, for example, when general principles, like solidarity and equality, clash with principles specific to the EMU context, such as price stability and sound finances? A second more intractable problem is whether these standards are justifiable from a normative perspective. Using specific EU law principles to analyse the accountability of EU institutions limits the scope of accountability research by begging the question of whether these principles *themselves* – and the institutional design that results from them – in fact meet basic accountability standards. To make an even bolder claim, the specific principles and institutional design of EMU may be precisely the problem in that the demand for accountability is precisely often a contestation of EMU's design and not just a contestation of the way that design is implemented and carried out.[13]

What we will describe in the first chapter as the impasse between deductive and inductive approaches to EMU accountability thus leaves a framework of accountability research that in our view demands either too little or too much of economic decision-makers. One is left either with national standards – that EU actors cannot realistically meet as they do not operate in the thick democratic setting of the nation-state. *Or*, one is left with EU and EMU-specific standards that economic decision-makers normally can easily meet because their institutions were calibrated to meet them (and which largely overlap with their functional missions). The impasse of a more powerful EMU, without

[12] See, for example, Markakis, *Accountability in the Economic and Monetary Union* (Oxford University Press, 2020); Zilioli, 'The ECB's Powers and Institutional Role in the Financial Crisis: A Confirmation from the Court of Justice of the European Union', 23 *Maastricht Journal of European and Comparative Law* 17 (2016).

[13] For a related argument regarding the OMT jurisprudence of the Court of Justice, see Schepel, 'The Bank, the Bond, and the Bail-out: On the Legal Construction of Market Discipline in the Eurozone', 44 *Journal of Law and Society* 79 (2017).

powerful accountability mechanisms, is therefore in our view matched with an academic literature unable to fully conceptually grasp EMU's accountability deficit.

This diagnosis was the starting point for the larger project on which this volume is founded. The project – 'Taming the Leviathan: Legal and Political Accountability in Post-crisis EU Economic Governance' – was sponsored by the European Research Council and carried out by four researchers, all of which have contributed their work to this volume. A large part of the project's work was empirical, examining the effectiveness of EMU accountability mechanisms in practice. This work – by Ana Bobić examining judicial review;[14] Adina Akbik, the European Parliament;[15] and Tomas Wozniakowski, national Parliaments[16] – empirically testifies to many of the accountability dilemmas mentioned above. The other empirical chapters contained in this volume expand this work yet further, examining other institutions and policy areas not examined by the core research team (thus providing an empirical picture across all of EMU's main fields).

A further goal of the project, however, was to advance the conceptual debate regarding EMU accountability. That debate is represented by a number of chapters in this volume (e.g. those of Heidelberg, Steinbach and Goldmann). Our own work makes two conceptual contributions. The first of these is to think about what accountability is *for* in EMU. As Akbik and Dawson argue, one way of approaching the academic impasse over EMU accountability is to develop a general framework for accountability understood in terms of the underlying normative claims being advanced in accountability research. Such a framework should be applicable to the EU and EMU context but not produced by it (in that it should also be applicable to other economic institutions and policy areas).[17] By examining what accountability is *for*, the framework shifts attention from actors, that is, who is accountable to whom (an often intractable problem in EU accountability research) to norms, that is, what kinds of demands are being made in accountability relations and have they in fact been met?

14 See, for example, Bobić, '(Re) Turning to Solidarity in EU Economic Governance: A Normative Proposal', in *Contesting Austerity: A Socio-Legal Inquiry Into Resistance to Austerity* (Hart, 2021), 115–134.

15 Akbik, *The European Parliament as an Accountability Forum: Overseeing the Economic and Monetary Union* (Cambridge University Press, 2022).

16 Woźniakowski, Maatsch and Miklin, 'Rising to a Challenge? Ten Years of Parliamentary Accountability of the European Semester', 9 *Politics and Governance* 3 (2021), 96–99.

17 See, for example, for an application of the framework to a different field, Dawson, 'The Accountability of Non-governmental Actors in the Digital Sphere: A Theoretical Framework', *European Law Journal* (forthcoming, 2022).

The framework disaggregates accountability into four main normative goods, which are drawn from the general accountability literature. The first – openness – is the demand that public action is open, transparent and contestable. The second – non-arbitrariness – is the use of accountability to place meaningful constraints on public power. The third – effectiveness – is the use of accountability to correct errors and to improve policy performance. The final good – publicness – is the use of accountability to ensure that public actors pursue the common (and not individual or sectional) good. The framework offers, therefore, a means to unpack different accountability claims in order to pinpoint more accurately across the fields and institutions of EMU where accountability deficits lie, and in which form. We have invited our authors to use the framework in this light.

The project and volume's second conceptual contribution is to think about *how* accountability is rendered in EMU. Here, we borrow a distinction from law. As is well known in judicial review, Courts often distinguish between reviewing policy measures procedurally and substantively, that is, they may either restrict themselves to the procedural steps followed by the policy-maker or, alternatively, might consider the legal worth or merit of the decision itself (e.g. whether a given law violates a fundamental right).[18] In our view, this distinction is also informative when considering accountability. Much of EMU's current construction considers accountability in procedural terms. Actors such as the Eurogroup or ECB are routinely therefore probed on *how* they reach their decisions, that is, which information they take into account, who they consult and how transparent they are. Such a procedural form of accountability has clear advantages in the EMU setting. Most notably, asking economic decision-makers to alter the *process* by which they arrive at decisions seems to respect (or at worst, marginally limit) their operational independence.

The politicization of EMU discussed above, however, also suggests both the presence and the need for a second, substantive form of accountability. Here, decision-makers must answer not for how they reached their decisions but for the decisions *themselves*. They are asked to defend the merit, efficiency and justness of their decisions. To give a prominent example, while there is now a debate about the 'greening' of the ECB,[19] at stake in this debate is not just whether the ECB consults environmental non-governmental organisations (NGOs) or releases figures on its environmental impacts. What matters

[18] See, for example, Lenaerts, 'The European Court of Justice and Process-Oriented Review', 31 *Yearbook of European Law* 1 (2012), 3–16.

[19] Ioannidis and Zilioli, 'Climate Change and the Mandate of the ECB: Potential and Limits of Monetary Contribution to European Green Policies', 59 *Common Market Law Review* 2 (2022).

is whether the ECB *should* in fact meet environmental targets *and whether it has done so*.

This latter substantive form of accountability – for precisely the reasons of independence outlined above – is much harder to realize in today's EMU. It is much more scarcely found in the explicit design of accountability institutions (such as the economic and supervisory dialogues, which ask officials to respond to parliamentarians without the possibility of sanction). At the same time, while we lack substantive accountability as a matter of design it is increasingly being asked for, and even demanded, of economic decision-makers. As highlighted in a number of the chapters of this volume (such as those by Akbik, Bobić, Violante and Wozniakowski), the distributive stakes and constitutional justness of economic decisions increasingly drive both important political accountability mechanisms and judicial review, with some of Europe's highest Courts frequently clashing over the standards to which economic decision-makers such as the ECB should be held. EMU's accountability deficit is also therefore a substantive accountability deficit – an inability to properly allow scrutiny of the justness, efficiency and worth of economic decisions (a key argument of the project and book as a whole).

## I.3 THE GOALS AND CHAPTERS OF THIS VOLUME

Accordingly, in the following chapters, authors in different disciplines investigate specific institutional contexts and subareas of the EMU in order to assess EMU accountability as reflected in this framework. Several research questions have guided their investigation. First, constituting the first part of the book, which normative goods and concepts should orient the accountability of trans-national economic decision-makers and should subsequently orient EMU? How in particular do the different normative goods identified in the opening chapter of Akbik and Dawson relate to one another and to related concepts, such as democracy, legitimacy, transparency and the rule of law? Examining the theoretical standards we can use to evaluate accountability – and the extent to which they require re-formulation in the EMU context – constitutes a first objection of our collection.

One perspective, adopted in the chapter of Roy Heidelberg, is to consider accountability as a cross-cutting and political concept, which must be understood well beyond the specific context of the EU. Heidelberg's chapter offers a critical perspective on accountability that finds echo in a number of other contributions. More particularly, Heidelberg questions the often-discussed nexus between accountability and democratic legitimacy. Many chapters assume a complementary relation between the two, that is, that accountability is a normative good because it ultimately serves democratic ends. Heidelberg asks us, however, to think again. We should understand accountability, for him, not as a tool of democratic governance but rather as a technique of bureaucratic control, concerned primarily with facilitating relations between experts rather than building a chain of answerability to the general public. As he puts it, '[U]ltimately, accountability is a practice that formalizes expertise into governing, an idea contrary to the prevailing notion of it as a value that ensures democratic control.'

Heidelberg's re-casting of democratic accountability connects well to a second theoretical chapter, by Armin Steinbach, that focuses on the specific form of accountability developing in EMU (yet which comes to quite different conclusions). Steinbach casts EMU's accountability regime in terms of a continuum between a market form of accountability introduced in the Maastricht settlement to a form of political accountability that is much more prominent in post-crisis EU economic governance. As Steinbach argues, both forms are connected to different ideas of democratic legitimacy: one focused on state sovereignty and market discipline, and the other on the legitimacy of EU institutions themselves, who must take a prominent role in the management of debt and deficits. For Steinbach, both forms are capable of meeting the normative goods of accountability, with market accountability similarly striving towards open financing conditions (openness), limiting unviable and therefore arbitrary fiscal policies (non-arbitrariness) and improving the overall stability of EMU (effectiveness) and its ability to achieve the common European good (publicness). Steinbach's chapter thus illustrates EU economic governance's attempt to re-model the very meaning of democratic accountability. When examining the 'substance' of accountability in EMU, we need to be conscious not just of the traditional accountability relation between public officials but between economic decision-makers and market actors, who may (for good or bad) displace public accountability relationships.

A final theoretical chapter is offered by Mathias Goldmann. Whereas Steinbach's focus is on fiscal policy, Goldmann's is on how we might adapt our understandings of accountability given the design of another crucial area of EMU: banking and financial supervision. The multi-level and regulatory nature of this field presents severe accountability challenges. As Goldmann demonstrates, even the seemingly technical field of banking supervision entails wide discretion, implying a deepened need for political control. The particular features both of the EU legal order (such as the applicable standard of review and preparatory nature of legal acts in Banking Union (BU)) and of the EU's political institutions (such as the limited role of the European Parliament and diverging positions of national Parliaments) leave little space for traditional forms of legal and political accountability. Goldmann's message retains, however, some optimism – precisely the institutional complexity of banking Union also provides greater scope for 'intra-executive accountability' (understood in terms of relations between executive institutions such as the ECB, Commission and European Court of Auditors). Whereas for Heidelberg, accountability is 'impossible', for Steinbach and Goldmann, there remain opportunities to close the accountability gap, so long as the institutions and meaning of democratic accountability are re-thought.

A further set of questions pursued in our volume concern how the normative goods of accountability are delivered in different areas of EMU and via different institutional settings. If we can understand accountability through the distinction between procedural and substantive means of rendering the normative goods of accountability, we require a comparative understanding of where different 'types' of accountability predominate across different fields of EMU. Furthermore, we require a more detailed understanding of how accountability is institutionalized in different settings, particularly through the two main sets of institutions on which we focus: Courts and Parliaments.

The second part of the book thus focuses on one particular variety of accountability – political accountability, understood as accountability to political and majoritarian institutions. This part begins with a chapter by Diane Fromage, in investigating both the legal form and practice of political accountability in the Banking Union (BU). Whereas Goldmann's earlier chapter pointed to the difficulties of operationalizing legal and political scrutiny in this area, Fromage points to a further challenge, namely the differentiated landscape in which the BU has been constructed (partly centred on the EU as such, partly on the Euro area and partly on the specific Member States participating in the Banking Union). This leaves a messy web of accountability relationships that can confuse the question of who is accountable to whom and for what (an example being the annual report of the single supervisory mechanism to the Eurogroup, which does not per se include all BU members and is itself a non-official institution of the Union). Members of the European Parliament (MEPs) thus demonstrate confusion as to whom they must address their questions – the ECB, national authorities, the Commission, the EBA or some other actor? A further problem concerns political salience as discussed above – there exist many accountability 'offers' in terms of ability of MEPs to ask questions of both the Single Resolution Board (SRB) and the supervisory board of the Single Supervisory Mechanism (SSM). The limited political salience of banking issues, and their complexity, however, mean that these offers are not always taken up. Fromage suggests reforms to tackle these gaps, from the ambitious (a Treaty change that would more rigorously legally ground Banking Union and the agencies it contains) to the more realizable in the short term (e.g. a dedicated sub-group of the ECON committee in which MEPs could specialize in this policy field).

Two further chapters in this section focus on one key institution across different areas of the EMU – the Eurogroup. In his chapter, Menalaos Markakis provides a broad overview of the available mechanisms to hold this uniquely powerful institution procedurally and substantively accountable. First, Markakis notes the limited political accountability of the Eurogroup, with the European Parliament carrying an ability to question the Eurogroup President but not meaningfully sanction its activities. This gap is in danger of being worsened by recent case law of the Court of Justice which, by declaring the Eurogroup a non-official EU institution, leaves a legal blackhole with no room for legal review of Eurogroup decisions.[20] This leaves important gaps in legal accountability, for example, when other organs lacking judicial review of their decisions, such as the European Stability Mechanism (ESM), give practical effect to Eurogroup decisions. For Markakis, quasi-legal institutions, such as the European Ombudsman have had more success in closing legal accountability gaps, by gradually prompting the Eurogroup and its preparatory working group to provide greater document access (i.e. to reach at least towards procedural openness).

While Markakis focuses on the available procedures to scrutinize Eurogroup decisions, an equally important question – and one at the centre of our focus on 'substantive accountability' – concerns the uses to which these mechanisms are put. As the chapter of Adina Akbik demonstrates, while one would expect the deficiencies which Markakis outlines to seriously inhibit substantive accountability, the practice of the main mechanism for political accountability of the Eurogroup – the economic dialogue – suggests a more nuanced picture. In spite of procedural and transparency hurdles, the European Parliament has used its regular dialogue with the Eurogroup President to throw a spotlight on substantive deficiencies in EMU (which Akbik demonstrates by categorizing MEP questions according to four accountability 'goods' discussed in Chapter 1). As Akbik shows, while openness and transparency are an important focus for MEPs, so is policy effectiveness, indicating an increasing willingness for parliamentarians to focus on the substantive outcomes of economic decisions. More worryingly, the answers of the Eurogroup President often indicate a reflex to defend and justify existing conduct rather than to re-consider policy

[20] See Joined Cases C-597/18 P, C-598/18 P, C-603/18 P and C-604/18 P, Council v K. Chrysostomides & Co. and Others, Judgment of the Court (Grand Chamber) of 16 December 2020, EU:C:2020:1028.

in response to critical feedback. As she puts it, '[O]verall the economic dialogues with the Eurogroup illustrate a unilateral accountability relationship in which substantive demands from the forum remain unmet by the actor.' Substantive accountability is thus sought but not delivered.

In his chapter, Tomasz Wozniakowski complements the analysis of Akbik and Markakis by adopting a national perspective on political accountability. His chapter thus investigates the accountability of fiscal governance from the perspective of National Parliaments, focusing on the scrutiny of economic decisions at EU level in the context of one crucial process, the European Semester. The chapter's in-depth study focuses on the scrutiny powers of the Polish Parliament. Here too, effectiveness is a main focus, that is, the use of accountability to shine a light on domestic and EU-level economic performance. As the chapter illustrates, however, there is no easy and automatic link between 'accountability as effectiveness' and policy implementation, that is, the fact that Parliaments scrutinize and demand answers regarding the Semester's Country Specific Recommendations (CSRs) seems to carry no obvious link in terms of the seriousness of the domestic government's commitment to actually implementing CSRs. Once again, we seem to have an example of substantive accountability being sought but not delivered, this time in respect of an important non-Eurozone Member State.

The final section of the book focuses on legal accountability, that is, the accountability of economic decision-makers towards Courts and legal institutions. If, as the chapters of the second section generally conclude, substantive political accountability is lacking in EMU, to what extent can legal institutions fill the gap? The section begins with Ana Bobić's chapter on the role of law in delivering accountability goods. One might expect this to be limited: courts are normally entrusted with the narrower task of ensuring the 'legality' of official action not with ensuring their accountability to the wider public. As Bobić's chapter shows, however, the current clashes between national and EU Courts about core features of the EMU are precisely conflicts about how to improve 'substantive' accountability in EMU. At the core, for example, of the German Constitutional Court's objection to the CJEU's appraisal of recent ECB programmes has been what it sees as a deficient standard of review, focused on procedural mechanisms (has the ECB given reasons to justify quantitative easing?) but without any substantive assessment of whether *in substance* these programmes lead to their intended results or carry burdensome effects. There is therefore an accountability conflict within the legal conflict – to whom is the ECB answerable and what does it have to demonstrate to meet its legal duties? If this is so, the conflict between legal institutions need not only be seen in a negative light – as a threat to the unity of the

EU legal order – but as an opportunity for judicial dialogue to improve the overall accountability set-up of EMU. Constitutional conflict, in her words, may be a feature, not a bug (and one able to improve key substantive goods, such as the non-arbitrariness and publicness of ECB action).[21]

Anuscheh Farahat's chapter is also interested in the three-way relationship between law, accountability and political conflict. In Farahat's case, her interest is in the trans-national solidarity conflicts precipitated by the Euro crisis. The increasing inter-dependence of the Euro area, as Farahat shows, dramatically diminishes the political agency of the Member States, making their ability to fight the negative effects of economic crises dependent not just on their own decisions but also those of other Member States on whom they have limited political influence. This leaves the crucial question of whether legal institutions carry the potential to limit the destructive potential of these conflicts. Such legal accountability might be considered as an important factor for two goods highlighted in this chapter – openness, understood as the ability of Courts to force policy-makers to reveal the reasoning behind decisions with cross-border impacts, and publicness, understood as the use of legal procedures to 'clarify in the first place which common goods are legitimate or ought to be considered according to the normative (constitutional) framework'. By examining the jurisprudence of national Courts, Farahat's accounts of the Portuguese and German Courts illustrate the tendency of national Courts to 'nationalize' what are in effect trans-national conflicts. In other words, the effort to ensure substantive legal accountability at the domestic level (e.g. with reference to equality and social rights provisions in the Portuguese Constitution) can cut against allowing it trans-nationally (by securing a legal outcome without reference to European law standards or CJEU guidance). In this pessimistic diagnosis, however, there is an optimistic under-current – the unimpressive contribution of Courts in limiting destructive trans-national conflict is not some deeply embedded structural feature of the EU legal order but rather, as Farahat shows us, often an explicit choice of the relevant legal institutions, that could be adjusted over time. Here, an awakening of national and European Courts to their inter-dependency – the fact that their decisions are inherently inter-connected – is a crucial task (one that Bobić and Farahat share).

While dealing with a different policy field – financial assistance – Teresa Violante's chapter follows the chapter of Fromage in focusing our attention on a different challenge: how the multi-level nature and complexity of EMU

[21] On the broader use of constitutional conflict, see Bobić, *The Jurisprudence of Constitutional Conflict in the European Union* (Oxford University Press, 2022).

can blunt (legal) accountability. In so far as financial assistance in bail-out states was conditional on compliance with terms laid out in a Memorandums of Understanding (MOUs), Violante's chapter demonstrates how the unclear legal foundations of financial assistance created a severe gap in legal accountability, namely a situation where neither national nor EU Courts could be turned to when seeking accountability for bail-out measures violating shared European fundamental rights. The chapter also crucially demonstrates the inter-linkages between the aftermath of the Euro crisis and the other great crisis of legal integration – the rule of law crisis. While, therefore, *Portuguese Judges* has been celebrated as a landmark judgment with respect to the fight against rule of law erosion, in Violante's words, it also established new divides between citizens: 'On the one hand, those that cannot resort to the protection afforded by EU law, that is, the communities that are treated as "deserts" of EU law. On the other, domestic judges, who enjoy not only the national level of protection but also the supranational guarantees, including the EU institutional machinery.' As with Farahat, Violante's chapter thus alters us to the importance (and failures) of legal accountability in addressing the crucial question of 'who is the public', that is, who are the citizens in whose name EU economic decisions are to be made, and who deserve redress when their rights are interfered with? Violante's conclusion based on the Portuguese case is certainly worrying from the perspective of 'substantive accountability' – while she shares Farahat's conclusion that Portuguese Courts nationalized the accountability question, she also points to the limited substantive lens under which the EU Courts analysed austerity measures, considering them in light of the Treaty's economic governance provisions but not via the full range of substantive goals the Treaties seek to protect.

In a second chapter on financial assistance, Anastasia Poulou places as her focus precisely the relation between legal and political accountability. Legal accountability may be particularly important when political accountability is lacking. As she demonstrates, the informal and rushed nature of financial assistance makes this area an important example. Her focus is accountability for human rights violations, primarily before the EU Courts. Human rights litigation therefore tracks the goods of non-arbitrariness and publicness in both their procedural and substantive dimensions. To take non-arbitrariness as an example, litigation has therefore concerned both the procedural steps followed in financial assistance, that is, the presence or otherwise of a human rights impact assessment, and the substantive impact, that is, was there a violation of the right even where procedural accountability was provided?

Poulou's chapter carries here two important arguments. The first concerns two distinct phases in the relationship between the CJEU and the other EU institutions: a first where the Court sees financial assistance as outside the scope of EU law, and a second, where the Court is more willing to bring measures within the scope of the Charter yet adopts a weak standard of review. The effect in both stages from a substantive point of view is the same: applicants are denied accountability, either because assistance is not seen as emerging from an EU source, or because it is seen as a discretionary matter where the Court cannot tie the hands of policy-makers. The second argument is a normative critique. As Poulou argues, loose, procedural forms of judicial review, may be justified in circumstances where policy-makers can demonstrate a robust policy process but not where this is lacking. Poulou therefore makes a robust normative defence of a more substantively ambitious form of legal accountability in particular cases. As she puts it, '[T]he basic principle is that, in order for the courts' judgement in disputed financial assistance cases to be legitimized, judges should assess the observance of the procedural dimension of human rights and, depending on the outcome, calibrate the standard of review on the basis of the substantive dimension of the respective rights accordingly.'

Finally, Joana Mendes completes the legal accountability section by examining a further area of EMU – the monetary policy of the ECB and its review by the EU Courts. This chapter is also closely concerned with the standard of review used by judges. Like Goldmann, Mendes is sceptical of the ability of judicial review to meaningfully limit the discretion of the ECB.[22] Analysing the Bank's 'constitutive powers' in the field of monetary policy, she demonstrates the difficulty both with a limited procedural form of review and the type of full substantive review demanded by the German Constitutional Court in its Public Sector Purchase Programme (PSPP) decision. Whereas the former demands too little of economic decision-makers, the latter demands the use of tools that Courts – with their ability merely to prohibit action or to conduct 'proportionality' analysis – simply lack. Cautious optimism is also, however, a feature of Mendes's chapter: the difficulty of achieving legal accountability through judicial review does not render law meaningless. In spite of the ECB's independence, Mendes points us to the use of the duty to give reasons as a device to structure ECB activity, to oblige economic decision-makers to explain their reasoning and to tie economic decisions more closely to the common good (or in the language of the introductory chapter, to improve the publicness of ECB activity). As Mendes argues in her conclusion, 'the constitutional dimension of the duty to give reasons highlighted here, if developed

[22] See also Goldmann, 'Adjudicating Economics: Central Bank Independence and the Appropriate Standard of Judicial Review', 15 *German Law Journal* 265 (2014).

institutionally, may secure public-interest based executive action understood in substantive terms, even if independence places clear limits to the ability of political accountability to induce substantive policy changes'.

## I.4 TOWARDS SUBSTANTIVE ACCOUNTABILITY

This collection of chapters provides a diverse and complex look into the practice of EMU accountability. In broad terms, it illustrates a system of accountability that is dynamic but also one that is in crisis. Political accountability mechanisms provide an important opportunity for parliamentarians to nudge economic decision-makers but classical problems of the EU's institutional set-up – its multi-level nature and the limited time and political horizons of MEPs and economic institutions – can often render political accountability a formal and administrative exercise. Legal institutions show indications of equally nudging economic decision-makers to improve their accountability practices, as demonstrated for example via the PSPP decision. At the same time, we have many examples of two-step forwards and one-step back – as highlighted by the refusal of the CJEU to fully recognize the Eurogroup's institutional power in *Chrysostomides*. While our chapters do not provide a uniform picture, our initial diagnosis – of an EMU that carries mechanisms of procedural accountability, without providing for accountability 'in substance' seems born out by the chapters.

This leads to a final set of questions the project was interested in, which concerns how our evaluation of EMU accountability should evolve in light of the theoretical concepts we introduce, and the empirical picture gathered through the chapters. If, for example, more substantive accountability in EMU is needed, given its increasingly distributive character, how can this be realistically fostered? How can the pay-offs and trade-offs (in terms of the costs to substantive accountability we have identified) be appropriately balanced? This forward-looking perspective – how to transform and re-build the accountability structure of EMU – constitutes a final objective of the volume.

A number of chapters take up these questions in specific ways. As already discussed, many authors see clarifying legal responsibilities as important. For Fromage, this would require providing a clear legal basis and division of labour between the institutions of the Banking Union. For Farahat and Bobić, it would require greater horizontal dialogue between national Courts, who need to better internalize the impacts of their constitutional jurisprudence on the options available to other states. For others, the work of improving substantive accountability must primarily be born by political institutions: for example, by economic dialogues in which the leaders of institutions like the

Eurogroup commit to engaging in a substantive discussion of the Eurozone's economic priorities with MEPs (a discussion inhibited by the marginal role they provide the European Parliament in setting the Union's economic goals when compared to the 'co-decision' enjoyed in other policy areas).

More broadly, our chapters suggest a need for all those actors engaged in holding economic decision-makers accountable to *prioritize* the substantive dimension of EMU. In simple terms, the EU has shifted decisively in its ambitions in the past decade. One can no longer speak of the Union as a 'regulatory state', where technocratic institutions can make decisions in which all win.[23] Instead, EMU involves distributive choices, in which winners and losers appear. In such a brave new world, accountability can no longer simply be a technical exercise of determining whether decision-makers followed practices of good governance but entails considering the justness of economic policies. Our volume's call for substantive accountability is a call to build an EU accountability structure for EMU within which questions of substantive justness and effectiveness can be posed, debated and answered.

[23] Dawson and Maricut-Akbik, 'Accountability in the EU's Para-regulatory State: The Case of the Economic and Monetary Union', *Regulation & Governance* (early-view, 2021).

# PART I

# (RE)THEORISING ACCOUNTABILITY IN EMU

# 1

# From Procedural to Substantive Accountability in EMU Governance

*Adina Akbik and Mark Dawson*[*]

## 1.1 INTRODUCTION: WHY WE NEED A DIFFERENT PERSPECTIVE ON ACCOUNTABILITY IN THE EMU

The Economic and Monetary Union (EMU) is a major achievement of European integration but also one of its major democratic accountability challenges. No other policy area of the European Union (EU) is as clear about 'who gets what, when, how'[1] as the EMU. No other policy area has laid bare the necessity of controls – political, legal and administrative – over the exercise of power at the EU level as much as the EMU did during the euro crisis.[2] And yet the academic and political debate about democratic accountability in this policy field has reached a stalemate. On the one hand, it is widely acknowledged that the EMU suffers from structural flaws determined by a multi-level system that blurs conventional accountability lines between those who hold political authority in a representative democracy (the citizens) and those who make decisions on their behalf (in this case EU institutions).[3] With respect to economic policy coordination, it remains difficult

[*] This chapter draws upon a theoretical framework developed in Mark Dawson and Adina Maricut-Akbik, 'Procedural vs Substantive Accountability in EMU Governance: Between Payoffs and Trade-offs' (2021) 28 *Journal of European Public Policy* 11, 1707–1726.

[1] Harold Dwight Lasswell, *Politics: Who Gets What, When, How* (Whittlesey House 1936).

[2] Mark Dawson, 'The Legal and Political Accountability Structure of "Post-Crisis" EU Economic Governance' (2015) 53 *Journal of Common Market Studies* 976; Frank Naert, 'The New European Union Economic Governance: What about Accountability?' (2016) 82 *International Review of Administrative Sciences* 638.

[3] This is an adaptation of the 'democratic deficit' argument in the EU: Giandomenico Majone, 'Europe's "Democratic Deficit": The Question of Standards' (1998) 4 *European Law Journal* 5; Andrew Moravcsik, 'In Defence of the "Democratic Deficit": Reassessing Legitimacy in the European Union' (2002) 40 *Journal of Common Market Studies* 603; Andreas Follesdal and Simon Hix, 'Why There Is a Democratic Deficit in the EU: A Response to Majone and Moravcsik' (2006) 44 *Journal of Common Market Studies* 533.

to disentangle the individual responsibility of finance ministers acting collectively in the Eurogroup and the Economic and Financial Affairs Council (ECOFIN), although their members are technically accountable to their respective national parliaments and electorates.[4] The same problem exists when considering decisions made by heads of state and government in the European Council – an institution which has taken a clear leadership role during the euro crisis.[5] The European Parliament (EP) has virtually no control over the intergovernmental institutions, while its legislative oversight of the European Commission in economic governance remains weak.[6] In parallel, the Commission saw its powers expanded during the euro crisis by assuming key responsibilities for the coordination of national budgets through the newly introduced European Semester.[7]

On the monetary union side, the European Central Bank (ECB) has always faced criticism from an accountability perspective because its establishment effectively took monetary policy decisions away from Eurozone Member States and entrusted them to a technocratic institution, which, by several accounts, is the most independent central bank in the world.[8] The expansion of the ECB mandate during the euro crisis has further complicated the situation, adding new accountability deficits with respect to unconventional monetary policies, financial assistance programmes and banking supervision.[9] Last but not least, the Eurozone Member States established in 2012 an intergovernmental organization – the European Stability Mechanism (ESM) – designed to provide financial assistance to countries experiencing sovereign debt problems. Given its status outside EU Treaties, the ESM is subject only to a limited extent to scrutiny by national parliaments and not at all to scrutiny

4 Article 10 TEU.

5 Adina Maricut and Uwe Puetter, 'Deciding on the European Semester: The European Council, the Council and the Enduring Asymmetry between Economic and Social Policy Issues' (2018) 25 *Journal of European Public Policy* 193, 199.

6 Sergio de la Parra, 'The Economic Dialogue: An Effective Accountability Mechanism?' in Luigi Daniele, Pierluigi Simone and Roberto Cisotta (eds.), *Democracy in the EMU in the Aftermath of the Crisis* (Springer International Publishing 2017).

7 Michael W Bauer and Stefan Becker, 'The Unexpected Winner of the Crisis: The European Commission's Strengthened Role in Economic Governance' (2014) 36 *Journal of European Integration* 213.

8 Jakob De Haan and Sylvester CW Eijffinger, 'The Democratic Accountability of the European Central Bank: A Comment on Two Fairy-Tales' (2000) 38 *Journal of Common Market Studies* 394, 396.

9 Mark Dawson, Adina Maricut-Akbik and Ana Bobić, 'Reconciling Independence and Accountability at the European Central Bank: The False Promise of Proceduralism' (2019) 25 *European Law Journal* 75; Diane Fromage and others, 'ECB Independence and Accountability Today: Towards a (Necessary) Redefinition?' (2019) 26 *Maastricht Journal of European and Comparative Law* 3.

by the EP.[10] To sum up, the EMU institutional structure illustrates in many ways the 'impossible accountability thesis' in the EU, according to which democratic accountability is simply incompatible with the EU's multi-level governance model.[11]

On the other hand, scholars have emphasized the need to improve EMU's democratic accountability since its inception.[12] Demands to make the EMU more accountable follow the standard discourse on accountability in modern governance: at the basic level, accountability requires public officials – whether elected or not – to justify their conduct in front of a higher authority;[13] at the next level, accountability ensures the possibility to punish those officials found lacking or allow them to make amends for past failures.[14] An accountability relationship thus involves two parties: an account-giver – henceforth 'the actor' – who can be a person (member of a legislature, executive, bureaucracy) or a public institution, and an account-holder – henceforth 'the forum' – who can also be an individual (a direct superior, a minister, a parliamentarian) or an institution (parliaments, courts, ombudsmen, audit offices).[15] In the policy discourse on accountability, the concept has multiple positive connotations, holding (1) the promise of democracy (by ensuring the answerability and responsiveness of elected officials), (2) the promise of control (through mechanisms designed to oversee executive and administrative action), (3) the promise of justice (through judicial and administrative review of government decisions), and (4) the promise of performance (through target-setting and incentivization of public officials).[16]

10 David Howarth and Aneta Spendzharova, 'Accountability in Post-Crisis Eurozone Governance: The Tricky Case of the European Stability Mechanism' (2019) 57 *Journal of Common Market Studies* 894, 908.

11 Gijs Jan Brandsma, Eva Heidbreder and Ellen Mastenbroek, 'Accountability in the Post-Lisbon European Union' (2016) 82 *International Review of Administrative Sciences* 621, 624.

12 Amy Verdun, 'The Institutional Design of EMU: A Democratic Deficit?' (1998) 18 *Journal of Public Policy* 107.

13 Patricia Day and Rudolf Klein, *Accountabilities: Five Public Services* (Tavistock 1987) 4; Barbara Romzek and Melvin J Dubnick, 'Accountability' in Jay M Shafritz (ed.), *International Encyclopedia of Public Policy and Administration* (Westview Press 1998) 6; Richard Mulgan, '"Accountability": An Ever-Expanding Concept?' (2000) 78 *Public Administration* 555, 555.

14 Robert D Behn, *Rethinking Democratic Accountability* (Brookings Institution Press 2001) 3; Dawn Oliver, *Government in the United Kingdom: The Search for Accountability, Effectiveness, and Citizenship* (Open University Press 1991) 22–28.

15 Mark Bovens, 'Analysing and Assessing Accountability: A Conceptual Framework' (2007) 13 *European Law Journal* 447, 450.

16 The four 'promises of accountability' are borrowed from Melvin J Dubnick, 'Accountability as a Cultural Keyword' in Mark Bovens, Robert E Goodin and Thomas Schillemans (eds.), *The Oxford Handbook Public Accountability* (Oxford University Press 2014) 29.

The problem, however, is that the institutional set-up of the EMU reduces the potential of such promises significantly. For example, in order to address the structural weaknesses of the EP in the EU political system, there is a proposal to institutionalize a subcommittee for Eurozone oversight that would call executive actors to account for their decisions.[17] It is doubtful, however, that such a committee would deliver on the 'promise of democracy', given the well-known disconnect between citizens and EP elections – despite the institutional empowerment of the EP in recent years.[18] In a similar vein, since the ECB mandate can only be altered through a cumbersome treaty change, there is pressure for the institution to narrow the mandate on its own – for instance, by excluding itself from financial assistance conditionality, limiting the purchase of government bonds to avoid redistribution or setting more specific objectives to measure the effectiveness of its banking supervision.[19] To put it differently, given the constraints of the ECB legal framework, the 'promise of control' present in accountability discourse is largely a voluntary exercise – dependent on the ECB's 'willingness for control' by oversight bodies like the EP and national parliaments, the European Ombudsman, the European Court of Auditors (ECA) or the European Anti-Fraud Office.

The mismatch between the structural flaws of EMU accountability and the incremental proposals put forth to reform the system suggests that academic thinking about accountability on the topic is at a stalemate. There is a gap between what is seen as necessary and what is feasible in the EMU governance framework – given the complications of multi-level decision-making within a hybrid institutional constellation of intergovernmental and supranational actors. In this chapter, we identify the cause of the stalemate in the parallel development of deductive and inductive approaches to accountability in the EU. Most deductive approaches typically apply national accountability benchmarks on EMU and subsequently find numerous shortcomings in their institutionalization at the EU level – especially when it comes to the role of parliaments. In contrast, inductive approaches start from the EU's

[17] Michele Chang and Dermot Hodson, 'Reforming the European Parliament's Monetary and Economic Dialogues: Creating Accountability Through a Euro Area Oversight Subcommittee' in Olivier Costa (ed.), *The European Parliament in Times of EU Crisis: Dynamics and Transformations* (Springer International Publishing 2019).

[18] Simon Hix and Bjørn Høyland, 'Empowerment of the European Parliament' (2013) 16 *Annual Review of Political Science* 171, 184.

[19] Paul Dermine, 'Out of the Comfort Zone? The ECB, Financial Assistance, Independence and Accountability' (2019) 26 *Maastricht Journal of European and Comparative Law* 108; Klaus Tuori, 'Has Euro Area Monetary Policy Become Redistribution by Monetary Means? "Unconventional" Monetary Policy as a Hidden Transfer Mechanism' (2016) 22 *European Law Journal* 838; Dawson, Maricut-Akbik and Bobić (n 9) 78.

Treaty framework on EMU and subsequently infer standards of accountable behaviour for different EU institutions. The problem is that the EU cannot meet national benchmarks for accountability, while the principles set in the EU Treaties are too narrow and hence decoupled from generally applicable accountability standards.

To break the stalemate, we propose a new deductive framework for studying accountability more suitable to EMU and the EU setting – which can be applied and drawn upon in subsequent theoretical and empirical chapters within this collection. Drawing on public administration literature, legal scholarship, and liberal and republican thinking in political theory, we develop a normative conceptualization of accountability that seeks to answer a basic question: 'what is accountability good for?' Accordingly, we identify four normative 'goods' of accountability: openness, non-arbitrariness, effectiveness and publicness. We show that existing mechanisms of accountability can address the normative 'goods' in two ways: one centred on the processes through which actors take decisions (procedural accountability) and the other focused on the merit of the decisions themselves (substantive accountability).[20] We argue that there are both pay-offs and trade-offs in choosing one alternative over the other. While procedural accountability brings clarity and predictability for the people involved in the process, it tends to detract from the underlying goals of accountability's four normative goods because it draws public attention away from the policies public officials pursue and their effects *to the procedures by which they do so*. In contrast, substantive accountability is more complex and costly to achieve but has the merit of maintaining the normative ethos of the concept. After analysing various aspects of EMU accountability, we conclude that procedural accountability dominates: a finding that we encourage our authors to critically explore.

The chapter is structured as follows. We begin by explaining the stalemate of the EMU accountability literature, caught between deductive approaches focused on national benchmarks of democratic accountability and inductive approaches emphasizing contrasting interpretations of different principles set by EU Treaties. We show the need for a deductive, normative perspective that is applicable to the EMU without being specific to it. The second section introduces the four normative goods of accountability and describes the possibilities to enforce them in a procedural or substantive way. The third section applies the new conceptualization to examples across the EMU in order to show how political and legal institutions deliver the normative goods

[20] We first developed the distinction in relation to the ECB; see Dawson, Maricut-Akbik and Bobić (n 9) 76.

of accountability procedurally and substantively – with an emphasis on the former. The fourth section highlights the limits of procedural accountability, making an argument against its prevalence in the EMU governance structure. We conclude with a call for both our authors and other scholars to apply the distinction between procedural and substantive accountability to different policy fields and institutions within EMU.

## 1.2 THE STALEMATE OF ACCOUNTABILITY RESEARCH ON EMU: BETWEEN DEDUCTIVE AND INDUCTIVE APPROACHES

To make sense of the accountability literature on EMU, we propose a distinction between deductive and inductive approaches to accountability. The basis of the classification is the reasoning behind accountability assessments: how do scholars judge whether an actor has acted accountably in the EMU? Do they start from general definitions and seek to apply them to specific institutions like the ECB? Or alternatively, do they first examine a given institutional setting, for example, the legal framework of the ECB, and then derive general accountability standards applicable thereof? The distinction between deductive and inductive methods is well known in scientific inquiry. From Aristotle to Francis Bacon to William Whewell, philosophers have discussed two directions of the scientific method: the first begins with general and fundamental principles that are then applied to specific cases (deduction), while the second starts with the specific of what is observed and then moves to general and fundamental principles (induction).[21] Although this chapter focuses on the EMU, the distinction between deductive and inductive approaches applies to accountability research more generally.

In fact, accountability research benefits from the new classification in two ways. First, the distinction between deductive and inductive approaches transcends regular disciplinary boundaries dividing the study of accountability[22] – especially visible between political scientists and legal scholars. Browsing through the relevant academic literature, we can identify deductive and inductive studies which examine all the classic institutional mechanisms of accountability, regardless if they are political (elections, parliamentary

[21] Hanne Andersen and Brian Hepburn, 'Scientific Method' in Edward N Zalta (ed.), *The Stanford Encyclopedia of Philosophy* (Summer 2016, Metaphysics Research Lab, Stanford University 2016) https://plato.stanford.edu/archives/sum2016/entries/scientific-method/ accessed 18 March 2020.

[22] Mark Bovens, Thomas Schillemans and Robert E Goodin, 'Public Accountability' in Mark Bovens, Robert E Goodin and Thomas Schillemans (eds.), *The Oxford Handbook Public Accountability* (Oxford University Press 2014) 6–7.

scrutiny of the executive), legal (judicial review), administrative (investigations by ombudsmen, auditing and anti-fraud offices) or managerial (hierarchy in a bureaucratic organization).[23] Second, the deductive/inductive dichotomy encompasses definitions of accountability that are either normative or descriptive, as distinguished by Mark Bovens.[24] From a normative standpoint, what matters are standards for accountable behaviour, which can be either general (deductive) or specific to a situation (inductive). From a descriptive perspective, the interest is in [the appropriate] institutional mechanisms of accountability, which can be borrowed from other contexts in a comparativist effort (deduction) or inferred on an ad hoc basis from the experience of selected actors (induction). Consequently, deductive or inductive studies can have an explicit normative focus on the accountable behaviour of actors or a more analytical focus on the institutional arrangements of accountability.

In the EMU accountability literature, deductive approaches revolve around two general standards of accountability: ensuring democratic control and preventing abuses of power.[25] This is visible among authors who underline the accumulation of executive power in economic governance after the euro crisis and the necessity to increase the role of parliaments as a countervailing power.[26] While the EP had been marginally involved in economic governance prior to the crisis, national parliaments actually saw their budgetary and fiscal monitoring powers reduced since the institutionalization of the European Semester.[27] The importance of parliaments for democratic accountability is grounded in an understanding of the concept as the counterpart to delegation in the ubiquitous principal–agent model. The logic is straightforward: if 'A is obliged to act in some way on behalf of B', then 'B is empowered … to sanction or reward A for her activities or performance in this capacity'.[28] Transposed to

[23] Ibid., 12. The authors also talk about professional peer review and social accountability mechanisms, but they cannot be considered part of the 'classic' accountability toolbox.

[24] Mark Bovens, 'Two Concepts of Accountability: Accountability as a Virtue and as a Mechanism' (2010) 33 *West European Politics* 946.

[25] Bovens (n 15) 462.

[26] Ben Crum, 'Parliamentary Accountability in Multilevel Governance: What Role for Parliaments in Post-Crisis EU Economic Governance?' (2018) 25 *Journal of European Public Policy* 268; Deirdre Curtin, 'Challenging Executive Dominance in European Democracy: Challenging Executive Dominance in European Democracy' (2014) 77 *The Modern Law Review* 1, 3.

[27] Katrin Auel and Oliver Höing, 'National Parliaments and the Eurozone Crisis: Taking Ownership in Difficult Times?' (2015) 38 *West European Politics* 375; Mette Buskjær Rasmussen, 'Accountability Challenges in EU Economic Governance? Parliamentary Scrutiny of the European Semester' (2018) 40 *Journal of European Integration* 341.

[28] James D Fearon, 'Electoral Accountability and the Control of Politicians: Selecting Good Types versus Sanctioning Poor Performance' in Adam Przeworski, Susan C Stokes and Bernard Manin (eds.), *Democracy, Accountability, and Representation* (Cambridge University Press 1999) 55.

the EU level, what is required is to (re-)build the democratic accountability chain from voters to elected representatives but especially from elected representatives to executive actors.[29] Parliaments are thus crucial in closing the gap between citizens as the ultimate principals of economic decisions and various executive agents such as the European Council, the Council or the Commission. Accordingly, scholars argue that the EMU could improve its democratic accountability credentials by empowering the EP[30] and national parliaments[31] in terms of both decision-making and legislative oversight of executive actors. Despite having different analytical foci, these studies share an implicit normative assumption that *parliamentary involvement in economic governance can help Member States – and hence the EU – 'meet their legitimacy obligations to their own publics'*.[32]

In monetary affairs, deductive studies focus on 'preventing the development of concentrations of power' and ensuring an appropriate system of checks and balances of the ECB.[33] The emphasis here is different because the ECB is a non-majoritarian institution whose need for independence from electoral competition has been one of the cornerstones of the EMU since its creation (Article 130 TFEU). The EP is thus often cited as an 'accountability forum' and not the principal of the ECB in monetary policy and banking supervision; consequently, the ECB 'owes' the EP transparency and justification of decisions but not obedience or even political responsiveness.[34] Conversely,

29 Kaare Strøm, 'Delegation and Accountability in Parliamentary Democracies' (2000) 37 *European Journal of Political Research* 261, 267.

30 On the EP, see Berthold Rittberger, 'Integration without Representation? The European Parliament and the Reform of Economic Governance in the EU' (2014) 52 *Journal of Common Market Studies* 1174; Diane Fromage, 'The European Parliament in the Post-Crisis Era: An Institution Empowered on Paper Only?' (2018) 40 *Journal of European Integration* 281; Cristina Fasone, 'European Economic Governance and Parliamentary Representation. What Place for the European Parliament?' (2014) 20 *European Law Journal* 164.

31 On national parliaments, see Aleksandra Maatsch, 'Effectiveness of the European Semester: Explaining Domestic Consent and Contestation' (2017) 70 *Parliamentary Affairs* 691; Davor Jančić, 'National Parliaments and EU Fiscal Integration' (2016) 22 *European Law Journal* 225; Mark Hallerberg, Benedicta Marzinotto and Guntram B Wolff, 'Explaining the Evolving Role of National Parliaments under the European Semester' (2018) 25 *Journal of European Public Policy* 250.

32 Christopher Lord, 'How Can Parliaments Contribute to the Legitimacy of the European Semester?' (2017) 70 *Parliamentary Affairs* 673, 676.

33 Bovens (n 15) 466.

34 Fabian Amtenbrink and Kees van Duin, 'The European Central Bank Before the European Parliament: Theory and Practice After Ten Years of Monetary Dialogue' (2009) 34 *European Law Review* 561; Stefan Collignon and Sebastian Diessner, 'The ECB's Monetary Dialogue with the European Parliament: Efficiency and Accountability during the Euro Crisis?' (2016) 54 *Journal of Common Market Studies* 1296; Adina Maricut-Akbik, 'Contesting the European Central Bank in Banking Supervision: Accountability in Practice at the European Parliament'

the importance of preventing abuses of power is much stronger in the area of legal accountability, that is, judicial review of ECB decisions by national and EU courts.[35] In legal accountability, deductive and inductive approaches are sometimes intertwined, as courts apply the general standard of 'curtailing the abuse of executive power' in reference to existing regulations.[36] A combination of deductive and inductive approaches can be found for instance in the work of Markakis, who examines the accountability of the ECB in relation to the price stability objective prescribed in Article 127(1) TFEU.[37]

Conversely, studies that are 'purely' inductive use the EMU legal and institutional architecture as the starting point for evaluating accountability. A clear example is offered by case-law analyses of ECB or ESM instruments. In this category, scholars do not apply an overarching accountability definition in order to evaluate judicial decisions; conversely, they selectively employ the Treaty framework in order to identify specific features, for example, the independence of the ECB, which are then connected to different headings and degrees of judicial review, for example, the duty to state reasons as displayed in *Gauweiler*.[38] As a result, there is room for contrasting interpretations of the stringency with which the Court of Justice of the European Union (CJEU) should uphold different Treaty principles. For instance, with respect to the ECB, the introduction of the first unconventional monetary instrument – the Outright Monetary Transactions (OMT, 2012) – divided lawyers on the question of the violation of the Treaty's 'no-bailout' clause[39] and the extent to which national courts and the CJEU should intervene to hold the ECB accountable for potentially acting *ultra vires*.[40] The 'no-bailout' clause had also featured

[2020] *Journal of Common Market Studies* https://onlinelibrary.wiley.com/doi/abs/10.1111/jcms.13024 accessed 4 March 2020; Menelaos Markakis, *Accountability in the Economic and Monetary Union: Foundations, Policy, and Governance* (Oxford University Press 2020).

35 Dawson, Maricut-Akbik and Bobić (n 9); Marco Goldoni, 'The Limits of Legal Accountability of the European Central Bank' (2017) 24 *George Mason Law Review* 595.

36 Bovens (n 15) 466.

37 Markakis (n 40).

38 Case C-62/14, *Peter Gauweiler et al. v Deutscher Bundestag*, EU:C:2015:400.

39 Article 125 TFEU.

40 Vestert Borger, 'Outright Monetary Transactions and the Stability Mandate of the ECB: Gauweiler' (2016) 53 *Common Market Law Review* 139; Matthias Goldmann, 'Adjudicating Economics: Central Bank Independence and the Appropriate Standard of Judicial Review' (2014) 15 *German Law Journal* 265; Heiko Sauer, 'Doubtful It Stood: Competence and Power in European Monetary and Constitutional Law in the Aftermath of the CJEU's OMT Judgment' (2015) 16 *German Law Journal* 971; Takis Tridimas and Napoleon Xanthoulis, 'A Legal Analysis of the Gauweiler Case: Between Monetary Policy and Constitutional Conflict' (2016) 23 *Maastricht Journal of European & Comparative Law* 1; Chiara Zilioli, 'The ECB's Powers and Institutional Role in the Financial Crisis: A Confirmation from the Court of Justice of the European Union' (2016) 23 *Maastricht Journal of European and Comparative Law* 171.

in *Pringle*[41] in relation to the establishment of the ESM, which similarly divided scholars on whether courts should interpret Treaty articles in light of background teleological expectations about current political circumstances.[42] In this context, several scholars emphasized the deferential approach of the CJEU towards EMU executive actors, as judicial decisions failed to question if austerity was indeed demanded by 'the logic of the market',[43] or whether the instruments adopted during the euro crisis were substantively justified by 'a logic of emergency'.[44] Regardless of whether studies criticize or endorse court decisions on the EMU, the inductive approach to evaluating accountability is obvious – as the benchmarks for accountable behaviour are derived from specific features of the EU Treaties.

Another variant of inductive studies examines the normative peculiarities of EMU governance. In a recent article further developed in this volume, Steinbach argued that the 'normative choice for accountability' in the EMU need not be democratic in the principal–agent sense of empowering political institutions (especially parliaments); conversely, EU economic governance has created an accountability regime of its own, subject to the judgement of the market.[45] According to Steinbach, the orientation towards the market is institutionalized in the EU Treaties, which highlight the Union's commitment to create 'an open market economy with free competition'.[46] Moreover, the emphasis on the 'free market' is seen as a constitutional norm which 'implies the absence of state intervention in the market-based price determination process'.[47] Accordingly, states and private actors in the EMU are/should be accountable to markets rather than attempt to create a political accountability regime in a flawed democratic system. In fact, Steinbach sees current criticism of EMU accountability as the result of attempting to substitute economic accountability with political accountability, for example, in

41 Case C-370/12, *Pringle v. Ireland*, ECLI:EU:C:2012:756.

42 See the exchange between Paul Craig and Gunnar Beck: Paul Craig, 'Pringle: Legal Reasoning, Text, Purpose and Teleology' (2013) 20 *Maastricht Journal of European and Comparative Law* 3; Gunnar Beck, 'The Legal Reasoning of the Court of Justice and the Euro Crisis – The Flexibility of the Court's Cumulative Approach and the Pringle Case' (2013) 20 *Maastricht Journal of European and Comparative Law* 635; Paul Craig, 'Pringle and the Nature of Legal Reasoning' (2014) *Maastricht Journal of European and Comparative Law*.

43 Harm Schepel, 'The Bank, the Bond, and the Bail-out: On the Legal Construction of Market Discipline in the Eurozone' (2017) 44 *Journal of Law and Society* 79.

44 Goldoni (n 41) 615.

45 Armin Steinbach, 'EU Economic Governance after the Crisis: Revisiting the Accountability Shift in EU Economic Governance' (2019) 26 *Journal of European Public Policy* 1354, 1357–1358.

46 Article 119(1–2), Article 120, Article 127(1) TFEU.

47 Steinbach (n 57) 1359.

financial assistance when creditor states and EU institutions have taken over the position of accountability forum from the market.[48] The issue is whether accountability to the market is normatively justifiable in a democratic system; after all, the belief that the market will hold actors accountable 'just the right amount' is rooted in ordoliberal assumptions of political economy that have been seriously challenged since the crisis.[49] As a recent study by the ECB acknowledges in relation to fiscal requirements for price stability, a certain paradigm of political economy 'became constitutional law in Europe before the economics profession could even prove [its] value'.[50]

Overall, the point of this review is to show that there are problems with both deductive and inductive approaches to EMU accountability. First, deductive studies drawing on principal–agent theory are stuck in a vision of accountability designed for the nation-state that is simply unattainable in the specific institutional setting of EMU governance. National parliaments and the EP are important accountability forums, but they cannot be expected to deliver in the same way as legislatures within national democratic systems of government. In the EMU, the delegation chain from voters to elected representatives to executive actors is either short-circuited (in the case of the EP) or too tortuous to function properly (in the case of national parliaments). In contrast, inductive studies display different problems, namely the replacement of general accountability standards with situation-specific benchmarks assessing the performance of an actor in a given setting. In EMU, the EU Treaties constitutionalize certain principles (like the 'no-bailout clause' or the 'free-market orientation') that remain open to political contestation and ordinary decision-making domestically.[51] One of the difficulties of this constitutionalization is that EU institutions can be held accountable for the extent to which their decisions comply with Treaty principles but not for the principles themselves. Political accountability, however, may concern the overall principles governing EMU (a level of contestation that inductive studies – as they are oriented by these principles themselves – cannot capture). Normative standards of accountability should be broader than policy-specific benchmarks for holding actors accountable in a particular context. We introduce such an approach in the next section in relation to the EU setting.

48 Ibid., 1368.

49 Magnus Ryner, 'Europe's Ordoliberal Iron Cage: Critical Political Economy, the Euro Area Crisis and Its Management' (2015) 22 *Journal of European Public Policy* 275.

50 Massimo Rostagno and others, 'A Tale of Two Decades: The ECB's Monetary Policy at 20' (2019) *ECB Working Paper Series* No 2346 52 www.ecb.europa.eu/pub/pdf/scpwps/ecb.wp2346~dd78042370.en.pdf accessed 20 March 2020.

51 Dieter Grimm, *The Constitution of European Democracy* (Oxford University Press 2017).

## 1.3 THE FOUR NORMATIVE GOODS OF ACCOUNTABILITY IN MODERN GOVERNANCE

The objective to conceptualize accountability beyond the nation-state is usually associated with global politics.[52] In this context, Michael Goodhart has observed that all approaches to global accountability share a similar understanding of the term, namely the 'question of making those who wield power answerable to the appropriate people'.[53] In his view, this standard definition is based on a Westphalian notion of the state that is unworkable in world politics. In the EU, the absence of a European *demos* and the resilience of national *demoi*[54] implies that accountability cannot be organized around the 'appropriate' forum because this is simply not feasible in a large-scale political unit where citizens have few opportunities to influence governing decisions.[55] In this context, Goodhart proposes to shift our thinking about accountability 'from *who* is entitled to hold power to account to the reasons *why* accountability is justified in democratic theory'.[56] His interest is in the nexus between democracy and human rights, linking accountability to emancipatory human rights norms that 'constrain the exercise of power and enable meaningful political agency' in the global arena.[57] We agree with Goodhart that the conceptualization of accountability beyond the nation-state must include normative standards for holding power to account. However, we believe that focusing on human rights reduces accountability to the role of an instrument necessary to achieve other democratic objectives rather than giving it credit as a democratic goal in itself. Accordingly, we hold that any meaningful conception of accountability must begin with an understanding of the normative goods to which accountability is aimed. Drawing on liberal and republican thinking from political theory and the broader public administration literature, we distinguish between four such goods.[58]

The first good is openness. Liberal thinkers from Bentham onwards have long argued that public confidence in official action is likely to be

[52] See, for example, Ruth W Grant and Robert O Keohane, 'Accountability and Abuses of Power in World Politics' (2005) 99 *American Political Science Review* 29.

[53] Michael Goodhart, 'Democratic Accountability in Global Politics: Norms, Not Agents' (2011) 73 *The Journal of Politics* 45, 45.

[54] Kalypso Nicolaïdis, 'European Democracy and Its Crisis' (2013) 51 *Journal of Common Market Studies* 351.

[55] Robert A Dahl, 'Can International Organizations Be Democratic? A Skeptic's View' in Casiano Hacker-Cordón and Ian Shapiro (eds.), *Democracy's Edges* (Cambridge University Press 1999).

[56] Goodhart (n 66) 51.

[57] Ibid., 52.

[58] For a similar attempt, with some diverging categories, see Dubnick (n 16); Bovens (n 15) 462–464.

increased where public policy is conducted under the public gaze (what he termed 'publicity').[59] The openness of public policy has thus been linked to a number of public goods, such as the avoidance of corruption,[60] the improvement of public knowledge and the republican demand that free citizens should enjoy 'non-domination' through the ability to question and contest official action.[61] We might therefore want accountability because we see it as a device to ensure that public action is open, transparent and contestable.

The second such good is non-arbitrariness. There is a deep tradition in accountability research of tying accountability to notions of principal–agent theory in which accountability is a device for (political) principles to control (administrative) agents to whom they have delegated powers.[62] This is a narrower instance of a broader accountability good, namely that those who wield public power should do so in a limited manner and that they should exercise coercion only to the degree necessary to achieve their goals.[63] Non-arbitrariness is also therefore linked to more general limits on public action such as human rights or due process guarantees that seek to regulate the relationship between the individual and the state.[64] Accountability – by making officials answer for conduct – provides a means by which arbitrary distinctions or applications of power can be identified and later remedied.

The third good which accountability seeks to render concerns effectiveness. While openness and non-arbitrariness seem highly normative values, accountability may be sought for more utilitarian reasons, namely that accountable officials are more likely to deliver high-quality services. From this perspective, accountability holds the promise of performance.[65] By making an official answer for their conduct, and by offering the possibility to correct potential errors, accountability is a mechanism to improve the efficacy and

59 Jeremy Bentham, 'Of Publicity' in Michael James, Cyprian Blamires and Catherine Pease-Watkin (eds.), *The Collected Works of Jeremy Bentham: Political Tactics* (Oxford University Press 1999).

60 Ivar Kolstad and Arne Wiig, 'Is Transparency the Key to Reducing Corruption in Resource-Rich Countries?' (2009) 37 *World Development* 521.

61 Roy L Heidelberg, 'Political Accountability and Spaces of Contestation' (2017) 49 *Administration & Society* 1379.

62 See, for example, Fearon (n 29).

63 In political theory, the importance to constrain arbitrariness is a key pillar in civic republicanism; see Philip Pettit, *Republicanism: A Theory of Freedom and Government* (Oxford University Press 1997) 55.

64 TRS Allan, 'Accountability to Law' in Nicholas Bamforth and Peter Leyland (eds.), *Accountability in the Contemporary Constitution* (Oxford University Press 2013) 77.

65 Melvin J Dubnick, 'Accountability and the Promise of Performance: In Search of the Mechanisms' (2005) 28 *Public Performance & Management Review* 376, 377.

responsiveness of public policy.[66] Here, the premise is that the need to justify and even correct conduct will likely improve, and encourage reflection upon, the design of policy-making or implementation.

The final such good is one of publicness or that official action should be oriented towards the common good (and therefore justified by public or universal reasons).[67] This involves demonstrating both that officials were not personally enriched and that their decisions are fairly balanced, taking into account different societal interests and perspectives. Once again, accountability is a key device for ensuring the publicness of official action in this sense – when parliamentarians scrutinize government agencies, or courts conduct judicial review, a key demand is that actors show how their activities forwarded the national or collective interest (with different accountability forums likely to disagree on what a fair balancing of societal interests would entail).[68] Accountability is thus a device to advance the normative good of public policy grounded in the *public* interest.

Having established the normative goods of accountability, the question is how they can be delivered in practice. Our proposal is to distinguish between procedural and substantive ways of providing the four normative goods of accountability. To put it simply, actors are procedurally accountable if they can demonstrate that *the processes or steps they followed in performing their tasks* were open, limited (non-arbitrary), effective and/or public. By contrast, actors are substantively accountable if they can demonstrate *that the decisions themselves or the outcomes to which they led* were open, limited, effective and public. We further explain the distinction below.

## 1.4 PROVIDING ACCOUNTABILITY GOODS: PROCEDURAL VERSUS SUBSTANTIVE WAYS

How can accountability be procedural, and how can it be substantive? The simplest way of understanding the distinction is through the categories of public law.[69] In this context, judges often distinguish between reviewing parliamentary acts on procedural or on substantive grounds.[70] When conducting

66 William F West, 'Formal Procedures, Informal Processes, Accountability, and Responsiveness in Bureaucratic Policy Making: An Institutional Policy Analysis' (2004) 64 *Public Administration Review* 66.

67 Jeremy Waldron, 'Accountability and Insolence' *Political Theory* (Harvard University Press, 2016).

68 Oliver (n 14) 28.

69 See, for example, Darren Harvey, 'Towards Process-Oriented Proportionality Review in The European Union' (2017) 23 *European Public Law* 93.

70 Colm O'Cinneide, 'Legal Accountability and Social Justice' in Nicholas Bamforth, Peter Leyland (eds.), *Accountability in the Contemporary Constitution* (Oxford University Press, 2013) 392.

a procedural review, a judge will enquire into the robustness of the process through which a parliamentary act was adopted.[71] When conducting a substantive review, what is important is not the process of adopting an act but its substantive provisions per se and their likely impact. To give an example, if a Court is enquiring whether a statute setting out minimum requirements for religious schools infringes the right to freedom of religion, it might assess the infringement either procedurally (did Parliament consider the impact of the bill on freedom of religion, or incorporate the views of religious minorities, when adopting it?) or substantively (is the statute likely to infringe religious freedom, or is it in fact neutral vis-à-vis different systems of belief?).

If we transport this distinction to the world of accountability, procedural accountability suggests an accountability relation oriented around the process by which a particular decision was rendered. If we are holding an actor to account procedurally, we are calling them to account for, and justify, the procedural steps they undertook in forming or executing a policy decision. If we are holding an actor to account substantively, by contrast, we are calling them to account for and justify *the substantive worth of the policy decision itself*. Thus, a parliamentary committee examining the implementation of the bill above might also seek to hold a school inspectorate either procedurally or substantively accountable. Procedurally, they might ask how often religious schools had been inspected or how parents of religious minorities had been consulted in drawing up guidelines for inspection. By asking such procedural questions, the committee is not calling into question the substantive worth of the inspectorate's decisions but confining itself to examining the steps the inspectorate took to fulfil its mandate.

Parliamentarians might also seek, however, to hold the inspectorate substantively accountable – did the implementation of the statute achieve the goals (e.g. of improving school standards) it originally sought, or why did the inspectorate choose to prioritize the inspection of one set of schools or one aspect of the school curriculum over another? In the latter case, what is at issue is not the *form* of decision-making but its *substance*, that is, did the actor being held accountable make substantively worthwhile, just or efficient decisions? The official is thus being held accountable against a substantive rather than procedural benchmark: they are being asked to explain and justify the *worth* of their action.

From a conceptual perspective, process is either unimportant or instrumental in this case – the inspectorate could be judged by parliamentarians to have

71 Koen Lenaerts, 'The European Court of Justice and Process-Oriented Review' (2012) 31 *Yearbook of European Law* 3.

implemented the statute justly or effectively even in circumstances where the procedure by which they had done so was inadequate just as the inspectorate could demonstrate a robust, transparent and inclusive procedure *yet still* be seen by parliamentarians as substantively failing to adequately explain the correctness or efficacy of their decisions. In simple terms, the two 'forms' of accountability carry different lenses through which to understand whether accountability has been adequately rendered.

The notions of procedural and substantive accountability overlap to a certain extent with the distinction between process and outcome accountability found in social psychology.[72] The interest there is in the micro-behaviour of individuals and how they respond to different types of evaluation standards set by accountability forums, which can focus on processes or outcomes. In contrast, we take a macro-level approach and discuss the abstract forms (procedural or substantive) through which the normative goods of accountability can be delivered in practice. Our concept of accountability is therefore not relative to a specific accountability forum, but it is centred on general democratic 'goods' considered inherent in the term. For the purposes of illustration, these are applied to the EMU context in the next section. The purpose of the edited collection is to expand and apply these goods in a manner more comprehensive than this schematic overview can provide.

## 1.5 PROCEDURAL AND SUBSTANTIVE ACCOUNTABILITY IN THE EMU

The four normative goods of accountability can be identified across the EMU governance architecture. The examples below focus on diverse cases that are 'representative in the minimal sense of representing the full variation of the population'.[73] The purpose is to show the predominance of procedural ways of providing the normative goods of accountability in the EMU.

Let us start with the first good – openness. Transparency has been for decades a key concern of accountability research.[74] Most importantly, however, transparency seems a good that can be fulfilled without a demand for substantive justification. An official can therefore satisfy the demand for openness

72 Shefali V Patil, Ferdinand Vieider and Philip E Tetlock, 'Process Versus Outcome Accountability' in Mark Bovens, Robert E Goodin and Thomas Schillemans (eds.), *The Oxford Handbook of Public Accountability* (Oxford University Press 2014).

73 Jason Seawright and John Gerring, 'Case Selection Techniques in Case Study Research: A Menu of Qualitative and Quantitative Options' (2008) 61 *Political Research Quarterly* 294, 297.

74 Christopher Hood, 'Accountability and Transparency: Siamese Twins, Matching Parts, Awkward Couple?' (2010) 33 *West European Politics* 989.

procedurally by providing the public with information and documents on a regular basis. In this scenario, the task of accountability forums, such as parliaments, auditors or courts, is to enquire into the procedures by which citizens can access official information and to demand reform if these procedures are found wanting. Many accountability requests in the field of EU economic governance are of this nature. To take a specific example from banking supervision, the largest number of questions asked by Members of the European Parliament (MEPs) to the ECB are requests for information, seeking to address information asymmetries between the two institutions.[75] Keeping in mind that 'transparency is a necessary but insufficient condition for accountability',[76] it would make sense for MEPs to first ask for information before acting on it substantively. But when political accountability does not move beyond transparency requests, the value of openness remains procedural.

The value of openness can also, however, be met substantively. The test of substantive openness is not the de jure but the de facto openness of official action. To be substantively open, an official must not simply provide information, or demonstrate transparent procedures, but provide information in a sufficiently relevant and timely way that it is *likely to be used* by accountability forums, such as parliaments, courts or citizens.[77] The test of substantive accountability is thus one of whether official action *is in fact* regularly probed and contested. This establishes an obligation on accountability forums too, namely that they utilize their information rights to understand policy decisions and to make clear to the public the substantive choices, including the achievements and errors, of public actors. To return to the example above, the key difficulty in the parliamentary accountability of the ECB is not only the availability of information but its volume and complexity.[78] MEPs simply do not have the expertise to identify the most relevant or salient questions that would allow them to substantively challenge ECB decisions.[79] *Substantive openness* often requires additional resources, raising difficult questions about who should bear its costs.

The second good – non-arbitrariness – also carries procedural and substantive elements. Procedurally, public actors are commonly bound by statutes or other rules which specify their substantive mission. When adopting legislation,

75 Maricut-Akbik (n 40) 9.

76 Deirdre Curtin, '"Accountable Independence" of the European Central Bank: Seeing the Logics of Transparency' (2017) 23 *European Law Journal* 28, 43.

77 Heidi Kitrosser, *Reclaiming Accountability: Transparency, Executive Power, and the U.S. Constitution* (University of Chicago Press 2015) 16.

78 Curtin (n 89) 33.

79 Maricut-Akbik (n 40).

or making specific decisions, officials are commonly under a duty to explain why particular decisions are necessary to fulfil their mandate (which may be subject to judicial review).[80] Similarly, public institutions may adopt procedures to 'mainstream' rights-based limitations into their policy-making, that is, to conduct impact assessments or other exercises by which officials may demonstrate that human rights have been taken into account.[81] Here, arbitrariness is limited procedurally in the sense that public actors bind themselves via process-based limits on their action; subsequently, accountability forums such as courts and parliaments are able to verify these limits; for example, was a rights-based impact assessment conducted? To provide an example from the EMU, the Commission committed, as part of the Juncker Commission's promise to improve the EMU's social dimension, to produce social impact assessments to assess and minimize detrimental social rights implications of future EU financial assistance. Such an assessment was conducted in relation to the third Greek bailout.[82]

Substantively, however, non-arbitrariness carries a higher bar. As with openness, the important element is whether public action was de facto limited and non-arbitrary. This would require not only that actors are bound by limits but that they demonstrate how limits *constrained* their activities. Non-arbitrariness also concerns whether a given policy arbitrarily discriminates against a given group in society or infringes an individual's rights. From the perspective of an accountability forum, the key question would be whether a particular group in society or (for a judge) a core autonomy right is disadvantaged by virtue of how a policy has been designed. To return to the definition of the procedural/substantive distinction of the previous section, the existence of a procedure to mainstream human rights considerations within an institution would not fulfil this requirement if the outcome of such mainstreaming violated a core right. To continue the example of financial assistance, while the Commission indeed conducted a social impact assessment for the third Greek bailout, academic commentary on this assessment has been highly critical.[83] These

80 Carol Harlow, 'Global Administrative Law: The Quest for Principles and Values' (2006) 17 *European Journal of International Law* 187.

81 Christopher McCrudden, 'Mainstreaming and Human Rights' in Colin Harvey (ed.), *Human Rights in the Community: Rights as Agents for Change* (Hart Publishing 2005).

82 European Commission, 'Assessment of the Social Impact of the New Stability Support Programme for Greece' (*Commission Staff Working Document SWD(2015) 162 final*, 2015) https://ec.europa.eu/info/sites/info/files/ecfin_assessment_social_impact_en.pdf accessed 20 March 2020.

83 Mark Dawson, *The Governance of EU Fundamental Rights* (Cambridge University Press 2017) 213; Paul Copeland, *Governance and the European Social Dimension: Politics, Power and the Social Deficit in a Post-2010 EU* (Routledge 2020).

criticisms range from the inadequacy of the assessment to the question of how it actually fed into policy-making (with no indication that it led to any meaningful changes in how the stability programme for Greece was designed or implemented). The key test for substantive accountability as non-arbitrariness is thus whether policy choices in EMU plausibly aimed for and achieved non-arbitrary results.

The third accountability good, effectiveness, would seem to be inherently substantive in nature – as it concerns whether planned policies resulted in particular outcomes. Nevertheless, the 'explosion' of auditing in the 1990s as a means to control the government suggests that effectiveness can also be implemented in a limited procedural way.[84] In 2016, the ECA evaluated the operational performance of the Single Supervisory Mechanism (SSM) and the role of the ECB thereof.[85] The evaluation report included a section on the 'difficulty in obtaining audit evidence', as the ECA officially complained that the ECB provided the auditing team 'very little' of the information required.[86] The ECB was given the chance to respond to the report, emphasizing its different understanding of 'sufficient information' for auditing purposes. Specifically, the ECB claimed that 'all audit evidence covered by the Court's mandate to audit the "operational efficiency of the management of the ECB" had been provided' and that any exception concerned documents that were not related to the SSM's operational efficiency.[87]

The problem here concerns the legal limits imposed on auditing the ECB's substantive effectiveness by the ECA. According to EU primary law, the ECA has 'full power to examine all books and accounts of the ECB' but only with respect to examining the 'operational efficiency of the management of the ECB' (Article 27, Protocol no. 4 TFEU). The conflict between the two institutions regarding the SSM report reflects the different interpretations of 'operational efficiency' and the substantive need for information to make such an assessment. In the absence of said information, the ECA's report was reduced to evaluating procedural aspects such as staffing, for example, whether on-site inspections of banks should be run by ECB staff as opposed to representatives of national supervisors.[88] Despite these legal limitations, the ECA clearly understood the value of substantive effectiveness, as the report recommended

84 Michael Power, 'Evaluating the Audit Explosion' (2003) 25 *Law & Policy* 185.

85 European Court of Auditors, 'Single Supervisory Mechanism – Good Start but Further Improvements Needed' (Publications Office of the European Union 2016) Special report No 29/2016 www.eca.europa.eu/en/Pages/DocItem.aspx?did=39744 accessed 22 January 2018.

86 Ibid., 20.

87 Ibid., 123.

88 Ibid., 11.

that the ECB develops a public and formal performance framework to assess the effectiveness of its supervisory activities.[89]

Lastly, the final accountability good of publicness can also be rendered procedurally or substantively. In both cases, publicness requires that public officials demonstrate the orientation of their conduct towards the common good. In the EU context, this may take on a specific meaning, namely the duty of EU actors to demonstrate that their policies (such as in EMU, country-specific recommendations) take the interests of the EU as a whole into account (and not just of selected industries or states). A common mechanism to achieve accountability as publicness concerns establishing procedures for public participation in government action from notice and comment procedures to more intensive forms of citizen participation.[90] An accountability forum may therefore assess whether a robust process of consultation existed when adopting public policies. This can also include proportionality review in the sense that such review commonly requires, in order for limitations on rights to be justified, that officials demonstrate that their policies restricted rights in pursuit of a 'legitimate aim'.

In the context of EMU, examples of both can be found. In the 2015 'Five Presidents Report', the leaders of the EU's main institutions committed to greater involvement of the social partners in fiscal coordination processes such as the European Semester, with some commentators arguing that this has led to a gradual 'socialization' or re-balancing of the Semester's policy priorities.[91] Elsewhere, several ECB programmes – most notably the OMT, the Asset Purchase Programme (APP) and the Public Sector Purchase Programme (PSPP) – have been subject to judicial challenge, with the CJEU asked to rule on whether their effects on national economic competencies were adequately grounded in the ECB's mandate of producing stable prices for the Eurozone as a whole.[92]

Substantively, publicness concerns not just the existence but the effects of participation and reason-giving. With respect to participatory governance,

89 Ibid., 12.

90 John Gaventa, 'Exploring Citizenship, Participation and Accountability' (2002) 33 *IDS Bulletin* 1; Richard B Stewart, 'Remedying Disregard in Global Regulatory Governance: Accountability, Participation, and Responsiveness' (2014) 108 *The American Journal of International Law* 211.

91 Jonathan Zeitlin and Bart Vanhercke, 'Socializing the European Semester: EU Social and Economic Policy Co-Ordination in Crisis and Beyond' (2018) 25 *Journal of European Public Policy* 149. For a contrary view, see Mark Dawson, 'New Governance and the Displacement of Social Europe: The Case of the European Semester' (2018) 14 *European Constitutional Law Review* 191.

92 Case C-62/14 Gauweiler and Others; Case C-493/17 *Weiss and Others*, ECLI:EU:C:2018:1000.

many studies of the phenomenon in different national and transnational settings complain of its elitist, or perfunctory character, questioning whether participation actually leads to policy change.[93] Substantive accountability regarding publicness would therefore concern the question of how participation affects outcomes, or how the knowledge garnered via participation was utilized in the policy process. In respect to proportionality review, substantive accountability would not merely require officials to posit the aim to which their policies were directed but would allow scrutiny of the suitability and necessity of those policies, given those negatively affected by them (such as those whose fundamental rights were infringed).

Once again, demands for substantive accountability as publicness can also be found in the EMU context. To return to the examples above, while the participation of civil society actors in the European Semester may be an end in itself, the tying of this participation to a debate about the Semester's policy priorities illustrates the weakness of accountability in this policy context. The real question is whether the involvement of civil society in the Semester *matters* or is simply another abstract commitment boldly stated in policy documents only to be safely disregarded when substantive decisions about EU fiscal policy are made. Similarly, those analysing proportionality review of the ECB have repeatedly questioned whether such review in the area of monetary policy is meaningful or whether the standard of review provides the ECB with such a margin of discretion as to make judicial review practically meaningless (or 'incomprehensible' as provocatively put by the German Constitutional Court).[94] In this sense, what matters for accountability as publicness is not the mere provision of reasons for action relating to the common good but whether these reasons meaningfully *orient the conduct* of economic policy-makers.

With all four categories, the guiding distinction between procedural and substantive accountability is between process and merit. For the former, the connecting point between actor and forum is the steps taken to make public action accountable; for the latter, the basis for interaction is the merit of official action vis-à-vis alternatives. This leaves a crucial question: from an institutional design perspective, why would anyone choose an accountability regime focused on one form of accountability, rather than the other? This is the subject of the next section.

93 Jens Newig and Oliver Fritsch, 'Environmental Governance: Participatory, Multi-Level – and Effective?' (2009) 19 *Environmental Policy and Governance* 197; Stijn Smismans, 'New Modes of Governance and the Participatory Myth' (2008) 31 *West European Politics* 874.

94 Harvey (n 82) 110; Mark Dawson and Ana Bobić, 'Quantitative Easing at the Court of Justice – Doing Whatever It Takes to Save the Euro: Weiss and Others' (2019) 56 *Common Market Law Review* 1005, 1025.

## 1.6 PROCEDURAL ACCOUNTABILITY – AND ITS LIMITS

There are good reasons why institutions may favour procedural accountability. The main reason concerns the clarity and predictability of the standards used to orient accountability. Under the substantive reading, a potentially broad set of standards are at play, with the actor under a heavy and potentially limitless justificatory burden. To take one of the four categories discussed above, requirements of publicness in public policy are complex and may be subject to significant disagreement.[95] This diversity in interpretation applies to both actors and accountability forums. Assuming that officials may be accountable – in a complex and 'networked' modern polity – to multiple accountability forums, representing an array of interests, finding an appropriate balance able to satisfy these interests can be an overwhelming task.[96] In the EMU context, the ECB's bond-buying programme was of such volume and complexity to have potentially limitless consequences on a wide variety of societal interests; under the circumstances, how could the ECB adequately demonstrate that this policy was non-arbitrary, effective and oriented towards the common good? Substantive accountability widens the set of standards orienting the conduct of the actor, potentially confusing both public officials themselves and the accountability forums that must scrutinize them.

In this regard, procedural accountability seems to be much more straightforward. Here, the primary duty of the actor is to follow an established process (under the assumption that, if followed, this process will lead to open, non-arbitrary and effective outcomes oriented towards the common good). The job of the forum is then to verify that the correct process has been implemented. As a result, a significant burden – of calculating and adjusting conduct according to its concrete effects – is lifted and externalized. This may be particularly important in a judicial context, where judges may lack both the knowledge and legitimacy to interfere in complex economic debates. In social psychology, experimental research has demonstrated that procedural (or process) accountability is linked to situations when actors lack knowledge about the specific outcomes they are expected to achieve; consequently, they shift their focus to the quality of the decision-making process.[97] This suggests that procedural accountability can easily become decoupled from substantive outcomes.

95 Jeremy Waldron, *Law and Disagreement* (Oxford University Press 1999).

96 Carol Harlow and Richard Rawlings, 'Promoting Accountability in Multilevel Governance: A Network Approach' (2007) 13 *European Law Journal* 542.

97 Thomas Schillemans, 'Calibrating Public Sector Accountability: Translating Experimental Findings to Public Sector Accountability' (2016) 18 *Public Management Review* 1400, 1412.

The potential 'replacement effect' of procedures for substance therefore represents the first major limitation of procedural accountability. Indeed, there are important implications to 'lifting the burden of substantive justification' *for actors*. Jane Mansbridge has famously discussed the interplay of material and moral incentives in the process of delegation.[98] As she argues, the introduction of material incentives may destroy moral incentives by making what was once a duty (to act in the right way) a material question (is this action in my interest?). A similar risk applies in relation to procedural accountability. As discussed above, procedural accountability is based on the assumption that, if actors follow the correct procedures, they will then orient their activities towards correct substantive outcomes. The risk is that the opposite applies – that if actors begin to care only about procedures at the expense of the substantive goods, those procedures are designed to secure (and without reflecting on their adequacy). According to Roy Heidelberg, this logic reflects a technical conception of accountability that 'allows for an actor to dismiss criticism of a policy or action by appealing to an obedience to procedural rules or, at worst, to justify doing the wrong thing in the right way'.[99]

In the EMU, the substitution effect of procedural for substantive accountability is significant. As we have argued elsewhere, ECB accountability in particular is grounded in procedural devices such as transparency, which are seen as better suited to the institution's operational independence.[100] Nevertheless, transparency obligations tend to carry the functional mission of the ECB to the outer limit, as accountability debates become hijacked by discussions over the secrecy regime of the ECB.[101] As a result, the focus on transparency limits the substantive contestation of the actual merit and distributive implications of ECB decisions. While accountability forums like the EP are thus permitted and even encouraged to ask questions of ECB officials, their ability to contest and seek to influence the direction of monetary and supervisory policy is minimal.[102] Accountability in substance seems needed but is also excluded a priori by the EMU institutional structure.

Second, procedural accountability is limiting from the perspective of accountability forums. As indicated by the classic accountability literature, one challenge faced by accountability forums is information asymmetry,

[98] Jane Mansbridge, 'A Contingency Theory of Accountability' in Mark Bovens, Robert E Goodin and Thomas Schillemans (eds.), *The Oxford Handbook Public Accountability* (Oxford University Press 2014).

[99] Heidelberg (n 74) 1386.

[100] Dawson, Maricut-Akbik and Bobić (n 9) 81.

[101] Curtin (n 89).

[102] Collignon and Diessner (n 40); Maricut-Akbik (n 40).

or the difficulty of holding accountable actors with greater knowledge of a specific topic. In principal–agent theory, agents are expected to 'shirk' their obligations before principals either by hiding information before they are appointed (adverse selection) or by hiding their behaviour while on the job (moral hazard).[103] Procedural accountability extends these problems, as explained by Heidelberg:

> Because the accountor is exposed to the rules and subject to them, it is not unusual for the accountor to have a better understanding of how the rule system works than the accountee, in which case, the rule system is as much an instrument for the accountor as the accountee.[104]

The discussion about the exceptions to the application of the Stability and Growth Pact (SGP) by the Commission is a clear example of an actor exploiting the rule-based system introduced by the excessive deficit and macroeconomic imbalance procedures. In fact, the Commission's past record of sanctioning some Member States but not others for budgetary or macroeconomic transgressions has raised important accountability questions of arbitrariness and equal treatment.[105] MEPs have regularly accused the Commission of unfair treatment of a few Member States, for example, for the failure to take action against France's excessive deficit in 2014 or Germany's macroeconomic imbalances in 2015.[106] The problem is that the relevant legislation – the Two-Pack and the Six-Pack – gives the Commission ample discretion to calculate budget deficits by deciding which expenditures, fluctuations and one-off investments are taken into account and which are excluded.[107] This has two important implications. On the one hand, the Commission benefits from information asymmetries in fiscal governance, as it is the only institution with the [expert] knowledge to navigate the 'maze of alternative or even-conflicting rules, part legislative, part non-legislative, which few understand'.[108] On the other hand, the Commission can make strategic use of these rules in order to explain away decisions not to

[103] Terry M Moe, 'The New Economics of Organization' (1984) 28 *American Journal of Political Science* 739, 754–755.

[104] Heidelberg (n 74) 1386.

[105] Damian Chalmers, 'The European Redistributive State and a European Law of Struggle' (2012) 18 *European Law Journal* 667, 684.

[106] de la Parra (n 6) 114.

[107] Mark Dawson, 'How Can EU Law Contain Economic Discretion?' in Joana Mendes (ed.), *EU Executive Discretion and the Limits of Law* (Oxford University Press 2019) 66.

[108] Päivi Leino and Tuomas Saarenheimo, 'Discretion, Economic Governance and the (New) Political Commission' in Joana Mendes (ed.), *EU Executive Discretion and the Limits of Law* (Oxford University Press 2019) 132 https://researchportal.helsinki.fi/en/publications/discretion-economic-governance-and-the-new-political-commission accessed 24 March 2020.

sanction some Member States, as shown by the justification given for the French and German decisions to MEPs during hearings in 2014 and 2015.[109] Overall, procedural accountability seems to favour the actor at the forum's expense.

To sum up, of the two forms of accountability, which is more suitable for the EMU? The argument of this section was not that procedural accountability is of limited value universally. In fact, there are advantages to procedural accountability, namely its clarity and predictability, which make it an important avenue for providing the normative goods of accountability in the EMU. This may be particularly important in an EMU constitutional settlement that gives particular institutions – namely the ECB – high operational independence. But without a substantive component, the normative goods of accountability remain focused on processes of decision-making, which are insufficient for evaluating decisions in a policy field that decides 'who gets what, when, how'[110] as much as EMU.

Substantive accountability can be more complex and costly to achieve; for instance, in order to balance information asymmetries between forums and actors, the former would need to acquire expertise in many fields, which requires additional resources. In some cases, this might be infeasible – no matter how desirable or demanded substantive accountability becomes. Under the circumstances, political architects of EMU accountability will have to decide if the costs of substantive accountability are worth the payoffs or, alternatively, if they are willing to accept the trade-offs between substantive and procedural accountability which the EMU's institutional set-up currently entails.

## 1.7 CONCLUSION

In this chapter, we introduced a new normative framework for analysing accountability in the EMU. The framework has been determined deductively by surveying the relevant literature in political theory, law and public administration in order to identify four goods that accountability is supposed to ensure: openness, non-arbitrariness, effectiveness and publicness. All of these can be achieved in a procedural or substantive way, but the latter imposes higher standards of accountable behaviour for actors – as they have to demonstrate the merit of their decisions rather than defend the process through which those decisions have been reached. Different types of accountability forums can examine an actor's conduct in line with the four goods: parliaments through

[109] Adina Maricut-Akbik, *Contesting Executive Power in EU Economic Governance: The European Parliament as an Accountability Forum* (Cambridge University Press forthcoming 2021).

[110] Lasswell (n 1).

legislative oversight, courts through judicial review, ombudsmen and court of auditors through administrative review. When transposed to the EMU, there seems to be a predominance of procedural accountability that remains limited because of the 'replacement effect' of procedures for substance and the weak position of accountability forums vis-à-vis actors with expert knowledge of the policy area. Our argument is that there is a clear need for more substantive accountability in the EMU across different mechanisms of accountability – political, legal and administrative: a claim that we invite our authors to question, probe and elaborate in the chapters that follow.

We have sought through the chapter to add to the academic literature on EMU accountability by constructing an approach that is deductive without being rooted in a nation-state view of the concept and which identifies normative standards of accountability that are not inductively derived from the EU Treaties alone. The benefit of the approach is that accountability is evaluated on the basis of norms, rather than owed to a specific principal – part of a would-be democratic chain of delegation. Acknowledging that the term is often used interchangeably with 'answerability' or 'responsiveness',[111] we argue in favour of a change of analytical optics: instead of obsessing about the appropriate forum to whom actors should answer or respond, scholars should focus on the question 'what should actors be accountable for?' This is particularly applicable at the EU level, where the distance between the ultimate democratic principal (the citizens) and their supposed agent (EU institutions) remains great. We thus call on other authors to break the stalemate of EMU accountability research by researching the extent to which national and EU institutions provide the four normative goods of accountability, and subsequently, by showing how account-giving by EU institutions can be made more substantive in the future. We hope to have provided useful conceptual tools for the more empirical papers that follow this chapter.

[111] Dubnick (n 16) 33.

# 2

# Reconsidering the Good of Improving Accountability

*Roy L. Heidelberg*

## 2.1 INTRODUCTION

One of the more curious developments of twentieth-century modern political thought is the laudatory treatment of accountability. Despite frequent debates over accountability, the general sense is that it is something to be preserved and improved for the sake of democracy.[1] Accountability has long been connected to democracy in the sense of representation, a feature that dates to JS Mill. But the modern notion of accountability is different in substance from the liberal idea, which is tied to representation. Accountability in its modern guise trends away from ideas of representation towards matters of technology and design. What I mean by this is that accountability is a derivative value that functions at the level of instrumentation. What makes accountability good is its use in achieving a goal. Accountability is still regarded as and spoken about as a *political* good, but this is generally a remnant of the liberal idea of accountability tied to representation. As Mill put it, perfecting accountability, in the sense that he meant it, depended on aligning the interests of rulers with that of the people.[2] Mill, however, did not have the insight into what accountability looks like in a modern bureaucratic state, which is the modern version upon which I will focus here.

The approbation of accountability derives from a sense that accountability is a promotional good of democracy. In other words, accountability has been framed over the past century as a feature of modern government that is essential to the broad success of realizing democratic government, which has lately been transformed into an idea of participatory governance. Achieving

1 See Anderson, "Illusions of Accountability," 31 *Administrative Theory & Praxis* 3 (2019), 322–339. See also Bovens, Schillemans and t'Hart, "Does Public Accountability Work? An Assessment Tool," 86 *Public Administration* 1 (2008), 225–242.

2 Mill, *Dissertations and Discussions*, Vol. 1 (London: John W. Parker and Son, 1859), p. 467.

accountability entails success in both realizing the increasingly complex objectives of the modern state and satisfying the values of democracy. As such, many regard promoting accountability as de rigueur of democracy. The idea carries a normative force that appears essential to addressing imbalances of power that favor experts against the public. As Dawson and Maricut-Akbik describe in their introductory chapter to this volume, the normative goods of accountability can help guide frameworks to address the nongovernmental, extra-nation-state institutions developed and developing alongside the increasingly complex demands of modern governance. They propose four normative goods: openness, nonarbitrariness (procedural limits on discretion), effectiveness through measured performance, and ensuring that actions are in the public interest (publicness). These goods underscore both the procedural and substantive qualities of accountability. Procedural accountability ensures that activities are done correctly (open, public, nonarbitrary) and lead to appropriate outcomes (effective). Substantive accountability places higher demands on the institutional setting, as Dawson and Maricut-Akbik describe, by requiring an explanation of the decisions behind the activities.

It is unusual not to be swept along in the laudation of accountability. I myself have described accountability in two previous essays, one in which I attempt to deepen the connection between accountability and democracy by incorporating practices of contestation and nondomination into its conceptual fold.[3] I see such matters slightly differently now, especially considering some of the distinctions I will address in this essay, namely the distinction between responsibility and accountability and the ways in which accountability serves bureaucracy and not democracy. I focus upon the concept as it applies to public administration and the political formations associated with it (i.e. the administrative state). The administrative idea of accountability is tied to design and performance, evident in the procedural sense of accountability, making accountability a concept that deepens technological systems of control. I also identify problems on the substantive side of accountability where actors are required to tell a story (give an account) of their decisions. The account itself is plagued by the dual problem that, first, it is the account itself that is subjected to procedural accountability through design and, second, that accountability as a practice does not permit a meaningful discourse

[3] In "Political Accountability and Spaces of Contestation," 49 *Administration and Society* 1379 (2017), I introduced a third component to the idea of accountability, what I described as *per factum* accountability (building on Dubnick and Frederickson, *Public Accountability: Performance Measurement, the Extended State, and the Search for Trust* (Washington: Kettering Foundation & National Academy of Public Administration, 2011), in which they theorize accountability as being based upon *pre factum* and *post factum* ideas).

between experts and the public. Ultimately, accountability is a practice that formalizes expertise into governing, an idea contrary to the prevailing notion of it as a value that ensures democratic control.

I doubt the integrity of ideas that connect modern accountability to democracy and see the rethinking of accountability against democracy as an important political problem of our time. Accountability is not an idea that promotes democracy. Contra democracy, the notion of accountability is found in strengthening bureaucracy, and it does so without explicit regard for ideas of democracy. Viewing accountability not as an institutional good but as a concept with relational consequences achieved through technology brings into question this largely uncriticized connection between democracy and accountability. In this essay, I question "the good" of accountability and identify how the concept of accountability in both the procedural and substantive sense reinforces the power of experts above the public.

## 2.2 RESPONSIBILITY AND ACCOUNTABILITY

I begin by distinguishing between accountability and the more common notion of responsibility. Responsibility partly entails giving an account of one's actions, meaning an explanation for what one did, why one did it, and what reasonable expectations were behind doing it. This does not mean that responsibility is the account itself. Responsibility is something that one can have in the sense of "my responsibility." We can speak of responsibility in a way that gives it a sense of character and connection with an individual.

On the other hand, accountability takes that element of the account as everything. For accountability, the details of the account prevail, so much so that in its reductive sense, accountability renders pointless the thinking and decision that lies behind the human act itself. One cannot speak of "my accountability." It is meaningless. Being accountable means being *held* accountable. This contrasts sharply with the quality of responsibility, which does not require an other to act upon me. One does not need another to make one responsible. The other can play a role in one's sense of responsibility, but it does not serve to make my actions objective to a preconceived principle, as a principal does in the sense of accountability.

The relationship between the holder and the one held that makes accountability – let us refer to them as principal and agent for the sake of simplicity – is entirely bound by an instrumental scheme. The principal wants beneficial actions done by the agent, who serves as a means to achievement. This arrangement of expectations is the core of the relationship between the principal and the agent. The principal is a principal insofar as she has expectations for an agent. The agent is an agent insofar as he acts under the oversight of the principal. This is a relationship in only a superficial sense. Each party does what serves himself/herself under the constraint of what the other desires or wants. There is no expectation of sincere consideration for the other in this relational schema, the absence of which minimizes, even eliminates, the relational sense of it. In other words, the moral or custom is dictated by a fully inward consideration of one's objectives. This collapses any real sense of morality, a feature that frequently plagues institutions and organizations premised on *impersonal relationships*.

What do I mean by an impersonal relationship? Simply put, it is one that is dictated by formal rules. The rules are not suggestions. They are prescriptions, stipulations on a course of action. The challenge for the principal is not to express the rules of action; the challenge for the principal is guaranteeing that the rules are followed. The agent can have been prescribed how to act, can be fully aware of the rules. But even then, the agent may not perform. It is at this point that accountability is thought to function. Accountability is imposed on the agent. It is an instrument of the principal. In other words, it is an instrument of power over another where formal rules determine how another must act. The starting point of any accountability relationship, then, is the objective of the principal. A perfect accountability scheme (we will revisit this idea of "perfect" below) requires that the agent perform a prescribed role. To the greatest extent possible, the complications involved in performing this prescribed role have been addressed through the formal rule scheme.

One way of thinking through this impersonal relationship is by seeing it as a contest over the decision. The agent is in a position through which his decision will have ramifications for the principal. The principal, meanwhile, wants to minimize the decision-making scope of the agent and enforce arrangements that accord with her decision (of what is to be done). A perfection of accountability is a condition of nondecision for the agent. This is one reason why substantive accountability is conceptually convoluted: procedural accountability designs away the substance of the decision itself.

The condition of nondecision is one facet of accountability. It is the condition that Dubnick and Frederickson refer to as *pre factum* accountability, or accountability before the deed.[4] They contrast this facet of accountability with *post factum* accountability, which places focus upon consequences as a

4 Dubnick and Frederickson, *Public Accountability: Performance Measurement, the Extended State, and the Search for Trust* (Washington: Kettering Foundation & National Academy of Public Administration, 2011).

facet of the principal–agent relationship. It is reasonable to see the necessity of consequences as made by a failure of control. When the condition of nondecision in *pre factum* accountability fails, the force of consequence in *post factum* accountability arises.

## 2.3 RECONSIDERING *PER FACTUM* ACCOUNTABILITY

In a previous essay,[5] I added to the dual concepts of *pre factum* and *post factum* accountability the idea of *per factum*, which I described as during or through the deed itself. Viewed through administrative logic, in particular the solutionism of technics, *per factum* accountability is better thought of in the sense of "thoroughly done," the sense bearing a connotation of perfection. Achieving the condition of nondecision through thorough design is perfect accountability. But the political consideration eschews perfection in that sense. The focus must be on the deed itself, the ongoing process of any activity that is supported by authority and involves power. In this respect, the *per factum* accountability should be viewed as ongoing, as being "through" the deed, in the same sense that "permeate" means to go through and "permit" means to send through. This meaning of *per factum* does not correlate with a sense of perfection, though, because of the contestable practices intrinsic to politics. Simply put, the administrative logic of accountability begins and ideally ends with *pre factum*, meaning a properly and thoroughly designed system or institution that minimizes the concern over the execution of the deed (*per factum*) and the possibility of incompletion (*post factum*). While this may itself appear impossible, it is the basis of accountability design: a system that functions impersonally does so without judgment or thought of its performing elements (in an organization's case, people are the elements). In other words, *perfection* renders moot the question of *performance*, and thus the *per factum* and *post factum* concerns are irrelevant.

We should not be distracted by the challenge and the fact that such design is not possible in many cases. Particularities will always make such "perfection" inconsistent with practice. But inconsistency is not inconceivability, and the point is that every error in the system is perceived as an opportunity for improving the *pre factum* system that is behind it. This is an ethos of technology. The question should never be posed in terms of a given state, a fixed condition, because at issue is the condition of perfectibility, not the state of perfection. The administrative sense that is behind solutionism is supported

5 Heidelberg, "Political Accountability and Spaces of Contestation," 49 *Administration & Society* 10 (2017), 1379–1402.

by a belief in a perfectible state or institution.[6] This belief is not hindered by the evidence of imperfection since that is considered evidence for what can be improved. Such is the logic of technics, and it is thus that accountability is realized as a concept of technology.

The idea that accountability is possible "during" the deed, as I imply with the sense of *per factum*, is conceptually inconsistent with how accountability is generally conceived within administrative logics. In other words, opening the deed is a direct challenge to accountability and exposes the problems with it. These problems are largely the result of accountability being a concept of and for technology, a concept in diametrical opposition to responsibility.

It is worth returning to the question of responsibility to clarify the claim that accountability is in both concept and practice against responsibility. The distinction hinges primarily on how accountability is premised on impersonal structures and institutions to facilitate preconceived actions. Responsibility, however, operates within ambiguity and uncertainty, conditions that require judgment about how to act in particular circumstances. As already mentioned, it is understandable to speak of "my responsibility" because one must take possession of the decision that corresponds with the action directed towards the particular concern. However, the grammar of accountability does not allow us to speak of "my accountability." This phrase is senseless. I can say, for example, "Raising my children is my responsibility." This connotes a relational understanding of my role, what we can call a caretaker, and its meaning is built upon this relationship. The actions that correspond with "raising my children" are not preconceived, even if I hold firmly to certain standards, morals, customs, or even principles. The point is that my responsibility may require me to act in a particular case *against* such standards and then to answer for doing so (hence the account within the concept of responsibility).

I am unable to say "Raising my children is my accountability" and to convey a sensible meaning. The reason is that accountability produces an object relationship so that the "I" that speaks cannot express something about the "I" through accountability, but only about the tasks and expected behaviors. To speak in this way of accountability requires me to say "I am accountable for raising my children," a remark that connotes a person or structure that "holds" me accountable and "possesses" my condition of accountability. The "I" then turns to the tasks necessary to fulfill the accountability relationship. What accountability enables above responsibility is an objective view on what is necessary to be done, objective to the extent that another party is charged

6 Heidelberg, "Public Administration and the Logic of Resolution," 11 *Critical Policy Studies* 3 (2017), 272–290.

with determining the appropriateness of the act based upon established standards. It is this last qualification that distinguishes "being held accountable" from "my responsibility," and this distinction is further clarified by the difference between action and tasks.

## 2.4 TASKS AND DESIGN

Consider what is connoted by *task*: a duty, a chore, an assignment, a charge. A task is something given to you based upon what is expected of you. It is often generalized by the expected conditions that demand activity. I want to contrast this with the idea of action, which I believe connotes a greater degree of ambiguity sufficient to support the judgment of the actor. A task is itself an idea that eschews judgment, while action demands it. The distinction is clarified by Arendt's description of action as being the *conditio per quam* (the condition by means) of political life, a category she contrasted with work (the category of artificial worldliness) and labor (the category of life in the sense of the biological).[7] What is specific to action is what Arendt called natality. Action is the condition by which a person can start something new, can bring about a beginning, and it is partly for this that action is a condition of freedom itself. Natality is first realized in the fact of our birth, that every birth is a new beginning, and our capacity to create something new is what makes us free.

Arendt's conception of action is diametrically opposed to the conditions that are fostered through the bureaucratic apparatus through which accountability functions. The actualization of freedom through action is the capacity to do the unexpected, which is how a new beginning is brought about. "It is in the nature of beginning that something new is started which cannot be expected from whatever may have happened before."[8] Routine, standards, and procedure all work against the conditions of action precisely so that expectations are realized, so that the unexpected does not happen.

But accountability and the associated administrative logics are not to be found in the other "human conditions" that Arendt discusses. There is no biological need for accountability, so it is not present in labor. Work, according to Arendt, is judged based upon the production of a world suitable for human use. It is associated primarily with the production of the material world, the kind of artifice that we associate with the Promethean violence against nature,[9] wresting from it the materials for our needs and goals. Work

7 Arendt, *The Human Condition* (Chicago: University of Chicago Press, 1958), p. 7.

8 Ibid., pp. 177–178.

9 See Hadot, *The Veil of Isis* (Michael Chase, Trans.) (Cambridge: The Belknap Press of Harvard University).

characterizes the condition of making the material world accommodate human life. Accountability is about task, not work. It is not premised on human use but on the use of humans. Accountability is complicit in the bureaucratic arrangement that prioritizes artificial production above human use, the quality of dehumanization that is especially associated with bureaucracy.

It does not have to be this way. There was a sense of accountability that was associated with representation and a liberal sense of government, an understanding that derived accountability from responsibility. But that idea no longer prevails in the meaning of accountability. The modern idea of accountability rests on notions of control over the administrative apparatus to ensure execution. It is a concept that follows the growth of bureaucracy and administration to such an extent that responsibility is conditioned by accountability. Action, as Arendt described it, is consistent with responsibility but not accountability. Accountability is a political concept only to the extent that it domesticates the components of politics to the point of erasure. What is done through accountability is not a space of contestation where the possibility of action might produce the unexpected; rather, what is done is a restricted space of behavior, where ultimately an algorithmic expression is possible, thus erasing action and responsibility. Behavior is the antithesis of action. It is produced by design, and behavior is to act in a way consistent with expectations.[10] Design implies expectation, and accountability is a concept of design insofar as the agent is given the procedures and the incentives to do as the design dictates. Actors properly embedded within an accountable institution do not act where their tasks are not prescribed, which is a way of saying that action is conceptually inconsistent with accountability itself. Prescription is the arena of behavior and the act of constraining action; or, more concisely, prescription erases action. Therefore, one can never say "my accountability"; the prescription of one's actions removes any ownership over the act itself.

The early debates over accountability were focused on what was called "administrative responsibility." The sense of administrative responsibility was eventually abandoned in favor of talking about accountability, and I argue elsewhere that this shift in language testifies to a changing idea of the meaning of "responsible government."[11] Carl Friedrich, who appeared to take the side of administrative discretion and deference to expertise, stated that

> if a responsible person is one who is answerable for his acts to some other person or body, who has to give an account of his doings (Oxford English

[10] This point is made in greater depth in Heidelberg, "Ten Theses on Accountability," 42 *Administrative Theory and Praxis* 1 (2020), 6.

[11] Ibid.

> Dictionary), it should be clear without further argument that there must be some agreement between such a responsible agent and his principal concerning the action in hand or at least the end to be achieved. When one considers the complexity of modern governmental activities, it is at once evident that such agreement can only be partial and incomplete, no matter who is involved.[12]

Friedrich's apparent defense of discretion in fact opened the door for design. He goes on to say immediately after this remark that a realistic consideration of the electorate and its representatives shows that, as principals, they are inadequate to the task of reaching such an agreement over administrative tasks. They are unable to bring about what Friedrich calls "responsible conduct of public affairs," by which he meant the alignment of required actions and defined ends, with one qualification: "unless elaborate techniques make explicit what purposes and activities are involved in all the many different phases of public policy." Indeed, the qualities associated with modern accountability – performance measurement, transparency, incentives of various sorts, rules, and procedures – are the elaborate techniques that fulfill this qualification. These techniques render moot the story from the "responsible person" since they address the problem from a design perspective, meaning the "many different phases of public policy" are considered in dictating how an agent acts under relevant conditions.

A fair rejoinder would point to the way that Friedrich himself defined responsible: one who is answerable for his acts to some other person or body, who must give an account of his doings. He cited the *Oxford English Dictionary*. The current version (*OED* Third Edition, March 2010; most recently modified version published online June 2021) offers the following as the first definition of responsible: "Capable of fulfilling an obligation or duty; reliable, trustworthy, sensible." The third, fourth, fifth, and sixth definitions under the adjectival use refer to some variation of answering a charge (even using "accountable for" and "to be held as"). There is no dispute here that responsibility includes some facet of account-giving, but the distinction between accountability and responsibility is the extent to which the account remains a story communicated between two people about what happened. Modern accountability takes the story as a component of control, as though the story must be written beforehand. Responsibility entails an account about why one decided to act as one did, which in some respect is the arena of "substantive accountability." In perfect form, though, accountability takes the

[12] Friedrich, "Public Policy and the Nature of Administrative Responsibility" in C. J. Friedrich and E. S. Mason (eds.), *Public Policy* (Cambridge: Harvard University Press, 1940), pp. 3–24.

account and makes it an *ex ante* concern that determines what is to be done. At issue is how accountability takes the component of the account and magnifies it. In responsibility, I may feel obligated to explain to someone why I did what I did. With accountability, that account is transformed so that I act as you intend, making the story itself not one that the account-giver tells but rather a story to be followed.

The emphasis on the account that coincides with modern accountability is not about the act of explaining one's action; the emphasis is on controlling the account itself, on dictating the story. To refer to accountability is not to refer to a human quality but to a technological quality in which systems are designed to guarantee outcomes. The "ability" in accountability is a quality of the institution or system, not the person. When we refer to an accountable actor, we refer not to a person capable of action and responsibility but instead to an agent performing within a designed institution or system. The perfection is aimed at the task, and the person is an instrument within a perfectible system. One could say that accountability seeks to solve the problem of responsibility by perfecting it. Responsibility conceptually retains the possibility that a person might act on their own discretion and judgment, and accountability removes this by and through design. It is not that accountability is *different* from responsibility. Rather, it is an extreme form of it expressed through the administrative logics of solution and technology. Referring back to the definition of responsibility above (capable of fulfilling an obligation or duty; reliable, trustworthy, sensible), the *-able* of accountability erases the uncertainty of the second part of the definition. The design approach seeks to exclude the variable effect of reliability, trustworthiness, and sensibility. The one holding the agent accountable is an institution.

## 2.5 PERFECTING BUREAUCRACY

Let us return to the question of perfection in accountability. The perfection of accountability rests in the same ideal condition of perfection identified more than a century ago in the bureaucratic system of order described by Weber: in dehumanization.[13] He defined this quality of the bureaucratic apparatus as being composed of agents acting *sine ira et studio*, a phrase he might have borrowed from Tacitus, meaning without anger or bias. Tacitus meant by this that a story of historical occurrence (an account) might be presented to an audience based solely on facts of what happened and without any flourishing

[13] Weber, *Economy and Society* (G. Roth and C. Wittich, Eds.) (Berkeley: University of California Press, 2013). esp. Ch. XI.

from the speaker. In this way, an orator is restrained from attempting to influence the audience. In essence, Tacitus refers to what we might consider an "objective viewpoint" and used this formulation in his early history of the Roman Empire. Weber's meaning is slightly different. His meaning refers to the acts of agents in a bureaucratic system. It is the deed, not the story, that concerns Weber's notion of objectivity behind *sine ira et studio*. Nevertheless, both Tacitus and Weber refer to a condition that is restricted by a conception of objectivity. Both sought to introduce a condition through which fact (that which is done) supersedes truth to such an extent that fact itself becomes truth. But Weber's description did something that Tacitus's did not. Tacitus's conception of an objective account allowed interpretation by the listener. A story can be told "faithful to the facts" but the meaning can remain open to the audience. Tacitus's *sine ira et studio* meant that the account must be given according to what *was* done. There thus remained some political element concerning how what was done could be relevant to current matters of action and deed. The *sine ira et studio* expressed by Weber is not concerned with what was done but rather what *is to be done*. Meaning, interpretation, and understanding are expressly removed from the question of fact, understood to mean deed or that which is done. The agent of the Weberian *sine ira et studio* is foremost an instrument of the design. This is the meaning of dehumanization: a prescription to ensure that design becomes fact. This quality is of utmost importance to bureaucracy and administration. Weber called it the special virtue in his description of the ideal-type bureaucracy.

Weber answered the issue of what is to be done by upholding the function of calculability in the deed itself. Here is how Weber expressed it:

> The peculiarity of modern culture, and specifically of its technical and economic basis, demands this very "calculability" of results. When fully developed, bureaucracy also stands, in a specific sense, under the principle of *sine ira ac studio*. Bureaucracy develops the more perfectly, the more it is "dehumanized," the more completely it succeeds in eliminating from official business love, hatred, and all purely personal, irrational, and emotional elements which escape calculation. This is appraised as its special virtue by capitalism.[14]

Perfection (fully developed or thoroughly done) requires dehumanization. This is the mode through which the bureaucratic apparatus exerts control, and it is precisely the condition of modern accountability. What is to be done is predetermined so that actors behave according to tasks. The story is told

[14] Weber, ibid., p. 975.

beforehand. This is markedly different from the sense of responsibility, which retains some sense of moral conduct by the individual, a conduct that depends upon the exercise of the faculty of judgment. Accountability operates where judgment is made obsolete.

Accountability is the moral expression of amoral conduct that marries the conditions of perfection in bureaucracy: dehumanization and calculability. How can one claim accountability to be a moral expression of amorality? The simple answer to this is that a moral expression is concerned with the central principles of right and wrong as pertains to right conduct; amoral conduct is carried out without regard to right or wrong. This is precisely the condition of calculability (morality as determined by calculable rules of conduct) and dehumanization (disregard for personal considerations of right and wrong). How does accountability marry these conditions together? A necessary premise of accountability is that the actor behaves in accordance with established rules and procedures and not according to their own judgment of appropriate conduct. In other words, "Objective discharge of business primarily means a discharge of business according to *calculable rules* and 'without regard for persons.'"[15]

## 2.6 CONTESTATION IS NOT A FIX

Modern accountability differs from responsibility. The key distinction is that accountability is conceptually linked to the use of humans as part of an instrumental institutional apparatus, which makes it an extreme version of certain components of responsibility. The apparatus, which in modern parlance is called bureaucracy, puts primary emphasis on the tasks and procedures for achieving defined goals. We may speak of an accountable person, but in effect we are describing the system in which the person operates. Persons cannot *have* accountability because in being accountable they relinquish action to the operations of tasks and thus to a power that holds them accountable. Accountability operates as a condition of perfectibility for bureaucracy.

Accountability cannot be political insofar as it is premised on the erasure of politics from the discharge of state operations. Conceiving of accountability as political has sparked interest among many scholars (the present author included), who hold that accountability is an essential precondition for democracy and that there is the possibility of *democratic accountability* in the modern sense of government. But there is not. Rather, accountability operates against democracy in the important sense that it perfects bureaucracy, not democracy. What I previously identified as *per factum* accountability – something

[15] Ibid.

between *pre factum* and *post factum* that took place during the deed – suffers the same problem as *post factum* accountability: everything depends on the perfection *before the deed*. Accountability operates against the unexpected; its functions seek fulfillment of expected outcomes through increasingly optimal designs. The unexpected of today becomes a bit of new information for the greater perfection of the system. That is what a thoroughly done (*per factum*) bureaucratic system is in practice. Accountability is a concept of and for technology and design, not a concept for human use but, at the risk of repetition, it is a concept for the use of humans. While it is the case that in its early stages humans (principals) use humans (agents), the logic persists in such a way that rules and algorithms ultimately prevail. In other words, the design is intended so that eventually the tasks of the agent are *compelled by evidence*.

This logic is one of the reasons that rethinking accountability by embedding contestation or by emphasizing a substantive orientation of account-giving fixes nothing. Modern accountability entails practices that absorb what was not used where and when it is useful to do so. The shift in focus that occurred with modern accountability was not a move away from representation but rather a step further into the direction set by representation where the state addresses the increasingly complicated and specialized conditions of modern culture that derive from the interests of the people. Accountability is its own solution. When things go wrong in modern mass society, the calls for accountability ring out almost immediately. Sometimes this means punishing the wrongdoers, but it is also a call for preventing it from happening again. What this ultimately looks like is no surprise: refinement of rules and procedures. Contestation is a value similar to transparency that can easily be normalized under the broader goals of accountability. This is in practice quite common. Public participation and transparency are both facets of modern accountability arrangements. The point is not that they are present in the arrangement. The important point is that they are subsumed under accountability itself.

The problem in accountability has always been *who is in control*. This is apparent from the earliest stages of the debate. It is at the very heart of the dispute between Carl Friedrich and Herman Finer: is a responsible administration better guided by experts or public representatives? The entry of "the public" into this debate is not a progressive step, nor is it necessarily a normative good.[16] Increasing the publicness of an accountability regime or arrangement does not address the issue of control. What it does, however, is

[16] This position contradicts the one posed by Dawson and Maricut-Akbik in the introductory chapter to this volume.

to highlight that the control falls to *nobody*. The public is not a somebody but a calculated political entity designated by its generality. It fits the essence of calculability (in, e.g. "public opinion"), the quality that provides bureaucracy its technical superiority: decisions are based on measurable criteria and not left to somebody. The decision must be for the "public benefit." The decision is what accountability addresses, and the modern form of it eschews representation in favor of objectivity, an objectivity that is realized in nobody deciding. Questions about the exception and the unexpected, the questions that constitute political concerns, are erased by design.[17]

An agent under an accountability regime asked to justify or defend a decision presents two problems. The first is that it is not the agent's decision. This is not meant in the banal sense that the agent is simply following orders from a principal because it is rarely so simple, although this is an issue of substantive accountability and is the source of perversions of accountability, such as scapegoating. More critically, though, the decision is increasingly determined by the measurable components of the substantive policy arena. The orders come from nobody. They can be based possibly on evidence, data or information. The second issue is to whom the decision must be defended or justified. The defense here must balance a finely tuned distinction between justification and manipulation through what can only be properly called propaganda.

For example, let us imagine an official in a national health department, such as a leading infectious disease expert. This expert identifies a highly infectious virus that leads to greater than average mortality. She briefs government officials and explains that certain difficult measures must be implemented in order to stem the spread of the disease. Cities shut down commerce, schools close, and only essential services are allowed to continue operating. The expert is then scheduled to speak on dozens of news programs to explain what she sees in the data and to exert her expertise in defending the judgment to take such drastic measures. She explains that this will save lives and that the sacrifices are necessary to stem the spread of the virus. She explains the decision with admirable clarity and cites data and evidence. But most people cannot understand the evidence and cannot interpret the data. They express doubt. They contradict the expert with their own data and evidence. They question the integrity of the expert. At some point, the attention turns from justification

[17] In some respects, Carl Schmitt anticipated this issue in his theorizing of sovereignty following the democratic movements leading into the twentieth century. But for Schmitt, the way to address this diminishing political agency that was necessary for sovereignty was to promote a modern Hobbesian leader who was charged with the power of decision. He did not anticipate the rising power of nobody. See Schmitt, *Political Theology* (G. Schwab, Trans.) (Chicago: University of Chicago Press, 2005).

to winning the argument. The expert is joined by other experts to spread a message and to counter "home remedies" and "alternative facts." Her status as an expert is questioned by her opponents, who claim that she is nothing but an opposition bully trying to undermine the people and destabilize society. Meanwhile, commercials and billboards and public service announcements encourage people to take the steps necessary to stem the spread of the virus: avoid socializing, wear a mask, and wash your hands.

One could tell a similar story about a monetary expert who faces a potential catastrophic financial collapse. During the 2008 financial crisis, the US Fed began a policy of quantitative easing, a monetary policy that had to that point been scarcely used in a few countries, including Japan in the early 2000s. The experts in the Federal Reserve Bank faced the challenge of explaining a complex purchasing practice that was intended to encourage banks to protect their balance sheets enough that they could make loans and, thus, send money into the economy. To nonexperts, this looked like the equivalent of printing money, which sparked fears of inflation, but the experts had to make nuanced arguments on the differences between money printing and quantitative easing. A little more than a decade later, facing another potential financial crisis from a global pandemic, the US Fed began purchasing Treasury bills again, but this time the leader of the Fed was adamant that the practice was not quantitative easing. Instead, the practice was framed as a way for the Fed to create reserves. They purchased short-term rather than long-term bills and were not making the purchases with the goal of increasing liquidity. As then Fed Chairman Jerome Powell said, "This is not QE. In no sense is this QE."[18]

Both descriptions of experts at work highlight the disparity of knowledge between the experts and the public at large. The expert health official case could be seen as an example of contestation, and it could be viewed as an example of substantive accountability. The expert is put in a position of justifying the activities (policies) that she deems necessary based on the evidence. On its face, this would seem to be an exercise of accountability. But, I think that it actually exemplifies a *failure* of accountability as I understand it. The example displays the justification of accountability as necessitated by the increasingly complicated conditions of modern government. To grasp the failure, consider the way that Mill described accountability:

> When the accountability is perfect, the interest of rulers approximates more and more to identity with that of the people, in proportion as the people

[18] Quoted in Timiraos, "The Fed Is Buying Treasurys Again. Just Don't Call It Quantitative Easing," *Wall Street Journal*, October 16, 2019. www.wsj.com/articles/the-fed-is-buying-bonds-again-just-dont-call-it-quantitative-easing-11571218200

> are more enlightened. The identity would be perfect, only if the people were so wise, that it should no longer be practicable to employ deceit as an instrument of government; a point of advancement only one stage below that at which they could do without government altogether; at least, without force, and penal sanctions, not (of course) without guidance and organized co-operation.[19]

Mill alluded to the ingredients necessary for going from representation to administration. Perfection approaches the point when the people could do without government, by which he seemed to mean the use of force and penalty. There will always be the need, one infers, for guidance and organization. The perfection of accountability in the liberal sense makes the purpose and function of representation unnecessary. If the interest of the representatives approximates the interests that identify the people, then the people do not need representation. This only works, though, to the extent (in proportion with) the enlightenment of the people. Mill's liberalism depended upon expertise and leadership of those who were knowledgeable, as he made clear in his advocacy for weighing voting rights based on education. For Mill, this was a solution to the problem of aristocratic power. He believed that knowledgeable voters would improve upon the political decisions made by property owners. By the early twentieth century (and into the twenty-first), this same argument of giving more political power to those who know would be used to tame democracy (which of course was the original target of this argument, dating back to ancient Greece). The perfection that Mill described in the nineteenth century had a different nuance by the middle of the twentieth century. The person who is accountable is not a representative but an administrator. They are not supposed to have interests (*sine ira et studio*) and are supposed to act according to calculability (measurable, evidence-based reasoning). The point at which an administrator must explain to the public the reasons for a policy decision is a failure of accountability precisely because the decision is under question. This activity is aimed at bringing the interests of the public into line with what the expert has deemed appropriate based upon evidence and data. As Mill himself described it, the perfection of accountability entails improving the wisdom of the public (since, *ab definitio*, the expert *knows*). When the public displays an ignorance about the issue at hand, we witness the imperfection of accountability.

This standpoint is clearer in the context of administrative accountability because, as described above, the – able of accountability rests in the institution, not an individual. At issue is the story about what is to be done, as in

[19] Mill, *supra* note 2, p. 467.

telling the story ahead of time. In other words, the ability of accountability situates power into the nobody of administration (*public* administration), and the expert is the remnant agency of this nobody. That the public is insufficient for the task of governing is a key premise of public administration. Woodrow Wilson regarded public opinion as being meddlesome and considered it the role of the reformer to "persuade [his fellow-citizens] to want the particular change he [the reformer] wants."[20] Walter Lippmann said that "the false ideal of democracy can lead only to disillusionment and to meddlesome tyranny.... The public must be put in its place, so that it may exercise its own powers."[21] Finally, consider Carl Friedrich, in his explication of what he called administrative responsibility:

> The pious formulas about the will of the people are all very well, but when it comes to these issues of social maladjustment the popular will has little content, except the desire to see such maladjustments removed.... Consequently, the responsible administrator is one who is responsive to these two dominant factors: technical knowledge and popular sentiment. Any policy which violates either standard or which fails to crystallize in spite of their urgent imperatives, renders the official responsible for it liable to the charge of irresponsible conduct.[22]

What Friedrich, Wilson, and Lippmann are describing is the arrangement for a technical civilization that, while being sensitive to public opinion or sentiment, also must, as Wilson put it, "make public opinion efficient without suffering it to be meddlesome."[23] And as Friedrich argued, this new kind of responsibility, which I have argued is modern accountability, must serve the double standard of adhering to technical knowledge and remaining sensitive to public opinion. These are the requirements that Friedrich described as a novel type of responsibility for the permanent administrator that we now call accountability.[24]

So how does this story about the health administrator indicate a failure of accountability rather than an exercise of it? The short answer is that it only fulfilled one of the two standards: it failed on the popular sentiment front. The example illustrates also how accountability operates ideally as a *pre factum* course of action: the tasks must be seen as necessary according to the

20 Wilson, "The Study of Administration," 2 *Political Science Quarterly* 2 (1887), 197–222, esp. p. 201.
21 Lippmann, *The Phantom Public* (New York: The Macmillan Company, 1927), p. 155.
22 Friedrich, *supra* note 12, at p. 12.
23 Wilson, *supra* note 20, at p. 215.
24 Friedrich, *supra* note 12, at p. 14.

evidence and information, or according to the technical details of the issue. Accountability is an operation that is primarily concerned with the decision, and in its perfect state, the decision is preordained by necessity. Popular sentiment must be "accounted for" in the decision itself. If it reaches the point of persuasion (force), then it is imperfect. Thus, a key part of public accountability is constructing what Mill called the identity of the people.

For Mill, this perfection of accountability centered upon the public sentiment merging with representative interests. The new sense of responsibility arising in the twentieth century that Friedrich remarked upon is not representative in nature but rather centered upon expertise and public sentiment. The difference is not negligible since, assuming the expert acts in good faith to her profession (a key proviso in Friedrich's model), the contest will inevitably favor the expert. Contestation in this regard contradicts the premise of expertise. Mill's notion of perfect accountability fits the administrative conception of accountability to the extent that the perfection of accountability requires an alignment of what is to be done with the enlightenment of the people – in other words, the people are in no position to dispute the necessity of evidence. The substantive accountability in which justification is required is an act of persuasion, but it may as well be an act of manipulation. The expert knows. The public doesn't. The expert has to convince the public. This is the justification. If the public disputes the expert, then the very premise of the expert's position flounders. Thus, contestation is not a way of improving or fixing accountability. It is an act of destruction. The contest calls into question the very legitimacy of the institutional arrangement by putting into question the premise of expertise. The Millian standpoint retains an element of the public sentiment that Friedrich mentioned, but the administrative concept of accountability incorporates public sentiment as another component of perfection, a problem to be solved. To contest the decision within an accountability framework is a destructive act, but as fits the logic of technology, destruction is constructive. There is the ongoing possibility of subsuming the content of the contest for the sake of improving accountability, to the extent that the contest reveals improvement or the possibility thereof. The accountable institution can incorporate the values or ideas into the accountability framework, whether that be through formalizing contestation in public participation or transparency or by using the problems raised in the contest to improve the impersonal operations of the accountable institution. Herein lies the perfection of accountability, a thoroughly done task achieved by design that will further alienate the nonexpert from the decision itself. The realization of *per factum* components of accountability deepens bureaucracy.

# 3

# Markets as an Accountability Mechanism in EU Economic Governance

*Armin Steinbach*[*]

## 3.1 INTRODUCTION

By upsetting traditional interdependencies between financial actors, the European sovereign debt crisis has engendered a range of accountability concerns. Prior to the crisis, treaty-based arrangements in the EU subjected both public and private entities to the discipline of market forces. Specifically, governments and financial institutions relied on liquidity furnished by private counterparties, and Member States met their financing needs without central bank intervention or assistance from other EU countries. However, the collapse of financial markets significantly reshaped relations between creditors and debtors. Indeed, a new regime now prevails in which central banks act as pivotal market makers and in which sovereign states backstop other sovereigns. For many years now, the European Central Bank (ECB) has been injecting massive liquidity into markets, which has had strong redistributive effects between EU states while also distorting private-sector competition.[1] As a result, bond rates have been effectively unmoored from practical realities, and the principle of strict national responsibility for public debt has been all but invalidated. In this way, market forces no longer determine the allocation of debt capital; this role is now performed by EU creditor states and the ECB. In exchange for financial assistance, EU creditors have imposed a range of obligations on debtor states in order to encourage their fiscal consolidation.

This shift has been associated with a 'derogation' of democratic governance, according to various legal and political scholars.[2] To be sure, the current structural arrangements did not arrive all at once but rather on a piecemeal basis as

* Professor of Law and Economics at HEC Paris.

1 Menéndez, 'The Crisis of Law and the European Crises', 44 *Journal of Law and Society* (2017), 56–78, at 59; Steinbach, 'The Lender of Last Resort in the Eurozone', 53 *CML Review* (2016), 361–383, at 368.

2 White, 'Authority After Emergency Rule', 78 *Modern Law Review* (2015), 585–610, at 587–591; Deters, 'National Constitutional Jurisprudence in a Post-National Europe: The ESM

part of numerous macroeconomic adjustment programmes, granular memoranda of understanding, and unconventional monetary policy measures, many of which are viewed by commentators as hostile to the democratic principle that parliament should be the progenitor of policy decisions – particularly when it comes to weighty matters of public interest. 'Intergovernmentalism', 'non-majoritarianism' and 'executivism' are just some of the terms that have been deployed in discussing this shift away from standard notions of democratic accountability.[3] However, rather than focus on assessing such developments from the perspective of democratic representation, an examination of how underlying accountability relationships have been transformed would appear to be a more fruitful line of inquiry. Since time immemorial states have been obligated to raise money to fulfil various functions, from waging war to providing infrastructure. Here, a distinction is illuminating, for there have traditionally been two main sources of public financing: specifically, direct taxation of domestic entities over which the state enjoys sovereign authority, and, alternatively, procurement of funding from other states or foreign organisations.[4] The second mode of financing is typically governed by market mechanisms, as states normally enter into a competitive market in which bond rates are free to rise or fall in line with demand and perceived risk. Accordingly, when states raise finance internationally, accountability is typically structured through market arrangements. By contrast, under the non-market model of domestic finance, the entities providing tax revenues exercise a disciplinary effect through political representation.

Notably, the foregoing distinction regarding forms of accountability coincides with the difference typically drawn between the 'tax state' (*Steuerstaat*) and 'debt state' (*Schuldenstaat*). The former term was coined by Schumpeter to draw attention to the crucial role played by taxation in enabling the activities of the state.[5] By contrast, the latter term emphasises the tendency of states to amass large public debts. While states have accrued enormous debt loads

Ruling of the German Federal Constitutional Court', 20 *European Law Journal* (2014), at 204–218.

3 Curtin, 'Challenging Executive Dominance in European Democracy', 77 *Modern Law Review* (2014), 1–32; Crum, 'Parliamentary Accountability in Multilevel Governance: What Role for Parliaments in Post-crisis EU Economic Governance?', 25 *Journal of European Public Policy* (2018), 268–286; Deters (n.2); Rittberger, 'Integration Without Representation? The European Parliament and the Reform of Economic Governance in the EU', 52 *Journal of Common Market Studies* (2014), 1174–1183.

4 Even though in these credit-based relationship, the debtor states must pay a price that may be linked to some market price level, the financial relationship between public entities follows non-market terms.

5 See the seminal contribution by Schumpeter, Die Krise des Steuerstaates, 1918.

in past eras – British national debt, for example, stood at 200 per cent of GDP at the end of the Napoleonic wars – Streeck argues that 1970 was a transitional moment, as the enormous post-war increases in the size of the public sector in all Western states heralded a new stage in the relationship between capitalism and democracy.[6] In Streeck's view, the growing dependence of governments on large-scale debt issuance entailed growing susceptibility to political influence by financiers. Streeck also undertakes a division between the tax and debt state, positing that under the former model, governments are predominantly accountable to their citizenry, or *Staatsvolk*, who enjoy political representation. Under the debt state model, by contrast, citizens have to compete with bondholders, or *Marktvolk*, who demand reliable debt service.[7] The accountability concept introduced previously reflects this point of distinction between the debt and tax state, while also situating them in wider categories. In particular, the tax state is one type of financing regime based on public relationships – that is, between the taxpayer and sovereign, but public relationships are also at stake in financing between states (e.g. bilateral lending between EU states through the European Financial Stability Facility, or EFSF) or between states and other public institutions (e.g. the International Monetary Fund (IMF) or European Stability Mechanism or, indirectly, the ECB when it purchases government debt). This wider notion of the relationship between public entities and political accountability in the domain of state financing transcends Streeck's notion of the tax state. At the same time, the notion of market accountability goes beyond concern with the debt state's dependence on tax revenues (thus creating accountability to *Marktvolk*) by also encompassing the private relationships of market participants who enter into lending and borrowing transactions without the involvement of the state (e.g. on credit markets or interbank markets). The notion of the tax state versus debt state thus differentiates between sources of government revenue (taxpayers versus market actors), while market versus non-market-based accountability attends to the conditions under which such financing is provided.

One key contribution of this chapter is to elaborate an alternative notion of accountability that furnishes a theoretical underpinning for how economic governance has evolved in the post-crisis setting. The theoretical framework that is developed here builds on the observation that states have the option of raising financing through relationships that depend on market accountability or political accountability, respectively, and that one can be substituted with the other. Furthermore, market accountability as a dominant mode of raising

6 Streeck, *Buying Time: The Delayed Crisis of Democratic Capitalism* (New York: Verso, 2014).

7 Ibid. at 81.

financing has been steadily supplanted in the EU by political accountability in the relationship between debtor states, on the one hand, and creditor states and the ECB, on the other, thus engendering the democratic tensions widely cited in the literature. My central claim is that this shift offers an explanation for the seemingly undemocratic evolution of EU economic governance that has been described by various scholars.[8] Consequently, it follows logically that one way of solving the widely maligned 'democratic deficits' within the Economic and Monetary Union (EMU) would be to restore the market accountability enshrined in the Treaties, as evident in part on the ban on monetary financing, bailouts and state aid. As part of a gradual return to market discipline, it would of course be necessary to enact institutional safeguards that limit the risk of excessive and destabilising market fluctuations. In this regard, with the European Stability Mechanism (ESM) effectively in place, the European Banking Union moving towards completion, and financial market regulations continuously being updated, important safeguards have been established to prevent a return to market accountability from triggering excessive turbulence.

A second contribution of this chapter is to relate the notion of accountability presented here with the accountability concept developed in the introductory chapter of this volume. While the distinction between market and political accountability primarily focuses on *whether* accountability relationships can be organised through market- or non-market-based arrangements, the introductory chapter focuses on *how* accountability standards can be determined and *how* political accountability should be designed. Specifically, Dawson and Maricut-Akbik develop a compelling subdivision between four normative goods of accountability in modern governance – namely: openness, non-arbitrariness, effectiveness and publicness. By reference to their accountability concept, my contribution shows how market accountability – as substitute for political accountability – meets all four of these standards.

## 3.2 THE EU'S ECONOMIC ACCOUNTABILITY REGIME AND ITS DISSOLUTION DURING THE CRISIS

Accountability can be defined as a 'liability to reveal, to explain and to justify what one does'.[9] *Bovens* offers a general understanding of accountability as a relationship between an actor and a forum – the *actor* has an obligation to

[8] Steinbach, 'EU Economic Governance After the Crisis: Revisiting the Accountability Shift in EU Economic Governance', 26 *Journal of European Public Policy* (2019), 1354–1372.

[9] Normaton, 'Public Accountability and Audit: A Reconnaissance', in Smith and Hague (eds.), *The Dilemma of Accountability in Modern Government: Independence Versus Control* (Macmillan, 1971), pp. 311–346.

explain and to justify his or her conduct, while the *forum* can pose questions and pass judgement, and the actor may face consequences.[10] Furthermore, this relationship is founded on three elements: *information* captures the actor's duty to provide information to the forum about his or her conduct. *Justification* expresses the forum's authority to demand that the actor justify his or her actions. And *consequences* denotes the forum's power to impose sanctions or offer rewards.[11]

The three elements of accountability – information, justification, consequences – are readily apparent in the normal exercise of public authority. The government in power (the actor) is accountable to the parliament (the forum); the government informs parliament about its actions and policies (*information*), which are subjected to open debate in parliamentary sessions and special committees (*justification*). On this basis, parliament may impose punishments or rewards (*consequences*).[12]

At this conceptual level, accountability is not limited to the exercise of public power. Rather, accountability more generally encompasses the notion of normative dependencies, which can be established in a formal or informal manner, through social norms or laws. In other words, the legal order may stipulate multiple checks and balances or supervisory mechanisms, which can be understood as normative dependencies. Recalling the above differentiation between market- and non-market-based methods of financing a sovereign state, we can infer that accountability as a normative dependency can be established through either market or political relationships.

### 3.2.1 *Market Accountability in the EU*

The EU is a market economy, which means that investment and spending decisions are guided by price signals. A key principle underlying a market-economic system is individual responsibility, in which companies and individuals reap the consequences of their decisions, whether they produce benefits or culminate in economic failure. If a company wishes to raise investment capital, it must convince investors of its merits. Similarly, when governments borrow money from financial markets, the interest rate they pay is determined by investor assessment of creditworthiness.

The EU Treaties enshrine the notion that both public and private actors should be exposed and accountable to market forces, asserting that economic

10 Bovens, 'Analysing and Assessing Accountability', 13 *European Law Journal* (2007), 447–468, at 447.
11 Bovens, 'Two Concepts of Accountability: Accountability as a Virtue and as a Mechanism', 33 *West European Politics* (2010), 946–967, at 952.
12 Bovens, *supra* note 11, at 952.

policy should be 'conducted in accordance with the principle of an open market economy with free competition'.[13] This commitment to free market principles applies not only to the private sector but also to the public sector, as governments seeking to raise financing must subject their fiscal conduct to the allocative judgements of the market. Similarly, state aid rules forbid government spending that would distort free competition, while the no-bailout principle and prohibition of monetary financing seek to expose governments to the disciplinary force of the market. A commitment to free competition and market-based accountability – including prohibitions against state aid and bailouts – has been a constitutive element of the European Treaties since Maastricht.[14] Thus, despite financial assistance for crisis-wracked Member States, the EU has not created a so-called Transfer Union in which debt obligations are shifted between Member States or to the EU level.[15] In this way, the EU remains committed at least in principle to the allocative wisdom of freely fluctuating price signals, not only as a means of organising economic activity in the private sector but also as a tool in sovereign debt markets for ensuring that Member States conduct sound fiscal policy.

Referring again to the model of market accountability presented above, the market acts as a 'forum' by which judgements are rendered concerning the behaviour of participating actors. Under the EU's legal framework, markets thus perform a crucial organising function, not only in the private sector, by preventing companies from relying on state aid, but also in the area of fiscal policy, as the prohibition of direct transfers between Member States or the EU is designed to prevent irresponsible fiscal behaviour. Under this framework, markets ultimately have the responsibility for rendering judgement on the fiscal viability of a Member State, based on economic criteria. This stands in sharp contrast to the supervisory function exercised by the citizenry and its democratically elected representatives, as various types of value judgements, rather than a purely economic calculus, typically inform assessments regarding the reasonableness of a given policy. Following Bovens's accountability concept, the state–market relationship corresponds to an agent–forum relationship. Public and private actors provide *information* in the sense that

[13] Articles 119, 120, 127 TFEU.

[14] Lechevalier, 'Why and How Has German Ordoliberalism Become a French Issue? Some Aspects About Ordoliberal Thoughts We Can Learn from the French Reception', in Hien and Joerges (eds.), *Ordoliberalism, Law and the Rule of Economics* (Hart, 2017), 23–48, at 42.

[15] Case C-62/14, *Peter Gauweiler and Others v Deutscher Bundestag*, ECLI:EU:C:2015:7, para. 100; Case C-370/12, *Thomas Pringle v Government of Ireland, Ireland and The Attorney General*, ECLI:EU:C:2012:756, para. 135; Case 2 BvR 2728/13, *Bundesverfassungsgericht*, judgment 14 January 2014.

both actors communicate signals concerning their performance (whether in the form of macroeconomic statistics or profit statements). The market (as a forum) processes the information provided by the actors (whether public or private) to assess economic viability and solvency. The *debating* element is less explicit, as states are not literally interrogated by markets in the same way that political authorities are. However, state actors do provide justification for their actions to markets at various levels.[16] Specifically, states testify to the soundness of their policies and to their solvency by publishing budgetary statistics and by adhering to certain accounting standards.[17] They comply with the bond issuance requirements requested by investors, and they cooperate with the rating agencies that scrutinise their policies in order to assess their solvency. Finally, *consequences* represent the forum's power to reward or punish actors for their performance;[18] market prices thus act as the disciplinary mechanism. Rising bond rates reflect riskier lending conditions and are an outcome of the assessment performed by market observers. States are thus held liable for their economic performance through interest rates, with sanctions or rewards taking the form of higher or lower risk premiums.[19]

### 3.2.2 *How the EU Replaced Market Accountability with Political Accountability*

Over the course of the crisis, the market orientation that previously served as a mechanism for ensuring sound fiscal policy was gradually supplanted by a new regime of political accountability, as Member State reliance on market financing was substituted with non-market-based support facilities. As the finances of some debtor states deteriorated, causing them to lose access to capital markets, the EU stepped in to prevent financial collapse, providing bilateral financial aid, which was later replaced by the ESM. The ESM and other forms of assistance were structured with conditions that can be ascribed

16 Steinbach, 'EU Economic Governance After the Crisis: Revisiting the Accountability Shift in EU Economic Governance', 26 *Journal of European Public Policy* (2019), 1354–1372, at 1361.

17 For example, Member States submit annual Stability and Convergence Programmes as part of the European Semester, which serve the Commission and finance ministers to assess whether Member States are on track towards reaching their Medium-Term Budgetary Objectives (MTOs).

18 Fearon, 'Electoral Accountability and the Control of Politicians: Selecting Good Types versus Sanctioning Poor Performance', in Przeworski, Stokes and B. Manin (eds.), *Democracy, Accountability, and Representation* (Cambridge University Press, 1999), pp. 55–97, at 55; Strøm, 'Delegation and Accountability in Parliamentary Democracies', 37 *European Journal of Political Research* (2000), 261–290, at 267.

19 Steinbach, *supra* note 8, at 1358.

to the categories of *information*, *justification* and *consequences*. Specifically, a Member State must apply for assistance and provide information that fulfils transparency standards (*information*); it must comply with a set of conditions, adopt policy changes, and demonstrate adherence to agreed terms (*justification*); and lastly, it may be subject to consequences – rewards in case of compliance, sanctions in case of non-compliance (*consequences*).[20]

Various policy tools subsequently developed by the EU also adhere to this logic. Prior to the outbreak of the COVID-19 pandemic, a 'reform delivery tool' was envisaged by the EU Commission, under which Member States would enact structural reforms in exchange for financial assistance.[21] In concrete terms, Member States wishing to receive support would submit a proposal for reform commitments to the Commission substantiating how it would address the challenges identified in the European Semester (i.e. *informing*).[22] The Commission would be entitled to request additional information and require the Member State to revise the proposal if needed (i.e. *justifying*).[23] During the implementation process, the Commission would assess compliance with milestones and would be able to suspend disbursement (i.e. *sanctioning*).[24] With the onset of the COVID-19 crisis, this tool was replaced by an even more financially potent instrument: the Next Generation EU (NGEU) and the Recover and Resilience Facility (RRF), which establish a quid pro quo mechanism in which grants are offered in return for compliance with a conditionality regime; financial assistance is made contingent on certain types of public expenditure.[25] The RRF allocation mechanism builds on *information* provided by Member States as they pitch eligible projects;[26] involves an element of *justification* by virtue of an assessment by the Commission, which may entail requests for changes or additional information;[27] and foresees the *sanction* of payment suspension if milestones or targets are not adequately fulfilled.[28]

Thus, rather than being exposed to the collective and (ostensibly) impassioned judgements of the market, ESM or RRF funding, recipients are subject

20 On the metric of implementation of financial assistance Ioannidis, 'EU Financial Assistance Conditionality after "Two Pack"', 74 *Zeitschrift für ausländisches öffentliches Recht und Völkerrecht* (2014), 61–104, at 76 et seq.

21 COM/2018/391, Proposal for a Regulation of the European Parliament and of the Council on the establishment of the Reform Support Programme.

22 Article 11 para. 3 of COM/2018/391.

23 Article 11 para. 5 of COM/2018/391.

24 Article 15.5 of COM/2018/391.

25 Regulation (EU) 2021/241 of the European Parliament and of the Council of 12 February 2021 establishing the Recovery and Resilience Facility, O.J. 2021, L 57/17 (hereinafter: RRF).

26 Article 17 para. 1, Article 18 para. 4, Article 27 of RRF.

27 Article 19 of RRF.

28 Article 24 of RRF.

to the discretion of the bureaucratic authorities administering these funding programmes.[29] In this way, market accountability has effectively been replaced with a new regime of political accountability. Accordingly, it stands to reason that insofar as a public authority (in this case, the European Commission) is rendering judgement on the policy decisions of a Member State, the principle of democratic representation would demand that Commission's decision be legitimised through an appeal to its proper authority as an elected body. While the relationship between markets and democracy has always been controversial,[30] this new accountability regime would be far less fraught if Member States were to subject their fiscal policy to the judgement of markets, for the abolishment of market accountability has raised major questions surrounding the proper role for EU institutions in the financing of Member States, including associated theoretical issues related to democratic legitimacy.

With fiscal and monetary support for crisis-racked countries undermining the principle of market accountability, strict national responsibility for national debt has been practically invalidated, thereby relaxing the economic accountability rule enshrined in EU Treaty arrangements. Moreover, the shift from market to political accountability has not been limited to state financing. The crisis-induced easing of EU restrictions on state aid illustrates how the decline of market accountability standards has also extended to the private sector. The numerous public–sector interventions that have been witnessed in past years – from bailouts to liquidity lifelines – are far from compatible with the regulatory ideal of free markets that are enshrined in the Treaties.[31]

In sum, with the principle of market exposure weakened by crisis and a greatly expanded role for the public sector in providing financing and ensuring liquidity, debt financing is now granted for political reasons under the logic of discretional conditionality, rather than for reasons of market economics. In this way, markets are no longer the motive force for states to engage in fiscal consolidation – rather, consolidation and restructuring are performed due to conditions attached to ESM, RRF or ECB aid.[32] Numerous observers have argued that the discontinuation of market accountability was predominantly driven by market failure: with bond spreads jumping erratically, fear of financial collapse triggering bank runs, and investors pulling out of crisis-roiled

[29] However, the conditionality type attached to the RRF is more modest than under the ESM, see De Witte, 'The European Union's Covid-19 Recovery Plan: The Legal Engineering of An Economic Policy Shift', 58 *CML Review* (2021), 635–681, at 676.

[30] Streeck, 'How Will Capitalism End?', 87 *New Left Review* (2014), at 35–64, 40 et seq.

[31] Menéndez, *supra* note 1, at 59.

[32] Viterbo, 'Legal and Accountability Issues Arising from the ECB's Conditionality', 1 European Papers (2016), at 501 et seq.

countries, policy officials enacted far-reaching interventions to clamp down on market turmoil and limit the economic fallout of the crisis. Legally, the ESM has a mandate to intervene if 'indispensable to safeguard the financial stability of the euro areas as a whole and of its Member States';[33] similarly, it has been argued that unconventional monetary policy measures were necessary to sustain the transmission of monetary impulses to the real economy.[34] In the wake of the crisis, should we therefore conclude that market accountability has failed as an organising principle for sovereign financing, and should thus be abandoned, as some have argued?[35] Insofar as one supports this view, one must contend with the limitations to state sovereignty that emerge from dependence on creditor countries and institutions, and associated challenges to democratic legitimacy. Accordingly, it would appear more promising to advocate the preservation of market accountability, yet in a modified form that limits risk market failure through sound regulatory and monetary policy in combination with limited backstopping and bailout measures.

## 3.3 THE NORMATIVE, PROCEDURAL AND SUBSTANTIVE DIMENSIONS OF MARKET ACCOUNTABILITY

In the introductory chapter, Dawson and Maricut-Akbik develop a standard of accountability with two-fold applicability: on the one hand, it can serve as analytical benchmark for assessing the degree and scope of accountability; and, on the other, it can serve as a normative standard for ensuring a high level of democratic accountability. This section engages in greater detail with the accountability concept presented in the introductory chapter. Specifically, I argue that market accountability can serve as a conceptual vehicle for 'four normative goods' doctrine developed by Dawson and Maricut-Akbik, not least because it also accommodates the procedural and substantive dimensions of this typology. Accordingly, market accountability is useful not only as an analytical category but also as a conceptual tool for framing an accountability regime grounded in normative ethics, one that supports subjecting public policy to the allocative wisdom of the market. I argue that, when properly regulated, market accountability promotes openness, incentivises impartiality among policy officials, augments the effectiveness of policy measures, and support decisions oriented to the common good. Yet this does not mean to elevate market accountability to

33 Article 3 ESM Treaty.

34 Case C-62/14, Peter Gauweiler and Others v Deutscher Bundestag, ECLI:EU:C:2015:7, para. 50.

35 Stiglitz, 'The Fundamental Flaws in the Euro Zone Framework', in da Costa Cabral, Gonçalves, and Rodrigues (eds.), *The Euro and the Crisis: Financial and Monetary Policy Studies* (Springer, 2017), 11–16.

the status of universal applicability at the expense of democratic accountability norms – market considerations should not trump democratic legitimacy where core matters of public interest are concerned.[36] However, market exposure would appear decidedly preferable to political accountability when multiple levels of governance confound clear lines of democratic control, as in the case of European sovereign debt financing.

### 3.3.1 *Market Accountability and the Four Normative Goods*

Dawson and Maricut-Akbik developed their accountability concept against the backdrop of the structurally flawed EMU accountability regime, subject as it is to a complex array of intergovernmental and supranational actors, who interact at multiple decision-making levels. The authors propose a new deductive framework for studying accountability that is more suitable to the EMU setting. Drawing on the public administration literature and liberal and republican strands in political theory, they develop a model of accountability that posits four normative 'goods' of accountability: openness, non-arbitrariness, effectiveness and publicness. They explore this normativity along the two normative dimensions of accountability typically recognised in public law – namely, procedural accountability, which focuses on the processes used by actors to take decisions, and substantive accountability, which focuses on the merits of the decisions themselves.

In a previous section, we discussed how Bovens's general characteristics of accountability – that is, information, justification and consequences – are evident not only in market accountability relationships but also in the political accountability relationships that structure EMU financial assistance and RRF support. Notably, there are clear parallels between Dawson's and Bovens's accountability standards: first, *openness* refers to the expectation that the workings of the state should be transparent. It is a defining feature of the democratic ideal that citizens should be in a position to observe the actions of public authority as a necessary prerequisite for rendering judgement on it. This relates directly to Bovens's notion of 'justification', according to which the actor must give an account of her actions in a public forum. Crucially, openness (and Bovens's 'information' and 'justification') can be found in both market and non-market accountability settings. For example, in federal systems, regional authorities who obtain financial transfers from the federal government are held politically accountable, as they are typically obliged to demonstrate their

36 Grauwe, *The Limits of the Market: The Pendulum Between Government and Market* (Oxford University Press, 2017).

financial need ('informing'), while accounting for how they have spent this funding in the past or will do so in future ('justifying').[37] Public entities are required to maintain open books and to report their expenditures to parliament and to the citizenry. Similarly, market accountability relies on openness – governments seeking to receive obtain financing through bond sales are expected to disclose their financial position so that market actors can assess associated lending risks, with more precarious macroeconomic and fiscal conditions leading to higher risk premiums and less favourable financing conditions, which can culminate in extreme cases in loss of access to financial markets.

The second good in the model posited by Dawson and Maricut-Akbik is *non-arbitrariness*. Drawing on principal–agent theory, non-arbitrariness limits the agent's scope of authority and links it to the principal's interest. Non-arbitrariness also encompasses the legal protection of the principal against non-compliant actions of the agent. Holding officials responsible for their conduct allows the arbitrary application of power to not only be discouraged but also remedied, should it occur.[38] The concept of non-arbitrariness is inherent to public fiscal relationships, as parliament approves and monitors budgets proposed by government, and citizens also exert an oversight function through elections. Similarly, under a market accountability regime, financing conditions are (in theory) determined by underlying economic fundamentals, thus compelling the state to pursue viable fiscal policies. Furthermore, if a state were to act arbitrarily or in opposition to the interests of the principal (i.e. investors) by defaulting on bond payments, the state in question would not only face legal attempts to force repayment but would witness a withdrawal of market confidence, and, by extension, rapidly deteriorating economic conditions.[39] However, the principle of non-arbitrariness in the domain of market accountability does have certain limitations, as markets can behave irrationally, such as when investors are seized by herd behaviour.[40] This is an important point of divergence from political accountability that is based on constitutional rights. When the relationship between economic fundamentals (as an outcome of policy) and bond rates (as a judgement rendered on that policy) becomes fundamentally disturbed or arbitrary, market accountability

37 Steinbach, *supra* note 8, at 1360.

38 Dawson and Maricut-Akbik, Introduction in this volume.

39 On the reputational function of markets, see Eaton and Gersovitz, 'Debt with Potential Repudiation: Theoretical and Empirical Analysis', *The Review of Economic Studies* 48 (1981), 289–309, at 290; Tomz, *Reputation and International Cooperation: Sovereign Debt across Three Centuries* (Princeton University Press, 2007).

40 De Grauwe, Ji and Steinbach, Armin. 'The Euro Debt Crisis: Testing and Revisiting Conventional Legal Doctrine', *International Review of Law and Economics* 51 (2017), 29–37.

as an operative principle breaks down. This underscores the importance of embedding market accountability in an adequate regulatory and institutional architecture that can limit and address such instances of market failure.

The third good that accountability seeks to ensure is *effectiveness*. Unlike the first two goods, effectiveness refers to a standard of performance: public officials are expected to enact policies of a satisfactory quality. Indeed, explicit efficiency benchmarks are not foreign to the accountability standards that are applied to government authorities. To be sure, the notion that public goods should be supplied in line with market mechanisms is a rich strand in the public administration literature, one that has stimulated numerous managerial reforms in the public sector.[41] Effectiveness may well be the aspect of accountability most closely related to market accountability, as functioning markets impose clear financial constraints on public-sector budgets. In this regard, effectiveness also mirrors Bovens's criterion of 'consequences' – as the agent (here, the state) suffers immediate disadvantages if its conduct does not conform with market expectations. Specifically, bond rates can be expected to fluctuate in line with a state's financial position and solvency. In this way, sovereign debt markets send price signals that act as a disciplinary mechanism, incentivising policymakers to adopt judicious policies.

The fourth and final normative good is 'publicness', which refers to the notion that policy should serve the *common good*. This aspect enshrines the notion that government authorities should not pursue selfish purposes but rather take into account collective interests. This does not mean, however, that each forum must pursue the same collective interests: for example, courts review public authority on the basis of certain legal standards; citizens vote in elections based on their political convictions; and parliaments monitor the executive with a view to the fulfilment of legislative goals. This criterion subsumes the notions of both 'justification' and 'consequences' contained in Bovens's model, as it implies officials are to be scrutinised and must also give an account of their actions. Regarding the mechanisms of market accountability, markets price the risk of default based on a country's ability to service a bond – and this risk depends on numerous factors, including the performance of the economy as a whole, which depends in part on inclusive growth. In this way, financial investors will punish countries that flout the interests of the society at large. However, the market may also be indifferent to ethical considerations when a country is otherwise fiscally sound. For example, authoritarian states may enjoy the full confidence of the market, particularly if they are rich in commodities, and high levels of inequality do not necessarily impair fiscal stability. However, as open

[41] Harlow, *Accountability in the European Union* (Oxford University Press, 2002), p. 24.

and stable societies with a strong tradition of individual rights are generally more prosperous, we often find a correlation between these characteristics and the market's valuation of a country's creditworthiness.

Against this backdrop, we infer that market accountability can be assessed within the normative framework proposed by Dawson and Maricut-Akbik and that the normative premises grounded in public law are not alien to market accountability. This does not mean to imply that political accountability can be substituted in all instances with market accountability, as the exercise of public power in line with democratic principles requires political legitimacy to traceable to the will of the citizenry.[42] However, in domains in which market actors and political actors supply an identical good – that is, financing – it is important to recognise that market accountability can fulfil all of the standards associated with political accountability – namely, openness, non-arbitrariness, effectiveness and publicness.

### 3.3.2 *Procedural and Substantive Dimensions of Market Accountability*

The concordance between market accountability and procedural and substantive notions of accountability also deserves our attention. The respective scope of procedural and substantive accountability emerges most clearly from the judicial review of parliamentary decisions, where courts exercise judicial restraint with regard to substance. Typically, the substantive and procedural dimensions of a legality review interact as communicating vessels: the more the court requires in procedural terms, the more it alleviates the judicial review on substantive grounds towards a 'manifestly inappropriate' standard.[43] Judicial procedural review implies a thorough assessment of the process by which a parliamentary act was adopted.[44] Not the substantive content of the decision is at stake but rather the procedural steps that led to the formation of a policy decision. Conversely, a substantive account would value the substantive worth of the policy decision itself.

Regarding the first normative good – openness – market accountability operates on the basis of procedural grounds: states periodically disclose statistics and

[42] Böckenförde, 'Demokratische Willensbildung und Repräsentation', in Isensee and Kirchhof (eds.), *Handbuch des Staatsrechts der Bundesrepublik Deutschland*, volume 3, 3rd ed. (C.F. Müller, 2005), pp. 31–54.

[43] Brenncke, Case Note (2010), 47 *CML Review* 1793, at 1809–1810; Mendes, 'Discretion, Care and Public Interests in the EU Administration: Probing the Limits of Law', 53 *CML Review* (2016), 419–452.

[44] Lenaerts, 'The European Court of Justice and Process-oriented Review', *Research Papers in Law* 1 (2012), at 15.

indicators that reveal their fiscal position and economic outlook. Also, public-sector emitters of bonds must comply with certain transparency requirements in order to protect investors.[45] The regulatory framework, which includes the requirement to publish transparent statistics and adhere to good accounting practices, generates trustworthiness through behavioural compliance. The second criterion – non-arbitrariness – also has a procedural and behavioural dimension. Rating agencies play an important role in this regard. While they do not perform a public policy function, rating agencies serve the interests of the principal (i.e. the market) by requiring the state to reveal the information necessary for markets to monitor the state's conduct. Rating agencies help to discipline states, dissuading them from putting their solvency at risk. There is a procedural dimension in the fact that rating agencies work through a web of more or less formalised interactions between actors and market institutions, by which they subject states to justification and transparency. Internally, rating agencies apply substantive standards, on the basis of which they form their solvency assessment and assign a bond credit rating. Rating grades are a substantive and quantifiable metric of fiscal viability – however, as a substantive standard, such ratings are not legally contestable, nor are they transparent or uniformly applicable.

Effectiveness as an accountability standard is of a substantive nature, as it mirrors the degree to which markets can hold states to be fiscally viable or not. The precise nature and scope of solvency in terms of market judgement may be hardly computable, but the market price for debt is the numerical tool through which markets impose fiscal discipline on states. Functioning markets translate the fundamental performance data of a state into a price that ultimately has an impact on the state's conduct. While price signals are a market-based tool for promoting effectiveness, reporting and disclosure practices are undertaken to fulfil demands imposed by market actors and public transparency expectations. As mentioned, public-sector emitters of bonds must comply with certain transparency rules. At the same time, states justify their fiscal expenditures in the public sphere, and they also publicise statistics through multiple channels, as required by EU reporting duties. These legally defined reporting duties (e.g. as imposed by the European Semester) seek to capture various dimensions of economic viability.[46]

Finally, publicness also contains both procedural and substantive dimensions. This criterion encapsulates the expectation that the state demonstrate

[45] Most recently, COM (2021) 391 final, Proposal for a Regulation of the European Parliament and of the Council on European green bonds.

[46] For example, the Semester requires Member States to submit Stability and Convergence Programmes on basis of which the Commission assesses whether Member States are on track towards reaching their Medium-Term Budgetary Objectives (MTOs).

its commitment to working towards the common good. Clearly, markets are not formally committed to promoting the general welfare, so it cannot be expected the market forces will necessarily encourage states to pursue the common good. While there are often political movements that aim to constrain markets and make them subject to the public will, markets do in fact promote virtuous policy to some extent, for they discourage kleptocratic fiscal management that is harmful to economic fundamentals or growth prospects. An economy will fare better over the long term if its resources are managed to encourage growth and prosperity, rather than to enrich a narrow segment of society. In this way, while market exposure can neither assure socioeconomic fairness nor prevent corrupt rulers from holding power, a market's assessment of a country's solvency may indirectly promote innovation and inclusive growth. As with the other normative goods, disclosure and transparency have an important signalling effect that a country is engaged in practices that are generally supportive of a healthy society.

## 3.4 CONCLUSION

With the outbreak of sovereign debt crisis, there was a gradual shift in European state financing from market-based accountability relationships to a political accountability regime. From the perspective of democratic accountability, there is a significant difference between, on the one hand, raising financing from financial markets, with bond rates determined by a dispassionate assessment of default risk, and, on the other hand, from accepting financing on conditions set by sovereign foreign or supranational entities, which, by virtue of their creditor position, can directly impinge upon the state's sovereignty. As part of the massive market interventions undertaken since the outbreak of the crisis, the ECB and EU lending facilities such as the ESM have extended financing to debtor nations at favourable rates unmoored from economic fundamentals while simultaneously imposing various forms of political conditionality, thus engendering numerous tensions related to democratic representation and legitimacy.[47] Specifically, the public authorities empowered to intervene in the affairs of debtor nations are not subject to the accountability controls normally ascribed to democratic systems. This situation is directly attributable to the regime shift from market accountability to (anaemic) political accountability, a shift that occurred in the absence of robust public discussion or debate.[48]

47 Heldt and Mueller, 'The (Self-)Empowerment of the European Central Bank During the Sovereign Debt Crisis', 43 *Journal of European Integration* (2021), 83–98.

48 Joerges and Kreuder-Sonnen, 'European Studies and the European Crisis: Legal and Political Science Between Critique and Complacency', *European Law Journal* 23 (2017), 118–139.

As shown in this chapter, market-based accountability exhibits strong congruence with other accountability regimes. Market accountability features both an actor and a forum, and relationships are structured based on information, justification and consequences. Our analysis suggests that market accountability may also undergird the supply of normative goods by promoting openness, non-arbitrariness, effectiveness and publicness. Markets exercise behavioural pressure on debtor states, encouraging transparency, fiscal stability and inclusive growth. Of course, there are strong limitations on the ability of international financial markets to encourage states to respect individual rights and the general welfare.[49] However, given the role ascribed to the market-based allocation of financial resources in the EU Treaties in tandem with ongoing concerns about the democratic deficits exhibited by alternative arrangements, reinvigorating market forces may in fact represent a solution for encouraging a more impartial and broadly accepted governance architecture in the EU.

While this discussion by no means aims to assert that market accountability should generally prevail over political accountability regimes, the major contribution of this chapter is to highlight that market accountability has theoretical underpinnings that are congruent with traditional accountability systems rooted in public law or political theory. At the same time, market-based modes of accountability are less intrusive and less susceptible to control by narrow interests than the EU economic governance regime that has emerged in the wake of the crisis.[50] Hence, in order to avoid economic and social policy in debtor states from being subjugated by the fiat decisions of creditor nations or supranational governance bodies, there is a need for an eventual retreat from political accountability as an organising principle in the domain of European sovereign debt financing. A return should be sought to the EU Treaties' choice of free market rules that subject the financing needs of private actors and states to the judgement of markets, rather than political actors.

As it stands, current trends indicate there could be a further weakening of market accountability in favour of an even greater role for EU institutions in the area of public-sector financing. Since the outbreak of the COVID-19 pandemic, the ECB has been purchasing sovereign debt on an expanded scale, and there has been an attendant growth in political conditionalities. More generally, Member State reliance on EU-based financing is slated to expand dramatically in the coming years as part of the general proliferation

49 Merkel, 'Is Capitalism Compatible with Democracy?', *Comparative Governance and Politics* 8 (2014), 109–128.

50 Steinbach, *supra* note 8, at 1368.

of lending facilities. This will increase the EU's exposure to market accountability while also increasing the political accountability of Member States to EU institutions.

Finally, drawing on the difference between market and political accountability, our analysis relates back to Streeck's critical view on the gradual shift from the tax state to the debt state. For Streeck, the shift from the publicly dominated tax state to the privately dominated dependence on markets is undemocratic, since the emergence of private creditors as a second constituency alongside national citizens requires public officials to balance between maintaining the loyalty of their citizens while at the same time preserving the confidence of private investors.[51] This contrasts with the finding of this study: starting from the vast body of literature that has spotlighted the democratic issues emerging from abandoning market exposure in sovereign debt financing,[52] this study argued that market accountability poses fewer issues from a democratic perspective, for it avoids the inevitable intrusions into national sovereignty that result from borrowing at preferred terms from EU bodies or other Member States. Clearly, market accountability comes with its own specific risks, which is why it is necessary to adopt an institutional framework that contains and combats the risks of market irrationality or Black Swan events. Ultimately, when properly managed, markets thus appear to be more compatible with responsible accountability and policy founded on a chain of legitimacy and stems from the citizenry.

[51] Streeck, Buying Time, 2014, p. 79.

[52] *Supra* notes 2 and 3.

# 4

# The Case for Intra-executive Accountability in the Banking Union

*Matthias Goldmann*[*]

## 4.1 INTRODUCTION

One remarkable, widespread trend in the European economic constitution since the financial crisis has been the rise of discretionary powers on the part of independent government agencies, specifically, the European Central Bank (ECB). The shift to unorthodox monetary policy, and in particular quantitative easing, has increased, or rather, brought to light the discretionary powers of the ECB within the four corners of its stability mandate.[1] Moreover, the competencies assigned to the Single Supervisory Mechanism (SSM) imply enormous leeway for the ECB in assessing the financial situation of banks throughout the European Union.[2] In times of radical uncertainty, it seems difficult to imagine carrying out monetary policy or supervisory functions without ample discretion at hand.[3]

Yet, many observers frown upon these powers as they undermine the technocratic narrative that has served as a justification for ECB independence so far.[4] A first boiling point was reached in the *Landesbank* case. According to

* Professor, EBS University Wiesbaden; Senior Research Fellow, Max Planck Institute for Comparative Public Law and International Law, Heidelberg, goldmann@mpil.de. This text is based on Matthias Goldmann, "Die Bedeutung intraexekutiver Kontrollen für die Gewaltenteilung in der Bankenunion," in Michael Sachs et al. (eds.), *Zentralbanken, Währungsunion und stabiles Finanzsystem. Festschrift für Helmut Siekmann* (Duncker & Humblot, 2019) 289.

1 BVerfG *PSPP*, 2 BvR 859/15, Judgment of 5 May 2020, ECLI:DE:BVerfG:2020:rs20200505.2bvr085915, para. 129.

2 Council Regulation (EU) No 1024/2013 of 15 October 2013 conferring specific tasks on the European Central Bank concerning policies relating to the prudential supervision of credit institutions, OJ L 278/63 of 29 October 2013 (hereinafter SSM Regulation).

3 Kay and King, *Radical Uncertainty: Decision-Making for an Unknowable Future* (Bridge Street Press 2020).

4 Tucker, *Unelected Power: The Quest for Legitimacy in Central Banking and the Regulatory State* (Princeton University Press 2018); Feichtner, 'The German Constitutional Court's PSPP

the Court of Justice of the European Union (CJEU), the SSM enjoys wide discretion to cede its supervisory competence over less significant institutions to national supervisory authorities.[5] This judgment provoked backlash not only in academia[6] but also at the German Constitutional Court (BVerfG). While ultimately accepting the CJEU judgment, it clearly drew a red line, pointing out that the CJEU narrowly missed an *ultra vires* verdict from Karlsruhe.[7] Moreover, members of domestic parliaments sense a loss of influence and are skeptical of the concentration of powers in the hands of the ECB, even though Article 21 SSM Regulation stipulates ample consultation rights for them.[8] On the other hand, nobody has come forward with a proposal to dismantle the ECB and shift its powers to the European Commission or, worse, the Council. Apart from well-known time-inconsistency problems, the ideas of expertise and reliability favor delegation to authorities enjoying some degree of autonomy.[9] Some therefore suggest that one should assign supervisory competencies to the European Banking Authority (EBA) instead of the ECB.[10]

This chapter argues that the accountability of the SSM may be better than the current debate suggests. While judicial and parliamentary modes of accountability – the focus of the present debate – do have certain limits, a set of intra-executive accountability mechanisms is often overlooked. It is adequate for politically salient decisions like the discretionary powers exercised by the SSM.

The chapter proceeds as follows. An overview of the breadth and depth of discretionary powers exercised by the SSM debunks any attempt to base the

Judgment: Impediment and Impetus for the Democratization of Europe', 21 *German Law Journal* 1090 (2020).

5 Cf. *Landeskreditbank Baden-Württemberg – Förderbank v European Central Bank*, Case T-122/15, Judgment of the General Court (Fourth Chamber, Extended Composition) of 16 May 2017, ECLI:EU:T:2017:337; confirmed by the CJEU in Case C-450/17 P, Judgment of 18 May 2019, ECLI:EU:C:2019:372, mn. 53 et seq.

6 Tröger, "How Not to Do Banking Law in the 21st Century: The Judgement of the European General Court (EGC) in the Case T-122/15-Landeskreditbank Baden-Württemberg-Förderbank V Euro-pean Central Bank (ECB)," SAFE Policy Letter No 56 (2017).

7 BVerfG *Banking Union*, 2 BvR 1685/14, Judgment of 30 July 2019, ECLI:DE:BVerfG:2019:rs20190730.2bvr168514, para. 203 et seq.

8 Cf. Deutscher Bundestag, Motion "Europäisches System der Finanzaufsicht effizient weiterentwickeln," BT-Drs. 18/7539 of 16 February 2016; see also the speech of MdB Radwan, 18 February 2016, Plenary Protocols, 18th term, session 155, pp. 15265–15266, http://dipbt.bundestag.de/dip21/btp/18/18155.pdf#P.15265.

9 Tucker, supra note 4, pp. 92 et seq.

10 Ramthun, "CSU-Vorstoß zur Trennung von EZB-Geldpolitik und Bankenaufsicht," Wirtschaftswoche, 11 January 2018, available at: www.wiwo.de/politik/deutschland/europaeische-zentralbank-csu-vorstoss-zur-trennung-von-ezb-geldpolitik-und-bankenaufsicht/20834002.html. This might require a treaty change, see Moloney, "European Banking Union: Assessing Its Risks and Resilience," 51 *Common Market Law Review* 1609 (2014), pp. 1653 et seq.; Ohler, *Bankenaufsicht und Geldpolitik in der Währungsunion* (Beck, 2015), pp. 145–146.

legitimacy of the SSM on a technocratic rationale (B.I.). Instead, the chapter argues that the legitimacy of independent institutions like the SSM is effectively a question of a level of accountability commensurate to the institutional position of the SSM and the authority exercised by it (B.II.). The specific authority exercised by the SSM requires judicial, parliamentary, and intra-executive accountability (B.III.).

The chapter then reviews the current framework of checks and balances applicable to the SSM. While judicial review is an effective accountability mechanism for standard administrative decisions that implement legal requirements, it has a limited function in respect of the highly policy-relevant, quasi-governmental powers of the SSM (C.I.). Parliamentary accountability is generally capable of dealing with politically salient issues that might require changes in the law or of keeping budgetary side effects of financial regulation under control. However, the control exercised by the parliament is rather general in nature and cannot address individual regulatory decisions. This impedes the review of policy-heavy, discretionary decisions addressing individual cases (C.II.). This turns the focus to intra-executive accountability mechanisms. These mechanisms comprise the review of individual, discretionary decisions with potentially far-reaching consequences. As the independence of the ECB prohibits the issuance of binding directives like in ordinary administrative review proceedings, the Commission and the European Court of Auditors (ECA) yield a nonbinding type of authority by reviewing the work of the SSM. Fortunately, obstacles initially preventing the work of ECA have been eliminated. Taken together with parliamentary accountability and judicial review, it does not appear that the SSM is suffering from a severe accountability gap (C.III.).

The chapter concludes by reviewing suggestions for strengthening intra-executive accountability. They range from reassigning the SSM to EBA, to increasing the Commission's powers of control. In fact, the latter scenario seems most advantageous. It is even possible to reconcile it with the treaty-guaranteed independence of the ECB. Despite the positive assessment of the present level of SSM accountability, increasing the powers of the Commission over the SSM might be in the ECB's best long-term interest (D.).

## 4.2 THE LEGITIMACY OF INDEPENDENT INSTITUTIONS

### 4.2.1 *The Limits of Technocratic Legitimacy*

Historically, the legitimacy of independent institutions has been based on the ideas of expertise and time inconsistency. Some decisions require too much technical expertise and a longer-term perspective to leave them to elected officials whose primary focus is on winning the next elections.[11] This, however, assumes that the issue in question is essentially a technical, low-politics one that does not shift major redistributive decisions to unelected institutions.[12]

I think that this justification is insufficient for independent supervisory authorities. The sheer extent of the SSM's discretionary powers debunks the attempt to adorn it with a technocratic varnish. Of course, not all SSM decisions raise similar concerns. To the extent that the SSM takes decisions of a rather narrow administrative character, that is, by applying a narrowly defined normative program to a specific case, it would be wild to assume a spectacular legitimacy gap. One example would be fit and proper decisions.[13] Rigorous judicial review appears to be sufficient for decisions of this type. The CJEU would even allow delegating such competencies to independent agencies.[14] However, there is another category of supervisory decisions, which are of far-reaching political significance. They involve crucial choices that might have relevance for the health of the entire financial sector. The following scenarios illustrate some of these decisions and their impact and potential for conflict.

First, supervisory decisions may include monetary policy considerations. While the SSM Regulation provides for the separation of monetary and supervisory powers,[15] in practice, the two fields are too closely related for a full separation to work out. It would create an impossible situation for the ECB if its monetary and supervisory prongs were pulling on the opposing ends of one and the same string.[16] Moreover, the legal frameworks of the Treaty on the Functioning of the EU (TFEU) and the SSM Regulation provide enough discretionary leeway for the ECB to take monetary concerns and concerns for financial stability into account in its prudential decisions.[17] The relevant rules define goals rather than setting out a precise normative program to be applied in a narrowly defined situation – a familiar feature of the provisions applicable in the scope of the Economic and Monetary Union.[18] Naturally, the application of goal-oriented provisions involves a wide margin of discretion.

[11] Tucker, supra note 4.; Goldmann, "United in Diversity? The Relationship between Monetary Policy and Prudential Supervision in the Banking Union," 14 *European Constitutional Law Review* 283 (2018).

[12] Tucker, *supra* note 4, at 569.

[13] Cf. Article 4(1)(e) SSM Regulation.

[14] *United Kingdom v Parliament and Council (ESMA)*, Case C-270/12, judgment of 22. January 2014, ECLI:EU:C:2014:18.

[15] Article 25, SSM Regulation.

[16] See Goldmann, supra note 11.

[17] Ibid.

[18] Bast, "Don't Act Beyond Your Powers: The Perils and Pitfalls of the German Constitutional Court's Ultra Vires Review," 15 *German Law Journal* 167 (2014), at p. 175.

Second, wide discretionary powers exist with respect to decisions on bank resolution. According to the Single Resolution Mechanism (SRM) Regulation, the Resolution Board decides about the resolution of a financial institution on the basis of the opinion of the ECB on the probability of default.[19] Although the Resolution Board may override the ECB's opinion, the ECB's decision structures the ultimate result in a decisive way.[20] In taking this decision, the ECB might have to balance conflicting interests. On the one hand, it might be cost-effective to resolve failing institutions as soon as the situation appears to be irreversible. On the other hand, supervisory concern for the stability of other institutions likely to be affected by the resolution might militate in favor of a delay until precautionary measures are in place or the other institutions have been stabilized. The wording of Article 18 SRM Resolution provides enough leeway for the ECB to tilt in one direction or another. In particular, to establish under Article 18(1)(c) SRM Regulation that a resolution action is in the public interest, Article 18(5) SRM Regulation refers to the broadly phrased objectives of Article 14(2) SRM Regulation, which comprise, among others, the objective to protect "financial stability."[21] This concept is hardly more concrete than the notion of price stability.[22]

The third scenario concerns the influence of the ECB on rulemaking. In the Banking Union, the EBA in cooperation with the Commission normally holds rulemaking powers, while the ECB is only a nonvoting member of the EBA board of supervisors.[23] However, the ECB has gained effective influence owing to its position as the institution hosting the SSM. In particular, the ECB and National Competent Authorities (NCAs) are charged with the implementation of EBA guidelines. For this purpose, the ECB and the NCAs have developed common policies reflected in guides, such as the guide for fit and proper decisions.[24] Of course, such guides are subordinate to, and need to be in compliance with, all applicable rules, including relevant EBA guidelines.

19 Article 18(1) subpara. 1 lit. a SRM Regulation.

20 Article 18(1) subpara. 2 SRM Regulation. Nothing else applies to decisions about alternatives to resolution, Article 18 (1) subpara. 1, lit. b SRM Regulation, or decisions on early intervention, Article 18(2) SRM Regulation.

21 Article 14(2)(b) SRM Regulation.

22 Actually, the ECB financial stability mandate is derivative of its price stability mandate, see Psaroudakis, "The Scope for Financial Stability Considerations in the Fulfilment of the Mandate of the ECB/Eurosystem," 4 *Journal of Financial Regulation* 119 (2018).

23 Article 40(1)(b), Regulation (EU) No 1093/2010 of the European Parliament and of the Council of 24 November 2010 establishing a European Supervisory Authority (European Banking Authority), amending Decision No 716/2009/EC and repealing Commission Decision 2009/78/EC, OJ L 331/12 of 15 December 2010 (hereinafter EBA Regulation).

24 ECB, Guide to fit and proper assessments, May 2018, www.bankingsupervision.europa.eu/ecb/pub/pdf/ssm.fap_guide_201705_rev_201805.en.pdf.

But apart from the fact that the ECB published its guide before the adoption of the relevant EBA guidelines,[25] the ECB's guide effectively reduces options available to NCAs under the regulatory framework.[26] The regulatory powers of the ECB under Article 4(3) SSM Regulation for its own supervisory powers, and under Article 6(5)(a) SSM Regulation with respect to the supervisory activities of NCAs, put the ECB in a competition with EBA.[27] Moreover, the development of a common "supervisory culture"[28] by the EBA is difficult to imagine without crucial support from the ECB. In fact, this culture is likely to be framed by ECB practice and through supervisory guidelines and recommendations pursuant to Article 4(3) SSM Regulation. One might therefore wonder who the master is and who the servant in this relationship.

The last scenario described here concerns the familiar interplay between financial stability and fiscal policy. The ECB is – still – involved in the design and implementation of adjustment policies of the European Stability Mechanism (ESM). According to Article 13 ESM Treaty, the ECB is charged with the production of debt sustainability analyses, the negotiation of MoUs, and, as part of the "troika," with compliance control (Article 13(7) ESM Treaty). In states where a spillover from problems in the banking sector is at the origin of trouble, the multiple roles of the ECB might be difficult to juggle. On the one hand, as a supervisor, the ECB sets the conditions relevant for the fiscal situation of member states. On the other hand, it is charged with playing crucial roles in fixing the very same crisis.[29]

Overall, this overview reveals the political salience of the ECB's supervisory powers. This regularly stems from the fact that the applicable legislation often holds the ECB to follow certain objectives rather than strict rules, or even to balance various potentially diverging objectives, thereby equipping the ECB

[25] Commission Staff Working Document accompanying the document Report from the Commission to the European Parliament and the Council on the Single Supervisory Mechanism established pursuant to Regulation (EU) 1024/2013, 11 October 2017, COM(2017) 591 final, 39.

[26] Instructive: Chiti and Recine, "The Single Supervisory Mechanism in Action: Institutional Adjustment and the Reinforcement of the ECB Position," 24 *European Public Law* 101 (2018), at p. 122.

[27] These tensions shine through in the Report from the Commission to the European Parliament and the Council on the Single Supervisory Mechanism established pursuant to Regulation (EU)No 1024/2013, SWD(2017) 336 final, 11 October 2017, 15.

[28] Article 8(1)(b) EBA Regulation.

[29] For similar reasons, Advocate General Cruz Villalón admonished the ECB should discontinue its involvement in the "troika" in countries where it would implement it Outright Market Transactions Program, see *Peter Gauweiler and Others v Deutscher Bundestag*, Case C-62/14, Opinion of Advocate General Cruz Villalón delivered on 14 January 2015, ECLI:EU:C:2015:7, para. 150.

with considerable authority.[30] These decisions are not merely of a technocratic nature but involve political judgment, including difficult discretionary choices and at times severe financial consequences. The ECB's supervisory powers therefore require more than a technical, expertise-driven kind of legitimacy based on narrowly defined mandates.[31]

### 4.2.2 *Democratic Legitimacy of Independent Institutions*

How to establish the legitimacy of independent authorities with considerable discretionary powers? At the outset, it is important to move beyond the familiar, yet mythological concept of technocratic legitimacy. This concept implies that independent institutions are a democratic pathology. In particular, in the view of the BVerfG, they are at loggerheads with the principle of representative democracy, undermining the principle of ministerial control, a core trajectory of legitimacy in parliamentary democracies.[32] The court therefore accepts them only under narrowly circumscribed conditions.[33] The result is no different if one understands the European Parliament (EP) as the ventricle of representative democracy, rather than national parliaments.[34] However, the pathological view tends to underestimate the significance of independent institutions for the Union. As Antoine Vauchez has argued, the Union's independent institutions – the Commission, the CJEU, and the ECB – have been its most effective ones, the ones that represent the Union's interest most clearly and have given the Union its contemporary shape.[35] The concept of technocratic legitimacy therefore not only fails to provide a satisfactory level of legitimacy for the existing discretionary powers of independent institutions; by

[30] Smits, "Accountability of the European Central Bank," *Ars Aequi* 27 (2019), at p. 29.

[31] Dawson, Bobić and Maricut-Akbik, "Reconciling Independence and Accountability at the European Central Bank: The false promise of Proceduralism," 25 *European Law Journal* 75 (2019), p. 77 et seq.

[32] Cf. Fichtmüller, "Zulässigkeit ministerialfreien Raums in der Bundesverwaltung," 91 *Archiv des öffentlichen Rechts* 297 (1966).

[33] For example, BVerfG *Maastricht*, 2 BvR 2134, 2159/92, Judgment of 12 October 1993, 89 BVerfGE 155, at 207 et seq.; Assigning exceptional status to the democratic legitimacy of the ECB: BVerfG *Gauweiler*, Case 2 BvR 2728/13, Judgment of 21 June 2016, para. 131, ECLI:DE:BVerfG:2016:rs20160621.2bvr272813; on supervisory powers: BVerfG *Banking Union*, 2 BvR 1685/14, Judgment of 30 July 2019, ECLI:DE:BVerfG:2019:rs20190730.2bvr168514, para. 132 et seq.

[34] Vibert, *The Rise of the Unelected: Democracy and the New Separation of Powers* (Cambridge University Press, 2007) 18, at p. 138 (on why independent agencies are more compatible with a constitution built around a separation of powers like the US constitution rather than the European constitution built around parliament).

[35] Vauchez, "The Appeal of Independence: Exploring Europe's Way of Political Legitimacy," TARN Working Paper 7/2016 (2016). <http://dx.doi.org/10.2139/ssrn.2881913>, at p. 19.

doing so, it also misses out on core features of the European Union's exercise of public authority, redefining the "normal" as an anomaly. It might occasionally go as far as echoing populist attacks on the administrative state.[36]

The point is therefore to ensure the democratic legitimacy of independent institutions in a genuine way, one that sees them as part of democratic institutional frameworks, rather than as pathologies. This is a challenge that certainly exceeds the analysis of the SSM. This chapter may only outline the broad contours of such a theory of democratic legitimacy for independent institutions. This theory is based on proposals in the literature. For the most part, they emerge from specific contexts other than the European Union, which one should keep in mind when analogizing from them.

As a first insight from this literature, it seems important to distinguish between different types of independent institutions. Bruce Ackerman proposed to distinguish regulatory and integrity institutions as specific emanations of the administrative state.[37] While integrity institutions, like courts of audit, would be justified by the significance of their task and the limitations of their mandate, regulatory institutions fulfill more executive functions, therefore requiring some level of democratic participation.[38] Tarunab Khaitan has recently extended the concept of integrity institutions by pointing out the specific role of "guarantor institutions," including ombudsmen and human rights commissions.[39] The kind of independent institution in the focus of this chapter is clearly different, given the political salience of SSM decisions.

A second recent proposal merits consideration. Cass Sunstein and Adrian Vermeule have suggested a strategy to redeem the administrative law by charging courts with the enforcement of the "inner morality" of the law against administrative agencies.[40] The concept of the "inner morality" stems from Lon Fuller's theory of government legitimacy and comprises a bunch of rule-of-law principles of an overly formal-procedural character. The authors argue that recent case law mostly revolves around obliging the administration to respect this inner morality. Their theory intends to dispel fears of the administrative state predominantly among the political right. This strategy deliberately restricts judicial control of allocative decisions[41] and does not consider the democratization of the administrative state as a particular

[36] Cf. Peters and Pierre, "Populism and Public Administration: Confronting the Administrative State," 51 *Administration & Society* 1521 (2019).

[37] Ackerman, "The New Separation of Powers," 113 *Harvard Law Review* 633 (2000), p. 693 et seq.

[38] Ackerman, ibid., at p. 697.

[39] Khaitan, "Guarantor Institutions," *Asian Journal of Comparative Law* 1 (2021).

[40] Sunstein and Vermeule, *Law and Leviathan* (Harvard University Press, 2020).

[41] Ibid., at p. 90 et seq.

urgency.[42] While this strategy might further Sunstein's and Vermeule's agendas of nudging and common good constitutionalism,[43] it seems hardly adequate for a pluralistic society.

A third proposal is Pierre Rosanvallon's theory of good government.[44] He argues that democratic struggles for representation prevailed during the nineteenth and early twentieth centuries. As the elected members of government became the predominant political power in the latter part of the twentieth century and traditional party systems began to erode, the struggles for representation became one for a better quality of government, for making the executive act in the people's best interest. It is therefore time to go beyond a conception of democracy as centered on elections and to understand democracy as a permanent process that requires transparency, responsibility, responsiveness, and truthfulness on the part of the executive power. In this respect, Rosanvallon points out the antipopulist potential of independent institutions and the function of integrity institutions to control the executive.[45] One could further extend this thought and even consider regulatory agencies as a way of establishing a separation of powers within the executive branch.

I believe that one can read the core constitutional provisions of the European Union as comprising both classical ideas of representative democracy and the trajectories for ensuring permanent democracy in line with Rosanvallon's theory. At the center of the core constitutional provisions sits Article 2 TEU, which stipulates the fundamental values of the Union, among them democracy and the rule of law.[46] Articles 9 to 12 TEU further specify these values for the interaction between citizens and Union institutions,[47] while Articles 13 to 19 TEU concretize them with respect to the institutional legal frameworks. There is no doubt that the core constitutional provisions of EU law also apply to the ECB.[48] From these provisions, one may derive various trajectories of legitimacy for independent institutions.

[42] On the democratic approach to the administrative state in historical context: Emerson, *The Public's Law: Origins and Architecture of Progressive Democracy* (Oxford University Press, 2019).

[43] Sunstein, *Why Nudge?: The Politics of Libertarian Paternalism* (Yale University Press, 2014); Adrian Vermeule, "Beyond Originalism" (31.3.2020) *The Atlantic*.

[44] Rosanvallon, *Good Government* (Harvard University Press, 2018).

[45] Ibid., at pp. 253 et seq.

[46] On Article 2 TEU as a fundamental value of EU law, see CJEU, Case C-64/16, Associação Sindical dos Juízes Portugueses (ASJP), Judgment of 27 February 2018, ECLI:EU:C:2018:117. On the significance of Article 2 for the identity of the EU, see Armin von Bogdandy, *Strukturwandel des öffentlichen Rechts* (Suhrkamp 2021) 16 et seq.

[47] Cf. BVerfG *Banking Union*, 2 BvR 1685/14, Judgment of 30 July 2019, ECLI:DE:BVerfG:2019:rs20190730.2bvr168514, para. 135. The BVerfG does not mention Articles 13 to 19 TEU, though.

[48] Haag, "Article 10," in von der Groeben, Schwarze, and Armin (eds.), *Europäisches Unionsrecht* 1, 7th edn (2015) mn 5.

The first trajectory is representative democracy as required by Article 10 TEU. While representative democracy is normally associated with Parliaments, there is no reason to exclude independent institutions from its scope. The members of their governing bodies are not subject to direct election, but their composition might still follow principles of representation. That, of course, requires seeing them as representatives of the diverging parts that form the Union interest, rather than as neutral experts.[49] The structure of the ECB governing council reflects this desire for representative expertise. It is important that different national traditions and sensitivities have a voice on the governing council and participate in the formation of the Union interest.

Second, besides representative democracy, Articles 10 (3) and 11 TEU stipulate principles for the direct interaction between institutions and the people. In light of Article 10(3) TEU, this implies for independent institutions like the ECB to engage in public discourse, explain their decisions and scientific basis, and interact with the public on these matters.[50] Since the beginning of the financial crisis, the ECB has much improved its practice in this regard.[51]

A third trajectory concerns the relationship between institutions as per Article 13(2) TEU. The principles of conferred powers and mutual sincere cooperation provide a basic framework for interinstitutional accountability, for mechanisms of mutual oversight and control as an essential aspect of the separation of powers in democracies.[52] As I will argue, this includes but goes beyond the control exercised by the EP. It is important to point out that interinstitutional forms of accountability are not per se limited to procedural checks. Depending on the institution exercising accountability, such mechanisms may well question the substance of an independent institution's decision. To safeguard an institution's independence, they may exercise deference and confine themselves to plausibility checks. The distinction between full

[49] Vauchez, *Démocratiser l'Europe* (Seuil, 2014) 90 et seq.

[50] On the parallel challenge for courts, see Bassok, "The Schmitelsen Court: The Question of Legitimacy," 21 *German Law Journal* 131 (2020).

[51] Curtin, "'Accountable Independence' of the European Central Bank: Seeing the Logics of Transparency," 23 *European Law Journal* 28 (2017).

[52] Vile, Constitutionalism and the Separation of Powers (2nd edn, Liberty Fund, 2012), 19; Habermas, Faktizität und Geltung (Suhrkamp, 1992) p. 229 et seq.; Möllers, *Die drei Gewalten. Legitimation der Gewaltengliederung in Verfassungsstaat, Europäischer Integration und Internationalisierung* (Velbrück, 2008), pp. 68–69: Trute, "Die Demokratische Legitimation der Verwaltung" in Hoffmann-Riem, Schmidt-Aßmann and Voßkuhle (eds.), *Grundlagen des Verwaltungsrechts*, vol 1 (2nd edn, Beck, 2012) § 6 mn 53, 108.

review and deference should, however, not be confused with one between procedure and substance.[53]

Lastly, Article 19 TEU establishes the need for both the Union and the member states to respect the rule of law. In case of the SSM, this comprises not only judicial review but also administrative review before the Administrative Board of Review.[54]

In principle, independent institutions need to respect all these trajectories of democratic legitimacy, but not to the same degree. Rather, the adequate legitimacy mix depends on two variables: the particular constitutional framework and the particular authority exercised by an independent institution.[55] Insightful in the latter respect is Habermas's theory of communicative action. Accordingly, one can distinguish different forms of power by the different types of reasons offered for their justification.[56] These reasons oscillate between pragmatic, ethical, and moral arguments in case of law-making, and the strictures of legal discourse in case of law enforcement.[57] The regulatory functions exercised by independent institutions will often display an amalgam of law-making and enforcement, involving legal as well as pragmatic, ethical, and moral arguments, depending on the specific decision taken. In a similar vein, Paul Tucker has proposed a matrix for independent institutions with three options each for who sets policies, and who implements them.[58] The next part will elaborate on how these different trajectories work out in relation to the SSM.

### 4.2.3 *Democratic Legitimacy of the SSM as a Question of Accountability*

Before assessing whether the SSM actually enjoys a sufficient level of legitimacy, it is necessary to establish a standard of legitimacy for the SSM in accordance with the specific form of authority it exercises. This standard will crucially depend on legal and political forms of accountability, that is on mutual checks and balances. Concerning the other trajectories, the Supervisory Board has a fairly representative structure that reflects a mix of expertise and national interests.[59] Moreover, the ECB has stepped up its

53 See, however, Dawson, Bobić and Maricut-Akbik, supra, note 31.

54 Article 24, Council Regulation (EU) 1024/2013.

55 Cf. Grzeszick, *Die Teilung der staatlichen Gewalt* (Verlag Ferdinand Schöningh, 2013), p. 47 et seq.

56 Habermas, supra note 52, at 213, 235.

57 On the different discursive modes, see Habermas, supra note 52, at p. 139 et seq., 187 et seq.

58 Tucker, supra note 4, p. 72 et seq. – This framework is somewhat insensitive to the specific constitutional context, though.

59 Article 26(1), Council Regulation (EU) 1024/2013.

interaction with the public considerably, in respect of both monetary policy and its supervisory activities, although there is disagreement as to whether the present level suffices.[60]

As concerns appropriate levels of accountability, the current literature focuses on two forms of accountability: judicial review and parliamentary oversight.[61] In explanation of the focus on parliamentary accountability, Menelaos Markakis submits that someone needs to define the public interest with respect to economic and monetary policy, and that should be the EP.[62] For analogous reasons, Paul Tucker is chiefly concerned about the interaction between parliaments and democratic legislatures.[63]

However, what is sufficient for monetary policy does not need to be good for supervisory authority. In this regard, it seems useful to take a closer look at similarities and differences between the two prongs of the ECB. A crucial difference between these two functions is often said to consist in the fact that monetary policy only pursues one objective, that of price stability, while financial supervision has to keep an eye on an array of objectives.[64] After the Public Sector Purchase Programme (PSPP) saga, this position no longer holds. According to the BVerfG, the ECB has to balance many factors to ensure the social impact of its monetary policy remains within

[60] Curtin, supra note 51. On the significance of transparency for accountability, see Tucker, supra n 4, p. 349 et seq.; cautioning that transparency is not an end in itself and might undermine the effective discharge of the ECB's mandate: Dawson, Bobić and Maricut-Akbik, supra note 31, at p. 82. More critical: Beroš, "ECB's Accountability within the SSM framework: Mind the (transparency) gap," 26 *Maastricht Journal of European and Comparative Law* 122 (2019). However, it stands to reason that supervisory powers require a different level of transparency.

[61] On judicial accountability, see Dawson, Bobić and Maricut-Akbik, supra note 31; Zilioli and Wojcik (eds.), *Judicial Review in the European Banking Union* (Edward Elgar Publishing, 2021). On parliamentary accountability: Magnette, "Towards 'Accountable Independence'? Parliamentary Controls of the European Central Bank and the Rise of a New Democratic Model," 6 *European Law Journal* 326 (2000); Amtenbrink and Markakis, "Towards a Meaningful Prudential Supervision Dialogue in the Euro Area? A Study of the Interaction between the European Parliament and the European Central Bank in the Single Supervisory Mechanism," 44 *European Law Review* 3 (2019); Fromage, 'Guaranteeing the ECB's Democratic Accountability in the Post-Banking Union era: An Ever More Difficult Task?', 26 *Maastricht Journal of European and Comparative Law* 48 (2019).

[62] Markakis, *Accountability in the Economic and Monetary Union: Foundations, Policy, and Governance* (Oxford University Press, 2020), p. 112 et seq.

[63] Tucker, supra note 4, pp. 569 et seq.

[64] Zilioli, "The Independence of the European Central Bank and Its New Banking Supervisory Competences" in Ritleng (ed.), *Independence and Legitimacy in the Institutional System of the European Union* (Oxford University Press, 2016), pp. 161–162; Amtenbrink and Lastra, "Securing Democratic Accountability of Financial Regulatory Agencies – A Theoretical Framework" in de Mulder (ed.), *Mitigating Risk in the Context of Safety and Security – How Relevant Is a Rational Approach?* (OMV, 2008), pp. 115, 125.

reasonable limits.[65] Although the proportionality analysis required by the CJEU differs on this point,[66] it turned out that considerations concerning the social impact actually do play a role in monetary policy decisions.[67] Hence, as concerns their policy implications, there is no longer much of a difference between monetary policy and financial supervision. While price stability is undeniably the primary objective of the ECB pursuant to Article 127(1) TFEU, it has the secondary objective to support the Union's economic policy. Whatever the precise relationship between the primary and secondary objectives, it shows that the complexity of monetary policy might not be inferior to that of financial supervision.

Nevertheless, there is indeed a difference between monetary policy and financial supervision with respect to the dimensions and the addressees of each policy. Monetary policy is macro policy. It affects everyone. The ECB sets only one policy rate for the Eurozone. Financial supervision has a more narrow scope. Decisions typically concern individual institutions or persons, or, in the case of guidelines and regulations, a specific industry, or part thereof. This applies even though the exercise of supervisory powers might involve a good deal of far-reaching policy considerations, as the initial examples have shown. Hence, accountability mechanisms for financial supervision need to take account of the comparatively narrow scope of supervisory powers.

This raises the question as to the institutions that should hold the SSM to account. While the SSM Regulation seems to understand accountability quite specifically as the relationship between the SSM on the one hand and the EP and Council on the other,[68] the treaty framework as applied to the SSM suggests a holistic view of accountability that comprises multiple accountability channels. Depending on the specific power exercised, accountability mechanisms operating within the executive branch might be particularly well-positioned to fill gaps left by judicial or parliamentary oversight.[69] This concerns particularly the gaps created by the comparatively narrow scope of supervision.

65 BVerfG *PSPP*, 2 BvR 859/15, Judgment of 5 May 2020, ECLI:DE:BVerfG:2020:rs20200505.2bvr085915; see Goldmann, "The European Economic Constitution after the PSPP Judgment: Towards Integrative Liberalism?" 21 *German Law Journal* 1058 (2020).

66 Wendel, "Paradoxes of Ultra-Vires Review: A Critical Review of the PSPP Decision and Its Initial Reception," 21 *German Law Journal* 979 (2020); Amtenbrink and Repasi, "The German Federal Constitutional Court's Decision in Weiss: A Contextual Analysis," 45 *European Law Review* 757 (2020), pp. 771 et seq.

67 Cf. Schnabel, "Necessary, Suitable, and Proportionate" ECB Blog, 28 June 2020, www.ecb.europa.eu/press/blog/date/2020/html/ecb.blog200628~d238a8970c.en.html.

68 Cf. Article 20(1) SSM Regulation.

69 Cf. Amtenbrink and Lastra, supra n 64, at p. 123; contra Dawson, Bobić and Maricut-Akbik, supra note 60, at p. 85; Egidy, "Proportionality and Procedure of Monetary Policy-Making," 19 *International Journal of Constitutional Law* 285 (2021).

With this in mind, the following part will analyze the different accountability relationships that operate within the legal framework of the SSM with a view to achieving an overall level of accountability that is commensurate to their powers.

## 4.3 ACCOUNTABILITY OF THE SSM

### 4.3.1 *Judicial Review*

Decisions of the SSM are subject to judicial review before the CJEU.[70] This follows from Article 263 TFEU, to which Recital 60 of the SSM Regulation makes explicit reference. In addition, persons concerned by SSM decisions have the option of lodging an internal review before the Administrative Board of Review pursuant to Article 24 SSM Regulation.[71] The scope of review to be carried out by the Administrative Board of Review is limited to assessing the procedural and substantive conformity with the SSM Regulation. It may adopt an opinion but cannot directly modify the challenged decision.[72]

Despite the seemingly far-reaching dimensions of judicial review, one can doubt for several reasons whether judicial review alone leads to a satisfactory level of accountability. First, the scope of acts subject to judicial review is limited, as the scenarios set out in the previous part usefully illustrate. For instance, the ECB's assessment of whether an institution is failing or likely to fail is a preparatory decision and therefore not subject to judicial review.[73]

Second, judicial review of the guides published by the ECB under the SSM Regulation faces the obstacle that these instruments are of nonbinding character. Article 263(1) TFEU requires actions for annulment to be directed against acts having "legal effect." In the case concerning the location of Central Counterparties, the General Court gave a wide reading to this term. While mere recommendations would not have "legal effect," the General Court considered it sufficient to assume legal effects that national competent

[70] Overview: de Lucia, "A Microphysics of European Administrative Law: Administrative Remedies in the EU after Lisbon," 20 *European Public Law* 277 (2014); Loosveld, "Appeals Against Decisions of the European Supervisory Authorities," 28 *Journal of International Banking Law & Regulation* 9 (2013).

[71] Cf. Decision of the European Central Bank of 14 April 2014 concerning the establishment of an Administrative Board of Review and its Operating Rules (ECB/2014/16).

[72] On administrative review, see particularly Zeitlin and Brito Bastos, "SSM and the SRB accountability at European level: room for improvements?: Banking Union Scrutiny," Economic Governance Support Unit (EGOV) PE 645747 (2020).

[73] Cf. Dörr, "Artikel 263 AEUV" in Grabitz and Hilf (eds.), *Das Recht der Europäischen Union: EUV/AEUV*, vol 3 (Beck, 2012) paras 39–40.

authorities might have reason to consider themselves obliged to implement the policy.[74] This might not be the case for guides like the one guide on fit and proper assessments, as it states explicitly that it is nonbinding.[75] Also, NCAs have to take relevant domestic law into account and might not be able to implement the guide in a strict manner. It therefore seems difficult to subject such guides to judicial review. In any event, only privileged applicants under Article 263(2) TFEU would be in the position to bring such a suit.

The third limitation of judicial review, and arguably the most important one, relates to the applicable standard of review, especially in case of discretionary SSM decisions. The exercise of such discretion depends to a large extent on economic projections, the balancing of complex, uncertain risks, and other policy choices, not on the interpretation of a legal rule. A case in point is the definition of financial stability. In Article 10(5) of the SRM Regulation, financial stability is defined as "a situation where the financial system is actually or potentially exposed to a disruption that may give rise to financial distress liable to jeopardize the orderly functioning, efficiency and integrity of the internal market or the economy or the financial system of one or more Member States."[76] The prognostic challenges implied in this definition are evident. One might reasonably disagree about the requisite data basis and methodology. Such decisions diverge significantly from the classical, Weberian ideal type of administrative activity guarded by legal rationality. It rather resembles a governmental type of decision-making, characterized by multiple, overlapping policy considerations.[77] In taking such decisions, independent institutions all but meet the expectation of rules-based, depoliticized governance.[78]

Such settings call for judicial deference and self-restraint. Courts need to respect the fact that the administration is in principle better positioned to take the requisite policy decisions and to assess risks under conditions of (radical) uncertainty.[79] Judicial review may still play a role, for example, by applying

74 *United Kingdom of Great Britain and Northern Ireland v ECB*, Case T-496/11, Judgment of 4 March 2015, ECLI:EU:T:2015:133, paras. 31–48.

75 *Supra* note 24, at p. 3.

76 Note that Article 14(2) SRM Regulation, which stipulates financial stability as the objective of resolution, does not explicitly refer to Article 10(5) SRM Regulation.

77 Schröder, "Die Bereiche der Regierung und Verwaltung" in Isensee and Kirchhof (eds.), *Handbuch des Staatsrechts*, vol 5 (C. F. Müller, 2007), para. 9.

78 Classical: Friedman, *Capitalism and Freedom* (University of Chicago Press, 1962), pp. 51–54; Tinbergen, *Centralization and Decentralization in Economic Policy* (North Holland Publishing Co., 1954); Kydland and Prescott, "Rules Rather Than Discretion: The Inconsistency of Optimal Plans," 85 *The Journal of Political Economy* 473 (1977).

79 For example, BVerwG, BVerwGE 106, 115 et seq., para. 80, Judgment of 14 January 1998, 11 C 11.96; for a UK perspective, see Poole, "United Kingdom: The Royal Prerogative," 8

plausibility checks of the reasons given by independent institutions and controlling their actions for manifest disproportionality and arbitrariness.[80] Those checks are substantive, not merely procedural; one cannot deduce from the fact that the CJEU has often accepted the reasons given by the ECB that the Court has not reached its own conclusions regarding their plausibility. The requirement to give *plausible* reasons is different from a requirement to give any reasons at all.[81] By contrast, full review of discretionary decisions would effectively replace the informed view of the SSM with the comparatively úninformed view of a court.[82] The PSPP saga has shown that this road should be avoided, not least because it might destabilize the Union.[83]

Notably, this limited standard of judicial review derives from the separation of powers doctrine and may apply to any kind of administrative decision, not just to the exercise of authority by independent institutions.[84] The functional limitation of judicial review is the flip side of the functional separation of powers between different branches of government, especially in highly uncertain, technical fields. Recognizing this policy salience, Recital 64 of the SSM Regulation explicitly states that the Administrative Board should check the legality of SSM decisions "while respecting the margin of discretion left to the ECB to decide on the opportunity to take those decisions."

To make matters worse, this limited standard of judicial review can even apply to routine, administrative-type decisions of the SSM. The decision by the General Court in the *Landeskreditbank* dispute is a case in point.[85] It turned around the qualification of the plaintiff institution as a systemically important one. This qualification involves many evaluative criteria that defy strict legal scrutiny, such as "particular circumstances" that might justify an exception according to Article 6(4) SSM Regulation. Again, courts might apply plausibility and proportionality checks that duly defer to the administration's higher

*International Journal of Constitutional Law* 146 (2010). On radical uncertainty, see Kay and King, supra note 3.

80 Notable: BVerfG, *Gauweiler*, Case 2 BvR 2728/13, Judgment of 14 January 2014, para. 60. See, however, Dawson, Bobić and Maricut-Akbik, supra note 31, at pp. 88 et seq.

81 But see above note 69 and accompanying text.

82 In the context of the Gauweiler case: Goldmann, "Adjudicating Economics: Central Bank Independence and the Appropriate Standard of Judicial Review," 15 *German Law Journal* 265 (2014).

83 Cf. Biernat, "How Far Is It from Warsaw to Luxembourg and Karlsruhe: The Impact of the PSPP Judgment on Poland," 21 *German Law Journal* 1104 (2020).

84 It is therefore misleading to invoke independence as the reason for discretion, see, for example, Fraccaroli, Giovannini and Jamet, "The Evolution of the ECB's Accountability Practices During the Crisis," *ECB Economic Bulletin* 47 (2018), at p. 49.

85 *Landeskreditbank Baden-Württemberg v ECB*, T-122/15, Judgment of 16 May 2017, ECLI: EU:T:2017:337.

level of expertise. The main value of judicial review might therefore lie in its preventive effect, in the impact it may have on decision-makers.[86]

In conclusion, it emerges that judicial review of SSM decisions stops short of an intense, substantive scrutiny of the discretionary powers of the SSM. This holds even after the BVerfG's Banking Union judgment, in which the BVerfG disagreed with the CJEU on competence issues, rather than on the right standard of judicial review. Accepting the limits of judicial review, it instead emphasized the need for democratic legitimacy of the SSM – the subject of the following section.[87]

### 4.3.2 *Parliamentary Accountability*

According to Article 20 SSM Regulation, the SSM needs to report to the EP and to the Council. The EP is also involved in the appointment of Supervisory Board and has a role to play in procedures for the removal of its chair or vice-chair, Article 26(4). The interinstitutional agreement between the ECB and the EP specifies the reporting requirements, establishes channels of communication (e.g. feedback), specifies public and confidential hearings and confidentiality requirements, etc. A similar agreement exists between the ECB and the Ecofin Council.[88] National parliaments have rights of information and control specified under Article 21 SSM Regulation, including the right to invite the Chair of the Supervisory Board for an exchange of views.

Many hail the "banking dialogue," which has developed since the establishment of the SSM on the basis of these provisions.[89] The ECB seems to understand it as its main form of accountability.[90] It is even pitched as a model for a refurbished monetary dialogue.[91] However, despite its popularity, even this form of accountability has certain limitations. Some of them stem from empirical issues; others are of a more theoretical character.

[86] Cf. Bobic, "Constitutional Pluralism Is Not Dead: An Analysis of Interactions between Constitutional Courts of Member States and the European Court of Justice," 18 *German Law Journal* 1395 (2018); Goldmann, 'Constitutional Pluralism as Mutually Assured Discretion: The Court of Justice, the German Federal Constitutional Court, and the ECB', 23 *Maastricht Journal of European and Comparative Law* 119 (2016).

[87] BVerfG *Banking Union*, 2 BvR 1685/14, Judgment of 30 July 2019, ECLI:DE:BVerfG:2019:rs20190730.2bvr168514, para. 216 et seq.

[88] See Smits, supra note 30.

[89] For example, Nicolaides, "Accountability of the ECB's Supervisory Activities (SSM): Evolving and Responsive," CERiM Online Paper Series Paper 10/2018.

[90] Cf. Fraccaroli, Giovannini and Jamet, supra note 84.

[91] Fromage and Ibrido, "The 'Banking Dialogue' as a Model to Improve Parliamentary Involvement in the Monetary Dialogue?" 40 *Journal of European Integration* 295 (2018).

Empirically, from a quantitative perspective, banking dialogue has seen an increasing frequency of interactions between the SSM and the EP, as well as more focused exchanges.[92] The ECB has stepped up its transparency by providing multiple reports, holding press conferences, publishing minutes, and making internal documents more accessible.[93] Qualitatively, according to an empirical survey of EP hearings of the Chair of the Supervisory Board, the quality of the questions asked varies, though. They often seem to address issues outside of the competence of the SSM, such as monetary policy, or the development of the banking sector in general or in specific countries, rather than questions relating to supervisory practice.[94] There has also been silencing of policy issues.[95]

Theoretically, one should not overestimate the potential of the EP to check the performance of the SSM. First, for the EP to be in the position to impose effective checks on the SSM would require consensus on the actual standard by which the SSM is to be measured.[96] The notion of financial stability does not become easier to apply when put in the hands of the heterogeneous group of members of the EP.

Second, effective accountability requires a congruence between the power of review and the power to impose consequences.[97] It therefore stands to reason that parliamentary control is most effective for tasks in respect of which the EP is a stakeholder because of its legislative, budgetary, or creative functions. However, the fact that the SMM Regulation has been adopted under Article 127(6) TFEU relegates the EP to an advisory body. Also, the EP does not control the budgets, which might suffer the most should the SSM err in its judgment. Any losses that require bail-out or compensation by the public purse will likely be covered by domestic budgets or the ESM. The only significant power of the EP over the SSM consists in its role in the appointment process of Supervisory Board members pursuant to Article 26(3) SSM Regulation. But for that, ex-post control is rather ineffective.

92 Fraccaroli, Giovannini and Jamet, supra note 84, at p. 70; Smits, supra note 30, at pp. 31–32.

93 Curtin, supra note 60; Smits, supra note 30, at p. 31.

94 Amtenbrink and Markakis, supra note 61, at pp. 18, 21 50. In the context of monetary policy, the monetary policy competence is used as a pretext for evasive questions, see Amtenbrink and Van Duin, "The European Central Bank before the European Parliament: Theory and Practice After 10 Years of Monetary Dialogue," 34 *European Law Review* 561 (2009).

95 Maricut-Akbik, "Contesting the European Central Bank in Banking Supervision: Accountability in Practice at the European Parliament," 58 *JCMS: Journal of Common Market Studies* 1199 (2020).

96 Amtenbrink and Markakis, supra note 61, at p. 11.

97 Cf. Grant and Keohane, 'Accountability and Abuses of Power in World Politics," 99 *American Political Science Review* 29 (2005).

By contrast, national parliaments do have reason to worry about the impact of banking supervision on their budgets. In this respect, however, Banking Dialogue suffers from a structural difficulty. In case of a conflict about bail-in or bail-out, national parliaments might take diametrically opposed positions, with the majority of the members of parliament in the member state affected being in favor of a bail-out backed up ultimately by the ESM, and the majority of the members of parliament in other member states likely to favor bail-in to protect their (short-term) domestic budgetary interests. Similar constellations can be expected for the balance between monetary policy and financial stability. Only the EP could assume a neutral position. The EP, however, is not responsible for the budgets that would need to ultimately provide financial support. There is thus an incoherence between control rights and potential financial implications of the EP, on the one hand, and national parliaments, on the other. While interparliamentary hearings might solve the information gap between the EP and domestic parliaments,[98] the problem persists that national parliaments might widely disagree on decisions that affect their constituencies differently.

One further limitation of parliamentary accountability derives from the fact that individual decisions involving specific credit institutions, such as fit and proper decisions concerning board members, or the view of the ECB regarding the regulatory capital of an institution, are usually confidential. It has been reported that while lots of questions relating to individual firms are asked in the EP, the Chair of the Supervisory Board invoke their confidentiality obligations.[99] This also shows that parliaments are not the right place for the review of individual decisions as their intervention would undercut the separation of powers between parliament and the executive branch of government.

### 4.3.3 *Intra-executive Checks and Balances*

This shifts the focus to accountability mechanisms within the executive branch of government. In many jurisdictions, the higher echelons of the executive branch have mechanisms at their disposal allowing them a certain level of control over administrative decisions, including discretionary ones. Administrative agencies in the United States (to the extent that they are not independent like the SEC or the FED) are under the control of the president. To a certain extent, this even comprises independent agencies, whose head is usually appointed by the President. In Germany, any administrative decision is subject to ministerial

98 Cf. Amtenbrink and Markakis, supra n 61, at p. 19.

99 Maricut-Akbik, supra note 95.

control.[100] Ministers might issue general or specific directions. While this power is rarely used, its activation usually takes place in cases with high political significance, reaching beyond the pay grade of the ordinary administration. A well-known example is the decision in the Kaiser-Tengelmann merger case by the Federal Minister of Economics, who allowed the merger against the advice of the Federal Cartel Office.[101] While some might consider ministerial intervention as being prone to capture by special interests, one needs to understand it in the context of the separation of powers. As the minister is directly answerable to parliament in a parliamentary democracy, ministerial intervention shifts political accountability from peripheral intra-executive relationships to the gravitational center of political accountability exercised by parliament over government.[102] In the end, ministerial intervention indirectly increases the leverage of parliament over executive decision-making, thereby contributing to democratic accountability. After all, the members of parliament likely have more influence on the minister than on members of the civil service, who are in the first place answerable to the higher echelons of the government.

Similar principles apply to European law. Article 17 TEU stipulates that the Commission is responsible for the implementation of legal acts by the Union. A corollary of this principle is the *Meroni* doctrine. Accordingly, no powers that include a discretionary element may be delegated to agencies.[103] The doctrine may have been partially restated in the *ESMA* case.[104] The CJEU decided that ESMA could independently exercise discretionary powers. However, the Court emphasized that these powers need to be restricted in various respects. In particular, ESMA may prohibit short selling only in specifically defined emergency situations, and the Commission may further define these situations through secondary rules.[105] The Court concluded that ESMA was ultimately not equipped with "a very large measure of discretion."[106]

As has been shown at the beginning of this chapter, this cannot be said about the SSM, which enjoys ample discretionary powers.[107] In fact, the SSM

[100] Herzog, "Artikel 65" in Maunz and Dürig (eds.), *Grundgesetz-Kommentar*, vol 5 (Beck, 2018), para. 61.

[101] Bundewirtschaftsministerium, Verfügung, 9 March 2016, available at: www.bmwi.de/Redaktion/DE/Downloads/M-O/oeffentliche-entscheidung-edeka-kaisers-tengelmann.pdf?__blob=publicationFile&v=2.

[102] See also BVerfG *Banking Union*, 2 BvR 1685/14, Judgment of 30 July 2019, ECLI:DE:BVerfG:2019:rs20190730.2bvr168514, para. 217.

[103] *Meroni v High Authority*, Case 9/56, [1957–1958] ECR 133, 152.

[104] *United Kingdom v Parliament and Council (ESMA)*, Case C-270/12, Judgment of 22 January 2014, ECLI:EU:C:2014:18.

[105] Ibid., para. 51.

[106] Ibid., para. 54.

[107] See above, B.I.

only escapes the Meroni doctrine because it was adopted under Article 127 (6) TFEU,[108] a move that evoked much criticism.[109] While the argument that the SSM powers exceeded the restriction of delegations under Article 127(6) TFEU to "specific tasks" is difficult to sustain as long as domestic supervisory authorities retain important supervisory competencies over insurance companies, securities, or investment firms, the critique has a point insofar as this legal basis obviates the need to satisfy the accountability requirements that form the true core of the *Meroni* doctrine.

Yet, even in case of authorities like the SSM enjoying wide discretionary powers exercised in independence from the administrative hierarchy, intra-executive accountability might make a decisive contribution to the overall accountability mix that might push their legitimacy to acceptable levels. Hence, it seems apposite to investigate whether the SSM is subject to a satisfactory level of intra-executive accountability. There are two potential yielders of such accountability: the Commission and the ECA.

As concerns the Commission, the independence of the SSM under Article 19 SSM Regulation prevents it from revoking, modifying, or otherwise affecting the decisions of the SSM. This also cuts off potential chains of legitimacy between the Supervisory Board and national governments, as representatives of NCAs on the Supervisory Board are obliged to act independently and in the Union interest.

Nevertheless, the Commission has powers to review the decisions of the SSM at a structural level. Article 32 SSM Regulation charges the Commission with triannual in-depth reviews of the performance of the SSM. The first report published under this provision in 2017 demonstrates the potential of this mechanism.[110] It covers the governance structure of the SSM, its instruments and processes, and checks the results for their cost-effectiveness. While the 2017 report understandably postpones a definite assessment of the ultimate impact of the SSM on financial stability and market integration to another day, this trajectory seems particularly apposite as an accountability mechanism for goal-oriented administrative power such as that of the SSM. One cannot review goal achievement by reviewing individual decisions, only by looking at the field in context. Issues of managerial effectiveness also require a holistic approach. In this respect, the Commission report scrutinizes the cooperation of the SSM with other stakeholders, the internal organization,

[108] Preamble, SSM Regulation.

[109] For many: Kämmerer, "Bahn frei der Bankenunion? Die neuen Aufsichtsbefugnisse der EZB im Lichte der EU-Kompetenzordnung," *Neue Zeitschrift für Verwaltungsrecht* 830 (2013), pp. 832 et seq.

[110] Report, supra note 27.

including the delegation of decision-making competencies, and the application of discretionary legal provisions, for example, the categorization of certain assets (which might desire more transparency) and waivers for capital requirements (which require further development).[111]

The ECA is charged with examining the operational efficiency of the ECB in accordance with Article 287 TFEU and Article 27.2 ECB Statute. According to Article 20(7) SSM Regulation, this also applies to the SSM. From the text of these provisions, it is unclear how far the ECA may review the practice of the SSM, in particular how far the mandate of the SSM to examine the operational efficiency of the ECB allows it to review supervisory practice.[112] This ambiguity gave rise to a conflict between the ECA and the ECB when ECA compiled information for its 2018 thematic report on the operational efficiency of the ECB's crisis management for banks. The ECB refused to disclose certain information to the ECA that it believed to fall outside the mandate of the latter.[113] On the insistence of the Commission, the ECB has meanwhile concluded a Memorandum of Understanding with the ECA on the issue.[114]

In substance, the ECA criticizes issues pertaining to supervision that are of a discretionary nature. For example, it submitted that the ECB did not set up specific indicators for crisis identification.[115] At this point, ECA and ECB seem to be following different supervisory philosophies: The ECA seems to favor a rules-based approach, while the ECB prefers a more discretionary approach.[116] This goes quite to the heart of the ECB's discretionary powers. One could argue that, instead of imposing a certain level of specificity, ECB should justify their absence. At least, instead of presenting its criticism of ECB as a piece of technical expertise, the ECA should have been more open about the political dimension of their disagreement. This would provide the Commission, the EP, or other stakeholders with a better basis for a decision on whether to follow up on this point.

111 Ibid., at pp. 9, 12.

112 See report by the Bundesrechnungshof, "Bericht an den Haushaltausschuss des Bundestages nach § 88 Abs. 2 BHO über die Verkürzung von Prüfungsrechten des Bundesrechnungshofes in den Bereichen Bankenaufsicht und bei Finanzinstituten," III 5 205103, of 20 January 2016.

113 See ECA, The operational efficiency of the ECB's crisis management (2018); ECA, Communication to the European Parliament concerning the European Parliament's request to be kept informed regarding the problem of access to information in relation to the European Central Bank, as laid down in paragraph 29 of the 2016 discharge procedure (2017/2188(DEC)), adopted by Chamber IV at its meeting of 13 December 2018.

114 Memorandum of Understanding between the ECA and the ECB regarding audits on the ECB's supervisory tasks, 9 October 2019, https://eur-lex.europa.eu/legal-content/EN/TXT/PDF/?uri=CELLAR:b44fbfa0-95f6-11ea-aac4-01aa75ed71a1&from=EN.

115 ECA, The operational efficiency of the ECB's crisis management (2018), para. 75 et seq.

116 On this age-old debate, see Kydland and Prescott, supra note 78.

Be this as it may, on the whole, these two reports by the Commission and the ECA seem to subject the SSM to more effective scrutiny than some hearings before the EP. The reports are systematic, focused, rigorous, and based on an intense study of the SSM practice. Also, the report by the Commission is not without direct consequences, as the commission has the power to recommend interpretations of the legal framework, or propose amendments to the legislature.[117] The interplay between the executive and legislative branches in the EU lends particular strength to intra-executive accountability. And even though the reports do not review individual decisions, they are well-positioned to identify structural problems. Individuals affected by decisions of the SSM therefore have the possibility of judicial review at their disposal as a remedy against arbitrary decisions, while intra-executive mechanisms, together with parliamentary accountability, will ensure the SSM stays focused on its objectives and puts in place an efficient management structure. It is this combination of the three branches of government that holds the SSM quite firmly to account.

## 4.4 OPTIONS FOR IMPROVING THE ACCOUNTABILITY OF THE SSM

While the overall level of accountability of the SSM appears satisfactory in light of the intra-executive accountability relations, one might ask for institutional alternatives that might deploy intra-executive accountability even better.

The option to reassign supervisory tasks to the EBA does not appear to be beneficial. While this would defeat the sometimes hegemonic position of ECB towards EBA, it would simply create a new hegemon – one that would combine the formal power to make rules with the power to implement them, and thereby remove an important dimension of intra-executive checks and balances. Apart from the fact that such a shift would possibly require a treaty change, it does not seem advantageous from an accountability perspective.

Another option might consist of integrating the SSM into the hierarchical structure of the Commission. This would correspond to the model of European administration envisaged by Article 17 TEU. However, this would require major shifts in the organizational setup of the SSM as it seems difficult to imagine the representatives of NCAs to be involved in decision-making in the frame of the Commission. From the perspective of the subsidiarity principle, the present constellation therefore appears as advantageous. It involves a certain amount of intra-federal checks and balances. Given that financial markets are heterogeneous across the EU, this should be an asset.

[117] Report, supra note 27, at p. 3.

As a third option, one might give the Commission the right to review, modify, or discard decisions by the SSM, or give directions to the SSM to act accordingly. This option would create a host of constitutional problems, as the ECB Governing Council has to take ultimate responsibility for the decisions of the ECB, including those of the SSM, pursuant to Article 282(2) TFEU. By way of a treaty amendment, an exception from this rule would have to be introduced for the SSM should it be subject to the Commission's direction. Moreover, this option would strip the SSM effectively of its independence. Whether this step would be economically advantageous or not,[118] as a matter of treaty law, it is not unthinkable. While it is argued that the *level* of independence enjoyed by the SSM under Article 19 SSM Regulation is equivalent to that of the ECB under Article 130 TFEU,[119] the latter does not require granting independence to the SSM, as independence was only intended to protect monetary policy. Independent supervisory agencies are a much more recent and much rarer phenomenon.[120] As a novelty in European administrative law at the time, Article 130 TFEU deserves a narrow reading. Nevertheless, the question is whether such a power of review would be advantageous. As the SSM would remain part of the ECB, the Commission would lack the requisite expertise to intervene in individual cases. By comparison, the present framework gives the Commission ample opportunity already by virtue of its right to initiate legislative amendments and adopt regulations.

On the whole, the present state of the SSM appears as advantageous from an accountability perspective. While the present arrangement owes its emergence to the contingency of a specific historical situation and might appear as a constitutional anomaly, it enables a reasonable level of checks and balances. Specifically, it offers a whole network of mutually interconnected accountability mechanisms that extend beyond the much-debated issue of parliamentary accountability. In this regard, intra-executive accountability appears as particularly relevant. Should stakeholders wish to strengthen the accountability of the SSM, this trajectory of accountability might bear some potential. For example, one could complement the periodic reports of the Commission with ongoing mechanisms of supervision and information exchange, or harmonize the cycles of the Banking Dialogue with the review exercised by the Commission or the ECA. But given the present state of the SSM, these improvements appear as options, rather than as stringent constitutional requirements.

118 Zilioli, supra note 64, at p. 158 et seq.

119 Ibid., at 161–164.

120 Cf. Quintyn and Taylor, "Regulatory and Supervisory Independence and Financial Stability," IMF Working Paper WP/02/46 (2002), 3.

# PART II

# POLITICAL ACCOUNTABILITY

# 5

# Democratic Accountability in the Banking Union

## *Is There Really a Gap?*

*Diane Fromage*[*]

### 5.1 INTRODUCTION

The creation of the Banking Union (BU) in 2012 represented an important change in the Economic and Monetary Union (EMU), and in the European Union (EU) in general. Indeed, it entailed the delegation of new competences in the areas of banking supervision and bank resolution to the EU level, and it demanded the creation of unique procedures and original governance mechanisms. It has no doubt represented a big step forward in the process of European integration as it is only the second area in which full integration is realised.[1] At the same time, it has also certainly increased the existing level of complexity within the EU. This is the case among other reasons because euro area Member States are part of the BU, but membership to the BU is also open to the rest of the Member States. In fact, in 2020, Bulgaria and Croatia availed themselves of this possibility to join the BU without having adopted the common currency. By creating a third category of Member States next to the EU27 and those that belong to the euro area within the EMU, the BU added a new layer of differentiation in an already largely differentiated Union.[2]

* Marie Sklodowska-Curie Individual Fellow, Law School, Sciences Po Paris. The present research was conducted as part of 'IMPACTEBU', a project that has received funding from the European Union's Horizon 2020 research and innovation programme under the Marie Sklodowska-Curie grant agreement No 895841. I would like to thank Cristina Dias and Daniela Quelhas for valuable comments, as well as all the participants of the LEVIATHAN Conference held on 23–24 September 2022.

1 Grundmann and Micklitz, 'The European Banking Union and Constitution – The Overall Challenge' in Grundmann and Micklitz (eds.), *The European Banking Union and Constitution – Beacon for Advanced Integration or Death-Kell for Democracy?* (Hart, 2019) 1–24.

2 As evidenced, for instance, by the different chapters contained in Fromage (forthcoming) and in ibid. 'Introduction' in Fromage (ed.), *(Re-)defining Membership: Differentiation in and Outside the European Union* (Oxford University Press, 2023).

As a result of this and of the (unaltered) EU legal framework on which basis it was created, the institutional architecture in which the BU is embedded, and the procedures that underpin it, are extremely complex. This is also the case because banking matters are of concern to all EU Member States since banks operate across the Internal market and are thus governed by its rules. Moreover, non-BU EU Member States are also naturally affected by the developments that happen within the BU, not least because BU banks commonly operate in non-BU Member States.[3] To make matters worse, whilst banking supervision and resolution are now the ultimate responsibility of an EU institution and agency (the European Central Bank (ECB) and the Single Resolution Board (SRB), respectively), national institutions continue to exercise part of the competences. A division of tasks is operated between various EU authorities, on the one hand, and the national ones, on the other.[4] Also, within the Single Supervisory Mechanism (SSM), the ECB, for instance, supervises Significant Institutions (SIs) directly, whereas National Competent Authorities (NCAs) remain in charge of the supervision of smaller credit institutions (or Less Significant Institutions, LSIs).[5]

The existing literature on democratic accountability in the BU has, so far, focused on the ECB in its quality as banking supervisor (ECB-SSM), and to a lesser extent on the SRB.[6] However, a comprehensive assessment of democratic

[3] See Smoleńska, 'Multilevel Cooperation in the EU Resolution of Cross-border Bank Groups: Lessons from the Non-euro Area Member States Joining the Single Resolution Mechanism (SRM)', *Journal of Banking Regulation* 23 (2022), 42–53.

[4] See further on this Della Negra and Lo Schiavo, 'The Relationship between the ECB and the National Competent Authorities in the Single Supervisory Mechanism: Problems and Perspectives' in Beukers, Fromage and Monti (eds.), *The 'New' European Central Bank: Taking Stock and Looking Ahead* (Oxford University Press, 2022).

[5] The specific role of the ECB and the NCAs has given rise to somewhat diverging interpretations by the Court of Justice of the EU and the German Federal Constitutional Court in their L-Bank and European Banking Union decisions, respectively. See *Landeskreditbank Baden-Württemberg – Förderbank V European Central Bank (ECB) and BVerfG* [2019] ECLI: DE: BVerfG:2019:RS20190730.2BVR168514, paras. 1–320; See for some comments on these cases: Annunziata, 'European Banking Supervision in the Age of the ECB: Landeskreditbank Baden-Württemberg – Förderbank v ECB', *European Business Organization Law Review* (2020) 21, 545–570; Schammo, 'Matching or Clashing? Landeskreditbank Baden-Württemberg v ECB and the Decision of the German Bundesverfassungsgericht on the Banking Union', Durham University, 28 November 2019. Accessed via http://dx.doi.org/10.2139/ssrn.3495226 (16.05.2022).

[6] In particular, to date no substantive analysis of the use of accountability mechanisms within the SRM have been performed. Recent analyses include: Amtenbrink and Menelaos, 'Towards a Meaningful Prudential Supervision Dialogue in the Euro Area? A Study of the Interaction between the European Parliament and the European Central Bank in the Single Supervisory Mechanism', *European Law Review* 1 (2019), 3–23; Fromage and Ibrido, 'Accountability and Democratic Oversight in the European Banking Union' in Schiavo (ed.), *The European Banking Union and the Role of Law* (Edward Elgar, 2019), 66–86; Vlachou,

accountability standards in this area of EU public policy requires that a more holistic, all-encompassing view is taken as only such an approach allows to determine whether the four goods that accountability should provide, which are openness, non-arbitrariness, effectiveness, and publicness, can be delivered.[7] This is precisely the perspective adopted in the present chapter, which aims at going beyond the mere analysis of the accountability mechanisms applicable to these two EU instances. Although both substantive and procedural accountability are considered, this chapter arguably already adds to the existing state of the art by providing a mapping of the accountability mechanisms in place considered altogether, that is from the inception – at the EU level – of the norms that are in force within the BU to their application by national and EU authorities.

To fulfil this objective, the present chapter is divided into four sub-sections: (1) It first examines how the BU operates and disentangles the various mechanisms in place, and the role of the different EU institutions and bodies within them. (2) It then proceeds to map the existing democratic accountability mechanisms. (3) The subsequent sub-section turns to the substantive part of the analysis, that is it considers how these mechanisms operate in practice. (4). The final section concludes by offering an assessment of the democratic accountability standards as they exist following the creation of the BU. It considers in particular whether any gap exists, whether in substance or in practice.

## 5.2 WHO DOES WHAT AND HOW? A MAPPING OF THE EXISTING PROCEDURES

The first substantive section of this chapter will detail the characteristics of the existing mechanisms and the specific role played by the various institutions and bodies involved therein.

For the purposes of this chapter, it suffices to note that European integration in the banking domain differs from what is the norm in other areas of the EMU, for instance, because different from what is the rule in the field of monetary policy, banking supervision is an area of shared competence in which the ECB does not adopt the necessary norms itself but, instead, applies those designed by the EU legislator and by the EU regulator. It is led to apply the standards primarily prepared – for the whole of the EU – by an EU agency,

'Ensuring the Democratic Accountability of the Single Resolution Board: Which role for the European Parliament and National Parliaments?', *Revue Internationale des Services Financiers/International Journal for Financial Services* 1 (2017), 8–20; Božina Beroš and Beroš, 'The Single Resolution Board: What About Accountability?', in Pollak and Slominski (eds.), *The Role of EU Agencies in the Eurozone and Migration Crisis*, pp. 127–148.

7 See further the introductory chapter to this edited volume.

the European Banking Authority (EBA), but which must be formally adopted by the European Commission to become legally binding. This notwithstanding, the ECB may itself also adopt certain norms such that the divide between supervisor and regulator is not as clear-cut as it could seem at first sight.[8]

As noted above, two EU authorities are primarily in charge of banking supervision and resolution within the BU. Their status, as well as the legal bases that underpin their existence, are however radically different. Whereas the ECB is an EU institution in its own right, the SRB is an EU agency. Powers in banking supervision could be conferred upon the ECB, thanks to the existence of a 'reserve of competence' contained in Article 127(6) Treaty on the Functioning of the EU (TFEU). It could nevertheless only be entrusted with new competences with regard to those BU Member States that also belong to the euro area, such that specific mechanisms had to be designed to allow the participation of non-euro area Member States in the BU.[9] By contrast, the SRB was created on the basis of Article 114 TFEU, an EU-wide Internal Market legal basis, even if only BU Member States participate in the Single Resolution Mechanism (SRM).[10]

Considering all this, studying the democratic accountability standards of the BU requires a substantive and a procedural analysis of several accountability mechanisms in place, that is those applicable to the ECB-SSM, to the SRB but also those applicable to the EBA, to the Commission and even to the ECB in as far as the ECB's Governing Council ultimately is the organ that formally approves the supervisory decisions prepared by the ECB's Supervisory Board.[11]

8 For instance: Brescia Morra 'From the Single Supervisory Mechanism to the Banking Union. The Role of the ECB and the EBA', LUISS Guido Carli School of European Political Economy, working papers, 13 June 2014. Accessed via https://papers.ssrn.com/sol3/papers.cfm?abstract_id=2448913 (16.05.2022); To ensure consistency between the actions pursued by the EU legislator and those pursued by the ECB, a specific procedure of cooperation has been established by means of the interinstitutional agreement concluded between the EP and the ECB. See: International agreements 2013/694/EU, Interinstitutional Agreement between the European Parliament and the European Central Bank on the practical modalities of the exercise of democratic accountability and oversight over the exercise of the tasks conferred on the ECB within the framework of the Single Supervisory Mechanism, OJ L320/1.

9 This is the so-called close cooperation regime defined in Article 7 SSM Regulation. See on practice to date: Beck and Bruno, 'The ECB's close cooperation on supervising banks in Bulgaria and Croatia', In-depth analysis for the EP ECON Committee, PE 699.521 (2022) and Darvas and Martins, 'Close cooperation for bank supervision: The cases of Bulgaria and Croatia', In-depth analysis for the EP ECON Committee, PE 699.523 (2022).

10 See for a discussion on the resort to this legal basis: Tuominen, 'The European Banking Union: A Shift in the Internal Market Paradigm?', 54 *Common Market Law Review* (2017), 1359–1380.

11 The exact role of the ECB in the approval of SRB decisions was also unclear, but eventually the Court of Justice designated the SRB as the sole decision maker. See *ABLV Bank AS and Others v European Central Bank* [2021] ECLI:EU:C:2021:369, paras 58f; Budinská,

To obtain a full picture of the existing situation, a multilevel perspective that considers the national dimension, as well as multilevel (administrative) cooperation and multilevel democratic accountability mechanisms, should also be adopted. Considering the limited space available here, however, this chapter will focus on the EU level and on the existing accountability mechanisms vis-à-vis EU institutions and bodies. The national and multilevel dimensions will only be underlined and considered in as far as it is necessary to assess the EU dimension of this issue.

## 5.3 ACCOUNTABILITY MECHANISMS IN PLACE

### 5.3.1 *Accountability Mechanisms Applicable to the ECB*

The question of the ECB's accountability plays a primary role in the guarantee of high (or adequate) democratic accountability standards in the BU because, as noted, the ECB is in charge of banking supervision. Its Supervisory Board – which is an internal organ of the ECB created for the specific purpose of banking supervision by the SSM Regulation –[12] is in charge of preparing supervisory decisions, which are later adopted by the Governing Council following a non-objection procedure. Its involvement is necessary because according to the Treaties, the Supervisory Board is not a decision-making organ of the ECB. As such, both the mechanisms in place to hold the ECB-SSM and the ECB to account are of importance when considering democratic accountability of and within the BU. However, because the role of the Governing Council is secondary to that of the Supervisory Board, the mechanisms in place vis-à-vis the latter will be examined first.

The accountability of the Supervisory Board is to be ensured following procedures defined in the SSM Regulation.[13] Its Article 20 is dedicated to '[a]ccountability and reporting'. According to this provision, the ECB is accountable to both the Council and the European Parliament (EP) for the implementation of this Regulation. To this end, it shall submit every year a

'Op-Ed: "Of Auctoritas and Potestas in the Banking Union: The ECB, the SRB, Failing Credit Institutions and Judicial Review"', *EU Law Live* (2021).

[12] Article 26(1), Regulation (EU) No 468/2014 of 16 April 2014 of the European central bank establishing the framework for cooperation within the Single Supervisory Mechanism between the European Central Bank and national competent authorities and with national designated authorities (SSM Framework Regulation), OJ L 141/1 (hereafter SSM Framework Regulation 2014).

[13] Council Regulation (EU) No 1024/2013 of 15 October 2013 conferring specific tasks on the European Central Bank concerning policies relating to the prudential supervision of credit institutions, OJ L 287/63.

'report on the execution of the tasks conferred on it by this Regulation, including information on the envisaged evolution of the structure and amount of the supervisory fees' to the EP, the Council, the European Commission and the Eurogroup. That report shall be presented by the Chair of the Supervisory Board to the EP and to the Eurogroup in presence of those Member States that participate in the BU but do not belong to the euro area (they are also involved in the procedures mentioned subsequently where reference to the Eurogroup is made). This format of the Eurogroup is known as the 'Eurogroup in BU format'. Both the Eurogroup and the EP also have the possibility (on an individual basis and independently from each other) to invite the Chair of the Supervisory Board to appear before them (or before the responsible committee in the case of the EP) to discuss the execution of its supervisory tasks. Oral or written questions may additionally be put to the ECB (i.e., the ECB-SSM) by both the Eurogroup and the EP.[14]

Next to these procedures, the possibility exists that, upon initiative of the Supervisory Board's Chair, confidential oral discussions behind closed doors be held with the Chair and the Vice-chairs of the responsible EP Committee, that is the Committee on Economic and Monetary Affairs (ECON Committee), where these 'are required for the exercise of the European Parliament's powers under the TFEU'. The details of these arrangements are to be defined in an interinstitutional agreement between the EP and the ECB, which was adopted in 2013.[15] Finally, a duty is set on the ECB to cooperate with the EP in its conduct of investigations. To this end,

> [t]he ECB and the European Parliament shall conclude appropriate arrangements on the practical modalities of the exercise of democratic accountability and oversight over the exercise of the tasks conferred on the ECB by this Regulation. Those arrangements shall cover, inter alia, access to information, cooperation in investigations and information on the selection procedure of the Chair of the Supervisory Board.

The interinstitutional agreement details the content of the annual report, which the ECB has to submit to the EP. It also specifies that the Chair of

[14] Note though that the questions submitted to the ECB in that framework are deducted from the total of six questions MEPs may ask every month as per Article 140 EP Rules of procedure. Likewise, the questions addressed by MEPs to the SRB – to which more below – are also deducted from this maximum number of six-monthly questions: See Rule 141, Rules of Procedure of the European Parliament (2019).

[15] International agreements 2013/694/EU, Interinstitutional Agreement between the European Parliament and the European Central Bank on the practical modalities of the exercise of democratic accountability and oversight over the exercise of the tasks conferred on the ECB within the framework of the Single Supervisory Mechanism, OJ L320/1.

the Supervisory Board shall be submitted at least to two ordinary hearings, although additional ad hoc exchanges of views may be organised too. Additionally, it specifies how confidential oral discussions have to take place in practical terms. Likewise, the modalities for the submission of written questions are specified, and the aim is that the ECB answers them within five weeks (as opposed to the six-week target set for the questions put to the ECB by MEPs on monetary policy issues as per the EP's Rules of procedure). Specific provisions furthermore detail how information on the ECB's tasks as a supervisor is to be made available. This includes, for example, access to the record of proceedings of the Supervisory Board by the ECON Committee or non-confidential information regarding a credit institution that has been wound up. The EP is to establish sufficient safeguards for the confidentiality of the ECB documents submitted to it to remain preserved.

As noted previously, also the EU executives (e.g. Commission, Council and Eurogroup) are addressees of the ECB-SSM's annual report. What may, however, appear as more surprising is the fact that it is with the Eurogroup and not the Council with which the true relationship of accountability is established. Indeed, the annual report shall be presented to the Eurogroup, which may invite the Chair of the Supervisory Board to appear before it and submit both written and oral questions to the ECB-SSM. This state of fact is disturbing for several reasons. As recalled by the Court of Justice on several occasions,[16] the Eurogroup is not an institution of the Union but an informal group whose *raison d'être* is to allow for the coordination of euro area Member States' policies. Neither the informal nature of the Eurogroup nor the purpose of its existence squares well with the role it is called to play in guaranteeing the ECB-SSM's democratic accountability.

Moreover, according to Article 10 TEU, democratic accountability rests upon two pillars within the EU since the entry into force of the Lisbon Treaty: the EP and Member States government representatives participating in the Council. Considering all this, the ECB-SSM could rather have been held accountable by the Council. This would have made all the more sense as the Council (and formally at least, not the Eurogroup) is involved in the approval of (part of) the secondary legislation the ECB has to apply in its quality as banking supervisor. Additionally, the argument can be made that developments within the BU are of interest to all of the EU Member States, as is

[16] *Joined Cases C-597/18 P, C-598/18 P, C-603/18 P and C-604/18 P Council of the European Union v Dr. K. Chrysostomides & Co. LLC, and the other parties whose names appear in Annex I* [2020] ECLI:EU:C:2020:390, paras 62f.; Markakis and Karatzia, 'Financial Assistance Conditionality and Effective Judicial Protection: Chrysostomides', *Common Market Law Review* 59 (2022), 501–542.

indeed confirmed by the fact that BU matters are, at least in some instances, discussed in Eurogroup meeting in inclusive format, that is with representatives from all EU27 Member States.[17] The Lisbon Treaty already opened the door to a 'differentiated Council', that is one within which on some occasions only euro area representatives may cast their vote, and thus the Council could have been used as an accountability forum. Admittedly, since the possibility formally exists that non-euro area (candidate) Member States may join the BU, an accountability forum that would only bring together BU representatives had to be set up, and only the Eurogroup (and not the Council) could easily be adapted for that purpose. But it remains the case that the solution found is largely unsatisfactory for the reasons outlined previously.

Next to these relationships of accountability with EU organs, 'relationships with national parliaments' are also foreseen in the SSM Regulation. Although formally, and according to the ECB itself, it is 'primarily accountable to the EP' and not to national parliaments, and although the question as to whether these relationships between the ECB-SSM and national parliaments serve the purpose of democratic accountability has been subject to debate,[18] there is little doubt that the powers with which parliaments have been entrusted vis-à-vis the ECB (written questions, reasoned observations on the annual report and exchange of views) resemble those that commonly exist between parliaments and any institution they hold accountable.

These relationships of accountability add to those that have existed between the EP (and the Council) and the ECB since the creation of the ECB. Indeed, the ECB's (strong) independence is to be compensated by its relationship of accountability towards the EP (primarily). It must therefore address an annual report on 'the activities of the ESCB [European System of Central Banks] and on the monetary policy of both the previous and the current year to the European Parliament, the Council and the Commission, and also to the European Council'.[19] This report shall be presented to the Council and to the EP, which 'may hold a general debate on that basis'. Additionally, the possibility exists for the President of the ECB or the other members of the Executive Board to be heard before the ECON Committee

[17] This was notably the case on the occasion of the meeting of 12 July 2021. See European Council, 'Meeting of Eurogroup, 12 July 2021', July 2021. Accessed via www.consilium.europa.eu/en/meetings/eurogroup/2021/07/12/ (16.05.2022).

[18] Fernández Bollo, 'Democratic Accountability Within the Framework of the SSM and the SRM as a Complement to Judicial Review' in Zilioli and Wojcik (ed.), *Judicial Review in the European Banking Union – Elgar Financial Law and Practice Series* (Edward Elgar Publishing, 2021).

[19] Article 15(3), Protocol (No 4) on the Statue of the European system of central banks and of the European Central Bank, OJ C 202/230, (here after ESCB Statute).

on their own initiative, or on that of the ECON Committee. MEPs are also entitled to submit six questions for written answers to the EP.[20] In the framework of monetary policy, although some exchanges were indeed organised in the past,[21] formally no relationship exists between the ECB and national parliaments, as may appear logical considering that monetary policy is a competence of the Union.[22]

The existence of a relationship of accountability between the ECB and the Council makes sense historically as, originally, the status of 'Member State with a derogation', that is that of Member State outside the euro area, was meant to remain temporary for all Member States bar Denmark and the United Kingdom which had obtained a permanent opt-out. Thus, correspondence largely existed between the geographical area within which the ECB's monetary policy would take effect (at that point in time or eventually), and the Member States represented in the Council. However, already at the time when the Lisbon Treaty was drafted, it may be argued that this had become wishful thinking. This notwithstanding, Member States did not choose to change the identity of the forum in charge of holding the ECB accountable and instead the Council kept this prerogative, despite the fact that it is precisely that Treaty (i.e. the Lisbon Treaty) which formalised the existence of the Eurogroup. The choice in favour of the Eurogroup when the SSM was established could point to the willingness to further empower the Eurogroup, a forum which had already been significantly reinforced as a result of the euro area crisis. Furthermore, to state the obvious, a choice in favour of the Eurogroup is also to the benefit of the Member States, since the accountability and transparency standards it is submitted to are much less stringent than those applicable to the Council.[23]

### 5.3.2 *Guaranteeing the SRB's Accountability*

The SRM was established a few years after the SSM, and the latter's accountability mechanisms no doubt inspired those of the former. Indeed, the obligations set on the SRB by the SRM Regulation are similar to those

[20] Rule 140 (1), Rules of Procedure of the European Parliament (2019)

[21] Jančić, 'Accountability of the European Central Bank in a Deepening EMU' in Jančić (ed.), *National Parliaments After the Lisbon Treaty and the Euro Crisis – Resilience or Resignation?* (Oxford University Press, 2017), 141–158.

[22] Relationships have still developed on an informal basis since the Eurocrisis. Whether they serve information/pedagogical purposes or are deemed to serve as an additional accountability channel for the ECB (or whether they ought to) is up for debate. See Fromage *Changing parliaments in a changing European Union* (Hart forthcoming).

[23] See further on the Eurogroup's accountability: Markakis in this volume.

set on the ECB-SSM by the SSM Regulation.[24] However, considering that the SRM is an agency and not an EU institution like the ECB, it is accountable not only to the EP and the Member States – coming together in the Council and not in the Eurogroup but also to the Commission. The annual report is submitted to the EP, the national parliaments of participating Member States, the Council, the Commission and the European Court of Auditors. As a result of this, differently from what is the case within the SSM, the Eurogroup is not supposed to be involved in any way in this instance, which could be the case because the SRB is an EU-wide agency. The report is then presented to the EP and the Council. The EP may additionally invite the Chair of the SRB to a hearing, and a minimum of one hearing per year is set by the SRM Regulation. Written and oral questions may be submitted to the SRB by the Council and the EP, and the possibility to hold confidential oral discussions is also provided. Like it is the case between the ECB-SSM and the EP, an agreement that details the modalities of these discussions shall be concluded,[25] and the SRB is set to cooperate in any investigation the EP may initiate.

Like the interinstitutional agreement between the ECB-SSM and the EP, the Agreement between the EP and the SRB details the content of the report that the SRB has to submit every year. The topics addressed in the ordinary public discussions are also defined, as is the possibility to organise ad hoc meetings and the practical modalities of the confidential oral discussions. A minimum of two ordinary hearings per year is set. The EP shall be kept duly informed as a 'comprehensive and meaningful record of the proceedings' of every executive or plenary meeting is to be submitted to it within the six weeks that follow said meeting. The rest of the provisions contained in the Agreement are similar to those included in the interinstitutional agreement between the ECB-SSM and the EP.

Likewise, the SRM Regulation establishes a direct relationship between the SRB and the national parliaments of the participating Member States. Their nature (i.e., whether they constitute a relationship of accountability) is also not specified, but as they are very similar to those established with the EP they

[24] Articles 45 and 46, Regulation (EU) No 806/2014 of the European Parliament and of the Council of 15 July 2014 establishing uniform rules and a uniform procedure for the resolution of credit institutions and certain investment firms in the framework of a Single Resolution Mechanism and a Single Resolution Fund and amending Regulation (EU) No 1093/2010, OJ L 225/1 (hereafter SRM Regulation).

[25] Agreement between the European Parliament and the Single Resolution Board on the practical modalities of the exercise of democratic accountability and oversight over the exercise of the tasks conferred on the Single Resolution Board within the framework of the Single Resolution Mechanism.

may also be viewed as contributing to the SRB's accountability credentials. The powers vested with national parliaments in this framework are indeed very similar to those attributed to them vis-à-vis the ECB. However, the SRB is set under stronger obligations towards them than the ECB is.[26]

### 5.3.3 *The EBA's Accountability Credentials*

Guaranteeing democratic accountability within the BU demands that also the EBA be submitted to democratic control. This is the case because it prepares technical standards that are officially adopted by the European Commission at a later stage, and because it still fosters coordination among National Competent Authorities, including but not only in areas closely linked to banking supervision.

The accountability mechanisms applicable to the EBA were significantly enhanced when the European Supervisory Authorities (ESAs) Regulations were amended in 2019.[27] In its original version, the ESAs Regulation only established that '[t]he Authorities referred to in points (a) to (d) of Article 2(2) [among which is the EBA] shall be accountable to the European Parliament and to the Council'. By contrast, it is now foreseen that the EBA be accountable to the EP and the Council but that it shall also cooperate with the EP in the event that the latter decides to conduct an investigation. Despite the EBA's quality as an agency – and differently from the SRB – the EBA is not accountable to the Commission. Several reasons could account for this. Perhaps the most evident one is that this provision concerns not only the EBA (or the ESAs) but also the European Systemic Risk Board (ESRB), which is not an agency but an independent body chaired by the President of the ECB. The EBA's prerogatives are also more circumscribed than those of the SRB. The Commission is called to formally adopt the

[26] Lamandini and Ramos Muñoz, 'Study Requested by the ECON Committee: SSM and SRB Accountability at European Level: What Room for Improvements? Banking Union Scrutiny', European Parliament, April 2020. Accessed via www.europarl.europa.eu/RegData/etudes/STUD/2020/645711/IPOL_STU(2020)645711_EN.pdf (11.5.2022).

[27] Regulation (EU) 2019/2175 of the European Parliament and of the Council of 18 December 2019 amending Regulation (EU) No 1093/2010 establishing a European Supervisory Authority (European Banking Authority), Regulation (EU) No 1094/2010 establishing a European Supervisory Authority (European Insurance and Occupational Pensions Authority), Regulation (EU) No 1095/2010 establishing a European Supervisory Authority (European Securities and Markets Authority), Regulation (EU) No 600/2014 on markets in financial instruments, Regulation (EU) 2016/1011 on indices used as benchmarks in financial instruments and financial contracts or to measure the performance of investment funds, and Regulation (EU) 2015/847 on information accompanying transfers of funds (Text with EEA relevance), OJ L 334/1.

normative acts, which the EBA prepares such that it already is in a position to exercise some form of control over its actions, although the procedures differ for non-normative acts.

The EBA's 'Board of Supervisors shall adopt an annual report on the activities of the Authority, including on the performance of the Chairperson's duties, and shall, by 15 June each year, transmit that report to the European Parliament, to the Council, to the Commission, to the Court of Auditors and to the European Economic and Social Committee'. As such, the duty that is now set on the Board of Supervisors is similar to that which the ECB-SSM and especially the SRB have to fulfil. However, in this case, a precise date is set by which the EBA has to fulfil its obligation. The European Economic and Social Committee is, too, an addressee of the report.

Additionally, it is prescribed that the EBA's Chairperson be heard by the EP – upon its request – at least once a year 'on the performance' of the EBA. The format of the hearing is quite precisely defined in the Regulation, as it calls for the Chairperson to make a statement and to answer the questions put to it by MEPs. The EP may ask the Chairperson to report on the activities of the EBA at least fifteen days before the hearing. Specific mention is also made to the possibility for the EP to request that the EBA reports on its participation in international forums, which is all the more welcome as those (which include, for instance, the Basel Committee on Banking Supervision[28]) have assumed an ever larger role following the outbreak of the Great Financial Crisis.

Next to these procedures, the possibility also exists for the Council or the EP to put written questions to the EBA, which it shall answer within five weeks. As with the ECB-SSM and the SRB, confidential oral discussions may be organised since the EBA Regulation was amended.

### 5.3.4 *The Commission*

One last actor that arguably plays an important role in the BU is the European Commission. This is the case for numerous reasons, chief of which are the facts that it is involved in several of the procedures that exist (for instance, in

[28] See on this: De Bellis, 'Reinforcing EU Financial Bodies Participation in Global Networks: Addressing Legitimacy Gaps?' in Hofmann et al. (eds.) *The External Dimension of EU Agencies and Bodies Law and Policy* (Cheltenham: Edward Elgar Publishing, 2019), 126–144; Fromage, 'The (multilevel) Articulation of the European Participation in International Financial for a: The Example of the Basel Accords', *Journal of Banking Regulation* 23 (2022), 54–65; Viterbo, 'The European Union in the Transnational Financial Regulatory Arena: The Case of the Basel Committee on Banking Supervision', 22 *Journal of International Economic Law* 2 (2019), 205–228.

banking resolution), that it has the last word on the standards developed by the EBA, and naturally also that it proposes the norms of secondary legislation that are of application within the BU.

In consequence, upholding suitable accountability standards within the BU demands that the Commission be submitted to sufficient controls. Put differently, in seeking to evaluate whether any accountability gap exists within the BU, one should also check whether the Commission's actions in this domain are sufficiently scrutinised by the EP.

The EP has numerous means to hold the European Commission to account. Its strongest power lies in its possibility to remove its confidence in the Commission and thus force it to resign collectively.[29] The EP and its members may also put some oral and written questions to the Commission or submit Commissioners to major interpellations,[30] organise hearings to provide the Commission an opportunity to explain its decisions,[31] and create committees of inquiry.[32]

### 5.3.5 *Conclusion*

The preceding analysis has evidenced that mechanisms exist to guarantee the democratic accountability of BU institutions. An evolution towards an enhancement of these mechanisms may additionally be witnessed, both in terms of their nature and in terms of their very existence. Indeed, the accountability of the EBA was significantly reinforced following the reform performed in 2019. Also, the mechanisms in place towards both the ECB-SSM and the SRB are more stringent than those applicable to the ECB. Several reasons may account for this. First, the ECB benefits from a stronger degree of independence in the area of monetary policy than it does in the field of banking supervision.[33] Second, accountability standards have evolved significantly over the past twenty years. For example, the EP is only consulted when the President of the ECB is appointed.

[29] Article 18(7) TEU.

[30] Article 230 TFEU and Rules 136, 137, 138 and 139, Rules of Procedure of the European Parliament (2019)

[31] Rule 133, Rules of Procedure of the European Parliament (2019).

[32] Article 227 TFEU and Rule 208, Rules of Procedure of the European Parliament (2019)

[33] As recalled, for instance, by Kerstin af Jochnick, Member of the Supervisory Board of the ECB on 1 March 2022. Supervisory independence and accountability. Af Jochnick, 'Speech by Kerstin af Jochnick, Member of the Supervisory Board of the ECB, at the IMF High-Level Regional Seminar in Sub-Saharan Africa', European Central Bank, 1 March 2022. Accessed via www.bankingsupervision.europa.eu/press/speeches/date/2022/html/ssm.sp220301~66eb4805eb.en.html (16.05.2022).

In contrast, its consent is necessary for the chair of the Supervisory Board to be nominated,[34] that is the EP's role has become larger over time.

Accountability mechanisms, be they formalised or not, make it more likely that democratic accountability is upheld. However, the mere existence of those mechanisms does not suffice, as there is, for example, no guarantee that they are used by the actors to which they are available. The next sub-section therefore turns to the practice of accountability in the BU to date.

## 5.4 THE PRACTICE OF DEMOCRATIC ACCOUNTABILITY SO FAR

To evaluate the practice of democratic accountability so far, two dimensions in particular will be considered: *formal* accountability, that is if and how the existing instruments have been used, and *substantive* accountability, that is what these mechanisms have been used for in terms of substance. The data examined in this sub-section covers the period between November 2014 and April 2022, that is from the start of the functioning of the SSM until the date of submission. It consists of minutes of EP debates, written questions and the responses they received, as well as the yearly reports produced severally by the institutions examined.[35] The focus is set on the ECB-SSM, the SRB and the EBA owing to the ECB and the European Commission playing a secondary role in the BU if compared to the ECB-SSM, the SRB and the EBA.

Before proceeding with the proposed analysis, it should be noted that any conclusion drawn at this stage may only be provisional since the two pillars of the BU have only been functioning for a short period of time. This notwithstanding, the proposed study is still valuable because it allows to gain some knowledge of how the existing mechanisms have been used and which shortcomings inherent to them or gaps among them may exist. The conclusion thus provides an assessment of the current situation, as well as some suggestions for improvement.

### 5.4.1 *Practice of Accountability to Date*

It must be said from the start that research reveals that the existing democratic accountability procedures have been used indeed: Parliamentary hearings

[34] See on this evolution: Fromage, 'Guaranteeing the ECB's Democratic Accountability in the Post-Banking Union Era: An Ever More Difficult Task?', 26 *Maastricht Journal of European and Comparative Law* 1 (2019), 48–62.

[35] This data was used either directly or via the proxy on analysis available in the literature duly referenced in footnotes.

and ad hoc exchanges of views have been organised, reports have been produced and parliamentary questions have been put to the ECB-SSM and to the SRB. However, differences in terms of frequency and fluctuations over time have existed. The following paragraphs first consider the ECB-SSM before turning to the SRB and to the EBA.

As regards parliamentary questions put by MEPs to the ECB-SSM, it must first be said that they were not very numerous in the first years of the functioning of the SSM, as is only logical. They peaked in 2017 and 2018 although they remained infrequent at approximately forty questions per year (by comparison, the number of questions put to the ECB as the European institution in charge of monetary policy was similar in 2017 but it rose to more than three times this amount in 2018).[36] The number of questions has since been decreasing and there was only a dozen of them in 2021. Perhaps this could be explained by the varying levels of interest among participating MEPs, with notably one of the most active of them, Sven Giegold, having ceased to be an MEP. Also, the SSM no longer is a new instrument, thus MEPs' interest could have faded with time, in particular seeing as no new banking crisis has emerged and the ECB thus seems to be fulfilling its tasks satisfactorily. It could be expected that MEPs' interest would rise again if the ECB-SSM were to deal more closely with controversial issues such as climate change. Despite recommendations in favour of the creation of a space dedicated to questions posed by MEPs to the ECB-SSM (and the SRB),[37] no such step has been taken by the EP to date, which is regrettable as it makes relevant information harder to find.

Also, some questions have been put by national members of parliaments, most often from the German Bundestag. It is perhaps unsurprising that the members of the Bundestag are those who have used this mechanism most, considering the fact that the creation of the BU had raised concerns that democratic accountability standards would be lowered as a consequence thereof. Indeed, the German NCA, the BaFin, is functionally placed below the responsibility of the ministry of finance, which may be held accountable for the actions of the NCA.[38] More generally, and perhaps most importantly, a tradition exists for German MPs to ask written questions. In terms of their

[36] These figures are extracted from the ECB's annual reports and from the dedicated sections of its website.

[37] Smits, 'Study Requested by the ECON Committee: SSM and the SRB Accountability at European Level: Room for Improvements?', European Parliament, April 2020. Accessed via www.europarl.europa.eu/RegData/etudes/STUD/2020/645726/IPOL_STU(2020)645726_EN.pdf (15.5.2022), p 26.

[38] Thiele, *Finanzaufsicht: der Staat und die Finanzmärkte* (1st Ed, Mohr Siebeck, 2014), p. 415f.

content, some of the questions are very specific and regard a specific credit institution, whilst others are much more general and address, for instance, non-performing loans, the implementation of the Basel standards or supervision in general. Such a mixed set of macro- and micro-topics seems to be healthy for the whole system of supervision.

Parliamentary hearings and ad hoc exchanges of views, as well as hearings before the Eurogroup, have taken place on a regular basis, and the annual reports were duly presented. Though some fluctuations over time may be observed in this regard as well – perhaps also due to the pandemic and the widespread 'Zoom-fatigue', it may generally be said that exchanges with MEPs have been more frequent than the minimum set by the SSM Regulation as they have often included a couple of ad hoc exchanges of views in addition to the standard bi-annual hearings.[39] The topics covered during these exchanges were varied as they ranged, for example, from the consequences of the pandemic to climate risks and the finalisation of Basel III.

Confidential oral discussions have taken place before hearings of the Chair of the Supervisory Board by the ECON Committee, and they have been 'reported to be much more confrontational than public hearings, with "tough" language that is often absent in public interactions between the two institutions'.[40]

Finally, the Chair of the Supervisory Board has regularly appeared before the Eurogroup, and these meetings have commonly been organised together with the Chair of the SRB (this is examined more in depth below). Fluctuations in their frequency have existed as well, with notably 2017 standing out as a year of particularly close exchanges, but this was also the year when the first resolution ever took place such that this is perhaps rather unsurprising. As these exchanges are not public, they are harder to assess. Nonetheless, the ECB had noted in the past that '[t]he topics of interest to the finance ministers overlapped to a large extent with those discussed in the European Parliament'[41] and the overall issues discussed may be found in the account of the main results of Eurogroup meetings since they exist. The topics covered have included, for example, broader issues such as non-performing loans and anti-money laundering.

39 2021 is a notable exception to this, which the need to resort to a virtual format could perhaps explain.

40 Akbik, *The European Parliament as an Accountability Forum: Overseeing the Economic and Monetary Union* (1st Ed, Cambridge University Press, 2022), p. 77f.

41 European Central Bank, 'Annual report on supervisory activities', March 2018. Accessed via www.bankingsupervision.europa.eu/press/publications/annual-report/html/ssm.ar2018~927cb99de4.en.html (14.05.2022).

If one considers the SRB, one may first regret that the part devoted to accountability in its annual reports remains particularly succinct. Also, it appears that its exchanges with the EP have been less frequent than those organised between the ECB-SSM and the EP as they have generally been limited to two exchanges per year in addition to the presentation of the annual reports. This could be explained by the fact that the SRM has only been activated on one occasion during the period considered here. On the other hand, the fact remains that the setting up of the SRM has raised questions indeed, in terms of its functioning and its financing but also in relation to questions related to the overall architecture of the BU and notably its missing pilar, the European Deposit Insurance Scheme, and the role the SRB could play therein. Therefore, more interest on the side of MEPs could have been reasonably expected.

MEPs have likewise devoted much less attention in their questions to the SRB than they have to the ECB-SSM. To date, they have addressed fifteen questions in total, of which seven were addressed by the same MEP (Sven Giegold).[42] These questions have sometimes consisted in requests for access to documents, or more general questions such as the architecture of the SRM in general, as well as questions on the Banco Popular case, for example.

Like was the case with the ECB-SSM as well, questions from national parliaments have not been numerous (ten in total) and only German MPs have asked questions to date. The identity of these MPs largely corresponds to those who raised questions to the ECB-SSM. Interestingly, although the answers to these questions are available on the SRB's website, they are not translated into English but are, instead, only available in German. Whilst this is understandable as translation is demanding on resources, one may wonder whether this does not, in fact, diminish the SRB's accountability potential vis-à-vis the larger public. Considering how few these questions are, it would be advisable for the SRB to make a courtesy translation available to all. As concerns the topics touched upon by these letters, they have regarded very factual issues, including the number of credit institutions whose resolution planning the SRB oversees, as well as questions related to specific credit institutions or related to findings of the European Court of Auditors.

The relationship between the SRB and the Eurogroup follows a similar pattern as the one between the ECB-SSM and the Eurogroup, not least because the Chair of the Supervisory Board and the Chair of the SRB commonly appear together before the Eurogroup. Issues addressed with the

[42] Some, like the one by MEP de Lange of 6 December 2016, were raised during hearings held before the EP.

Chair of the SRB have included resolution planning, the built-up of the Single Resolution Fund or resolvability (continuity seems to exist in the topics discussed, which is only logical as the SRB's main task in normal times is to prepare for potential resolution cases such that the issues that need addressing are rather recurrent as opposed to being individual events). It must be noted that although this practice of joint hearings with the Chair of the Supervisory Board and the Chair of the SRB makes perfect sense as they allow for a more comprehensive control by the EP of what is going on in the BU, it remains that it contradicts the content of the SRM Regulation, which foresees that the SRB – an EU-wide agency – be held to account by the Council. As noted above, it probably would have been best to entrust the Council with the task of controlling both the ECB-SSM and the SRB in the first place, also to guarantee higher transparency and thus higher accountability standards.

The relationship between the SRB and the Commission seems to unfold on a smooth basis, as the SRB noted, for instance, in its annual report for the year 2020 that it 'continued to maintain its close cooperation with the relevant directorates-general of the Commission, in particular with the Directorate-General for Financial Stability, Financial Services and Capital Markets Union (DG FISMA) and the Directorate-General for Competition (DG COMP) at all levels on various aspects, which are relevant to the SRB's work and functions, and participated actively in the meetings of the Expert Group on Banking Payments and Insurance (EGBPI)'.[43] Further details are not available.

Finally, one may regret that the information regarding the EBA's accountability is not much detailed; its annual reports and its website indeed only contain scarce information on this topic, and it is not easy to find. The EBA fulfils its duty to present its annual report to the EP, and it entertains relationships with other EU institutions.[44] Most of the correspondence publicly available is addressed to the European Commission, and it covers issues that go beyond banking supervision owing to the EBA's broad mandate. This notwithstanding, some of the letters are indeed addressed to MEPs, but they remain scarce.[45]

43 Single Resolution Board, 'Annual Report 2020', June 2021. Accessed via: www.srb.europa.eu/system/files/media/document/Annual%20Report%202020_Final_web.pdf (14.05.2022).

44 See the section dedicated to 'Correspondence with EU institutions' of the EBA's website. www.eba.europa.eu/about-us/missions-and-tasks/correspondence-with-eu-institutions

45 It is however not clear whether these letters are addressed to the EBA on the basis of Article 3(7) EBA Regulation, that the possibility open to MEPs to address questions to the EBA. As these questions do not appear when using the search function of the EP's website, it would seem as though formally these are not parliamentary questions.

### 5.4.2 *Conclusion*

The preceding analysis of the use of the existing accountability mechanisms to date reveals first that information on this issue is scattered around the various websites and uneasy to find. This is regrettable, and efforts should be made to improve this situation, as already proposed by René Smits.[46]

Second, it appears that, at the EU level, the existing procedures are being used indeed, as hearings and exchanges of views are organised, questions are posed, and reports are produced. The EP additionally produces annual reports on BU.[47] Parliamentary questions are, though rather infrequent, and fluctuations have existed over time in the frequency of the oral exchanges held. It is interesting to note that despite its duty to hold the EBA accountable too, the EP only keeps regular records of practice of accountability towards the ECB-SSM and the SRB but not towards the EBA (or any of the European Supervisory Agencies).[48] This is regrettable as the EBA and these agencies in general play an increasingly important role in financial supervision within the EU, and as the acts of soft law they adopt produce significant effects for banks and have been the object of litigation before the Court of Justice.[49]

In any event, shortcomings exist in the practice of accountability: despite the fact that external experts are regularly invited to produce briefings, the questions put by MEPs are not always sufficiently to the point.[50] Most importantly, the same questions are not consistently picked up during debates.[51] Also, MEPs are not always clear about the appropriate forum or addressee for

46 *Supra* note 37.

47 See, for instance, European Parliament, 'Draft Report on Banking Union – Annual Report 2020 (2020/2122(INI))', April 2021. Accessed via www.europarl.europa.eu/doceo/document/ECON-PR-658703_EN.pdf (13.05.2022).

48 These take the form of briefings, which are regularly updated. See for instance: European Parliament, 'Single Supervisory Mechanism: Accountability Arrangements (9th Parliamentary Term)', November 2021. Accessed via www.europarl.europa.eu/RegData/etudes/BRIE/2020/659623/IPOL_BRI(2020)659623_EN.pdf (13.05.2022) and European Parliament, 'Single Resolution Board: Accountability Arrangements (9th Parliamentary Term)', November 2021. Accessed via www.europarl.europa.eu/RegData/etudes/BRIE/2020/659621/IPOL_BRI(2020)659621_EN.pdf (13.05.2022).

49 *Fédération bancaire française (FBF) v Autorité de contrôle prudentiel et de résolution (ACPR)* [2021] ECLI:EU:C:2021:599; See for a comment of the case: Quelhas, 'The EBA Guidelines on Retail Banking Products' Saga Lessons from an Attempted Judicial Review of European Supervisory Authority Guidelines', *EU Law Live Weekend Edition* (2022) 97.

50 This was notably noted by Fabian Amtenbrink and Menelaos Markakis, as well as by Adina Maricut-Akbik, *supra* note 6 and Maricut-Akbik, 'Contesting the European Central Bank in Banking Supervision: Accountability in Practice at the European Parliament', 58 *JCMS: Journal of Common Market Studies* 5 (2020), 1083–1358.

51 Lamandini and Ramos Muñoz, *supra* note 26, at p. 35.

a specific issue. For instance, some of the questions put to the ECB were not addressed to it in the right setup, that is MEPs mixed up the setup designed for dialogue on monetary policy issues with the one reserved to banking supervision. Although this confusion could have been due to the very numerous forums in which MEPs have the opportunity to debate with the ECB, it could also be the case that they deliberately chose not to care for political reasons and simply use any channel they had at their disposal.

Beyond all this, it has been found that, in effect, MEPs only have had limited influence on the ECB-SSM's policy, although this is because MEPs only rarely require such changes but rather use their interaction with the ECB to request information on policy views.[52] This could point to a usage of public hearings and questions primarily for communication purposes, as opposed to their being used for accountability purposes.[53] Confidentiality in banking supervision is a further hindrance in MEPs' quest for accountability,[54] and reform proposals have been made to improve this situation.[55]

Finally, and although this issue is only subsidiary to the analysis conducted here, one may observe that very limited use has been made by national parliaments of the possibility they now have to directly interact with the ECB-SSM and the SRB. To assess whether this results in an accountability gap, research should determine whether this is compensated by adequate mechanisms of accountability towards NCAs and the use thereof by parliaments at the national level.

## 5.5 CONCLUSION: IS THERE A GAP AND IF SO, HOW TO BRIDGE IT

This chapter intended to adopt a holistic view of democratic accountability in the BU with a view to determining whether any gap exists. Some gaps appear to exist indeed, and they derive from (a) the EU's constitutional framework, (b) the BU's architecture and its characteristics, and (c) from practice, that is how the existing accountability mechanisms are used.

### 5.5.1 *The EU's Constitutional Framework Has Become Unfit for Purpose*

The existing flaws are generally related to both the EU's architecture and functioning, and specific to EMU. The shortcomings inherent to the EU's architecture are twofold, and are caused by, on the one hand, the trend of

[52] *Supra* note 50.
[53] *Supra* note 51.
[54] *Supra* note 50.
[55] *Supra* note 37.

agencification within the EU,[56] and relatedly to the absence of specific and precise legal basis for EU agencies, which would allow a much necessary update and adjustment of the Meroni doctrine. On the other hand, they derive from the gap that has grown between the existing legal framework, and the degree and the variety of differentiation within today's EU (where differentiated integration is understood in the largest possible sense). As noted above, the co-existence of the BU, the euro area and the EU27 and the corresponding institutional variations of the meetings of national ministers at the EU level certainly blur the boundaries between the various groups of Member States, and thus the accountability channels applicable to the various procedures. This then must bring back to a reflection on the question of (internal and external) differentiation and membership within the EU more generally.

Some of the existing shortcomings are, though, specific to the EMU and its sub-area the BU. Whereas differentiation is a feature commonly observed within the EU and not specific to the EMU, the EMU is arguably the most extreme example of differentiation in terms of its breadth and reach with, among others, the ECB conducting the euro area's monetary policy, or the existence of an intergovernmental European Stability Mechanism as an emergency safety net reserved to euro area Member States but one that also serves as a backstop to the (EU) BU. Differentiation within the EMU is then also visible in terms of its institutional embedding with the Eurogroup as a *quasi* institution, the existence of Euro Summit, of specific voting rules in the Council, and the recurrent proposals in favour of a euro area parliament or at least a euro area sub-committee to the ECON Committee,[57] to the point that the principle of institutional unity that used to be a requirement to any initiative of enhanced cooperation under Amsterdam could come under threat.[58] As has been evidenced in this chapter, the mechanisms formally in place within the BU are oftentimes pragmatic solutions to the lack of suitability of the existing legal framework as is illustrated by the Eurogroup's role in

56 On which see, among many others: Busuioc et al., *The Agency Phenomenon in the European Union: Emergence, Institutionalisation and Everyday Decision-Making* (1st Ed, Manchester University Press, 2012).

57 Curtin and Fasone, 'Differentiated Representation: Is a Flexible European Parliament Desirable?' in de Witte et al. (eds.) *Between Flexibility and Disintegration. The Trajectory of Differentiation in the EU* (Edward Elgar, 2017), pp. 118–145; Henette et al., 'Draft Treaty on the Democratization of the Governance of the Euro Area (T-Dem)' in Ibid. *How Democratize Europe* (Cambridge: Harvard University Press, 2019), pp. 63–86.

58 See on this question of institutional unity in the framework of EMU: Fromage 'Moving beyond "institutional unity" within the EU? Euro area versus non-Euro area representation in the EU institutions', Maastricht University Law Faculty Working paper, 2019. Accessed via www.maastrichtuniversity.nl/maastricht-faculty-law-working-paper-series-2019 (16.05.2022).

guaranteeing the ECB-SSM's accountability. Practice shows a further adaptation of the established mechanisms as in the case of the Eurogroup, which also serves as accountability forum for the SRB. Both of these phenomena nonetheless only illustrate that the existing institutional framework is unfit for purpose, because it has not been adapted to match the evolutions that have happened in the breadth of the policies conducted at the EU level and to the form that these take, even if it must be admitted that the framework currently in place has proven to be sufficiently flexible for informal arrangements to be developed.

### 5.5.2 *Flaws Inherent to the BU*

Next to these shortcomings related to the EU's institutional framework, there are also shortcomings that are specific to the BU, although they partially derive from the problems that exist within the EU's constitutional structure generally.

The BU is in-between the EU27 and the euro area, and relies on both structures. From this derives inherent complexity that in turn makes guaranteeing democratic accountability particularly challenging. Accordingly, democratic accountability standards within the BU may not be assessed by only looking at the ECB-SSM and the SRB. As this chapter has posited, other actors including the Commission and the EBA play an important role as well, and their accountability credentials must, too, be taken into consideration.

Mark Bovens has defined accountability as 'a relationship between an actor and a forum, in which the actor has an obligation to explain and to justify his or her conduct, the forum can pose questions and pass judgment, and the actor may face consequences'.[59] When the last step is taken within the framework of the BU, that is when the forum that holds the agent to account is to take actions based on its assessment of how the principle has performed, it must hold not only the ECB-SSM or the SRB to account but also the Commission and the EBA because of their role as regulator. The ECB's nature as an independent EU institution and as a central bank also acting as banking supervisor complicates matters further, as does the EBA's and the SRB's nature as independent agencies. As a result of the ECB's numerous functions, accountability becomes more difficult to ensure because the same group of MEPs are called to regularly interact with the ECB in different capacities, thus demanding from them that they first identify in which forum they must ask which kinds of questions. In any event, however, as recently noted by the former Governor

[59] Bovens, 'New Forms of Accountability and EU-Governance', 5 *Comparative European Politics* 1 (2007), 104–120.

of England Paul Tucker, '[t]he European Parliament's Econ committee is too big to conduct effective oversight of the ECB's stewardship of the monetary regime'.[60] The same could be said of the ECON Committee when it is called to hold the ECB-SSM to account although in that context, the possibility for smaller meetings to be organised in the form of confidential oral discussions may partially contribute to solve this problem. Be this as it may, even if Paul Tucker is certainly right in considering the EP ECON Committee to be too large an accountability forum, it is difficult to imagine which other format would have sufficient legitimacy based on its representativeness of the (large) euro area to play such a role. Furthermore, other practical problems outlined below may in fact be a bigger hindrance to effective accountability than the ECON Committee's large size.

Beyond all this, because the EU does not have exclusive competence in the field of banking supervision and bank resolution, national authorities continue to play a large role. Additionally, harmonisation is only partial such that the applicable rules vary across the BU. EU organs, and primarily the ECB, have to apply national norms upon whose content and legality they have no control.[61]

Finally, democratic accountability within the BU does not solely rest on EU institutions and bodies; national institutions, too, play a large role. This is the case because they approve national legislation as noted previously, because they remain competent in areas that are closely linked to BU matters (for instance: anti-money laundering) and because they are closely involved in the functioning and the operation of both the SSM and the SRM.

### 5.5.3 *How to Bridge the Existing Gaps?*

If all were best in the best of possible worlds, differentiation within the EU would vanish, that is the three currently co-existing categories of Member States, which the EU27, the euro area and the BU form would disappear. Thus, some of the regulatory gaps and of the institutional complexity would cease to exist.

Likewise, if Treaty change were a realistic option, a better design for EU agencies could be introduced, a proper legal basis for the BU could be created,

60 Tucker, 'How the European Central Bank and Other Independent Agencies Reveal a Gap in Constitutionalism; A Spectrum of Institutions for Commitment', 22 *German Law Journal* 6 (2021), 999–1027.

61 See on this the section dedicated to the application of national law by the ECB in the proceedings of the ECB Legal Conference 2019. European Central Bank, 'Building Bridges: Central Banking Law in an Interconnected World – ECB Legal Conference 2019', December 2019. Accessed via www.ecb.europa.eu/pub/pdf/other/ecb.ecblegalconferenceproceedings201912~9325c45957.en.pdf (12.05.2022).

including the formal acknowledgement of a third category of Member States next to the euro area and the EU27, that is that of BU Member States. A true discussion on whether the ECB should be the BU's supervisor could be had, and the Chinese wall that separates its monetary policy from its banking supervision functions better designed.

However, unfortunately, none of these options seem to be realistic at this stage of European integration. Even the Conference on the future of Europe is unlikely to lead to the full opening of Pandora's box, as it might do so but only in specific areas with a specific objective.[62] It is true that following Brexit the most adamant advocate of the interests of non-euro area Member States is gone, and no non-euro area Member State has as large a financial market as the UK used to have. Consequently, none of them has the UK's leverage in EU27-negotiations. But a discussion on Treaty change would likely regard many areas other than the BU, and taking account of all the challenges they are already facing internally, including the economic recovery post-COVID, the threats to the rule of law and to EU values, or the ecological and digital transition, EU Member States may not want to take this path at this point in time. Neither would they realistically be in a position to find a compromise solution at this stage if one considers how long they have been unable to come to a compromise solution on the completion of the BU, for instance.

If Treaty change is not an option, what is, then? In addition to the solutions already included in the main sections of this chapter, one could consider additional avenues to improve the existing situation.

First, institutional engineering, that is the improvement of existing practice through the actions of the institutions involved themselves should continue to be exploited. Institutional engineering commonly takes the form of arrangements put in place by institutions on an informal basis or their promoting regulatory change. In a nutshell, it means that institutions use their margin of discretion and action to the largest extent possible. One form this could take would consist in the creation of a dedicated BU sub-committee of the ECON Committee, a possibility that was already considered for the euro area in 2013–2014.[63] This would allow for some of the MEPs to become more specialised in BU matters, and they would not necessarily all have to stem from BU Member States.

[62] The EP did call for the constitution of a Convention, but it is unclear whether it will be constituted. European Parliament, 'Treaty Review Necessary to Implement Conference Proposals, Parliament Declares', European Parliament Press Releases, 4 May 2022. Accessed via www.europarl.europa.eu/news/en/press-room/20220429IPR28227/treaty-review-necessary-to-implement-conference-proposals-parliament-declares (12.05.2022)

[63] See Fasone and Curtin, *supra*, note 57.

Changes in secondary legislation (and in primary law where this is easily feasible) should also be considered with a view to upgrading the mechanisms in place, and to simplifying the existing architecture where possible.

Further harmonisation at the EU level should be pursued too, not only in terms of the norms applicable but also perhaps in terms of the minimum requirements set with respect to the features of the national institutions involved. At present, NCAs and NRAs are hosted by very different institutions that correspond to different national traditions and rules. Arguably, if for instance the applicable standards of independence were more strongly defined at the EU level, it would be easier to guarantee democratic accountability in this area, as the institutional setups would be less complex.[64] It may thus only be hoped that the Court of Justice will be called to continue to perform its duty of clarification and definition of the tasks and responsibilities of the different institutions involved within the BU.

Lastly, it may also only be hoped for that MEPs and MPs will improve the use they make of the existing mechanisms. This would include, as mentioned, asking more informed questions, making more demands for policy changes where necessary, and ensuring better synergies between the mechanisms that exist in parallel. To this end, interparliamentary cooperation should also be fostered, for instance, the Interparliamentary Conference on Stability, Coordination and Governance could be better exploited: to date, it has only rarely addressed BU-related matters. But other mechanisms should be established too, in the form of interparliamentary committee meetings hosted by the EP, and on the initiative of the Presidency parliament and with the involvement of national parliaments only.

As reforms to improve and complete the BU are high on the EU's agenda again,[65] it is urgent that they be also accompanied by matching improvements of the democratic accountability mechanisms in place in the whole of the BU.

64 The institutional embodiment of NCAs and NRAs is an issue, which has been largely neglected by research to date in the sense that there have not been large comparative studies of it. The EBA recently published the outcome of a survey on independence, which allows to gain some insights. Additionally, in the proposal of reform of the Capital Requirements Directive issued in October 2021, the requirements in terms of the independence of the NCAs are significantly enhanced. Proposal (COM/2021/663 final) for a directive of the European Parliament of the Council amending Directive 2013/36/EU as regards supervisory powers, sanctions, third-country branches, and environmental, social and governance risks, and amending Directive 2014/59/EU.

65 Ammann, 'Eurogroup President Launches New Push to Complete Banking Union', euractiv .com, 4 May 2022. Accessed via www.euractiv.com/section/economy-jobs/news/eurogroup-president-launches-new-push-to-complete-banking-union/ (13.05.2022).

# 6

# The Political and Legal Accountability of the Eurogroup

*Menelaos Markakis*[*]

## 6.1 INTRODUCTION

In perhaps one of the most memorable quotes from the Economic and Monetary Union (EMU) literature, Paul Craig once commented, 'The Eurogroup can lay good claim to being the EU body that is least understood'.[1] This does not mean that it has not played a central role in decision-making in this area since its very inception.[2] On the contrary, it is, as recognized by the Euro-area leaders, 'at the core of the daily management of the euro area'.[3] The Eurogroup partakes in deciding 'who gets what, when, how', which is rightly regarded as a key feature of EMU as a policy area.[4] Accordingly, this lays bare the necessity of controls over its activities in the EMU.[5]

* The author is the recipient of the EUR Fellowship by Erasmus University Rotterdam. He is grateful to Adina Akbik, Ana Bobić, Deirdre Curtin, Mark Dawson and the participants of the workshop held on 23–24 Sept. 2021 for their helpful comments. The usual disclaimer applies. The manuscript was completed on 10 February 2022.

1 Craig, 'The Eurogroup, Power and Accountability', 23 *European Law Journal* (2017), 234–249, at 234.

2 See also ibid., at 234. On the history of the creation of the Eurogroup, see Puetter, *The Eurogroup: How a Secretive Circle of Finance Ministers Shape European Economic Governance* (Manchester University Press, 2006), pp. 54–61.

3 Euro Summit Statement, 26 Oct. 2011, available at: <www.consilium.europa.eu/uedocs/cms_data/docs/pressdata/en/ec/125644.pdf> (last visited 17 Sept. 2021), para 32.

4 See the introductory chapter by Akbik and Dawson, 'From Procedural to Substantive Accountability in EMU Governance'. Throughout this contribution, we will be referring to the introductory chapter by Akbik and Dawson in lieu of Dawson, Maricut-Akbik and Bobić, 'Reconciling Independence and Accountability at the European Central Bank: The False Promise of Proceduralism', 25 *European Law Journal* (2019), 75–93, where this framework was initially developed and applied to the ECB. See also Dawson and Maricut-Akbik, 'Procedural vs Substantive Accountability in EMU Governance: Between Payoffs and Trade-offs', 28 *Journal of European Public Policy* (2021), 1707–1726.

5 See the chapter by Akbik and Dawson.

This chapter looks at the political and legal accountability of the Eurogroup. The discussion begins with the foundations and tasks of the Eurogroup (Section 6.2). The focus then shifts to the political accountability of the Eurogroup (Section 6.3), the emphasis being on its relationship with the European Council and the Economic Dialogues with the European Parliament (Section 6.3.1). The chapter further looks at its legal accountability, in light of the relevant case law of the Court of Justice of the European Union (CJEU) (Section 6.3.2). The penultimate section of the chapter provides an assessment of the Eurogroup's accountability in light of the framework laid down in the introductory chapter to this volume, namely in terms of procedural and substantive ways of delivering the normative goods of accountability (Section 6.4). Section 6.5 concludes by outlining the key features of the accountability arrangements and practices pertaining to the Eurogroup.

## 6.2 FOUNDATIONS AND TASKS

The Eurogroup is recognized in Article 137 TFEU, according to which 'Arrangements for meetings between ministers of those Member States whose currency is the euro are laid down by the Protocol on the Euro Group'. In turn, the preamble to Protocol (No 14) on the Euro Group mentions the High Contracting Parties' desire 'to promote conditions for stronger economic growth in the European Union and, to that end, to develop ever-closer coordination of economic policies within the euro area'. As such, it lays down 'special provisions for enhanced dialogue between the Member States whose currency is the euro, pending the euro becoming the currency of all Member States of the Union'.

Article 1 of the Protocol sets out the composition of the Eurogroup and the purpose of its meetings. It provides that the finance ministers of the Euro-area Member States shall meet informally, when necessary, to discuss questions related to the specific responsibilities they share with regard to the single currency.[6] The Commission shall take part in the meetings, whereas the European Central Bank (ECB) shall be invited to take part in such meetings.[7]

6 The Eurogroup can also meet in inclusive format, thereby comprising the ministers of finance from non-Euro-area Member States as well, in order to address issues that are also relevant to Member States outside the Euro-area. See Dias, Hagelstam and Lehofer, 'The role (and accountability) of the President of the Eurogroup', Jan. 2022, available at: <www.europarl.europa.eu/RegData/etudes/BRIE/2018/602116/IPOL_BRI(2018)602116_EN.pdf> (last visited 29 Jan. 2022), at p. 2.

7 Executive Vice-President Valdis Dombrovskis currently represents the Commission in the Eurogroup, whereas the ECB is represented by its President Christine Lagarde.

The meetings shall be prepared by the representatives of the finance ministers of the Euro-area Member States and of the Commission. Further, Article 2 of the Protocol provides that the finance ministers of the Euro-area Member States shall elect a President for two and a half years, by a majority of those States. The post is currently held by Paschal Donohoe, who is also the finance minister of Ireland.

The real-world picture is conveyed more accurately by the Eurogroup's webpage: the agenda and discussions for each Eurogroup meeting are prepared by its President, with the assistance of the Eurogroup Working Group (EWG),[8] the latter being composed of representatives of the Euro-area Member States of the Economic and Financial Committee (EFC), the European Commission and the ECB.[9] The EWG members elect a President for a period of two years, which may be extended. The post is currently held by Tuomas Saarenheimo, who is also Chairman of the EFC. The office of the EWG President is at the General Secretariat of the Council of the EU in Brussels. 'The secretariat tasks in relation to the Euro Group are divided between the General Secretariat of the Council (which is in charge, beyond the assistance to the President, of logistics) and the EFC Secretariat (which is responsible for the substance).'[10]

According to its webpage, 'The Eurogroup's discussions ... cover specific euro-related matters as well as broader issues that have an impact on the fiscal, monetary and structural policies of the euro area member states. It aims to identify common challenges and find common approaches to them.'[11] Craig comments that the Eurogroup is 'central to all major initiatives relating

The Managing Director of the European Stability Mechanism is also invited to participate in the meetings, and the International Monetary Fund is invited to participate in discussions on the economic programmes in which it is involved. See Council of the European Union, 'How the Eurogroup works', available at: <www.consilium.europa.eu/en/council-eu/eurogroup/how-the-eurogroup-works/> (last visited 17 Sept. 2021). For the full list of officials attending the Eurogroup meetings, see the Working Methods of the Eurogroup, 3 Oct. 2008, available at: <www.consilium.europa.eu/media/21457/08-10-03-eurogroup-working-methods.pdf> (last visited 18 Sept. 2021), at pp. 4–5.

8 Council of the European Union, op. cit. *supra* note 7.

9 Council of the European Union, 'Eurogroup Working Group', available at: <www.consilium.europa.eu/en/council-eu/eurogroup/eurogroup-working-group/> (last visited 17 Sept. 2021). On the EWG, see Puetter, *The European Council and the Council: New Intergovernmentalism and Institutional Change* (OUP, 2014), at pp. 192 et seq.

10 Dumitriu-Segnana and De Gregorio Merino, 'EU Institutions Representing Member States' Governments' in Amtenbrink and Herrmann (eds.), assisted by Repasi, *The EU Law of Economic and Monetary Union* (OUP, 2020), pp. 428–455, at para 16.106.

11 See Council of the European Union, op. cit. *supra* note 7, which draws heavily on the language of the Working Methods of the Eurogroup, op. cit. *supra* note 7.

to the euro area, broadly conceived' and that its role is central to EU macroeconomic planning.[12] More specifically, 'it brokers the agreements necessary for policy to become reality; it fosters implementation through close oversight; it plays a role in ensuring that EU legislation in the financial sector is properly implemented; and it is part of the accountability mechanism in the banking union.'[13] The activities of the Eurogroup may also have an impact on internal market issues more generally, which are not straightforwardly related to the single currency.[14]

Apart from the primary EU law provisions that were set out above, there are various other provisions that confer tasks on the Eurogroup which are scattered throughout secondary EU law and even intergovernmental agreements. Space precludes a detailed exegesis of those legal provisions, such that we will only refer selectively to perhaps the most important of them. The Treaty on Stability, Coordination and Governance (also known as the Fiscal Compact, from its most impactful part) provides that the Eurogroup is charged with the preparation of and follow-up to the Euro Summit meetings.[15] It will be recalled that the Euro Summit brings together the Heads of State or Government of Euro-area Member States, as well as the President of the Commission and the President of the ECB, 'to discuss questions relating to the specific responsibilities which the Contracting Parties whose currency is the euro share with regard to the single currency, other issues concerning the governance of the euro area and the rules that apply to it, and strategic orientations for the conduct of economic policies to increase convergence in the euro area'.[16] Moreover, according to 'two-pack' legislation, the Euro-area Member States shall

[12] Craig, op. cit. *supra* note 1, at 235–236.

[13] Ibid., at 236–237. See further ibid., at 237–238.

[14] See further Craig and Markakis, 'The Euro Area, Its Regulation and Impact on Non-Euro Member States' in Koutrakos and Snell (eds.), *Research Handbook on the Law of the EU's Internal Market* (Elgar Publishing, 2017), pp. 289–316, at pp. 312–315.

[15] Treaty on Stability, Coordination and Governance in the Economic and Monetary Union (TSCG), available at: <https://eur-lex.europa.eu/legal-content/EN/TXT/PDF/?uri=CELEX:42012A0302(01)&from=EN> (last visited 14 June 2021), Article 12(4). On the Eurogroup's relationship with the European Council and the Euro Summit, see Puetter, op. cit. *supra* note 9, Ch. 4.

[16] TSCG, Article 12(1)–(2). It should be added that, according to Article 12(3), 'The Heads of State or Government of the Contracting Parties other than those whose currency is the euro, which have ratified this Treaty, shall participate in discussions of Euro Summit meetings concerning competitiveness for the Contracting Parties, the modification of the global architecture of the euro area and the fundamental rules that will apply to it in the future, as well as, when appropriate and at least once a year, in discussions on specific issues of implementation of this Treaty.'

submit annually a draft budgetary plan for the forthcoming year to the Commission and to the Eurogroup.[17] The Eurogroup shall discuss opinions of the Commission on the draft budgetary plans and the budgetary situation and prospects in the Euro-area as a whole on the basis of the overall assessment made by the Commission.[18] The Euro-area Member States shall further report *ex ante* on their public debt issuance plans to the Eurogroup and the Commission.[19]

Furthermore, the Eurogroup forms part of the accountability mechanisms in the Banking Union.[20] More specifically, the Eurogroup receives a report from the ECB on the execution of its tasks in the Single Supervisory Mechanism, which shall also be presented to it by the Chair of the Supervisory Board of the ECB.[21] Moreover, the Chair of the Supervisory Board of the ECB may, at the request of the Eurogroup, be heard on the execution of its supervisory tasks, and the ECB shall reply orally or in writing to questions put to it by the Eurogroup.[22]

## 6.3 ACCOUNTABILITY ARRANGEMENTS AND PRACTICE

### 6.3.1 *Political Accountability*

The political accountability of the Eurogroup is described as 'thin'.[23] Craig comments that:

> Its principal political accountability runs to the European Council, as attested to by its role in preparing Euro Area Summits and having the responsibility for ensuring that the recommendations from such meetings are followed up. The reality is, however, … that the Eurogroup has considerable power in shaping macroeconomic policy broadly conceived for euro-area states.

[17] Regulation (EU) 473/2013 of the European Parliament and of the Council of 21 May 2013 on common provisions for monitoring and assessing draft budgetary plans and ensuring the correction of excessive deficit of the Member States in the euro area, O.J. 2013, L 140/11, Article 6(1).

[18] Ibid., Article 7(5).

[19] Ibid., Article 8(1).

[20] See among many others Amtenbrink and Markakis, 'The Legitimacy and Accountability of the European Central Bank at the Age of Twenty' in Beukers, Fromage and Monti (eds.), *The 'New' European Central Bank: Taking Stock and Looking Ahead* (OUP, 2022), pp. 265–291. See also the chapter by Fromage in this volume.

[21] Council Regulation (EU) 1024/2013 of 15 October 2013 conferring specific tasks on the European Central Bank concerning policies relating to the prudential supervision of credit institutions, O.J. 2013, L 287/63, Article 20(2)–(3).

[22] Ibid., Articles 20(4) and (6), respectively.

[23] Craig, op. cit. *supra* note 1, at 241.

> The recommendations that emanate from the European Council will often be at a relatively abstract level, and it will be the Eurogroup that imbues them with greater policy specificity.[24]

The latter case is exemplified by the Eurogroup's actions during and in response to the COVID-19 crisis.[25] Overall, '[t]here is little by way of formal accountability for the Eurogroup's input into the Euro Summits, and equally little by way of accountability check as to how it implements Euro Summit policy, more especially when the conclusions from such Summits require interpretation and choice in the implementation.'[26] This does not, however, preclude the possibility that the Eurogroup may be 'held to account in the European Council for the more detailed policy initiatives that the Eurogroup embraces when fulfilling European Council policy recommendations'.[27]

This answers the question of whom account is to be (primarily) rendered to, but does not speak of the standards against which its performance is to be assessed. After all, the Protocol on the Eurogroup merely provides that its main task is to ensure close coordination of economic policies among the Euro-area Member States, in order to promote conditions for stronger economic growth.[28] It is rightly argued that a meaningful accountability relationship

> is more difficult to achieve where the criteria against which the Eurogroup is being judged are relatively abstract recommendations from the European Council; where it is intended that these should be fleshed out by the Eurogroup; where all institutional players are mindful of the difficult political and economic determinations that have to be made; and where evaluation of success or failure may be difficult, and may not be apparent for some considerable time.[29]

[24] Ibid., at 240.

[25] See generally Dermine and Markakis, 'The EU Fiscal, Economic and Monetary Policy Response to the COVID-19 Crisis', *EU Law Live*, 27 March 2020, available at: <https://eulawlive.com/long-read-the-eu-fiscal-economic-and-monetary-policy-response-to-the-covid-19-crisis-by-paul-dermine-and-menelaos-markakis/> (last visited 17 Sept. 2021); Dermine and Markakis, 'EU Economic Governance and the COVID-19 Crisis: Between Path-Dependency and Paradigmatic Shift', 6 *International Journal of Public Law and Policy* (2020), 326–345. See also De Witte, 'The European Union's COVID-19 Recovery Plan: The Legal Engineering of an Economic Policy Shift', 58 *CML Review* (2021), 635–682, esp. at 638–644, 669–670.

[26] Craig and Markakis, op. cit. *supra* note 14, at p. 300.

[27] Craig, op. cit. *supra* note 1, at 240.

[28] See also Council of the European Union, 'Eurogroup', available at: <www.consilium.europa.eu/en/council-eu/eurogroup/> (last visited 17 Sept. 2021).

[29] Craig, op. cit. *supra* note 1, at 240–241.

The Eurogroup's role during the Euro-crisis, notably with regard to financial assistance programmes, provides a good illustration of this.[30] 'The [Eurogroup] was the body coordinating and, *de facto*, deciding whether financial assistance would be granted, and under which conditions, to a requesting Euro Area Member State. It is again gaining specific relevance in the context of the Recovery and Resilience Facility.'[31] The Eurogroup assesses the national implementation of the Euro-area recommendation through national recovery and resilience plans.[32] It is also evolved in coordinating the implementation of these plans.[33]

The 'six-pack' and 'two-pack' of EU legislation further make provision for *Economic Dialogues*.[34] Economic Dialogues are held in order to enhance the dialogue between the EU institutions on the application of economic governance rules and with Member States, if appropriate, and to ensure greater transparency and accountability. The competent committee of the European Parliament, that is, the Committee on Economic and Monetary Affairs (ECON), may invite representatives of Member States, the European Commission, the President of the Council, the President of the European Council and the President of the Eurogroup, to discuss

[30] Ibid., at 241; Markakis, *Accountability in the Economic and Monetary Union: Foundations, Policy, and Governance* (OUP, 2020), Ch. 3.

[31] Dias, Hagelstam and Lehofer, op. cit. *supra* note 6, at p. 1.

[32] Ibid., at p. 2.

[33] See Dias, Grigaitė and Cunha, 'Recommendation on the Economic Policy of the Euro Area – February 2022', available at: <www.europarl.europa.eu/RegData/etudes/IDAN/2020/651379/IPOL_IDA(2020)651379_EN.pdf> (last visited 2 Feb. 2022), at p. 2.

[34] See Council Regulation (EC) 1466/97 of 7 July 1997 on the strengthening of the surveillance of budgetary positions and the surveillance and coordination of economic policies, O.J. 1997, L 209/1, as currently in force, Article 2-ab; Council Regulation (EC) 1467/97 of 7 July 1997 on speeding up and clarifying the implementation of the excessive deficit procedure, O.J. 1997, L 209/6, as currently in force, Article 2a; Regulation (EU) 1176/2011 of the European Parliament and of the Council of 16 November 2011 on the prevention and correction of macroeconomic imbalances, O.J. 2011, L 306/25, Article 14; Regulation (EU) 1173/2011 of the European Parliament and of the Council of 16 November 2011 on the effective enforcement of budgetary surveillance in the euro area, O.J. 2011, L 306/1, Article 3; Regulation (EU) 1174/2011 of the European Parliament and of the Council of 16 November 2011 on enforcement measures to correct excessive macroeconomic imbalances in the euro area, O.J. 2011, L 306/8, Article 6; Regulation (EU) 472/2013 of the European Parliament and of the Council of 21 May 2013 on the strengthening of economic and budgetary surveillance of Member States in the euro area experiencing or threatened with serious difficulties with respect to their financial stability, O.J. 2013, L 140/1, Arts. 3, 7, 14 and 18; Regulation 473/2013, op. cit. *supra* note 17, Arts. 7(3), 15. On the legal basis for these dialogues, see also Hagelstam, 'Economic Dialogues with the other EU Institutions under the European Semester Cycles during the 9th legislative term', Jan. 2022, available at: <www.europarl.europa.eu/RegData/etudes/BRIE/2019/624436/IPOL_BRI(2019)624436_EN.pdf> (last visited 29 Jan. 2022), at pp. 3–6.

economic and policy issues.[35] According to the relevant EU rules, the competent committee of the European Parliament may invite the President of the Eurogroup for an Economic Dialogue during certain stages of the implementation of the European Semester for economic policy coordination and in the context of macroeconomic adjustment programmes, including the post-programme surveillance phase.[36] It should be stressed that, under the existing rules, the European Parliament has no powers to 'sanction' the Eurogroup for its performance or to amend any of the decisions taken. The relevant provisions instead focus on the information and debate stages of accountability.[37] There is further the expectation that finance ministers participating in the Eurogroup will be held separately to account by their respective national parliaments, in accordance with national constitutional requirements.

The Eurogroup President takes part in an Economic Dialogue twice a year (in spring and in autumn) and, if needed, on an ad hoc basis. This practice was agreed during the 7th legislative term through an exchange of letters between the competent Committee and the Eurogroup President.[38] Nine dialogues were held with the President of the Eurogroup in the ECON Committee during the 8th legislative term (autumn 2014 to spring 2019). Furthermore, the President of the Eurogroup occasionally participated in an exchange of views in plenary as well as in interparliamentary meetings relating to economic governance.[39] The Economic Governance Support Unit (EGOV) of the European Parliament provided members of the ECON a briefing in advance of these dialogues, as well as papers written by external experts.[40] This is important from the perspective of substantive accountability, because it helps address any information asymmetries between the European Parliament and the Eurogroup.[41] Five economic dialogues with

35 European Parliament, 'Economic Governance', available at: <www.europarl.europa.eu/committees/en/econ/econ-policies/economic-governance?tabCode=economic-dialogues> (last visited 17 Sept. 2021).

36 Dias, Hagelstam and Lehofer, op. cit. *supra* note 6, at p. 4.

37 See also Markakis, op. cit. *supra* note 30, at pp. 128–129.

38 Dias, Hagelstam and Lehofer, op. cit. *supra* note 6, at p. 4.

39 Hagelstam, De Biase and Navarini, 'Economic Dialogues with the President of the Eurogroup during 2014–2019', available at: <www.europarl.europa.eu/RegData/etudes/IDAN/2019/634367/IPOL_IDA(2019)634367_EN.pdf> (last visited 18 Sept. 2021), at pp. 1, 14.

40 Ibid., at p. 1. For a summary of external expert papers, see Angerer and Zoppè, 'Euro Area Scrutiny: External Expertise on Economic Governance during the 8th Parliamentary Term', June 2019, available at: <www.europarl.europa.eu/RegData/etudes/IDAN/2019/624421/IPOL_IDA(2019)624421_EN.pdf> (last visited 2 Feb. 2022).

41 See the introductory chapter by Akbik and Dawson.

the President of the Eurogroup have taken place thus far during the current (9th) legislative term.[42] In contrast to previous practice where only web streaming was available, a transcript of the dialogues is now made available to the public.[43]

In line with agreed practices, the following procedure is applied for the exchanges of views with the Eurogroup President. First, there are introductory remarks by the Eurogroup President for about ten minutes. These are followed by five-minute question-and-answer slots, with the possibility of a follow-up question, time permitting, within the same slot. Two minutes maximum are allocated for the question, and then three minutes maximum for the answer. In the first round of questions, each political group has one slot. Thereafter, the d'Hondt system is applied, which determines the order of questions by political groups. Any time for additional slots is allocated on a catch-the-eye basis.

Overall, the MEPs ask well-informed questions. In terms of the topics discussed, these are very much the issues of the day (whether it is, for example, financial assistance programmes back in the day or, nowadays, the assessment of recovery and resilience plans or the future of the EU fiscal rules). The MEPs also address structural issues pertaining to the EMU architecture, such as the completion of the Banking Union. Obviously, these two sets of issues sometimes intersect (as was the case, for example, with questions regarding the postponement of the work plan for the Banking Union). Further, there are questions about the Capital Markets Union, the digital euro, the enlargement of the Euro-area, as well as plenty of other issues. Whenever questions are not (adequately) answered by the Eurogroup President, it is common for the MEPs to return to the point made by their colleagues previously.[44] It is clear that the questions asked focus not only on the procedure by means of which a particular decision or policy choice was made but also on the substantive worth of the policy decision itself.[45]

[42] See Hagelstam, op. cit. *supra* note 34. As noted above, this manuscript was completed on 10 February 2022.

[43] This is with the exception of the meeting of 21 April 2020.

[44] A good example is provided by the follow-up questions asked by MEPs on gender balance in the Governing Council of the ECB at the meeting of 18 November 2019. For an extensive analysis of the questions asked by MEPs and the responsiveness of the Eurogroup President to the questions asked during Economic Dialogues, see Akbik, *The European Parliament as an Accountability Forum: Overseeing the Economic and Monetary Union* (CUP, 2022), at p. 159 et seq. (covering fourteen Economic Dialogues in the parliamentary terms 2013–2014 and 2014–2019).

[45] On the extent to which the MEPs focus on procedural or substantive accountability when questioning the Eurogroup President, as well as the accountability claims made by MEPs, see the chapter by Akbik in this volume, which examines the fourteen dialogues with the Eurogroup President between 2013 and the European elections of May 2019.

The Economic Governance Support Unit has conducted an extensive analysis of the Economic Dialogues with the President of the Eurogroup during the 8th legislative term (autumn 2014 to spring 2019). Nine dialogues were held in ECON during the said period. 'As a general conclusion, one can say that issues raised during the dialogues reflected on-going policy work by the Eurogroup and other topical issues related to the well-functioning of the euro area, including the public attention given to a specific policy issue at the time of the dialogue.'[46] The following figure provides an overview of the topics discussed during the 8th legislative term.

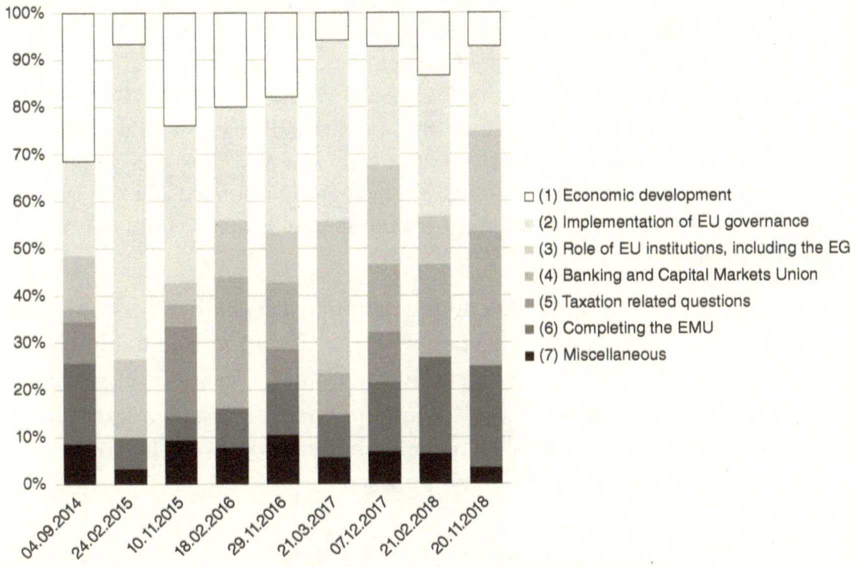


*Reproduced with permission from EGOV. Source: Hagelstam, De Biase and Navarini, 'Economic Dialogues with the President of the Eurogroup during 2014–2019', available at: <www.europarl.europa.eu/RegData/etudes/IDAN/2019/634367/IPOL_IDA(2019)634367_EN.pdf> (last visited 18 Sept. 2021), at p. 2.*

The Economic Dialogues with the Eurogroup President are rife with comments on accountability.[47] It is clear that the European Parliament, and the ECON Committee in specific, wants more on part of the Eurogroup in terms of accountability and transparency. Moreover, it is clear that the MEPs take

[46] Hagelstam, De Biase and Navarini, op. cit. *supra* note 39, at p. 3.

[47] See, for example, the remarks by Siegfried Mureşan (EPP), Jonás Fernández (S&D) and Luis Garicano (Renew) at the meeting of 21 June 2021.

issue with the frequency of those meetings with the Eurogroup President.[48] The Chair of the ECON Committee, Irene Tinagli, has opened the first two Dialogues with Eurogroup President Paschal Donohoe with an, to all intents and purposes, identical remark:

> President Donohoe, we were very pleased to read in your motivation letter as candidate for the Eurogroup President that, and I quote you: 'effectively communicating to our citizens and to the European Parliament the steps we are taking in the euro area will be a priority of my term'. So I would like to take this opportunity to reiterate ECON's request for enhanced cooperation with yourself and with the Eurogroup, and invite you to put forward how you would like to follow up on these. Due to the key role of the Eurogroup in steering the policy work of the euro area as a whole, we would like to stress the importance of a well-established cooperation practice with the European Parliament, notably our Committee. One way would be to go in the direction of the practice that we have for the monetary dialogue with the ECB President, which has been working very nicely in enhancing our cooperation. In these very challenging times, the Eurogroup is indeed at a key position. Therefore I think that the need for transparency and accountability is particularly important for us.[49]

The Eurogroup President replied, on the second occasion that this comment was made, thus: 'I'll certainly reflect on what the Chair just said there regarding how we can structure our dialogue in the future.' Overall, strengthening the (political) accountability of the Eurogroup remains work in progress. This places added emphasis on its legal accountability, which, as seen in the following section, is – at best – scant and indirect.[50]

### 6.3.2 *Legal Accountability*

The legal accountability of the Eurogroup has been the subject of lengthy litigation before the EU courts and remained ill-defined for a number of years. The leading authorities are *Mallis* and *Chrysostomides*. In very simple

[48] Among the many remarks made along these lines, the quip made by Mick Wallace (The Left) at the meeting of 21 June 2021 clearly stands out: 'How's it going Paschal? Long time no see!' In this connection, Akbik, op. cit. *supra* note 44, at p. 159 notes that, in comparison with the ECB, the Commission and the ECOFIN Council, 'the Eurogroup clearly has the fewest direct interactions with the [European Parliament]'.

[49] See the transcript for the meeting of 21 June 2021, available at: <www.europarl.europa.eu/cmsdata/238001/CRE_Eurogroup_President_21062021_EN.pdf> (last visited 30 Jan. 2022). See also the transcript for the meeting of 25 Jan. 2021, available at: <www.europarl.europa.eu/cmsdata/227559/CRE_Public%20hearing_Donohoe_25.01.2021.pdf> (last visited 30 Jan. 2022).

[50] See also Craig, op. cit. *supra* note 1, at 241.

terms, it was held in *Mallis* that litigants cannot admissibly bring actions for annulment under Article 263 TFEU against the acts of the Eurogroup.[51] The Court noted that the term 'informally' is used in Protocol (No 14) on the Euro Group and that the Eurogroup is not a configuration of the Council pursuant to the latter's Rules of Procedure. Accordingly, it could not be equated with a configuration of the Council or be classified as a body, office or agency of the EU within the meaning of Article 263 TFEU.[52]

In *Chrysostomides*, the Court held that the Eurogroup is not an 'institution' within the meaning of the second paragraph of Article 340 TFEU, such that its actions cannot trigger the non-contractual liability of the Union.[53] What renders this judgment uniquely important for the accountability of the Eurogroup is the reasoning provided by the Court for its judgment denying that the Eurogroup is an EU entity established by the Treaties. The Court held that 'the Euro Group was created as an intergovernmental body – outside the institutional framework of the European Union' and that 'Article 137 TFEU and Protocol No 14 … did not alter its intergovernmental nature in the slightest'.[54] The Court further held that 'the Euro Group is characterized by its informality, which … can be explained by the purpose pursued by its creation

[51] Joined Cases C-105/15 P to C-109/15 P, *Konstantinos Mallis and Others* v *European Commission and European Central Bank*, EU:C:2016:702. See further Lauhlé Shaelou and Karatzia, 'Some Preliminary Thoughts on the Cyprus Bail-in Litigation: A Commentary on Mallis and Ledra', 43 *EL Review* (2018), 249–268; Dermine, 'The End of Impunity? The Legal Duties of "Borrowed" EU Institutions under the European Stability Mechanism Framework', 13 *EuConst* (2017), 369–382; Poulou, 'Financial Assistance Conditionality and Human Rights Protection: What Is the Role of the EU Charter of Fundamental Rights?', 54 *CML Rev.* (2017), 991–1026; Repasi, 'Judicial Protection against Austerity Measures in the Euro Area: *Ledra* and *Mallis*', 54 *CML Review* (2017), 1123–1156; Xanthoulis 'ESM, Union Institutions and EU Treaties: A Symbiotic Relationship – Joint Cases C-8/15 P to C-10/15 P (*Ledra Advertising Ltd et al*) and Joint Cases C-105/15 P to C-109/15 P (*Mallis and Malli et al*)', 1 *Revue Internationale des Services Financiers* (2017), 21–33; Markakis, op. cit. *supra* note 30, Ch. 6. See also the chapter by Poulou in this volume.

[52] Joined Cases C-105/15 P to C-109/15 P, *Mallis*, para 61.

[53] Joined Cases C-597/18 P, C-598/18 P, C-603/18 P and C-604/18 P, *Council* v *K. Chrysostomides & Co. and Others*, EU:C:2020:1028. See Staudinger, 'The Court of Justice's Self-restraint of Reviewing Financial Assistance Conditionality in the *Chrysostomides* Case', 6 *European Papers* (2021), 177–188; Chamon, 'De procesrechtelijke positie van de Eurogroep uitgeklaard: Gevoegde zaken C-597/18 P, C-598/18 P, C-603/18 P en C-604/18 P, Raad e.a./ Chrysostomides e.a.', 69 *SEW: Tijdschrift voor Europees en economisch recht* (2021), 276–282; Rugge, 'The Euro Group's Informality and Locus Standi before the European Court of Justice: Council v. K. Chrysostomides & Co. and Others', 81 *ZaöRV* (2021), 917–936; Karatzia and Markakis, 'Financial Assistance Conditionality and Effective Judicial Protection: *Chrysostomides*', 59 *CML Review* (2022), 501–542.

[54] Joined Cases C-597/18 P, C-598/18 P, C-603/18 P and C-604/18 P, *Chrysostomides*, paras. 84 and 87, respectively.

of endowing economic and monetary union with an instrument of intergovernmental coordination but without affecting the role of the Council – which is the fulcrum of the European Union's decision-making process in economic matters – or the independence of the ECB'.[55] It also held that

> the Euro Group does not have any competence of its own in the EU legal order, as Article 1 of Protocol No 14 merely states that its meetings are to take place, when necessary, to discuss questions related to the specific responsibilities that the ministers of the [Member States whose currency is the euro] share with regard to the single currency – responsibilities which they owe solely on account of their competence at national level.[56]

As argued extensively elsewhere, the Court's reasoning in *Chrysostomides* is unconvincing.[57] First, it is not adequately explained in the judgment why Article 137 TFEU and Protocol No 14 did not alter the Eurogroup's intergovernmental nature in the slightest. Insofar as the Court refers selectively to arguments provided by the Advocate General, notably his literal and teleological interpretation, this interpretation of the provisions of the Protocol is not straightforward in textual terms, and that whatever the origins of the Eurogroup and its functions prior to the Treaty of Lisbon may have been, they do not seem to warrant the conclusion that, following the entry into force of the Treaty of Lisbon, the Eurogroup remains an entity situated outside the EU legal and institutional framework. Second, it is not clear from the judgment why the informal nature of the Eurogroup means that it is not an EU entity established by the Treaties for the purposes of non-contractual liability. In reality, formally recognizing the Eurogroup by means of primary law provisions would not affect the role of the Council, insofar as those Treaty provisions which confer powers on the Council remained unchanged. It is perfectly possible to recognize the existence of an entity *within* the EU institutional framework which would not encroach on the powers of the Council. It is also unclear why the informal nature of the Eurogroup is necessary to preserve the ECB's independence. Third, contrary to what the Court stated, we have seen that various EU law provisions confer powers on the Eurogroup. This also prompts the question of whether secondary EU law may confer powers or tasks on informal, non-EU bodies, especially to the point of involving them in the accountability mechanisms for a formal EU institution, the ECB.

According to the Court in *Chrysostomides*, individuals may bring before the EU courts an action to establish non-contractual liability of the EU

[55] Ibid., para 88.
[56] Ibid., para 89.
[57] Karatzia and Markakis, op. cit. *supra* note 53, esp. at 520–527.

against the Council, the Commission and the ECB in respect of the acts or conduct that those EU institutions adopt following the political agreements concluded within the Eurogroup.[58] Moreover, the principle established in *Ledra Advertising* applies,[59] meaning that an action for damages is admissible insofar as it is directed against the Commission and the ECB on account of their alleged unlawful conduct at the time of the negotiation and signing of the Memorandum of Understanding (MoU) with the European Stability Mechanism (ESM).[60] Furthermore, the Court *extended* the *Ledra* principle to the participation of the Commission in the activities of the Eurogroup. It held that

> the Commission … retains, in the context of its participation in the activities of the Euro Group, its role of guardian of the Treaties. It follows that any failure on its part to check that the political agreements concluded within the Euro Group are in conformity with EU law is liable to result in non-contractual liability of the European Union being invoked under the second paragraph of Article 340 TFEU.[61]

The Court is effectively arguing that there is a complete system of remedies and procedures, such that litigants in this area are ensured effective judicial protection. Unfortunately, this is most certainly not the case when the agreements reached in the Eurogroup are implemented by non-EU bodies, such as is the case when the MoU with the ESM gives concrete expression to a macroeconomic adjustment programme. The ESM Treaty, as it currently stands, gives jurisdiction to the CJEU only when an ESM Member contests the internal resolution of disputes (with another ESM Member or the ESM itself) on the interpretation and application of the ESM Treaty or the compatibility of ESM decisions with the ESM Treaty.[62] Private litigants have no standing to challenge the decisions of the ESM organs. What is more, as explained extensively elsewhere, there may be no measures adopted by formal EU institutions incorporating the specific harmful measures that litigants wish to challenge.[63] The relevant Council Decision, whether adopted on the basis of Articles 136(1) and 126(6) TFEU as was the case in *Chrysostomides* or – nowadays – on

58 Joined Cases C-597/18 P, C-598/18 P, C-603/18 P and C-604/18 P, *Chrysostomides*, paras. 93–94.

59 Joined Cases C-8/15 P to C-10/15 P, *Ledra Advertising Ltd and Others* v *European Commission and European Central Bank*, EU:C:2016:701. See the literature cited *supra* note 51.

60 Joined Cases C-597/18 P, C-598/18 P, C-603/18 P and C-604/18 P, *Chrysostomides*, para 95.

61 Ibid., para 96.

62 Treaty Establishing the European Stability Mechanism, available at: <www.esm.europa.eu/sites/default/files/migration_files/20150203_-_esm_treaty_-_en.pdf> (last visited 8 Feb. 2022), Article 37.

63 Karatzia and Markakis, op. cit. *supra* note 53, esp. at 533–534.

the basis of 'two-pack' legislation,[64] may not include all the terms from the Eurogroup statement and/or the MoU with the ESM. *Chrysostomides* is a case in point here, as only some of the harmful measures were mentioned in the impugned Council Decision. EU courts may or may not be able to read any terms that are not (fully) replicated into the relevant Council Decision.[65]

It should be noted that the Court in *Chrysostomides* recognized, for the first time, that EU law measures (*in casu*, a Council Decision) that *post-dated* the adoption of the harmful measures by the national authorities concerned may nevertheless trigger the non-contractual liability of the Union, provided that the relevant Union institution (the Council) had required the maintenance or continued implementation of the harmful measures and that the national authorities concerned had no margin of discretion to escape that requirement.[66] However, as explained elsewhere, the terms of those measures are often vague, such that the national authorities concerned have a margin of discretion for the purpose of laying down the impugned rules.[67] *Chrysostomides* is again a case in point, and the actions for damages were declared inadmissible insofar as they were directed against the relevant Council Decision. The extension of the *Ledra* principle to the Commission's participation in the activities of the Eurogroup may appear more promising, but, as argued elsewhere, its scope of application remains uncertain.[68] It seems that the Commission retains its role of guardian of the Treaties as regards *all* the activities of the Eurogroup, such that any failure on its part to check that (*any* of) the political agreements concluded within the Eurogroup are in conformity with EU law may give rise to non-contractual liability of the Union. This is a much broader scope of application for the *Ledra* principle than the financial assistance context in which it was first elaborated. Further, it is not clear what the Commission should do if, according to its assessment, a political agreement concluded within the Eurogroup is not in conformity with EU law.

## 6.4 AN ASSESSMENT OF THE EUROGROUP'S ACCOUNTABILITY

The status quo with regard to the accountability of the Eurogroup is probably problematic by *any* standards. This is rather self-evident, especially if

64 Regulation 472/2013, Article 7.

65 Kilpatrick, 'Are the Bailouts Immune to EU Social Challenge Because They Are Not EU Law?', 10 *EuConst* (2014), 393–421, at 409–412.

66 Joined Cases C-597/18 P, C-598/18 P, C-603/18 P and C-604/18 P, *Chrysostomides*, paras. 112–117.

67 Karatzia and Markakis, op. cit. *supra* note 53, at 533.

68 See ibid., at 534–538.

one were to apply national accountability benchmarks to EMU and look into any shortcomings that might exist in their institutionalization at the EU level, notably as regards the role of parliaments but also courts (thereby following a *deductive approach*, as per Akbik and Dawson).[69] It is equally true in case standards of accountable behaviour that are inferred from the EU's Treaty framework are applied to the Eurogroup (which would constitute an *inductive approach*, according to Akbik and Dawson).[70] The latter case is exemplified by the transparency arrangements pertaining to the Eurogroup, as well as the judicial protection accorded to individuals affected by its actions, especially after *Mallis* and *Chrysostomides*.

To be sure, there is considerable disagreement among scholars with regard to accountability, not only in the specific area of EMU, but also with regard to the EU in general. This disagreement normally centres on four dimensions which frame the accountability discourse.

> There is significant divergence of view at the normative level as to the framework against which EU accountability should be judged. There can be real dispute as to what the positive rules prescribe, which can shape different conclusions as to whether the normative vision is properly reflected in those rules. There are differences yet again at the empirical level, as to whether the legal rules, given their natural textual interpretation, capture the reality of how the institutions operate in practice, with consequential implications for assessment of accountability. Temporal change can, moreover, impact radically on the powers possessed by a particular institution, with consequential implications for the suitability and efficacy of accountability mechanisms.[71]

Notwithstanding any disagreements between scholars, it may be disputed whether academic discourse about accountability in EMU is 'at a stalemate'.[72] This is so, notwithstanding the fact that there could be said to be 'a gap between what is seen as necessary and what is feasible in the EMU governance framework'.[73] For the avoidance of any doubt, the framework introduced by Akbik and Dawson in the introductory chapter to this volume is extremely valuable in analysing the accountability discourse on EMU and in evaluating the existing arrangements as well as their practical application, also beyond the confines of EMU for that matter. It is no coincidence that it is also utilized in this chapter. However, it seems that it is principally the

[69] See the chapter by Akbik and Dawson in this volume.

[70] Ibid.

[71] Craig, op. cit. *supra* note 1, at 239.

[72] As claimed by Akbik and Dawson in the introductory chapter of this volume.

[73] Ibid.

*politics* of EMU that have reached a stalemate. Enhancing the accountability and transparency arrangements in the EMU is seemingly not on the agenda. It does not appear to be a (top) priority. This could be said to be explained by the fact that national leaders and EU institutions often had to respond swiftly to the various crises that the EU has faced in the past decade. However, this would not explain away the fact that, after all these years, there is no concrete plan to enhance accountability and transparency in the workings of EMU. Nor is there yet a 'grand plan' for enhancing accountability and transparency in a *reformed* (or *deepened*) EMU either. It has been argued elsewhere that:

> high-level reports on EMU reform only discuss accountability as an afterthought. The relevant section in those reports often conflates different issues, thereby mixing accountability with concepts and issues such as: transparency; national ownership; effective implementation; institutional reform more broadly conceived; and the external representation of EMU. We do not yet have a 'grand design' for enhancing accountability in a deep and genuine EMU. Instead, one has to trawl through the documents accompanying the Commission's Roadmap to get a glimpse of the accountability (and transparency) arrangements that would obtain in a reformed EMU.[74]

This remains true, in my opinion, to this day. This is so, notwithstanding the limited improvements that were made when the EU's recovery plan was introduced.[75]

It could be said to be true that we should not expect the EU institutions to produce such a plan, as this would not be in the interests of those controlled and assessed.[76] Nevertheless, this approach entails 'pay-offs and trade-offs'. On the one hand, it obviates the need for Treaty revision and various amendments to secondary law, and avoids any difficult interinstitutional conflicts and/or discussions between the Member States. On the

[74] Craig and Markakis, 'EMU Reform' in Amtenbrink and Herrmann (eds.), assisted by Repasi, *The EU Law of Economic and Monetary Union* (OUP, 2020), pp. 1400–1448, at para 42.103. See also Crum, 'Parliamentary Accountability in Multilevel Governance: What Role for Parliaments in Post-crisis EU Economic Governance?', 25 *JEPP* (2018), 268–286, at 268–269. For the Commission's Roadmap and accompanying documents, see European Commission, 'Commission sets out roadmap for deepening Europe's Economic and Monetary Union', 6 Dec. 2017, available at: <https://ec.europa.eu/info/publications/completing-europes-economic-and-monetary-union-factsheets_en> (last visited 5 Feb. 2022).

[75] See further De Witte, op. cit. *supra* note 25, esp. at 674–678; Crowe, 'An EU Budget of States and Citizens', 26 *ELJ* (2020), 331–344, esp. at 338–340; Fromage and Markakis, 'The European Parliament in the Economic and Monetary Union after COVID: Towards a Slow Empowerment?', 28 *Journal of Legislative Studies* (2022), 385–401.

[76] I am grateful to Deirdre Curtin for this observation.

other hand, it is doubtful whether the existing accountability arrangements in the area of EMU are enough 'to provide a democratic means to monitor and control government conduct, for preventing the development of concentrations of power, and to enhance the learning capacity and effectiveness of public administration'.[77] At a broader level, it is doubtful whether they 'can help to ensure that the legitimacy of governance remains intact or is increased'.[78] As shown in this chapter, this is all the more true in the case of the Eurogroup.

As regards the EMU, the predominance of procedural ways of providing the normative goods of accountability, identified in the introductory chapter to this volume, viz. openness, non-arbitrariness, effectiveness and publicness,[79] is not fortuitous. Take the first normative good of accountability, for example, openness. 'We might … want accountability because we see it as a device to ensure that public action is open, transparent, and contestable.'[80] In the EMU, it is often the case that either the relevant procedures for gaining access to information and documents do not exist at all or that they are found wanting.[81] In which case, it is only natural that the debate principally focuses on having the right procedures in place, which is a step *logically prior* to regularly probing and contesting official action.[82] To be sure, the debate should not stop there, and the accountability holders concerned should use the information and documents provided to regularly probe and contest the conduct of the 'EMU executive'. Nevertheless, it remains the case that accountability holders (and the general public) first have to exert considerable energy to pierce the veil of secrecy or non-transparency behind which the work of the 'EMU executive' is sometimes carried out.

The very body that forms the subject matter of this chapter provides a fine example of this, notably as regards the lack of transparency of Eurogroup meetings and requests for public access to Eurogroup documents. Nevertheless, the 2016 Transparency Initiative by the Eurogroup President has covered some ground. More specifically, in the Eurogroup meeting of 11 February 2016, 'Ministers agreed as a first step to make public

77 Bovens, 'Analysing and Assessing Accountability: A Conceptual Framework', 13 *ELJ* (2007), 447–468, at 462.

78 Ibid., at 464.

79 See the chapter by Akbik and Dawson in this volume.

80 Ibid.

81 Examples are plentiful. On access to documents related to the ESM, see, for example, Karatzia and Markakis, 'What Role for the Commission and the ECB in the European Stability Mechanism?', 6 *CILJ* (2017), 232–252, at 235–237. On access to information in the area of Banking Union, see among others Markakis, op. cit. *supra* note 30, at pp. 182–199.

82 See the chapter by Akbik and Dawson.

the annotated agendas for Eurogroup meetings and the summaries of their discussions'.[83] Moreover, the Eurogroup decided on 7 March 2016 that 'in future, Eurogroup meeting documents would be published shortly after the meetings … unless the institutions which drafted them object'.[84] 'Documents which have not been finalised or which contain market-sensitive information will not be made public.'[85] The European Ombudsman Emily O'Reilly notes that transparency is 'an issue of prime importance for further legitimacy and public trust' and has asked the Eurogroup President to make further improvements as regards access to documents relating to the work of the Eurogroup that are not published proactively; transparency in the workings of bodies and services that prepare Eurogroup meetings and notably in the EWG (notices and provisional agendas of meetings); and the publication of draft programme country-related documents prior to Eurogroup meetings.[86] However, Jeroen Dijsselbloem, then President of the Eurogroup, expressed the view that the Eurogroup is not a Union institution, body, office or agency, such that neither Article 15(3) TFEU and Article 42 of the EU Charter nor Regulation 1049/2001 applies to it.[87] He nevertheless noted, 'Despite these legal considerations, the Eurogroup's recent initiatives respond to perceived shortcomings in transparency and reflect the political will to adhere to the principles stated in Article 15(3) TFEU and Regulation 1049/2001.'[88] In his response to the Ombudsman letters, the Eurogroup President highlighted the need to protect the internal discussions that take place in the EWG to prepare the Eurogroup at *technical* level, whilst emphasizing that the Eurogroup's proactive transparency

83 Council of the European Union, 'Eurogroup, 11 February 2016', available at: <www.consilium.europa.eu/en/meetings/eurogroup/2016/02/11/> (last visited 4 Sept. 2021).

84 Council of the European Union, 'Eurogroup, 7 March 2016', available at: <www.consilium.europa.eu/en/meetings/eurogroup/2016/03/07/> (last visited 4 Sept. 2021).

85 Ibid.

86 European Ombudsman, 'Recent initiative to improve Eurogroup transparency', 14 March 2016, available at: <www.ombudsman.europa.eu/en/doc/correspondence/en/65359> (last visited 2 Feb. 2022); Council of the European Union, 'Reply from the Eurogroup President to the European Ombudsman's letter on Eurogroup transparency', 31 May 2016, available at: <www.consilium.europa.eu/en/press/press-releases/2016/05/31-peg-letter-ombudsman/> (last visited 2 Feb. 2022); European Ombudsman, 'Follow-up response from the European Ombudsman to the reply of President Dijsselbloem to her letter concerning Eurogroup transparency', 30 Aug. 2016, available at: <www.ombudsman.europa.eu/en/correspondence/en/70708> (last visited 2 Feb. 2022); Council of the European Union, 'Reply from the Eurogroup President to the European Ombudsman's letter on Eurogroup transparency', 1 Dec. 2016, available at: <www.consilium.europa.eu/en/press/press-releases/2016/12/01-eurogroup-peg-letter-ombudsman/> (last visited 2 Feb. 2022).

87 Eurogroup President letter, 31 May 2016, op. cit. *supra* note 86.

88 Ibid. See also the Eurogroup President letter, 1 Dec. 2016, op. cit. *supra* note 86.

regime in principle applies to all documents on which the *political* debate in the Eurogroup is based.[89] Further, he noted that the publication of programme documentation prior to the Eurogroup meetings was not deemed appropriate by the Eurogroup since they can be subject to change and are part of a negotiation process.[90] It may be observed that it is hard to separate 'technical' from 'political' aspects with regard to MoU conditionality. Moreover, the provision of programme-related documents in a sufficiently timely manner is crucial so that they be used by accountability fora in their scrutiny of the activities of the 'EMU executive'.[91]

The most recent developments regarding transparency in the work of the Eurogroup and its satellite bodies are as follows. The previous Eurogroup President, Mário Centeno, informed ministers at the Eurogroup meeting held on 7 September 2018 of his intention to review the transparency initiative adopted by the Eurogroup in 2016 and consider further improvements.[92] In her letter to the Eurogroup President dated 13 May 2019, the European Ombudsman noted, 'One outstanding matter is the transparency of the bodies involved in preparing Eurogroup meetings, in particular the Eurogroup Working Group.'[93] The European Ombudsman has launched a strategic inquiry into how requests for public access to documents of the Eurogroup, the EWG, the EFC and the Economic Policy Committee have been handled by the Council and the Commission under the EU rules on public access to documents. She further welcomed the Eurogroup President's views 'on the possibility of adopting a more ambitious approach to the transparency of the EWG, extending for example to the proactive publication of EWG meeting documents'.[94] In response to this as well as other calls,[95] the Euro-area finance ministers agreed in September 2019 'on some additional proposals to increase transparency … while paying particular attention to respect the

89 Eurogroup President letter, 31 May 2016, op. cit. *supra* note 86. See also the Eurogroup President letter, 1 Dec. 2016, op. cit. *supra* note 86.

90 Eurogroup President letter, 1 Dec. 2016, op. cit. *supra* note 86.

91 See also the chapter by Akbik and Dawson.

92 See the summing-up letter for the Eurogroup meeting of 7 Sept. 2018, available at: <www.consilium.europa.eu/media/36401/summing-up-letter-eurogroup-7-september.pdf> (last visited 2 Feb. 2022).

93 European Ombudsman, 'Request for information in Strategic initiative SI/2/2019/EA on transparency of the Eurogroup Working Group', 13 May 2019, available at: <www.ombudsman.europa.eu/en/correspondence/en/113770#_ftn3> (last visited 2 Feb. 2022).

94 Ibid.

95 See, for example, Braun and Hübner, 'VANISHING ACT: The Eurogroup's accountability', Transparency International EU, 5 Feb. 2019, available at: <https://transparency.eu/wp-content/uploads/2019/02/TI-EU-Eurogroup-report.pdf> (last visited 2 Feb. 2022).

requirement of confidentiality of the Eurogroup'.[96] These include improving the EWG webpage by providing more information, publishing the EWG's calendar meeting, expanding Eurogroup summing-up letters where relevant, bringing forward the publication of the draft Eurogroup (non-annotated) agenda, creating an online repository of publicly available Eurogroup documents, and providing more information on the Eurogroup's webpage on how the right of access to documents may be exercised with respect to documents held by other EU institutions.[97] These are by no means cosmetic changes, and the Eurogroup and its members are to be commended for introducing them. Whether this meets the higher demands that *substantive openness* would place on the Eurogroup and its accountability holders is up for debate.[98] Furthermore, it is not a foregone conclusion that the other 'accountability goods' are also delivered, such that it may be contested whether certain Eurogroup decisions are not arbitrary, are effective, and/or are taken in the public interest.[99]

Last, as regards the Eurogroup's legal accountability, there is no question whether there is a predominance of procedural accountability or whether there is a clearer need for more substantive accountability, because the acts and conduct of the Eurogroup are simply not subject to review by the CJEU. We have seen that the rulings in *Mallis* and *Chrysostomides* have rendered the Eurogroup immune to two key judicial accountability mechanisms in the Treaties, viz. actions for annulment and actions for damages. What is more, the *Chrystostomides* ruling might have wider ramifications for the application of EU rules to the Eurogroup. The reasons provided by the Court for its judgment could be seen to lend credence to arguments that the EU's transparency regime does not apply to the Eurogroup, examined *supra* in this chapter with respect to access to documents.

## 6.5 CONCLUSION

The preceding discussion has illustrated that the Eurogroup is an informal body with a vague mandate, which exercises an increasing amount of executive power. It is not, however, subject to the accountability checks that exist when executive power is exercised by the Commission or by the

96 Eurogroup, 'Eurogroup transparency policy review and way forward', available at: <www.consilium.europa.eu/media/40702/eurogroup-transparency-policy-review-and-way-forward.pdf> (last visited 2 Feb. 2022).

97 Ibid.

98 See the chapter by Akbik and Dawson.

99 I am grateful to Adina Akbik for this observation.

formal Council configurations.[100] Its principal political responsibility runs to the European Council, but there is little by way of accountability checks as to its input into European Council/Euro Summit meetings and the manner in which it follows up on the recommendations from such meetings. Further, there is certainly scope to improve the Eurogroup's interactions with the European Parliament, not least in the eyes of the MEPs themselves. As regards legal accountability, we have seen that actions for annulment may not be brought admissibly against the acts of the Eurogroup, and that the CJEU cannot hear a claim for compensation that is directed against the EU and based on the unlawfulness of an act or conduct the author of which is the Eurogroup. The remaining avenues for judicial review are insufficient to ensure that litigants are accorded effective judicial protection in this area.

Ultimately, the Eurogroup's accountability regime is currently stuck somewhere on the road between procedural and substantive accountability, with various improvements made over the years (following considerable pressure exerted by other institutions and actors), but also crucial preconditions for more robust accountability mechanisms missing altogether. Strengthening the accountability of the Eurogroup in EU fiscal and economic governance, as well as of the 'EMU executive' more broadly, remains work in progress. However, it is seemingly not accorded the political priority that it ought to be given in the various reform plans and blueprints. What is more, if it is indeed the case that the Eurogroup is a non-EU entity (as per *Chrysostomides*), some key changes to its accountability and transparency may no longer be possible within the framework of the existing EU Treaties.

[100] Craig and Markakis, op. cit. *supra* note 14, at p. 300.

# 7

# The Economic Dialogues with the Eurogroup

## *Substantive Accountability Claimed, but Unmet*

*Adina Akbik*

## 7.1 INTRODUCTION

The Eurogroup is the most infamous (non-)institution of the Economic and Monetary Union (EMU). As a key decision-maker on financial assistance programmes during the euro crisis, the Eurogroup has attracted significant criticism for its lack of transparency and accountability.[1] As an informal body which meets outside regular Council configurations, the Eurogroup cannot be legally found liable for its decisions because it is not an official institution of the European Union (EU).[2] Established in the late 1990s, the Eurogroup has always been an elusive body, with an agenda and proceedings that remained secret for most of its existence.[3] The Lisbon Treaty (2009) recognised the Eurogroup as an informal reunion of finance ministers of the euro area with a permanent president, elected for two and a half years.[4] Within the EMU, the powers of the Eurogroup revolve around the implementation of the Stability and Growth Pact (SGP), ensuring the coordination of national and economic policies in view of avoiding 'excessive government deficits'.[5] Outside the Treaty framework, the Eurogroup sits on the Board of Governors of the European Stability Mechanism (ESM) and takes crucial

1 Braun and Hübner, *Vanishing Act: The Eurogroups Accountability* (Transparency International EU, 2019); Craig, 'The Eurogroup, Power and Accountability', 23 *European Law Journal* (2017), 234–249.

2 See Joined Cases C-597/18 P, C-598/18 P, C-603/18 P and C-604/18 P, *Council v K. Chrysostomides & Co. and Others* EU:C:2020:1028.

3 Puetter, *The Eurogroup: How a Secretive Circle of Finance Ministers Shape European Economic Governance* (Manchester University Press, 2006); Puetter, *The European Council and the Council: New Intergovernmentalism and Institutional Change* (Oxford University Press, 2014).

4 Protocol 14 TFEU.

5 Articles 121 and 126 TFEU.

decisions on financial assistance.[6] In many ways, the Eurogroup acts as the 'economic government' of the euro area, a political counterweight to the European Central Bank (ECB).[7]

In the past decade, the increased power of the Eurogroup went hand in hand with calls to increase its transparency and democratic accountability.[8] Against this background, the legislative packages adopted during the euro crisis – the Six-Pack (2011) and the Two-Pack (2013) – institutionalised a new mechanism of parliamentary scrutiny of the Eurogroup. Benignly titled 'Economic Dialogues', the mechanism consisted of regular meetings between the Eurogroup President and the European Parliament (the 'Parliament'), where members of the Economic and Monetary Affairs (ECON) Committee could ask questions about various aspects of the Eurogroup's activity. In parallel, the Parliament organised Economic Dialogues with other executive actors such as the Commission, the Economic and Financial Affairs (ECOFIN) Council, and individual national governments.[9] So far, academic analyses of the Economic Dialogues have focused on their legal provisions[10] or made general observations regarding their functioning.[11] Less is known about the actual content of Economic Dialogues and the extent to which they ensure the accountability of the Eurogroup.[12]

6 Article 5 ESM Treaty.

7 Howarth, 'Making and Breaking the Rules: French Policy on EU "gouvernement économique"', 14 *Journal of European Public Policy* (2007), 1061–1078, at 1075.

8 Dias, Hagelstam, and Lehofer, 'The Role (and Accountability) of the President of the Eurogroup', PE 602.116 *European Parliament Briefing* (2021), <www.europarl.europa.eu/RegData/etudes/BRIE/2018/602116/IPOL_BRI(2018)602116_EN.pdf> (last visited 7 December 2021); *Smith-Mayer and Heath*, Eurogroup confronts own deficit: governance, Politico Europe, 24/05/2017, <www.politico.eu/article/eurogroup-urged-to-tackle-its-own-deficit-governance/> (last visited 7 December 2021).

9 Economic Governance Support Unit, At a glance: Dialogues and hearings in the European Parliament in the area of monetary, economic and financial affairs, 15 November 2016, <www.europarl.europa.eu/RegData/etudes/divers/join/2014/528738/IPOL-ECON_DV(2014)528738_EN.pdf> (last visited 7 December 2021).

10 Fasone, 'European Economic Governance and Parliamentary Representation. What Place for the European Parliament?', 20 *European Law Journal* (2014), 164–185; Fromage, 'The European Parliament in the Post-crisis Era: An Institution Empowered on Paper Only?', 40 *Journal of European Integration* (2018), 281–294.

11 Crum, 'Parliamentary Accountability in Multilevel Governance: What Role for Parliaments in Post-crisis EU Economic Governance?', 25 *Journal of European Public Policy* (2018), 268–286; de la Parra, 'The Economic Dialogue: An Effective Accountability Mechanism?' in Daniele, Simone, and Cisotta (eds.), *Democracy in the EMU in the Aftermath of the Crisis* (Springer International Publishing, 2017), pp. 101–120.

12 Such analyses exist, for example, in relation to the 'Monetary Dialogues' with the ECB and the 'Banking Dialogues' organised in the framework of the Single Supervisory Mechanism. See Amtenbrink and Markakis, 'Towards a Meaningful Prudential Supervision Dialogue in the

The effectiveness of the Economic Dialogues in holding the Eurogroup accountable is important for at least three reasons. First, given the informality of the intergovernmental body, the Parliament is the only political or legal forum that can make the Eurogroup President give a public account of decisions taken collectively by finance ministers of the euro area (see Section 7.2). Second, given the redistributive and politicised nature of EU economic and fiscal decisions,[13] the Parliament has the advantage of representing all Member States as opposed to the interests of one national electorate. Third, when it comes to the main question asked by this volume regarding substantive accountability in EU economic governance, the Economic Dialogues with the Eurogroup represent an essential 'most-likely' case.[14] Specifically, if Members of the European Parliament (MEPs) do not make substantive accountability claims towards the Eurogroup, they are unlikely to make them towards other EU executive actors.

This chapter investigates the Economic Dialogues with the Eurogroup since they were initially formalised in January 2013 until the end of the 8th parliamentary term (May 2019). The purpose is to assess the type of accountability claims made by MEPs vis-à-vis the Eurogroup as reflected in the parliamentary questions they pose during Economic Dialogues. Based on the conceptualisation set at the outset of this volume,[15] are MEPs more interested in procedural or substantive accountability in their interactions with the Eurogroup President? Which accountability goods – openness, non-arbitrariness, effectiveness, or publicness – do they prioritise in the oversight of the Eurogroup? Bearing in mind the political character of both actors under investigation, we can expect an emphasis on substantive accountability, with an express interest in the effectiveness and publicness of Eurogroup decisions. Unlike courts of law, ombudsmen, or auditors, members of parliaments can substantively assess the merit and impact of

Euro Area? A Study of the Interaction between the European Parliament and the European Central Bank in the Single Supervisory Mechanism', 44 *European Law Review* (2019), 3–23; Amtenbrink and van Duin, 'The European Central Bank Before the European Parliament: Theory and Practice After Ten Years of Monetary Dialogue', 34 *European Law Review* (2009), 561–583; Fraccaroli, Giovannini, and Jamet, 'The Evolution of the ECB's Accountability Practices During the Crisis', *ECB Economic Bulletin* (2018), 47–71.

13 Genschel and Jachtenfuchs, 'From Market Integration to Core State Powers: The Eurozone Crisis, the Refugee Crisis and Integration Theory', 56 *Journal of Common Market Studies* (2018), 178–196, at 181.

14 Gerring, 'Is There a (Viable) Crucial-Case Method?', 40 *Comparative Political Studies* (2007), 231–253.

15 Akbik and Dawson, 'From Procedural to Substantive Accountability in EMU Governance' in Dawson (ed.), *Substantive Accountability in Europe's New Economic Governance* (Cambridge University Press, 2022).

executive decisions as well as their effectiveness and the extent to which they reflect the public interest.

The chapter is structured as follows. The first section discusses the relationship between the Eurogroup and the European Parliament in conjunction with the legal framework of the Economic Dialogues. The second section transposes the theoretical notions of Chapter 2 to the context of parliamentary oversight, explaining how the four accountability goods can be identified in parliamentary questions in their procedural and substantive form. The rest of the chapter is dedicated to presenting the results of the empirical analysis, which includes a total of 474 questions (and corresponding answers) categorised according to the four accountability goods.

## 7.2 THE EUROGROUP AND THE EUROPEAN PARLIAMENT

The relationship between the Eurogroup and the European Parliament is only minimally comparable to the dynamic between a finance ministry and a legislature at the national level. From a principal–agent perspective, the European Parliament is not the principal of the Eurogroup in the EMU, as finance ministers of the euro area are individual agents of their own national parliaments and voters. Moreover, since the Eurogroup is an informal body, the counterpart of the European Parliament in the legislative process is the ECOFIN Council, not the Eurogroup. In a broad comparison to presidential systems of government,[16] one could say that the European Parliament and ECOFIN play the role of 'multiple competing agents'[17] in the EMU because they are supposed to represent citizens and Member States respectively at the EU level.[18] Although the Eurogroup contributes to legislative dossiers, its main activities are executive, concerning the implementation of fiscal and macroeconomic rules in the euro area and the management of financial assistance programmes in the ESM. For its part, the Parliament lacks formal powers to veto or even influence the executive decisions of the Eurogroup.[19]

[16] Lupia and McCubbins, 'Learning from Oversight: Fire Alarms and Police Patrols Reconstructed', 10 *Journal of Law, Economics, & Organization* (1994), 96–125; McCubbins and Schwartz, 'Congressional Oversight Overlooked: Police Patrols versus Fire Alarms', 28 *American Journal of Political Science* (1984), 165.

[17] Strøm, 'Delegation and Accountability in Parliamentary Democracies', 37 *European Journal of Political Research* (2000), 261–289, at 268.

[18] Article 10 TEU.

[19] Crum and Merlo, 'Democratic Legitimacy in the Post-crisis EMU', 42 *Journal of European Integration* (2020), 399–413; Rittberger, 'Integration without Representation? The European Parliament and the Reform of Economic Governance in the EU', 52 *Journal of Common Market Studies* (2014), 1174–1183.

Furthermore, the situation is further complicated by the informal status of the Eurogroup as an EU institution. For accountability purposes, informality is problematic in two ways. On the one hand, the Eurogroup cannot be held liable legally because its decisions do not count as EU acts until they are endorsed by the ECOFIN Council. According to recent judgments of the Court of Justice in the *Chrysostomides* and *Bourdouvali* cases, the Eurogroup 'cannot be equated with a configuration of the Council',[20] it 'does not have any competence of its own', and actions cannot be brought against it 'to establish non-contractual liability of the European Union'.[21] On the other hand, the informality of the Eurogroup facilitates strict confidentiality of its proceedings, that is, there are no minutes, conclusions,[22] or public votes as in regular Council meetings.[23] The lack of transparency makes accountability difficult for obvious reasons: if MEPs do not know how the Eurogroup reaches its decisions, they cannot establish which national governments pushed for or against the final outcome.

Against this background, the Economic Dialogues promised to increase the accountability of the Eurogroup by providing a regular mechanism through which the European Parliament could publicly discuss and question various Eurogroup activities.[24] One key policy instrument here was the European Semester – the EU's framework for economic and fiscal coordination – which included, among others, stricter rules for enforcing debt and deficit rules set in the SGP.[25] In respect to the euro area, the Six-Pack listed, as possible topics of the Economic Dialogues, the sanctions and fines applicable in the Excessive Deficit Procedure (EDP) and the Macroeconomic Imbalances Procedure (MIP).[26] The Two-Pack added two elements to the list of potential subjects: (1) the monitoring and assessing of budgetary plans in the Eurozone,[27] and (2) the special procedures for countries experiencing financial difficulties – procedures which included enhanced surveillance,

[20] Joined Cases C-597/18 P, C-598/18 P, C-603/18 P and C-604/18 P, *Council v K. Chrysostomides & Co. and Others* EU:C:2020:1028, para 87.

[21] Ibid., paras 89–90.

[22] Since 2017, the Eurogroup publishes agendas of its meetings and general summaries of its discussions, without attributing country positions.

[23] Puetter, *The Eurogroup: How a Secretive Circle of Finance Ministers Shape European Economic Governance* (Manchester University Press, 2006), chap. 3.

[24] Fromage, 'The European Parliament in the Post-crisis era: An Institution Empowered on Paper Only?', 40 *Journal of European Integration* (2018), 281–294, at 285–288.

[25] European Commission, The EU's economic governance explained, <https://ec.europa.eu/info/business-economy-euro/economic-and-fiscal-policy-coordination/eu-economic-governance-monitoring-prevention-correction/european-semester/framework/eus-economic-governance-explained_en> (last visited 7 December 2021).

[26] Article 3, Regulation (EU) No 1173/2011, Article 6, Regulation (EU) No 1174/2011.

[27] Article 15, Regulation (EU) No 473/2013.

macroeconomic adjustment programmes, or post-programme surveillance.[28] In fact, according to Markakis, the Two-Pack 'lays down the most detailed accountability and transparency requirements [in the EMU] to date'.[29]

While the tasks of the ECOFIN Council and the Eurogroup are difficult to separate in the European Semester (e.g. their role in the EDP and the MIP), it was clear that the Eurogroup would be the Parliament's main interlocutor for questions related to financial assistance. Even though the ESM was not an EU institution, the composition of its Board of Governors coincided with the Eurogroup, while the Eurogroup President served as the Chair.[30] Effectively, the Eurogroup brokered ESM agreements and supervised the implementation of aid packages,[31] which made it uniquely competent to discuss the details and approach of financial assistance programmes. By contrast, the practical administration and monitoring of programme countries fell to the 'Troika' – an informal alliance comprising the European Commission, the ECB, and the International Monetary Fund (IMF).[32]

The next section discusses ways in which the European Parliament could hold the Eurogroup accountable in the Economic Dialogues, in connection with the theoretical framework outlined in Chapter 2.

## 7.3 ACCOUNTABILITY GOODS IN PARLIAMENTARY OVERSIGHT

In the universe of political accountability in a democratic system of government, the Economic Dialogues correspond to parliamentary oversight – part of a legislature's controlling functions of the executive.[33] In the academic literature, the notion of 'oversight' gained traction in the 1970s, in parallel to empirical developments in the United States Congress regarding the growing importance of 'keeping a watchful eye' over the administration.[34]

28 Articles 3, 7, 14, and 18, Regulation (EU) No 472/2013.

29 Markakis, *Accountability in the Economic and Monetary Union: Foundations, Policy, and Governance* (Oxford University Press, 2020), at 128.

30 Article 5, ESM Treaty.

31 Craig, op. cit. *supra* note 1, at 237; Dijsselbloem, Letter to Ms Bowles, Chairwoman of the Committee of Economic and Monetary Affairs, <www.europarl.europa.eu/cmsdata/59958/att_20140114ATT77339-6443094514033203696.pdf> (last visited January 2014).

32 European Stability Mechanism, *Safeguarding the Euro in Times of Crisis: The Inside Story of the ESM* (Publications Office of the European Union, 2019), at 77.

33 Beyme, von, 'Functions of Parliaments' in Beyme, von (ed.), *Parliamentary Democracy: Democratization, Destabilization, Reconsolidation, 1789–1999* (Palgrave Macmillan UK, 2000), pp. 72–107, at 72.

34 Aberbach, *Keeping a Watchful Eye: The Politics of Congressional Oversight* (Brookings Institution Press, 1990).

However, the idea of legislative oversight was hardly new; in fact, congressional oversight has always been an integral part of the American system of checks and balances in connection to the question of 'who rules the rulers'.[35] The objective of oversight was to prevent abuses by the administration, including but not limited to dishonesty, waste, arbitrariness, unresponsiveness, or deviation from legislative intent.[36] Although definitions varied, the notion of 'oversight' implied an ex-post focus ('review after the fact') – that is, 'inquiries about policies that are or have been in effect, investigations of past administrative actions, and the calling of executive officers to account for their financial transactions'.[37]

One of the main tools in the repertoire of legislative oversight is the right to ask questions to the executive, either in writing or orally in hearings and plenary debates.[38] In fact, parliamentary questions constitute a field of studies on their own, with scholars interested in the behaviour of legislators and the reasons why members of parliaments choose to raise specific questions.[39] The connection between parliamentary questions and the ability of legislatures to control executives has always been implicit, following the logic that questions allow parliaments to 'check, verify, scrutinise, inspect, examine, … criticise, censure, challenge, [and] call to account' the government and public administration.[40] In fact, parliamentary questions can easily be connected to the four accountability goods described at the beginning of the volume.[41] The point is that parliamentary questions can make different accountability claims – openness, non-arbitrariness, effectiveness, or publicness – depending on the interest of the questioner. Moreover, members of parliaments can focus on procedural or substantive issues, in line with the four goods. The next pages describe the operationalisation of each good in turn.

First, openness overlaps with notions of transparency, which in the context of parliamentary questions means either requesting details about decision-making processes (procedural openness) or demanding information about the content

35 Ogul, *Congress Oversees the Bureaucracy*, 1st edition (University of Pittsburgh Press, 1976), at 3.

36 MacMahon, 'Congressional Oversight of Administration: The Power of the Purse. I', 58 *Political Science Quarterly* (1943), 161–190, at 162–163.

37 Harris, *Congressional Control of Administration* (Brookings Institution Press, 1964), at 6.

38 Pelizzo and Stapenhurst, *Parliamentary Oversight Tools: A Comparative Analysis* (Routledge, 2012); Yamamoto, *Tools for Parliamentary Oversight: A Comparative Study of 88 National Parliaments* (Inter-Parliamentary Union, 2007).

39 For a review, see Martin, 'Parliamentary Questions, the Behaviour of Legislators, and the Function of Legislatures: An Introduction', 17 *The Journal of Legislative Studies* (2011), 259–270.

40 Gregory, 'Parliamentary Control and the Use of English', 43 *Parliamentary Affairs* (1990), 59–76, at 64.

41 Akbik and Dawson, op. cit., *supra* note 15.

of decisions and their expected impact (substantive openness). Second, non-arbitrariness varies in line with the nature of the actor to be held accountable. Accordingly, non-majoritarian institutions are likely to be questioned about their compliance with decision-making processes (procedural non-arbitrariness) or potential deviations from their legal mandate (substantive non-arbitrariness). By contrast, political bodies are more often questioned on aspects regarding the equal treatment of different groups in decision-making processes (procedural non-arbitrariness) or the discriminatory effect of their decisions (substantive non-arbitrariness). Third, the interest in effectiveness is straightforward: legislators can either inquire about the speed and hurdles of decision-making processes (procedural effectiveness) or they can ask about the impact of decisions, that is, why policies failed to reach the intended results and what can be done to improve the outcome in the future (substantive effectiveness). Fourth, publicness can refer to the balance of interests involved in decision-making (procedural publicness) or the balance between groups affected by decisions (substantive publicness). In this respect, publicness is linked to the democratic character of decision-making processes, for instance, whether parliaments are involved or whether decisions are fair vis-à-vis specific groups. Table 7.1 provides an overview of the direction of parliamentary questions that can be found across the four goods in both their procedural and substantive forms.

Keeping in mind that oversight is a two-way process – composed of parliamentary questions and answers – it is important to assess the responsiveness of executive answers when engaging with members of parliaments. For the purposes of this chapter, I employ a simplified version of measuring responsiveness, drawing on previous work.[42] Accordingly, in response to parliamentary questions, executive actors can (1) agree with the member of parliament or simply provide the information requested, (2) disagree with the member of parliament and/or defend existing policies or conducts, or (3) evade the question either intentionally or because of lack of time[43] (in both cases, no concrete answer can be identified). Based on this categorisation, *the more executive actors evade parliamentary questions, the least responsive they are in oversight*. The distinction between agreement and disagreement with members of parliaments is more complex because it depends on government-opposition dynamics and political ideologies. What is important for the analysis of Economic Dialogues

[42] Maricut-Akbik, 'Q&A in Legislative Oversight: A Framework for Analysis', 60 *European Journal of Political Research* (2021), 539–559; Maricut-Akbik, 'Contesting the European Central Bank in Banking Supervision: Accountability in Practice at the European Parliament', 58 *Journal of Common Market Studies* (2020), 1199–1214.

[43] Empirically, it is difficult to distinguish the intention to not answer questions from lack of time, as they can present in the same way.

TABLE 7.1 *Accountability goods in parliamentary oversight. Own account, based on Akbik and Dawson*[44]

| Accountability good | How it is rendered | Focus of parliamentary questions |
|---|---|---|
| Openness | Procedurally | Who was involved in the decision-making process and in what way? When was/will a decision (be) taken? |
| | Substantively | What was/is/will be the content of a decision or policy? What will happen as a result of the decision?<br>What is your evaluation of the decision?<br>How and when will the decision be implemented? |
| Non-arbitrariness | Procedurally | Is the decision-making process in line with the rules? How can we make sure that rules are respected?<br>Are countries/groups of people treated equally in the decision-making process? |
| | Substantively | Are decisions in line with the mandate of an institution?<br>Does the decision result in equal treatment of countries or actors? Is the outcome biased against certain groups? |
| Effectiveness | Procedurally | Why did the decision-making process take so long?<br>How likely is it that a decision will be taken? |
| | Substantively | Has the decision achieved the intended result? Why not?<br>What is the strategy to reach the desired results?<br>Is X the right solution to the problem? |
| Publicness | Procedurally | Why does the decision-making process fail to take into account institution/group X? Have all legitimate interests been taken into consideration? Is the process democratic? |
| | Substantively | Is the outcome of a decision fair for different groups?<br>Will disadvantaged groups be compensated?<br>How can you restore confidence that the decision taken was/is in everyone's interest? |

44 Ibid.

is the type of issues raised by MEPs and whether the Eurogroup attempts to systematically evade questions. The next section illustrates the application of this framework to the questions asked by MEPs during 2013–2019.

## 7.4 THE ECONOMIC DIALOGUES IN PRACTICE

Although the ECON Committee held informal sessions with the Eurogroup President before the Two-Pack, such meetings only became formalised in 2013. Sharon Bowles, the Chair of the ECON Committee at the time, explained that the Economic Dialogues were being institutionalised twice per year: once in January to introduce the annual working programme of the Eurogroup, and once in September to take stock of progress on the working programme and follow up on Country-Specific Recommendations (CSRs) adopted in July; she also emphasised that the meetings are 'all legal now (…) no longer off Treaty'.[45] Depending on the schedule of the Eurogroup President in a year, meetings were sometimes postponed to February/March and October/November, respectively. In 2013, a special Dialogue took place in May on the ESM adjustment programme for Cyprus. In November 2015, the ESM Director Klaus Regling joined the Eurogroup President to discuss the details of the recently adopted third adjustment programme for Greece.

From the start of 2013 until the European Parliament elections of May 2019,[46] the ECON Committee organised fourteen Economic Dialogues with the Eurogroup. Throughout the period, the Eurogroup had three Presidents, who attended the meetings as follows: Jean-Claude Juncker (once in 2013), Jeroen Dijsselbloem (11 times between 2013 and 2017), and Mário Centeno (twice in 2018). Not only was Dijsselbloem the main interlocutor of MEPs in the period under focus, but he also led the Eurogroup during difficult times – including the ESM programmes for Cyprus (in 2013) and Greece (in 2015). By contrast, Juncker attended a Dialogue that was his last as Eurogroup President, in which MEPs mostly praised his performance as head of the group and asked him about future career plans in view of the 2014 European Parliament elections. Centeno's mandate was less eventful because the euro area was in the middle of an economic recovery and no further ESM programmes were agreed since 2016.

45 European Parliament, Economic Dialogue with the Eurogroup President, Jean-Claude Juncker, <https://multimedia.europarl.europa.eu/en/committee-on-economic-and-monetary-affairs_20130110-0900-COMMITTEE-ECON_vd> (last visited 10 January 2013).

46 However, in 2019, the ECON Committee did not hold an Economic Dialogue due to preparations for the European Parliament elections in May.

As with other hearings in the ECON Committee, the format of Economic Dialogues allocates a five-minute slot for each MEP to ask a question and receive an answer. The longer the question, the higher the likelihood that the Chair would cut off the Eurogroup President halfway through the answer. Most MEPs seem used to this format and seek to get concrete answers to their questions. In line with the Parliament's Rules of Procedure,[47] MEPs get the floor in the order of the size of their political groups, starting with the European People's Party (EPP) and the Socialists and Democrats (S&D). As with other Economic Dialogues, the coordinators of political groups took the floor in almost every meeting: for example, Jean-Paul Gauzès (EPP, France) and Elisa Ferreira (S&D, Portugal) for the 2009–2014 parliamentary term, and Burkhard Balz (EPP, Germany) and Pervenche Bères (S&D, France) during 2014–2019.

In total, the analysis identified 474 single-topic questions asked by MEPs in the fourteen Dialogues examined.[48] In terms of the issues covered, Figure 7.1 shows that the most frequent topic of questions concerned financial assistance programmes (17 per cent overall), mostly in relation to Cyprus (9 per cent) and Greece (5 per cent). MEPs also had the tendency to connect financial assistance programmes to ongoing developments in the Member States that captured economic and social indicators (15 per cent of questions). The next topic (also found in 15 per cent of all questions) referred to the internal organisation of EMU, which covered the 2015 'Five Presidents Report' as well as the Commission's 'Roadmap for completing EMU' in 2017. Such questions often included the democratic accountability of the Eurogroup and the possible transformation of the ESM into a European Monetary Fund (EMF) under EU law. Legislative files were also an important topic for MEPs (present in 9 per cent of all questions), especially in relation to the completion of the Banking Union and the Capital Markets Union (7 per cent of all questions). Finally, fiscal consolidation and specific instruments of the European Semester feature frequently in parliamentary questions (6 per cent each), showing that the Eurogroup is considered the main interlocutor on the implementation of the SGP – although formally the ECOFIN Council is responsible.[49]

47 *European Parliament*, Rules of Procedure 8th parliamentary term – January 2017, 01/2017.

48 Videos of the Economic Dialogues are publicly available on the Parliament's website. Transcripts of the videos were provided by the Parliament's EGOV Unit, thanks to Marcel Magnus. The transcripts were then manually categorised by the author using the software for qualitative data analysis Atlas.ti.

49 See also Akbik, *The European Parliament as an Accountability Forum: Overseeing the Economic and Monetary Union* (Cambridge University Press (forthcoming), 2022), chap. 6.

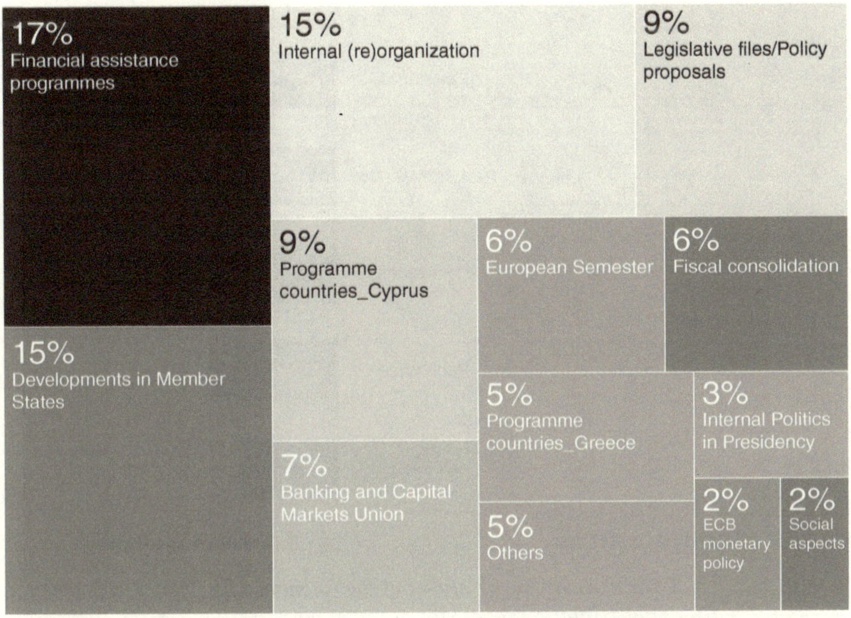


FIGURE 7.1 *Types of issues raised in the Economic Dialogues with the Eurogroup (January 2013–May 2019). Most questions have two codes, except those that address ESM programmes in Greece and Cyprus (which have 3 codes). Total codes assigned: 1095.*

Over time, MEPs asked fewer questions on ESM financial assistance, which is consistent with the lack of new programmes since 2016. In the last years (2016–2019), the focus shifted towards legislative proposals in the Capital Markets Union, general reform proposals of the economic governance framework, or economic recovery in the Member States. Having established the main areas of discussion in the Economic Dialogues with the Eurogroup, the next step is to discuss the types of questions and answers identified, in line with the theoretical framework outlined above.

### 7.4.1 *Which Accountability Goods Do MEPs Prioritise?*

Figure 7.2 shows the number of questions identified across the four goods in absolute numbers. In terms of percentages, the highest value – 52 per cent of all questions – prioritises substantive issues regarding the merit of policy decisions or measures. Next, 42 per cent of all questions are deemed procedural because they cover various aspects of the process through which decisions were taken. Finally, 6 per cent of all questions do not have a clear

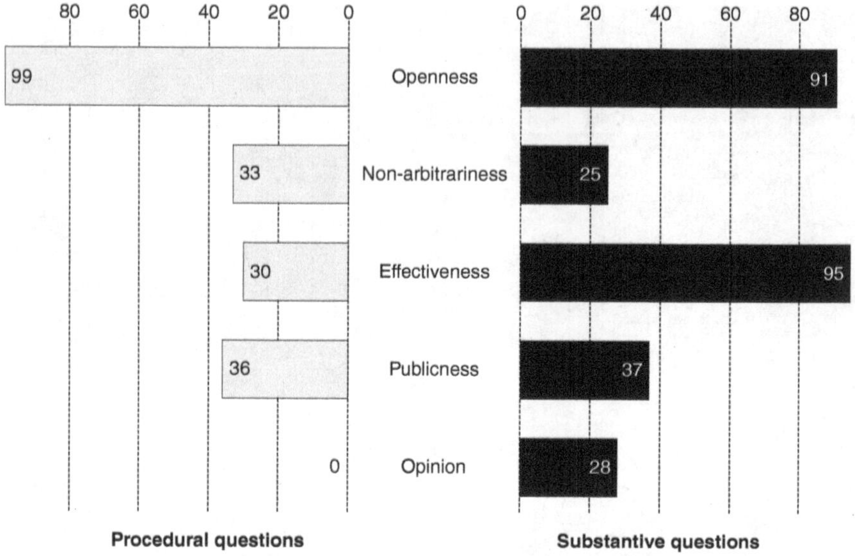


FIGURE 7.2 *Types of questions identified in the Economic Dialogues with the Eurogroup (January 2013–May 2019), in absolute numbers.*

accountability claim and are considered opinion questions about developments in the Member States or ongoing policy debates.

Among the four accountability goods, openness is the most frequent, not only in respect to decision-making processes but also when it comes to the content and outcomes of decisions. Requests for transparency make 40 per cent of all questions, with a slightly higher emphasis on procedural as opposed to substantive issues (ninety-nine versus ninety-one occurrences). In terms of procedural openness, one important example comes from the special Dialogue on Cyprus in May 2013, when MEPs questioned a controversial Eurogroup decision to ensure financing for the Cypriot economy by imposing a 6.75 per cent levy on all bank depositors, regardless of the protection offered by EU deposit insurance guidelines to small deposits under 100,000 euros.[50] While the Eurogroup soon backtracked on the measure – not least because the Cypriot parliament rejected it – MEPs wanted to know how the Eurogroup reached the decision in the first place and who supported the move:

> **Sharon Bowles (Chair, ECON Committee)**: How did the Euro Summit meeting on the night of the 15th and 16th of March reach its conclusions? (…) How was the meeting prepared and by whom? And actually, we're still a

[50] European Stability Mechanism, op. cit., *supra* note 32, at 269.

little bit curious about who was in the room and how many in particular from the IMF and whether there were any subrooms. (…) Did the Cyprus authorities provide or withhold all relevant information at all stages of the crisis?[51]

Another memorable question on the same matter is posed by Sven Giegold from the Greens, a long-standing advocate of more transparency in the EMU:

**Sven Giegold (Greens-EFA, Germany):** we as a Parliament have the right to know more from you how it came to this wrong decision. And we ask this in writing. And I would like to know whether you will respond in writing precisely why this process didn't deliver. And we have the right to know. The citizens have the right to know. And it's too cheap simply to say, I will not answer and I am the king of the Eurogroup.[52]

Leaving the political rhetoric aside, the interest in procedural openness featured throughout the period and went beyond transparency about negotiating positions in the Eurogroup: more generally, MEPs asked questions about the stage and timing of negotiations or about the evidence used as a basis for taking decisions. At the same time, MEPs made numerous requests for information about the substantive policy position of the Eurogroup on different matters. For instance, MEPs inquired whether the Cypriot bank levy on deposits could be applied to different countries as well[53] or whether the Eurogroup President Mario Centeno meant what he said to the Greek finance minister that 'the ball is [now] in your court'.[54] Other subjects of substantive openness concerned future EMU reforms planned in the 'Five Presidents Report' (2015) and the Commission's 2017 'Roadmap for completing EMU', as well as the risks posed to the euro area economy by Brexit and steps taken to prevent them. At times, MEPs just asked the Eurogroup President to clarify points about policy:

**Paul Tang (S&D, Netherlands):** Now I'd come back to an earlier exchange you had with Udo Bullman where you said you see ways to combine flexibility and credibility. You said structural reforms, maybe public investments, can be given more time for targeting the fiscal deficit. I would advise you to

51 European Parliament, Economic Dialogue with the Eurogroup President, Jeroen Dijsselbloem, <https://multimedia.europarl.europa.eu/en/committee-on-economic-and-monetary-affairs_20130507-1430-COMMITTEE-ECON_vd> (last visited 7 May 2013).

52 Ibid.

53 Ibid.

54 European Parliament, Economic Dialogue with the Eurogroup President, Mario Centeno, <https://multimedia.europarl.europa.eu/en/committee-on-economic-and-monetary-affairs_20180221-0900-COMMITTEE-ECON_vd> (last visited 21 February 2018).

be more specific on this. Do you want to have a formal procedure, or do you want to take the initiative to enshrine flexibility in the Pact and to combine flexibility and credibility at the same time?[55]

The second-most frequent category is made of questions concerning the effectiveness of policy decisions – 26 per cent in total – with a clear prioritisation of substantive aspects over procedural ones (95 as opposed to 30 occurrences). Many questions in this category concern the effectiveness of the European Semester and the implementation of CSRs by national governments. For example:

> **Elisa Ferreira (S&D, Portugal):** I'd like to know whether or not with the new powers that are conferred on you, we're going to get a careful and thorough assessment of the quality of these recommendations, which are then imposed on countries. And this [should be] depending on the effective results, not the theoretical results that the recommendations are based on or aiming at.[56]

Other questions concern strategies to improve the current effectiveness of EU policies, for instance, 'if you are a responsible policymaker, you have to have contingency plans; what is your contingency plan if growth would not come back?'[57] The effectiveness of the Troika and of austerity policies in particular are also questioned, as MEPs point to the lack of growth in Greece as a sign that the Eurogroup's approach has failed.[58] Conversely, procedural effectiveness has to do with the swiftness of decision-making processes and strategies to prioritise certain files or issues in order to reach agreements. For example, MEPs questioned the wisdom of not having a strategy in case Greece had left the euro area in 2015, under the Tsipras government.[59] Another long-standing aspect has been the proposal to create a European Deposit Insurance Scheme (EDIS), the final step of the Banking Union, which was deadlocked time and again since 2015.

Next, there are questions regarding publicness (15 per cent overall) and non-arbitrariness (12 per cent overall). The interest in publicness is almost equally procedural as it is substantive (36 and 37 occurrences, respectively). One

55 European Parliament, Economic Dialogue with the Eurogroup President, Jeroen Dijsselbloem, <https://multimedia.europarl.europa.eu/en/committee-on-economic-and-monetary-affairs_20140904-0900-COMMITTEE-ECON_vd> (last visited 9 April 2014).

56 European Parliament, op. cit., *supra* note 45.

57 Belgian MEP Philippe Lamberts from the Greens, cited in European Parliament, op. cit., *supra* note 55.

58 Ibid.

59 European Parliament, Economic Dialogue with the Eurogroup President, Jeroen Dijsselbloem, <https://multimedia.europarl.europa.eu/en/committee-on-economic-and-monetary-affairs_20150224-0900-COMMITTEE-ECON_vd> (last visited 24 February 2015).

recurrent issue concerns the transformation of the ESM into an Economic Monetary Fund under EU law, with the involvement of the European Parliament. Another aspect refers to the Parliament's opposition to the creation of an independent fiscal council to monitor national budgets, as captured below:

> **Jonás Fernández (S&D, Spain):** Do you know the name of the independent body that controls fiscal policy? The name of this chamber is the parliament. I have read with interest your letter in which, in the context of presenting the Five Presidents Report, you took the opportunity to defend a personal idea that I don't share at all. … you defended the creation of an independent fiscal body in charge of supervising and intervening in member states' national budgets, maybe in the European budget too, as if you were reacting against the supposed politicisation of the Commission. Something that I interpret as a direct, unfair and uncalled for criticisms of the current Commission. You should know that since the beginning of time there are institutions that look after governments budget policies, and they are the parliaments, whether the national ones or the European Parliament.[60]

A similar criticism about the Eurogroup's lack of democratic accountability referred to substantive issues and thus fell under 'substantive publicness'. One area of conflict concerned representing the public interest of a Member State (e.g. Alexis Tsipras after winning the election in Greece) as opposed to safeguarding the interest of the euro area as a whole:

> **Marco Valli (EFDD, Italy):** First of all, I would like to congratulate the President of the Eurogroup because I think what you have mentioned is incredible. A few weeks ago, we were facing a democratically elected government which had made promises to Greece and obviously that meant a 70 per cent haircut to the debt. The end of the program, they promised that, and reimbursing war debts on the part of Germany. And just a few weeks ago that's what we heard and now we've got this result. So well done then for showing that we are really in a sort of technocratic dictatorship. I'm sure that's going to increase Euroscepticism and the consensus about people who don't believe in this Europe.[61]

In respect to non-arbitrariness, there are more procedural questions encountered than substantive ones, but the difference is not significant (33 vs. 25

[60] European Parliament, Economic Dialogue with the Eurogroup President, Jeroen Dijsselbloem, <https://multimedia.europarl.europa.eu/en/committee-on-economic-and-monetary-affairs_20151110-1720-COMMITTEE-ECON22_vd?EPV_REPLAY=true&EPV_PHOTO=true&EPV_AUDIO=true&EPV_EDITED_VIDEOS=false> (last visited 11 October 2015).

[61] European Parliament, op. cit., *supra* note 59.

occurrences). On the procedural side, multiple questions address the uniform application of rules on the SGP and the 'special treatment' granted to large countries like France and even Spain. An interesting issue is raised regarding the duplicity of national ministers, who agree to CSRs in the ECOFIN Council/Eurogroup and then make public statements against the Commission to their domestic audiences:

> **Astrid Lulling (EPP, Luxembourg):** On the European Semester you said, if I understand correctly, that the Commission recommendations were passed unanimously by the Council. I'm quite surprised by that. Because immediately following the publication of the recommendations by the Commission, there were very negative reactions … by national politicians, [who] said that there would be no question of Brussels being allowed to dictate what member states had to do. This is almost hypocrisy. And as representatives of Europe, as the Eurogroup, should we not be calling them out on this hypocrisy?[62]

The point is not about the Eurogroup President specifically but by members of his institution, which is important because it shows that the Eurogroup President cannot be held accountable for the conduct of other finance ministers, especially when such conduct occurred in a domestic setting.

Finally, there are also questions focused on substantive non-arbitrariness, which focus mainly on equal treatment (of citizens, economic actors, or countries) in the context of ESM or EU measures. For example, in relation to the ESM programme in Cyprus, the Chair of the ECON Committee, Sharon Bowles asked how 'can we establish that there has been equality of citizens and member states in the various bailouts? And is this within both the spirit and the letter of the Treaties and legislation?'[63] Overall, non-arbitrariness plays a limited role among the accountability concerns of MEPs, not least because the legal mandate of the Eurogroup is ambiguous while the relationship with the Parliament is not strictly defined. It is difficult for MEPs to constrain the discretion of the Eurogroup if (1) the boundaries of that discretion are fluid, and (2) the Parliament does not set or review the tasks of the Eurogroup in the EMU.

To sum up, the European Parliament uses the Economic Dialogues to make a variety of accountability claims vis-à-vis the Eurogroup. However, most questions focus on openness (both procedural and substantive) as well

62 European Parliament, Economic Dialogue with the Eurogroup President, Jeroen Dijsselbloem, <https://multimedia.europarl.europa.eu/en/committee-on-economic-and-monetary-affairs_20130905-0900-COMMITTEE-ECON_vd> (last visited 9 May 2013).

63 European Parliament, op. cit., *supra* note 51.

as substantive effectiveness, revealing a systematic parliamentary interest in the transparency of the Eurogroup and the economic impact of its decisions. Ultimately, MEPs prioritise knowing what the Eurogroup is doing, and whether its actions achieve the intended results. While there is some questioning of the publicness and arbitrariness of Eurogroup decisions, such concerns are secondary to openness and effectiveness. The next section discusses how Eurogroup President responds to parliamentary questions in the Economic Dialogues.

### 7.4.2 *The Answerability of the Eurogroup*

When it comes to the types of answers provided by the Eurogroup Presidents, there is a clear trend observable across the four accountability goods. Regardless of the questions addressed by MEPs, Eurogroup Presidents have the tendency to disagree with the points raised or defend the conduct of their institution in respect to both procedural and substantive aspects. Disagreement or defence of conduct was identified in 55 per cent of all answers, with a higher incidence in response to questions on substantive issues (32 per cent) as opposed to procedural ones (23 per cent). Excluding opinion questions (which have no accountability claim), the frequency of answers in agreement with MEPs or simply providing the information is 20 per cent. On the other hand, evasion or lack of replies due to time constraints was identified in 18 per cent of all cases (also excluding opinion questions). In terms of specific accountability goods, answerability is similar. Figure 7.3 provides a snapshot of the various types of replies encountered.

To start with, answers that agree with points raised by MEPs or simply provide the information requested are categorised as 'agree/provide' [a reply]. Most of these answers concern openness in either its procedural (22 occurrences) or substantive form (24 occurrences). When the Eurogroup President is asked about the sequence of decision-making regarding the 2013 Cypriot programme, he is transparent about the process and considerations at the time but not about the specific positions of different Member States, which he feels he needs to protect as chairman of the Eurogroup.[64] Calls for decision-making transparency are finally met in 2016, when several reforms are passed:

> **Jeroen Dijsselbloem:** First on the transparency of the Eurogroup. We have agreed that we will put out in advance of our meetings and annotated agenda which is a lot more information than was accustomed. Secondly, we will put

[64] Ibid.

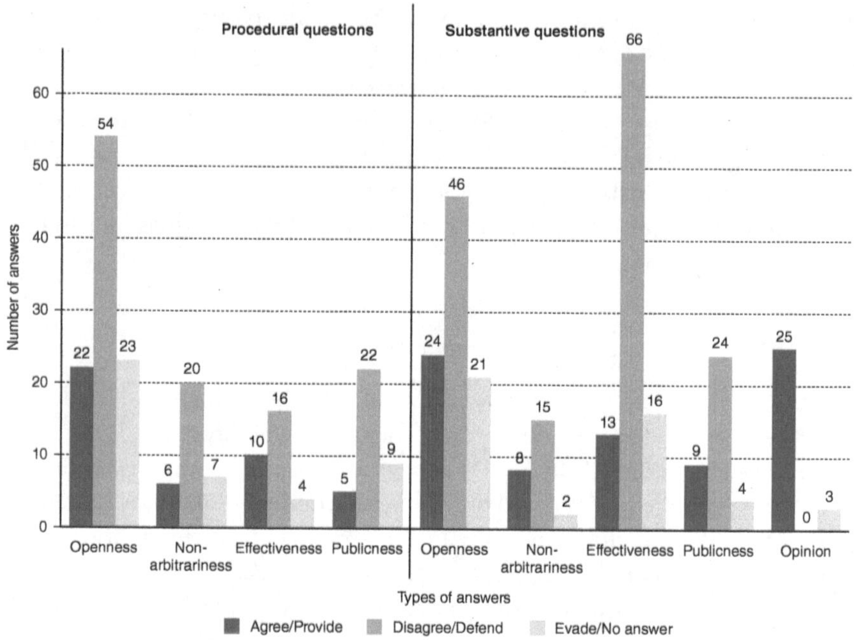


FIGURE 7.3 *Types of answers identified in the Economic Dialogues with the Eurogroup (January 2013–May 2019).*

> out what is called a summing up letter so it's not minutes in the sense that you can read who says what but it's a summing up letter which will give you an idea of the kind of discussion we had and the conclusions that we have come to on all the relevant issues.[65]

In respect to substantive issues, the Eurogroup President is generally open to clarifying the Eurogroup's policy stances or views on the future reforms of the EMU. For instance, in response to the question about the relationship between flexibility and credibility in relation to structural reforms (posed by Paul Tang), Dijsselbloem provides a lengthy answer and explains his position in respect to the preventive and corrective arms of the SGP.[66] Eurogroup Presidents also seem happy to provide their own opinions about lessons learned from holding the position, advice to their successors, or ongoing policy debates (see opinion questions, with answers provided in 25 out of 28 occurrences).

65 European Parliament, Economic Dialogue with the Eurogroup President, Jeroen Dijsselbloem, <https://multimedia.europarl.europa.eu/en/committee-on-economic-and-monetary-affairs_20160218-0900-COMMITTEE-ECON_vd> (last visited 18 February 2016).

66 European Parliament, op. cit., *supra* note 55.

The next pages illustrate the range of replies found in the dataset, corresponding to the questions listed in Section 7.4.1. For instance, in response to the question by MEP Astrid Lulling on the effectiveness of CSRs in the European Semester, the Eurogroup President explains that the problem is not 'the quality of recommendations, but the quality of the implementation and the progress being made where budgets are concerned'.[67] Years later, in 2017, Dijsselbloem still defended the effectiveness of the Semester:

> **Jeroen Dijsselbloem:** If you look at the OECD reports on structural reforms that have been implemented throughout the eurozone, it's quite impressive but it varies very much per country. Some countries have done very little. And some countries have been forced by circumstance and sometimes forced by programmes to do very difficult structural reforms. And interestingly enough if you look across the eurozone, now the countries with the highest growth are the countries that did the difficult structural adjustments in the past years. Ireland of course, Spain, Portugal, the Baltics, even the Netherlands. … So I think it's much more about ownership and we should really think about how we can improve ownership in [other] countries.[68]

Furthermore, the Eurogroup President also defends the democratic accountability of the ESM, arguing that each finance minister is accountable to her own national parliaments. In the Dialogue on 20 February 2014, he also refers to a letter sent by his predecessor Jean-Claude Juncker pledging to report to the European Parliament on a regular basis on the workings of the ESM. In his view: 'The easy thing is I am here now you can ask me anything you want on the ESM.' The MEP who originally asked the question (Bas Eickhout from the Greens/the Netherlands) retorts that this is not the same because 'for example the Dutch Parliament does not have a veto on any payment … whereas the German Parliament has because of the voting rules. So there is a democratic gap in the ESM and … that [needs] more than just that you are here coming.' The minister replies that the Dutch parliament can fulfil its accountability obligations without the formal voting rules because 'There is no subject that is debated that much and that often in the Dutch Parliament as the Eurozone agenda including all the programs and all the money that comes from the ESM.'[69]

67 European Parliament, op. cit., *supra* note 62.

68 European Parliament, Economic Dialogue with the Eurogroup President, Jeroen Dijsselbloem, <https://multimedia.europarl.europa.eu/en/committee-on-economic-and-monetary-affairs_20171207-0900-COMMITTEE-ECON_vd> (last visited 12 July 2017).

69 European Parliament, Economic Dialogue with the Eurogroup President, Jeroen Dijsselbloem, <https://multimedia.europarl.europa.eu/en/committee-on-economic-and-monetary-affairs_20140220-0900-COMMITTEE-ECON_vd> (last visited 20 February 2014).

Furthermore, reacting to the question of MEP Jonás Fernández about creating an independent fiscal council, the Eurogroup President rejects ever saying that such an institution 'should intervene in national procedures' on budgets or 'step into the authority of the Commission'. He argues that it would be good to have 'a European Fiscal Council that could independently assess whether we are taking the Pact seriously; sometimes criticise us, sometimes evaluate what we've done, … but also advise on what we discussed just now, the fiscal stance in the Euro zone'.[70] In response to Marco Valli's question about the Greek elections and respecting the democratic wishes of the voters, Dijsselbloem defends the intergovernmental nature of the Eurogroup and the need 'to deal with 19 ministers who have 19 mandates from 19 electorates'.[71] Last but not least, on the question of Astrid Lulling regarding the hypocrisy of national governments who berate CSRs after voting for them in the Council, the Eurogroup President defends the right of Member States to implement reforms their own way – as long as they engage seriously with the Commission's recommendations.[72]

Elsewhere, the point about the equality of citizens and Member States in the various bailouts (raised by Sharon Bowles) is first dodged by the Eurogroup President until it is picked up again by another MEP. At that point, Jeroen Dijsselbloem agrees that 'every country can be treated different, but it should be done on the same principles and one of the guiding principles is debt sustainability – that the country should be able to recover'.[73] Speaking of evasions more generally, Mario Centeno has the worst record in the dataset (with 26 out of 60 questions evaded). In fact, Centeno tends to answer questions in very general terms, without going into any details about the specific questions raised by MEPs. He is also inclined to defend Eurogroup positions through examples with Portugal – and how things worked domestically – although his country was not part of the questions raised by MEPs.[74]

Overall, the answerability of Eurogroup Presidents varies depending on the personality and experience of the incumbent, but there is a broader trend observable across time. In general, Eurogroup Presidents defend the conduct of their institution or openly disagree with the points of MEPs almost three times more often than they provide the answer requested or agree to parliamentary demands. This is not surprising in itself: after all, the job of Eurogroup Presidents is to represent – and by implication protect – the interests of the executive body that they are chairing. This trend,

[70] European Parliament, op. cit, *supra* note 60.

[71] European Parliament, op. cit, *supra* note 59.

[72] European Parliament, op. cit, *supra* note 62.

[73] Ibid.

[74] European Parliament, op. cit, *supra* note 54.

however, is more problematic in the context of the legal framework of the EMU and the Eurogroup in particular. Since the European Parliament cannot impose sanctions on the Eurogroup or force euro area finance ministers to take specific decisions, the type of accountability at play remains limited. The Eurogroup is not responsive to the European Parliament; if anything, the analysis above shows a form of selective transparency and willingness to justify (but not change) decisions already taken. The final section discusses the implications of these findings.

## 7.5 CONCLUSIONS

To sum up, can the European Parliament hold the Eurogroup accountable in substantive terms? The analysis of Economic Dialogues from 2013 to 2019 showed that MEPs are eager to question the extent to which Eurogroup decisions are substantively open and effective, and to a lesser extent whether they are arbitrary or protect the interests of the euro area/the EU as a whole. Among the four accountability goods highlighted at the start of this volume,[75] the openness of the Eurogroup is the leading concern of MEPs in both procedural and substantive terms (decision-making processes and the content of policy decisions). The next major accountability claim is substantive effectiveness, as MEPs are interested in the concrete impact of Eurogroup decisions on the economies and public finances of Member States. Publicness and non-arbitrariness feature less frequently and are equally found in questions focusing on procedural or substantive issues. For their part, Eurogroup Presidents engage with parliamentary questions in the Economic Dialogues, yet their emphasis is on justification of conduct and a limited form of transparency. While parliamentary exchanges can get heated, MEPs cannot make the Eurogroup do anything. Ultimately, the legal consequences of the Economic Dialogues are vague. As Fasone put it, 'it is not clear what happens if an Economic Dialogue fails'.[76]

There are crucial implications to this lack of connection between the substantive interest of MEPs in the activities of the Eurogroup and their ability to influence decisions of euro area finance ministers. Unlike in the accountability relationship with the ECB, which tends to focus on procedural issues,[77]

75 Akbik and Dawson, op. cit. *supra* note 15.

76 Fasone, op cit, *supra* note 7, at 175.

77 Dawson and Maricut-Akbik, 'Procedural vs Substantive Accountability in EMU Governance: Between Payoffs and Trade-offs', 28 *Journal of European Public Policy* (2021), 1707–1726; Dawson, Maricut-Akbik, and Bobić, 'Reconciling Independence and Accountability at the European Central Bank: The False Promise of Proceduralism', 25 *European Law Journal* (2019), 75–93; Maricut-Akbik, op. cit, *supra* note 43.

the European Parliament makes substantive accountability claims towards the Eurogroup in the Economic Dialogues. Especially in crisis situations, MEPs are likely to solicit additional information and demand public justification from the Eurogroup. Nevertheless, the Parliament cannot impose sanctions on the Eurogroup or force finance ministers to adopt a different course of action[78] than the one already announced. Even if MEPs were to follow up on Economic Dialogues with specific parliamentary resolutions listing demands for change, the Eurogroup could simply ignore them. In the end, the most successful Economic Dialogue can only put pressure on the Eurogroup President to defend the conduct of the intergovernmental body and give an economic reasoning for decisions taken. Overall, the Economic Dialogues with the Eurogroup illustrate a unilateral accountability relationship in which substantive demands from the forum remain unmet by the actor.

[78] Bovens, 'Analysing and Assessing Accountability: A Conceptual Framework', 13 *European Law Journal* (2007), 447–468, at 450.

# 8

# Parliamentary Accountability of the Country-Specific Recommendations

## *Effectiveness and Substance*

*Tomasz P. Wozniakowski*

## 8.1 INTRODUCTION

This chapter sheds light on the role of non-euro area national parliaments (NPs) in holding their governments to account in the EU's economic governance, making a contribution to the literature on the role of NPs in economic coordination.[1] The parliamentary accountability embedded in the EU context has been subject of scholarly attention for many years,[2] but the main emphasis was often on the EU as a whole, rather than economic coordination, and included mainly the euro-area member states.[3] Moreover, the

[1] Cooper, Maatsch, and Smith (eds.), 'Analysing the Role of Parliaments in European Economic Governance', 70:4, *Special Section of Parliamentary Affairs* (2017); Crum, 'Parliamentary Accountability in Multilevel Governance: What Role for Parliaments in Post-Crisis EU Economic Governance?' *Journal of European Public Policy* (2018), 268–286; Pernice, 'Financial Crisis, National Parliaments, and the Reform of the Economic and Monetary Union' in Jancic (ed.), *National Parliaments After the Lisbon Treaty and the Euro Crisis Resilience or Resignation?* (Oxford University Press 2017), pp. 115–140.

[2] Maurer and Wessels (eds.), *National Parliaments on Their Ways to Europe: Losers or Latecomers?* (Nomos 2001); Hefftler, Neuhold, Rozenberg, and Smith (eds.), *The Palgrave Handbook of National Parliaments and the European Union* (Palgrave Macmillan 2015); Miklin, Maatsch, and Woźniakowski (eds.), 'Special Issue: Rising to a Challenge? Ten Years of Parliamentary Accountability of the European Semester', 9 *Politics and Governance* 3 (2021).

[3] Auel, 'Democratic Accountability and National Parliaments: Redefining the Impact of Parliamentary Scrutiny in EU Affairs', 13 *European Law Journal* 4 (2007), 487–504; Bergman and Damgaard (eds.), Delegation and Accountability in European Integration: The Nordic Parliamentary Democracies and the European Union [Special Issue], 6 *Journal of Legislative Studies* 1 (2000); Jancic, National parliaments and European constitutionalism: Accountability beyond borders [Doctoral thesis, Utrecht University]. Utrecht University Repository. http://dspace.library.uu.nl/handle/1874/211177; MacCarthaigh, 'Accountability Through National Parliaments: Practice and problems' in O'Brennan and Raunio (eds.), *National Parliaments Within the Enlarged European Union: From 'Victims' of Integration to Competitive Actors?*

analysis focusing on the engagement of the NPs in EU economic governance of the non-euro member states is limited to mainly Western countries,[4] and Eastern members of the EU are largely excluded from the analysis. For instance, the available empirical research regarding parliamentary accountability of economic governance in Poland, the biggest country in the CEE region and the fifth-largest EU member state by population, (after Germany, France, Italy and Spain) is rather scarce.[5] However, most recently Schweiger[6] analysed parliamentary scrutiny of the European Semester in Poland as a case study, but he focused on the hearings devoted to the Convergence and National Reform Programmes and not on those devoted solely to the Country Specific Recommendations (CSRs) issued for Poland. Additionally, his analysis did not analyse the impact of accountability on the effectiveness of the whole process. In contrast, this chapter qualitatively analyses the parliamentary hearings concerning the EU's economic recommendations – the CSRs, as well as their policy effects regarding the implementation rate of those recommendations. It uses an explicit definition of parliamentary accountability, as described in the analytical framework, which will be guiding the empirical analysis.

How can the government be held accountable by a Polish NP in the area of economic governance? In order to answer this research question, the relevant debates in the NP are explored, which allow for the discovery of patterns along the chain of accountability. To this end, the parliamentary discussions in the context of specific area of economic governance are examined in depth – the European Semester, which is an annual cycle of economic and fiscal coordination of EU member states, focusing on its important part – the CSRs. Are the CSRs salient enough for the NP to invest its time and political capital in

(Routledge 2007), pp. 29–45; Raunio, 'The Parliament of Finland: A Model Case for Effective Scrutiny?' in Maurer and Wessels (eds.), *National Parliaments on Their Ways to Europe: Losers or Latecomers?* (Nomos 2001), pp. 173–198.

4 For example, Buskjaer Rasmussen, 'Accountability Challenges in EU Economic Governance? Parliamentary Scrutiny of the European Semester', 40 *Journal of European Integration* 3 (2018), 341–357.

5 Serowaniec, *Parlamentarne Komisje do Spraw Europejskich [Parliamentary European Union Affairs Committees]*, Wydawnictwo Sejmowe 2016, 195–199, 263–264; Woźniakowski, 'Accountability in EU Economic Governance: European Commissioners in Polish Parliament' in Miklin, Maatsch, and Woźniakowski (eds.), '*Special Issue: Rising to a Challenge? Ten Years of Parliamentary Accountability of the European Semester*', 9 Politics and Governance 3 (2021), 155–162.

6 Schweiger, 'Parliamentary Scrutiny of the European Semester: The Case of Poland' in Miklin, Maatsch, and Woźniakowski (eds.), '*Special Issue: Rising to a Challenge? Ten Years of Parliamentary Accountability of the European Semester*', 9 Politics and Governance 3 (2021), 124–134.

discussing these guidelines? What exactly is scrutinized? The second objective is to investigate the link between accountability and 'effectiveness' of the EU's economic coordination, as one of the normative goods which accountability could bring, as identified by Dawson and Maricut-Akbik in the Introduction to this Volume: 'Here, the premise is that the need to justify and even correct conduct will likely improve, and encourage reflection upon, the design of policy-making or implementation.'[7] The authors of the Introduction do not claim that there is a direct causality line between a forum's accountability claims and the behaviour of actors, as they focus more on types of claims that accountability forums can make vis-a-vis executive actors. Nevertheless, I will try to analyse if such a link can be established, even if it may not be a causal link, as the implementation of CSRs depends on many other domestic factors, the analysis of which would go beyond the scope of the chapter. Hence, in this chapter, effectiveness is understood through the prism of the implementation of CSRs at the national level, seen as one of key goals of the Semester. Indeed, in the case of the economic coordination, it was argued that 'greater parliamentary accountability should eventually contribute to the collective ownership of the European Semester'.[8] This idea is also present among policy-makers. For instance, the European Parliament in 2018 stated that it 'believes that more national ownership through genuine public debates at national level would lead to better implementation of the CSRs'.[9] By conducting an in-depth case study and comparing the specific policy issues that were debated with the CSRs and their implementation rate, I aim to contribute to this debate.

## 8.2 ANALYTICAL FRAMEWORK

The positions of Members of Parliament (MPs) towards CSRs and connected arguments expressed in parliamentary discussions will be explained by applying an analytical framework of justification and contestation as two basic forms of accountability as developed by Wozniakowski, Maatsch and Miklin[10]

7 Dawson and Maricut-Akbik, 'From Procedural to Substantive Accountability in EMU Governance', introduction to this volume.

8 Crum, 'Parliamentary Accountability in Multi-Level Governance: What Role for Parliaments in Post-crisis EU Economic Governance?' 25 *Journal of European Public Policy* 2 (2018), p. 283.

9 Hagelstam, Lehofer, and Ciucci, *The Role of National Parliaments in the European Semester for Economic Policy Coordination: In-depth Analysis*. (European Parliament 2018). www.europarl.europa.eu/RegData/etudes/IDAN/2018/614494/IPOL_IDA(2018)614494_EN.pdf, p.2.

10 Woźniakowski, Maatsch, and Miklin, 'Rising to a Challenge? Ten years of Parliamentary Accountability of the European Semester', 9 *Politics & Governance* 3 (2021), 96–99.

who drew from the concept of monitoring and political scrutiny developed by Auel[11] and consequently distinguished:

1. Justification, or the lighter form of accountability, including questions demanding information and explanation;
2. Contestation, or the heavier form of accountability, including statements of disagreement, requests for change, and sanctions.

Therefore, it investigates substantive accountability mechanisms, putting special emphasis on whether the interactions take lighter or heavier form of accountability, depending on the type of question asked.[12] Additionally, accountability will be defined 'through the distinction between procedural and substantive means of rendering the normative goods of accountability',[13] with a special emphasis on effectiveness. Therefore, my expectation is that if the CSR is scrutinized in parliament, then it is more likely that it will be implemented. While this chapter will focus on effectiveness as one of the four accountability goods as identified by Dawson and Maricut-Akbik in the Introduction to this edited volume, I will also try to explore the finding of the editors who concluded that procedural, rather than substantive, accountability dominates in EMU accountability.

## 8.3 PARLIAMENTARY SCRUTINY OF CSRS IN POLAND

Poland is a non-euro-zone country and its parliament, whose two chambers are the Sejm and the Senat, has medium-range budgetary powers, but the Sejm holds regular hearings within the Semester framework. What are the arguments used in those discussions? To this end, the deliberations of meetings of the Committees on the EU Affairs, Public Finance, and Economy and Development, which jointly discuss the European Semester are examined. In particular, I will focus on how the issues pointed in the CSRs played out during the hearings.

The hearings explored in this chapter cover the years between 2015 and 2019. This time frame covers both the Euro-enthusiastic centre-right PO-PSL governing coalition, which ended in 2015, and Euro-sceptic right-wing PiS government, which was created in late 2015 after winning the

[11] Auel, 'Democratic Accountability and National Parliaments: Redefining the Impact of Parliamentary Scrutiny in EU Affairs', 13 *European Law Journal* 4 (2007), 487–504.

[12] For a similar conceptualization, see Maricut-Akbik, 'Contesting the European Central Bank in Banking Supervision: Accountability in Practice at the European Parliament', 58 *JCMS* 5 (2020), 1199–1214.

[13] Dawson and Maricut-Akbik, introduction this volume, p. 22.

parliamentary elections. The regular hearings in parliament with the ministers started in 2015. Before that, the CSRs were discussed, but the hearings were organized with either the European Commissioners alone, such as Valdis Dombrovskis, or with both ministers and the Commissioners, such as Janusz Lewandowski – for this reason, it was difficult to distinguish who exactly is held to account by the MPs during the pre-2015 hearings. The hearings were held in the summer (June or July) and were attended by the deputy ministers, usually from two ministries responsible for finance and economic development. Table A.8.1 in the Appendix presents the CSRs issued for Poland between 2015 and 2019, which were subject of those hearings. Table A.8.2 in the Appendix summarizes the thirty-two questions related to CSRs which were asked during the five analysed hearings, which are divided both thematically and based on two types of accountability mechanisms: justification/contestation, followed by their detailed analysis in the following section, subdivided between three main CSRs.

### 8.3.1 *Questions Related to the 'Fiscal' CSR 1*

#### 8.3.1.1 Fiscal Council

The recommendation to establish an independent fiscal council appeared in both 2015 and 2016, as Poland remains the only EU country which did not formally introduce such a body. Both PO-PSL and PiS governments failed to implement this recommendation, and the reasoning was similar – Poland already has a set of institutions which do monitor the budget, especially the Supreme Audit Office (or NIK). Two questions about fiscal councils were asked during the 2016 hearing: by Joanna Mucha (Civic Platform – PO), who wanted to make sure that the government clearly says 'no' to this recommendation and by Marcin Święcicki (PO), who was contesting the minister's statement that Poland already has institutions which are functionally similar to the fiscal council:

> Well, I do not quite agree with the fact that the bodies that already exist, like for example, the Supreme Audit Office or the Social Dialogue Council are sufficient substitutes of the fiscal council.... I believe that it was a bad position [i.e. not to create a council in the past] and that such a council may be of helpful for the Ministry of Finance. The ministry is under pressure from a variety of other ministries, various political goals et cetera and the fiscal council, which would look at the long-term consequences, long-term balance, can only strengthen the position of the ministry and be an additional, I would say, argument or an additional source of information on this matter, guarding the long-term fiscal balance. So, I would suggest that you rethink

> the recommendation concerning the fiscal council, as it would make sense and would be of added value, because, as I say, the current institutions do not provide this long-term role expert assessment.[14]

In her answer Hanna Majszczyk, a deputy minister (undersecretary of state) in the Ministry of Finance (MF), confirmed the reluctance of the government to introduce such an institution and replied that the differences with the European Commission are mainly semantic, as the Commission recognizes the fact that the various functions which fiscal council hold should have been conducted by a number of independent institutions. The pressure is to create one intuition, but the government is in a dialogue with the Commission about that and remains optimistic about the prospects of diminishing this pressure.

This recommendation disappeared in 2017 from the list of CSRs, even if it was never implemented. Nevertheless, Święcicki raised this issue again two years later. After providing similar arguments, that is, that the fiscal council could be a source of valuable long-term assessment of various policies, for instance, regarding the retirement age, he asked if the government plans to come back to this topic. This time it was Piotr Nowak, deputy minister of MF, who responded by emphasizing that the Commission stopped recommending the creation of a fiscal council, after it understood that those functions are performed by different institutions, such as Monetary Policy Council and Supreme Audit Office. Hence, in this case, there is no link between the level of scrutiny and implementation.

#### 8.3.1.2 Deficit

Deficit (and related topics, such as benchmark rule) was by far the topic that was most often raised during the hearings as there were nine questions about it in total. For instance, in 2016 Joanna Mucha (PO) from the opposition asked if the government intends to implement CSR1, which recommends reduction of structural deficit by 0.5 per cent, because in the update of the convergence program, there is no such information. MF representative, Hanna Majszczyk, replied extensively and emphasized the fact that Poland aims to reduce this deficit in 2018. She also highlighted the fact that nominal deficit is the most important factor and, in this regard, Poland is implementing the recommendations. A year later, in 2017, Janusz Cichoń (PO), clearly contested the government fiscal policy by highlighting the fact that in both 2016 and 2017, the government failed to implement recommendations regarding MTO and

[14] *Full record of the course of the meeting European Union Affairs Committee* (No.60), *Public Finance Committee* (No. 63), *Economic Committee* (No. 33), Sejm 2016, pp. 6–7.

structural deficit and asked how the government plans to react to those recommendations in the next budgetary year of 2018. In the same round of questions, his demand was repeated by Święcicki (PO). The government representative did not react to those questions, perhaps due to the fact that in 2017 it was represented solely by a deputy minister from the Ministry of Development as this time a minister from MF did not take part in the hearing.

In the following year of 2018, there were four questions concerning the deficit, all of them asked by two opposition MPs: Święcicki (PO) and Henning-Kloska (N or Modern party). Święcicki asked two explanation-demanding questions in this regard: he wondered if the government plans to correct the planned deficit level and if the expenditure benchmark of 4.2 per cent will be met. A similar question, but much more elaborated (with examples of other countries and statistics illustrating the points being made), was asked by Hennig-Kloska, who worried that the slower economic growth than expected may even lead to an increase of the planned deficit. The response was provided by both a Deputy Minister in MF Piotr Nowak, and then via a much more technical response by a Deputy Director of the Department of Macroeconomic Policy Joanna Bęza-Bojanowska. While the latter focused on the detailed description of MTO and Polish efforts aiming at achieving the expenditure benchmark of 4.2 per cent and reducing the structural deficit by 0.5 per cent of GDP, the latter emphasized the differences between nominal deficit and the deficit and in relation to GDP and asked to focus the discussions on the deficit-to-GDP ratio, as it has fallen last year. Henning-Kloska was not satisfied with this answer and challenged the minister by stating that the fall of the deficit-to-GDP ratio was due to the growth of GDP and strengthening of the Polish zloty at the end of the year. She also reminded him that the debt of public healthcare and pension institutions such as ZUS is not included in the deficit calculations. In his second reply, Nowak agreed that the exchange rates had an impact on public debt, but only in nominal terms, and focused on its relation to the GDP.

In 2019 two questions concerned the deficit. Firstly, Janusz Cichoń (PO), after criticizing the current fiscal policy, asked if the government will implement CSR1 regarding the expenditure benchmark. In his response, Deputy Minister Marcin Ociepa stressed that Poland keeps receiving the same types of CSRs since 2011 and if the opposition criticises the government now it should do the same for the previous governments. The difference is that now Poland does not have a recommendation regarding VAT compliance. Secondly, Izabela Leszczyna (PO) asked about a discrepancy between the Convergence Programme and Multiannual State Financial Plan and the bills that the government sent to the parliament, especially on the reduction of PIT rate from 18 to 17 per cent and to 0 per cent for young people. It was the

Director of Department in MF Sławomir Dudek who admitted that there are differences between those documents, but this was because the budgetary cost of the tax proposals changed in the actual budget as for the first time these proposals could be assessed together.

#### 8.3.1.3 Reduced VAT Rates

In a 2016 hearing, Paweł Lisiecki (PiS) asked how the European Commission justified its recommendation to eliminate reduced VAT rates as in his opinion the higher the taxes the higher the tax avoidance. Deputy Minister in MF, Hanna Majszczyk, provided a detailed answer where she explained the positions of both the Commission and the government:

> The arguments regarded indeed the revenue side. It [the European Commission] noted that Poland continues to apply reduced VAT rates to many goods and services. This practice, according to the Commission, contributes to the loss of income and reduces the effectiveness of the VAT system (…). As I said before, in our exchange of views with the European Commission we insisted that we do not see this loss of income on the side of reduced rates of VAT, but on the fraud side. We focus our activities here in order to rebuild the tax base and eliminate abuses. In addition, we emphasize (…) the fact that many countries use reduced rates and, as a rule, the rates applied are in line with the EU directives. Thus, those tax solutions do not violate European law[15]

In the following year, in 2017, Krystyna Skowrońska (PO) asked what the government wrote in its reply to the Commission about this recommendation on reduced VAT rates. However, Adam Hamryszczak, MF's Deputy Minister only stressed that the Commission for the first time appreciated Polish efforts in fighting VAT compliance and did not refer to the reduced rates specifically. In both 2016 and 2017, the implementation of this CSR was assessed as 'no progress' (Table A.8.2).

### 8.3.2 *Questions Related to the 'Social' CSR 2*

#### 8.3.2.1 Increase of the Effective Retirement Age

In 2018 two MPs asked about the recommendation to increase the effective retirement age. Święcicki (PO) was wondering about the government's assessment of the various measures which could go in the opposite direction

[15] *Full record of the course of the meeting European Union Affairs Committee* (No. 60), *Public Finance Committee* (No. 63), *Economic Committee* (No. 33), Sejm 2016, p. 5.

to the one which is recommended. An MP from PiS, Kazimierz Smoliński, worried that Poland will be outvoted on this issue as a consequence of the reversed qualified majority voting and asked if Poland will need to implement this CSR in such a scenario. Marcin Ociepa, a Deputy Minister, started his answer with a general remark that CSRs are only recommendations which are supposed to help economic growth and some of them relate more to a sphere of politics rather than policy, and he would rather focus on the latter sphere:

> The essence of the process known as the European Semester is to help by supporting member states in achieving economic growth, and consequently for the EU as a whole to achieve economic growth, [there are] not the rigid orders from some external authority which we must obey. The philosophy of this instrument is completely different. Because in the end you have to answer the question of who creates and is responsible [accountable] for the economic policy of the state. Well it is a government of that country. So we take these recommendations as a good, kind advice, we often discuss them, argue, and agree with most of them, because they are rational directions, but elsewhere – well, here comes another distinction which should be mentioned. That is, we are dealing with elements that we would call policy versus politics. So the distinction between public politicians and a certain politics sensu stricto. What does it mean? Social policies or public policies can go one way or the other, and we can talk about some effectiveness, but there are such issues – and they appear here and there in the European Semester – which are, I would say, a political dispute that is also going on in Poland. Because the issue of 500+, the issue of approach to KRUS, the issue of lowering or increasing the retirement age, these are also political issues in Poland. So, I think that it should also be borne in mind. It is not my job to address the political element of this process or dispute, for example the question of the retirement age.[16]

But then he focused on the word 'effective' in the CSR concerning retirement age and that Poland agrees with this recommendation and tries to encourage people to work longer and thus to increase an *effective* retirement age and not the statutory retirement age, which was a CSR for some other countries, as he noted.

In the next year, 2019, this issue came up again, as Izabela Leszczyna (PO) asked what the government plans to do in order to increase the age when people over sixty or sixty-five retire and so they do not have to support themselves with pensions on which they could 'starve'. Minister Ociepa failed to

[16] *Full record of the course of the meeting European Union Affairs Committee* (No. 213), *Public Finance Committee* (No. 331), *Economic Committee* (No. 115), Sejm 2018, pp. 11–12.

answer this question, but in the next round of questions Święcicki pushed him on this topic. This time, Ociepa replied and provided some data supporting his claim:

> Let me start with an answer for Mr Święcicki regarding professional activity of elderly people. It is not true that this activity has started to decline. I quote the data: in 2017, because I understand that from that moment on, the MP said that from 2017 so we can possibly talk about a slowdown in growth, while 2017 that's 50.1%, 2018 that's 50.3%. Quarterly, Q1 2017 – 49.1%, first quarter of this year 2019 – 50%. So there's growth everywhere, even in 2019. We will be happy to share this data, with the Economic Analysis Department, this data clearly shows that we have an increase in activity all the time and we have to do everything to keep this growth at a high level.[17]

In both 2018 and 2019, the implementation of this CSR was assessed as 'no progress' (Table A.8.2).

#### 8.3.2.2 Reform of the Preferential Pension Arrangements

A CSR which advised to reform preferential pension schemes, especially a scheme for farmers ('KRUS' as it is called from its Polish abbreviation from Kasa Rolniczego Ubezpieczenia Społecznego or Agricultural Social Insurance Fund) was quite contested in the Sejm. For instance, in a 2015 hearing, MP Stanislaw Kalemba from a coalition partner PSL asked if in other countries similar pension schemes for farmers exists and if similar recommendations to reduce them were issued for those countries. Artur Radziwiłł, a Deputy Minister in the MF, replied that even though farmers were not mentioned specifically, for France and Germany the Commission recommended to take steps aiming to encourage people to retire later in life (Germany) and to balance the pension system, especially those schemes which are outside of the universal system (France).

In 2018, Święcicki asked if the government will have the courage to change the farmers' pension scheme (KRUS), which turn young farmers into 'economic invalids':

> Another thing that keeps coming back here is the issue of the unfortunate KRUS. Well, ladies and gentlemen, we are in such a paradoxical situation. At the moment, many young people farmers have higher education, know the languages, they are well prepared. We let them into KRUS, into a system

[17] *Full record of the course of the meeting European Union Affairs Committee* (No. 276), *Public Finance Committee* (No. 477), *Economic Committee* (No. 167), Sejm 2019, p. 18.

> in which they become economic invalids. (…) However, new farmers, those who enter agriculture, these educated, fully capable people don't need to be admitted for a lifetime, for several dozen years, like some economic invalids, who are unable to either retire or pay taxes, like all the rest of the adult population must do. It is even more proper as the agriculture remains one quite solidly subsidized sector (…).[18]

A Deputy Minister of Entrepreneurship and Technology, Marcin Ociepa, gave an extensive answer and focused on the fact that the number of farmers covered by KRUS dropped by 4.8 per cent in 2017 compared to 2016. He stressed that this is an example of philosophy of the government as it tries to create a system which would encourage people to do a certain thing, rather than to force them to do it by hard law means, which would be controversial. In both 2015 and 2018, the implementation of this CSR was assessed as 'no progress' (Table A.8.2).

#### 8.3.2.3 Participation in the Labour Market

A CSR advising Poland to increase labour market participation appeared consistently from 2016 to 2019. For instance, in 2017 it was quite detailed: 'Take steps to increase labour market participation, in particular for women, low-qualified and older people, including by fostering adequate skills and removing obstacles to more permanent types of employment' (see Table A.8.2). Two questions related to participation in the labour market CSR were asked – in 2017 and 2019. In 2017 Henning-Kloska worried that the current social policy leads to the exclusion of women from the labour market and asked about the plans to change it:

> Indicator the activity of women aged 35–44 during the year decreased by more than 1%. It is a lot, considering that we are directly in the period in which our unemployment is falling. So an increasing part of the working-age society should be professionally active, and here in the case of women aged 35–44, during the crucial time for the development of professional life for these women, this indicator goes completely the other way. And my question is: what ideas will you have for women excluded from the labour market to return to this labour market at the age of 45, when they will very often be without experience or will remain for ten years or more outside the labour market.[19]

[18] *Full record of the course of the meeting European Union Affairs Committee* (No. 213), *Public Finance Committee* (No. 331), *Economic Committee* (No.115), Sejm 2018, p. 17.

[19] *Full record of the course of the meeting European Union Affairs Committee* (No. 136), *Public Finance Committee* (No. 212), *Economic Committee* (No. 76), Sejm 2017, p. 18.

Deputy Minister Hamryszczak replied that the group of women who quit their job because of the program Family+ (500PLN child benefit introduced by PiS) is not substantial. He cited the data from 2016 to support his claim. In 2019 Święcicki asked about planned policies regarding the participation in the labour market of older adults and disabled people. Deputy Minister Ociepa replied by citing data which showed that there is a positive trend when it comes to both older adults and disabled people:

> With regard to the professional activity of, for example, people with disabilities, in 2015 – 25%, 2018 – 28%. As for activity of older people, i.e. aged 55–64: in 2015 – 46.9%, in 2018 – already: 50.3%. In all the indicators we have an increase, we are improving the state of affairs. This is what the European Commission appreciates, but we have no regrets as professionals that what is expected of us is to do even more, even better, because we ourselves expect to do even better. But please don't say that the Polish government is failing when it comes to economic policy, because in all of these areas we have growth, we have progress and we are successful.[20]

In both 2017 and 2019, the implementation of this CSR was assessed as 'limited progress' (Table A.8.2).

### 8.3.3 *Questions Related to the 'Business' CSR 3/4*

#### 8.3.3.1 Barriers in Railway Investments

One opposition MP Maria Zuba (PiS) in 2015 asked about CSR4 on the barriers in railway investments and what the government plans to do in order to improve the quality of railways and the use of EU funds. Deputy Minister of Economy, Grażyna Henclewska, gave a detailed answer, citing the legislative bills introduced in order to improve the situation and the amount of funding which will be used for railways from the EU programs. Limited progress was made in this policy area (Table A.8.2).

#### 8.3.3.2 Public Healthcare

In 2019 three questions on public healthcare were asked. Henning-Kloska focused on the state of public healthcare. She asked if the government will be able to increase funding on healthcare in the next two or three years. After her question was ignored by Minister Ociepa in the first round, she asked it

[20] *Full record of the course of the meeting European Union Affairs Committee* (No. 276), *Public Finance Committee* (No. 477), *Economic Committee* (No. 167), Sejm 2019, pp. 11–12.

again and insisted on getting an answer. In the same round, Izabela Leszczyna asked when the target of 6 per cent of GDP will be reached – in 2024 or 2050 as indicated in the document submitted by the government. Ociepa this time replied but provided rather generic answer. He cited PM Morawiecki who said that reforming the public healthcare system is the number one priority and that improvements are being made, even if we are still below the EU average. Limited progress was made in this policy area (Table A.8.2).

## 8.4 DISCUSSION AND CONCLUSIONS

On the accountability dimension, it is undoubtedly positive that the hearings on CSRs take place regularly and there is a lively debate where both majority and opposition MPs ask questions and (usually) the representatives from the two ministries responsible for finance and development attend and must provide answers. Most questions fall within the justification category (22 out of 37), in which the demands for explanation or information were made. Certainly, the accountability exercised is substantial and not purely procedural. However, there are certain areas which could be improved. Firstly, the type of interaction – MPs could ask a direct question, rather than simply criticizing the government. This would allow them to push the ministers in case their questions would not be answered. By not asking a clear question, they allow a minister to simply ignore their comments. It seems that more effort should be made towards making explicit demands and possible follow-ups, if the answer is not given. This is what MP Henning-Kloska did in 2019, when she complained that the minister ignored her question on the healthcare expenditures and demanded an answer. Secondly, the relevant ministers themselves should appear in front of the committees, rather than their deputies and high-level civil servants (i.e. at the level of directors of departments, which sometimes replied to more detailed questions). This would allow having a discussion on politics also and not only policies, as some CSR required a change in the former, as in the case of the pension systems. Thirdly, more MPs from the three committees could be active, as only a handful of MPs were actively engaged in the hearings, like Święcicki, Henning-Kloska or Leszczyna. Precisely, only nine MPs asked at least one question during these CSR-focused hearings in 2015–2019, which equals to one-fifth of the European Affairs Committee (42–43 members), not to mention the members of the other two sectoral committees.

On the efficiency dimension, one can hardly see any link at all as the scrutiny of the CSRs has a limited impact on their implementation. One of the objectives of this chapter was to analyse if the level of scrutiny corresponded in any way with the level of implementation. In this case, it was quite limited in delivering a normative good of efficiency understood as the level of implementation of CSRs. Most CSRs were assessed in the Country Reports as 'no progress', as only in the CSRs on the participation in the labour market, public health and barriers in railway investments one could observe a 'limited progress' assessment. Nevertheless, the Commission was determined in issuing very similar CSRs year after year (only occasionally it gave up, like with the case of a fiscal council, despite a complete lack of progress). This finding suggests that accountability may not necessarily bring about effectiveness understood as the implementation of CSRs.

# APPENDIX

TABLE A.8.1 *Commission's CSRs for Poland 2015–2019*

| Article I. CSRs | 2015 | 2016 | 2017 | 2018 | 2019 |
|---|---|---|---|---|---|
| 1 | Following the correction of the excessive deficit, achieve a fiscal adjustment of 0.5% of GDP towards the medium-term objective both in 2015 and 2016. Establish an independent fiscal council. Limit the use of reduced VAT rates. | Achieve an annual fiscal adjustment of 0.5% of GDP towards the medium-term budgetary objective in 2016 and in 2017. Strengthen the fiscal framework, including by establishing an independent fiscal council. Improve tax collection by ensuring better VAT compliance, and limit the extensive use of reduced VAT rates. | Pursue its fiscal policy in line with the requirements of the preventive arm of the Stability and Growth Pact, which translates into a substantial fiscal effort for 2018. When taking policy action, consideration should be given to achieving a fiscal stance that contributes to both strengthening the ongoing recovery and ensuring the sustainability of Poland's public finances. Take steps to improve the efficiency of public spending and limit the use of reduced VAT rates. | Ensure that the nominal growth rate of net primary government expenditure does not exceed 4.2% in 2019, corresponding to an annual structural adjustment of 0.6% of GDP. Take steps to improve the efficiency of public spending, including by improving the budgetary process. | Ensure that the nominal growth rate of net primary government expenditure does not exceed 4.4% in 2020, corresponding to an annual structural adjustment of 0.6% of GDP. Take further steps to improve the efficiency of public spending, including by improving the budgetary process. |

(*continued*)

TABLE A.8.1 (*continued*)

| Article I. CSRs | 2015 | 2016 | 2017 | 2018 | 2019 |
|---|---|---|---|---|---|
| 2 | Start the process of aligning the pension arrangements for farmers and miners with those of other workers, and adopt a timetable for progressive full alignment; put in place a system for assessing and recording farmers' incomes. | Ensure the sustainability and adequacy of the pension system and increase participation in the labour market, by starting to reform the preferential pension arrangements, removing obstacles to more permanent types of employment and improving the labour market relevance of education and training. | Take steps to increase labour market participation, in particular for women, low-qualified and older people, including by fostering adequate skills and removing obstacles to more permanent types of employment. Ensure the sustainability and adequacy of the pension system by taking measures to increase the effective retirement age and by starting to reform the preferential pension arrangements. | Take steps to increase labour market participation, including by improving access to childcare and by fostering labour market relevant skills, especially through adult learning, and remove remaining obstacles to more permanent types of employment. Ensure the sustainability and adequacy of the pension system by taking measures to increase the effective retirement age and by reforming the preferential pension schemes. | Ensure the adequacy of future pension benefits and the sustainability of the pension system by taking measures to increase the effective retirement age and by reforming the preferential pension schemes. Take steps to increase labour market participation, including by improving access to childcare and long-term care, and remove remaining obstacles to more permanent types of employment. Foster quality education and skills relevant to the labour market, especially through adult learning. |

| | | | | | |
|---|---|---|---|---|---|
| 3 | Take measures to reduce the excessive use of temporary and civil law contracts in the labour market. | Take measures to remove obstacles to investment in transport, construction, and energy infrastructure, and increase the coverage of spatial planning at local level. | Take measures to remove barriers to investment, particularly in the transport sector. | Strengthen the innovative capacity of the economy, including by supporting closer collaboration between business and research institutions. Improve the regulatory environment, in particular by ensuring effective public and social consultations in the legislative process. | Strengthen the innovative capacity of the economy, including by supporting research institutions and their closer collaboration with business. Focus investment-related economic policy on innovation, transport, notably on its sustainability, digital and energy infrastructure, healthcare and cleaner energy, taking into account regional disparities. Improve the regulatory environment, in particular by strengthening the role of consultations of social partners and public consultations in the legislative process. |
| 4 | Remove obstacles to investment in railway projects. | | | | |

*Note:* This table contains Commission recommendations, issued usually in May, because those recommendations are subject to parliamentary discussions. Commission recommendations have to be approved by the Council, which happens usually in July. Very rarely does the Council change the Commission recommendations.
*Source:* https://ec.europa.eu/. In bold titles of subsections which correspond to the subsections of the CSRs debated in Sejm.

TABLE A.8.2 *Questions asked during CSR hearings in Sejm 2015–2019*

| Question | 2015 | 2016 | 2017 | 2018 | 2019 |
|---|---|---|---|---|---|
| Total | 2 (0)* | 4 (1)* | 7 (2)* | 12 (5)* | 12 (7)* |
| Fiscal council (CSR1) | | 2 (1) (no progress) | | 1 | |
| Deficit (CSR1) | | 1 | 2 (1)* | 4 (2)* | 1 (1)* |
| Reduced VAT rates (CSR1) | | 1 (no progress) | 1 (no progress) | | |
| Preferential pension schemes (CSR2) | 1 (no progress) | | | 1 (no progress) | |
| Retirement age (CSR2) | | | | 2 (no progress) | 2 (1) (no progress) |
| Participation in the labour market (CSR2) | | | 1 (Limited progress)† | | 1 (0) (limited progress)‡ |
| Public health (CSR3) | | | | | 3 (2) (limited progress)§ |
| Barriers in railway investments (CSR4) | 1 (limited progress)¶ | – | – | – | – |
| Varia – not related to CSR | | | 3# | 4 (3)♠ | 5 (3)♥ |

* In brackets number of contestation type of questions. Assessment of the Implementation rate is provided based on Country Report Poland from the following year (Annex A, Overview Table).†† If there was at least limited progress, a justification is provided in the footnotes. The assessment of compliance with the Stability and Growth Pact is not included in the Country Reports and for this reason, the implementation rate of deficit recommendation is not provided.‡‡

† 'Limited progress has been made as regards measures to increase labour market participation. Some policy measures can be expected to increase activity. In particular the creation of nurseries should become easier and the public funding for them was increased. The number of places in kindergartens was also increased. Some barriers to permanent employment may potentially be removed by new labour codes, but the drafts have not yet been published. No government decision has been made on the higher education reform. Simultaneously, the lowered statutory retirement age acts towards limiting labour market participation. Labour market participation of the respective groups increased during the last 3–4 quarters thanks to a strong cyclical position of the economy', CR Poland 2018, p. 37.

‡ 'Limited Progress. Labour market participation increased, although for certain groups it is still below EU average. Access to childcare increased but still constitutes a major challenge for the age group 0–3. Access to long-term care still remains very limited, as this is mainly provided within families. Poland did not undertake major actions removing the remaining obstacles to more permanent types of employment', CR Poland 2020, p. 47.

§ 'Limited Progress. The National Strategy of Regional Development 2030 was adopted in September 2019. It includes investment activities related to the health care system. The Partnership Agreement and the Operational Programmes for 2021–2027 Programming Period are being drafted', CR Poland 2020, p. 50.

¶ 'Poland has made limited progress in addressing CSR 4: In September 2015 the National Rail Programme 2023 was adopted. An amendment to the Railway Act of 15/01/2015 aims to facilitate procedures for investing in railway infrastructure. Regarding the period 2014–2020, accelerating the processes for project preparation has not yet resulted in investments getting off the ground', CR Poland 2016, p. 36.

# Legal risks, economic consequences of government policies; salary freeze for civil servants.

♠ Private investments (2 questions) and VAT compliance (2 questions).

♥ Rule of law (4 questions) and VAT compliance.

†† *Country report Poland*, European Commission 2016; *Country report Poland*, European Commission 2017; *Country report Poland*, European Commission 2018; *Country report Poland*, European Commission 2019; *Country report Poland*, European Commission 2020.

‡‡ 'The following categories are used to assess progress in implementing 2015 [and in the following years] CSRs:

**No progress:** The Member State (MS) has neither announced nor adopted measures to address the CSR. This category also applies if the MS has commissioned a study group to evaluate possible measures.

**Limited progress:** The MS has announced some measures to address the CSR, but these appear insufficient and/or their adoption/implementation is at risk.

**Some progress:** The MS has announced or adopted measures to address the CSR. These are promising, but not all of them have been implemented and it is not certain that all will be. **Substantial progress**: The MS has adopted measures, most of which have been implemented. They go a long way towards addressing the CSR.

**Fully implemented**: The MS has adopted and implemented measures that address the CSR appropriately.' (Country Report Poland 2016, p. 36.)

# PART III

# LEGAL ACCOUNTABILITY

# 9

# Constructive Constitutional Conflict as an Accountability Device in Monetary Policy

*Ana Bobić*

## 9.1 INTRODUCTION

The year is 1974. In Karlsruhe, the Second Senate of the Bundesverfassungsgericht just informed the Court of Justice that the way in which the latter is safeguarding fundamental rights is subpar to the standard of protection provided in the Grundgesetz.[1] *Solange*, the Court of Justice, does not step up its fundamental rights protection game; the Bundesverfassungsgericht will continue to do so despite the possibility of EU law requiring otherwise.[2] Theories and commentaries abounded, so much so that this instance of constitutional conflict is still used as the ideal type guiding our academic thought in the area of judicial interactions in the EU. For example, the doctrines of 'Reverse Solange'[3] and 'Horizontal Solange'[4] are an unavoidable reading for anyone attempting to make sense of judicial interactions in the EU.[5] Substantively, an important consequence of *Solange* is an increase in the level of fundamental

[1] Case 37 BVerfGE 271 *Internationale Handelsgesellschaft (Solange I)*, Judgment of 29 May 1974.

[2] In its response, in Case C-4/73, *Nold*, EU:C:1974:51, para 13, the Court of Justice used the common constitutional traditions of Member States as the source of inspiration and the level of protection of fundamental rights that will be accorded on the Union level. Finally, the Bundesverfassungsgericht accepted such a level of protection in the *Solange II* judgment. Case 73 BVerfGE 339 *Wünsche Handelsgesellschaft (Solange II)* Judgment of 22 October 1986, (1987) 3 CMLR 225.

[3] von Bogdandy and Spieker, 'Countering the Judicial Silencing of Critics: Article 2 TEU Values, Reverse Solange, and the Responsibilities of National Judges', 15 *European Constitutional Law Review* 3 (2019) 391.

[4] Canor, 'My Brother's Keeper? Horizontal Solange: "An Ever Closer Distrust among the Peoples of Europe"', 50 *Common Market Law Review* 2 (2013) 383.

[5] For a summary, see Spieker, 'Breathing Life into the Union's Common Values: On the Judicial Application of Article 2 TEU in the EU Value Crisis', 20 *German Law Journal* 8 (2019) 1182.

rights protection in the EU, incrementally and dynamically developing through contestation between the EU and the national level.[6]

Fast forward to 2020, and the Court of Justice is being reprimanded by the Bundesverfassungsgericht yet again, this time for not properly controlling the European Central Bank (ECB) in respecting the limits of the law of the Economic and Monetary Union (EMU).[7] The ECB acting in excess of what the Treaties allow for is, according to the Bundesverfassungsgericht, not permitted by the Basic Law. This time around, the reaction to the German decision appears to me to suffer from a certain conflict fatigue: the attacks on the rule of law coming from Poland and Hungary are causing a strain in the ability of EU institutions[8] to ensure the respect of the values contained in Article 2 TEU, and the ultra vires finding of the Bundesverfassungsgericht is seen as unnecessarily adding fuel to the flames. This would explain the conceptually flawed, yet overwhelmingly present, conflation of the German and the Polish/Hungarian situations as both representing a rule of law issue that is an existential threat to the EU.[9] Constitutional conflict is thus considered a disruptive factor in the scholarship that regards the EU as a federal or quasi-federal system.[10]

Conversely, the EU's constitutional sphere is comprised of multiple constitutional sites of discourse and authority,[11] where the mutual recognition and respect between these sites is 'the only acceptable ethic of political responsibility for the new Europe'.[12] In consequence, constitutional conflict is not a bug but an important feature contributing to the system's functioning and incremental development.[13] So long as the conflict remains within the possible

[6] Schimmelfennig, 'Competition and Community: Constitutional Courts, Rhetorical Action, and the Institutionalisation of Human Rights in the European Union', 13 *Journal of European Public Policy* 8 (2006) 1247.

[7] Cases 2 BvR 859/15, 2 BvR 980/16, 2 BvR 2006/15, 2 BvR 1651/15, *Weiss II*, Judgment of 5 May 2020, para 116.

[8] Kelemen, 'The European Union's Authoritarian Equilibrium', 27 *Journal of European Public Policy* 3 (2020) 481.

[9] Editorial Comments, 'Not Mastering the Treaties: The German Federal Constitutional Court's PSPP Judgment', 57 *Common Market Law Review* (2020) 965; Mayer, 'To Boldly Go Where No Court Has Gone Before. The German Federal Constitutional Court's Ultra Vires Decision of May 5, 2020', 21 *German Law Journal* (2020) 1116, at 1124.

[10] Editorial Comments, op. cit. *supra* note 9; Kelemen and Pech, 'The Uses and Abuses of Constitutional Pluralism: Undermining the Rule of Law in the Name of Constitutional Identity in Hungary and Poland', 21 *Cambridge Yearbook of European Legal Studies* 1 (2019).

[11] Walker, 'The Idea of Constitutional Pluralism', 65 *Modern Law Review* 3 (2002) 317, at 337.

[12] Ibid. Similarly, Maduro stresses the importance of the discursive element between different sites of constitutional authority, who then jointly and coherently strive to create the shared European legal space. Maduro, 'Contrapunctual Law: Europe's Constitutional Pluralism in Action' in Walker (ed.), *Sovereignty in Transition* (Hart Publishing, 2003), pp. 513–514, 518.

[13] Bobić, 'Constructive versus Destructive Conflict: Taking Stock of the Recent Constitutional Jurisprudence in the EU'. 22 *Cambridge Yearbook of European Legal Studies* (2020) 60.

interpretation of values contained in Article 2 TEU, the conflict is contained within the 'constitutional' but remains 'pluralist'.[14] Ultimately, a heterarchical setup is achieved through the system's in-built auto-correct function, which serves to incrementally accommodate points of conflict through mutual respect and sincere cooperation of all courts involved.[15]

Taking this context as the starting point, my aim is to answer what role does constitutional conflict, as a feature of the EU's constitutional framework, play when it comes to achieving accountability goods presented in the theoretical framework of this book? And in unpacking the goods further, are (and should) they better achieved through procedural or substantive means? I will more specifically refer to three accountability goods. First, the analysis of the jurisprudence of constitutional conflict in the monetary field will show the way in which courts can contribute to non-arbitrariness, by imposing on the decision-makers more stringent standards for justifying their policies. There is of course a procedural as well as a substantive dimension to such judicial demands. As I will show below, a common critique of the Court of Justice is that it remains on the procedural side of ensuring the non-arbitrariness in ECB decision-making. On the other hand, the Bundesverfassungsgericht is also criticised for holding too firm a grasp on the ECB in terms of its substantive demands to demonstrate the ways in which its action is constrained. There is thus a need to take a closer look at the potential of constitutional conflict to act as a discursive mechanism between the EU and national courts in devising a standard of judicial review that ensures the good of non-arbitrariness that goes beyond its procedural facet.

The second accountability good that can be achieved through judicial review characterised by constitutional conflict is effectiveness. How can courts ensure that the decisions of the ECB are in fact correct? Another common critique of judicial review in monetary policy is that the courts necessarily lack the expertise required to in fact substantively ensure that the ECB's decisions are sound. The analysis below will thus aim to show the ways in which effectiveness has featured in judicial review in the monetary field.

Finally, I will also show the ways in which judicial review and the resulting constitutional conflicts flesh out how the ECB can be accountable by delivering the good of publicness. What is particularly interesting in this regard is that publicness might mean different things to different courts, and the role of constitutional conflict is particularly important here to ensure that for

[14] Ibid., at p. 70.

[15] Bobić, 'Constitutional Pluralism Is Not Dead: An Analysis of Interactions between the European Court of Justice and Constitutional Courts of Member States', 18 *German Law Journal* 6 (2017) 1395, at p. 1423.

areas where the EU has competence, the good of publicness contributes to the common interest of the entire Union.

In answering these questions, I will focus on the judgment of the Bundesverfassungsgericht in *Weiss II* through an incremental lens, forming part of a broader conversation on accountability in the EMU between the two courts that began with the earlier *Gauweiler* litigation. After a brief presentation of the broader ECB-related jurisprudence of the two courts in Section 9.2, I will address, first, the question of the role of the principle of proportionality in assessing the legality of ECB action (Section 9.3); and, second, the competition between the Court of Justice and national constitutional courts in competence control (Section 9.4). The final Section (9.5) will offer some conclusions on how these judicial interactions fared in achieving the procedural and/or substantive facets of the three accountability goods, as well as the remaining dangers of the *Weiss II* decision for the European judicial space.

## 9.2 THE MONETARY POLICY LITIGATION

From the perspective of constitutional conflict, the two courts have been discussing the appropriate level of control of the ECB as an idiosyncratically independent institution for some time now,[16] beginning with the Outright Monetary Transactions (OMT) mechanism that was at the centre of the *Gauweiler* litigation. The decision of the German court in *Weiss II* is at present the last instance of this back and forth. Three main threads run through and shape these interactions: the legality of ECB action, ultra vires review, and the role of constitutional identity, culminating in the German rejection of the interpretation provided by the Court of Justice.

In *Gauweiler*, the Bundesverfassungsgericht raised doubts concerning the compatibility of the OMT mechanism with primary EU law. More specifically, for the OMT to be ultra vires, it needed to exceed the monetary policy mandate of the ECB and the prohibition of monetary financing, resulting in an encroachment of Member States' economic policy.[17] The Court of Justice's response confirmed the legality of the OMT programme: it first analysed the powers of the ECB and concluded that indirect effects of monetary policy on economic policy do not make them equivalent, leading to the

[16] See also, Grimm, 'A Long Time Coming', 21 *German Law Journal* (2020) 944.

[17] Case 2 BvR 2728/13 *Gauweiler*, Order of 14 January 2014, paras 36, 39, 63 and 80. It is important to note here that the clear distinction between the two areas of competence is grounded in the Treaty text. However, as will be seen below, precisely this formal division that does not correspond to economic reality is one of the causes for the issues related to ECB's competence and accountability.

conclusion that the ECB was acting within the boundaries of its mandate.[18] The Court of Justice further provided an interpretation setting out some of the conditions necessary for compliance with the Treaties,[19] albeit differently than what the Bundesverfassungsgericht stated in its order for reference.[20] In relation to the judicial relationship between the two courts, the Court of Justice omitted any analysis of the claims to constitutional identity and ultra vires review of the Bundesverfassungsgericht, stating only that the decisions provided by way of the preliminary reference procedure concerning the interpretation and validity of Union acts are binding on the national court.[21] The Bundesverfassungsgericht accepted the findings of the Court of Justice, by setting out the relationship between the principle of primacy and the Basic Law, addressing also the identity and ultra vires review it carries out in relation to EU acts. It concluded that any such review must be done cautiously, with restraint, and in a way that is open to European integration.[22]

It is against this background that the Bundesverfassungsgericht submitted its second preliminary reference concerning the scope of ECB's mandate. This reference revolved around three issues: whether the ECB had complied with its obligation to state reasons in devising the Public Sector Purchase Programme (PSPP), whether said programme falls within the monetary policy mandate of the ECB, and whether it is contrary to the Treaty prohibition of monetary financing. The principle of proportionality was mentioned by the Bundesverfassungsgericht only in relation to the first two issues. After receiving the response from the Court of Justice, the Bundesverfassungsgericht found that the proportionality test as applied by the Court of Justice deprives the said principle of its ability to protect Member State competence.[23] It declared the judgment of the Court of Justice[24] and the PSPP[25] of the ECB ultra vires.

Having rejected the findings of the Court of Justice, the Bundesverfassungsgericht then took it upon itself to interpret the scope of the monetary policy mandate of the ECB. The ECB failed to take into account the economic policy effects of the PSPP and, importantly, balance a number

[18] Case C-62/14, *Gauweiler*, EU:C:2015:400, paras 52, 56, relying on its findings in Case C-370/12, *Pringle*, EU:C:2012:756.

[19] For a more detailed analysis of each of these conditions, see Tridimas and Xanthoulis, 'A Legal Analysis of the Gauweiler Case. Between Monetary Policy and Constitutional Conflict', 23 *Maastricht Journal of European & Comparative Law* 1 (2016) 17, at 23–30.

[20] Ibid., at 30–31.

[21] Case C-62/14 *Gauweiler*, op. cit. *supra* note 18, para 16.

[22] Case 2 BvR 2728/13 *Gauweiler*, Judgment of 21 June 2016, paras 121, 154, 156.

[23] *Weiss II*, op. cit. *supra* note 7, para 123.

[24] Ibid., paras 116, 163.

[25] Ibid., paras 117, 178.

of competing interests against each other.[26] In defining the relevant steps of the proportionality test, the Bundesverfassungsgericht stated that the fourth *stricto sensu* step has been omitted by the Court of Justice,[27] and there was no review of the sufficiency of information provided by the ECB in balancing the relevant interests.[28] The ECB thus failed in its duty to state reasons concerning the proportionality of the PSPP.[29] In relation to the prohibition of monetary financing, the Bundesverfassungsgericht raised some doubts as to the scrutiny applied by the Court of Justice, again related to the duty to state reasons,[30] but ultimately decided that the programme is in line with the Treaty prohibition of monetary financing and does not breach the constitutional identity of Germany.[31]

In consequence, the Bundesverfassungsgericht provided the Bundesbank with a three-month deadline during which it is obliged to work together with the ECB in ensuring the programme meets the principle of proportionality as interpreted by the German court. Otherwise, the Bundesbank will no longer be allowed to participate in the PSPP.[32] Since then, the ECB has decided to comply with the request of the Bundesverfassungsgericht,[33] which the President of the Bundesbank deemed to be in compliance with the demands on the proportionality analysis to be carried out and published by the ECB.[34]

## 9.3 PROPORTIONALITY AND ECB ACCOUNTABILITY

One of the central criticisms directed to the decision in *Weiss II* revolves around whether proportionality is the correct answer when the question is how competences are divided between the EU and the national levels.[35]

26 Ibid., paras 133, 138–145.

27 Here the Bundesverfassungsgericht infamously stated that the decision of the Court of Justice is 'simply not comprehensible'. Ibid., paras 116.

28 Ibid., paras 169, 176.

29 Ibid., para 177.

30 Ibid., para 190.

31 Ibid., paras 228–229.

32 Ibid., para 235.

33 See the letter by ECB President Christine Lagarde to MEP Sven Simon on 29 June 2020, <www.ecb.europa.eu/pub/pdf/other/ecb.mepletter200629_Simon~ece6ead766.en.pdf>, (last visited 16 Aug. 2022); Speech by Yves Mersch, Member of the Executive Board of the ECB, 'In the spirit of European cooperation', 2 July 2020, <www.ecb.europa.eu/press/key/date/2020/html/ecb.sp200702~87ce377373.en.html>, (last visited 16 Aug. 2022).

34 Frankfurter Allgemeine Zeitung, 'Weidmann sieht Forderungen des Verfassungsgerichts als erfüllt an', 3 August 2020, <www.faz.net/aktuell/finanzen/jens-weidmann-verfassungsgerichtsurteil-zur-ezb-erfuellt-16887907.html?GEPC=s3>, (last visited 16 Aug. 2022).

35 Mayer, op. cit. *supra* note 9, at 1119; Editorial Comments, op. cit. *supra* note 9, at 969.

It refers to Bundesverfassungsgericht's use of the principle of proportionality in delineating competences between the EU and the national levels, rather than applying it to the way in which these competences are exercised. This criticism is grounded in the wording of the Treaty, where Article 5(1) TEU clearly separates existence of competence to be guided by the principle of conferral and its exercise by the principle of proportionality. However, as I hope to show by analysing the interpretation of the two courts across *Gauweiler* and *Weiss*, this separation is not as straightforward when it comes to the mandate of the ECB, and the nature of separation between monetary and economic policy. In turn, this has important consequences for the accountability of the ECB as it allows the courts to better limit the arbitrariness of the ECB by connecting more closely the existence and exercise of competence in combination.[36] The conflict concerning the role of the principle of proportionality in holding the ECB to account thus seems to me to lose its pertinence. As I hope to show, it is less important to which stage, formally, it is being applied. What is relevant from the perspective of the good of non-arbitrariness in a substantive sense is that it places demands of justification on the ECB.

It is easy to say that the principle of conferral can be straightforwardly applied to whether something is, for example, an action in the area of competition law under Article 3(1)(b) TFEU, further specified in its content in Articles 101 and 102 TFEU. The European Commission, tasked with implementing competition law, does not have the mandate to define that it is agreements between undertakings that are prohibited by competition law, nor can it include or exclude the abuse of a dominant position from the scope of competition law. How it applies these concepts in the *exercise* of its competence is then subject to the principle of proportionality. However, when it comes to the ECB, Article 119(2) TFEU states that the competence itself includes 'the *definition* and conduct of a single monetary policy' (emphasis added).[37] In other words, the very *existence* of monetary policy is almost impossible to separate from and already forms part of its *exercise*: in order to find out whether the ECB acted *within* its mandate, we need to find out *how* it defined its mandate.[38] That this self-imposed and specific mandate has important consequences for

36 See also the chapter of Joana Mendes in this volume on the existence/exercise distinction.

37 See also Article 127(2) TFEU.

38 See also de Boer and van't Klooster, 'The ECB, the Courts and the Issue of Democratic Legitimacy After Weiss', 57 *Common Market Law Review* 6 (2020), 1689. They argue that the crisis has changed the operation of the ECB in such a way that judicial review has shifted from assessing the limits of its mandate, to reviewing measures with significant choices even within its mandate that might still lack democratic legitimacy.

the accountability of the ECB has been highlighted by the Court of Justice,[39] the Bundesverfassungsgericht,[40] as well as in the literature.[41] In the specific context of the ECB, then, both should in my view be subject to the principle of proportionality as reviewed by courts.

Let us then take a closer look at how the Court of Justice separates the analysis of existence and exercise of monetary policy competence for the ECB. In both *Gauweiler* and *Weiss*, 'delimitation of monetary policy' and 'proportionality' are separate headings, keeping in line with the division of Article 5(1) TEU.[42] However, in substance, a proportionality analysis can be discerned under both headings. In the proportionality section in *Gauweiler*, the Court of Justice defines it as requiring that acts of EU institutions be appropriate for attaining the objectives pursued and not go beyond what is necessary in achieving those objectives.[43] Back to the section on delimiting the monetary policy, the Court of Justice analysed whether the OMT mechanism *contributes to* achieving the objective of singleness of monetary policy and maintaining price stability.[44] Furthermore, the Court went on to assess whether the *means* to achieve the objectives of the OMT are in line with the objectives of monetary policy[45] – finding itself on the thin line separating existence from exercise of monetary policy. Precisely because a measure may have both monetary policy and economic policy effects,[46] and these are difficult to separate,[47] the Court is inevitably engaging in an assessment of whether the decision-maker (the ECB) by enacting its measures (the OMT, the PSPP) exceeded the scope of their mandate (monetary policy).[48] The inability of separating the question of existence versus exercise

[39] Case C-11/00, *Commission v ECB*, EU:C:2003:395, paras 134, 137.

[40] Case 2 BvR 2728/13 *Gauweiler* (Order), op. cit. *supra* note 17, para 187.

[41] Violante, 'Bring Back the Politics: The PSPP Ruling in Its Institutional Context', 21 *German Law Journal* (2020) 1045, at 1053–1056; Dawson, Maricut-Akbik, and Bobić, 'Reconciling Independence and Accountability at the European Central Bank: The False Promise of Proceduralism', 25 *European Law Journal* 1 (2019), 75, at 77–80.

[42] The literature does not seem to dispute this formalist division in the analysis. See, for example, Wendel, 'Paradoxes of Ultra-Vires Review: A Critical Review of the PSPP Decision and Its Initial Reception', 21 *German Law Journal* (2020), 979, at 985.

[43] Case C-62/14 *Gauweiler*, op. cit. *supra* note 18, para 67.

[44] Ibid., paras 48, 49.

[45] Ibid., para 53.

[46] Ibid., paras 51, 52.

[47] Ibid., para 110. See also, Case C-493/17, *Weiss*, EU:C:2018:1000, paras 60, 64.

[48] On balancing as central to the structural approach of the Court of Justice in applying the principle of proportionality when reviewing EU measures, see Harbo, 'The Function of the Proportionality Principle in EU Law', 16 *European Law Journal* 2 (2020), 158, at 177–180; Craig, *EU Administrative Law* (Oxford University Press, 2012), at 656.

is more explicitly apparent in *Weiss*, when the Court of Justice analysed the delimitation of monetary policy:

> It does not appear that the specification of the objective of maintaining price stability as the maintenance of inflation rates at levels below, but close to, 2% over the medium term, which the ESCB chose to adopt in 2003, is *vitiated by a manifest error of assessment and goes beyond* the framework established by the FEU Treaty.[49] (emphasis added)

A manifest error of assessment is a well-established standard for assessing the proportionality of exercise of competence of EU institutions in EU law.[50] Going beyond what is necessary is the explicitly stated third step of the proportionality test.[51] This approach is in fact not different from the way in which the Bundesverfassungsgericht phrased its standard in its Order for reference: 'a manifest and structurally significant exceeding of competences'.[52] The argument here is not that the two tests correspond to each other in their precise content but that both carry a logic of proportionality in assessing the ECB's compliance with its monetary policy mandate. From the perspective of ensuring the accountability of the ECB in a setup where it is empowered to define its own mandate, it thus seems inherently impossible to separate the existence and the exercise stage of competence control. The European System of Central Banks (ESCB), when determining the inflation target – which arguably should act as the outer limit of the monetary policy competence – is in fact already also *exercising* it. Otherwise, would it at all be possible that the Court of Justice says such a determination is in compliance with the TFEU unless a manifest error of assessment is made?[53]

A somewhat positive consequence of applying the principle of proportionality to the existence of competence in monetary policy is an increased standard in competence monitoring that has arguably been at the source of the preliminary references in both *Gauweiler* and *Weiss*. Once applied to the PSPP, proportionality does have the potential of increasing the accountability of the ECB through a more stringent obligation of giving account, even in the stage of defining the inflation target. This arguably has direct influence on the ability of courts to ensure the accountability good of non-arbitrariness. In the area of self-defined mandates, then, a conflation of existence and

49 Case C-493/17 *Weiss*, op. cit. *supra* note 47, para 56.

50 Harbo, op. cit. *supra* note 48, at 177.

51 Craig, op. cit. *supra* note 48, at 656–657.

52 Cases 2 BvR 859/15, 2 BvR 980/16, 2 BvR 2006/15, 2 BvR 1651/15 *Weiss*, Order of 18 July 2017, para 64.

53 Case C-493/17 *Weiss*, op. cit. *supra* note 47, para 56.

exercise of competence seems useful in delivering the non-arbitrariness good of accountability. The very existence of the need for the ECB to take action will thus be subject to scrutiny. By extension, the effectiveness and publicness of such decisions will also be controlled at an earlier stage and on a more in-depth level.

The Court of Justice has been subject to ample critique concerning its light touch proportionality review in both *Gauweiler*[54] and *Weiss*,[55] reducing its review to the duty to state reasons, and accepting any and all reasons provided by the ESCB as sufficient. The proportionality analysis in *Gauweiler* did not properly engage in the assessment of less burdensome alternatives, and was reduced to the Court of Justice analysing and ultimately accepting solely the information provided by the ESCB, thus concluding:

> the ESCB weighed up the various interests in play so as to actually prevent disadvantages from arising, when the programme in question is implemented, which are manifestly disproportionate to the programme's objectives.[56]

In *Weiss*, the Court of Justice was equally one-sided in the choice of information that it found relevant for assessing the proportionality of the PSPP, again accepting the information provided by the ESCB as the only relevant one.[57] In essence, the Court of Justice does not allow for a pluralist peer review of the duty to state reasons on the part of the ESCB.[58] This criticism has been picked up directly by the Bundesverfassungsgericht,[59] demanding that less burdensome alternatives be considered, and a wide array of interests included in such considerations. But who is in the best position to make such an assessment? Surely the ECB, both due to its Treaty role and the necessary expertise. Still, in order to ensure the effectiveness good of accountability, the ECB is not unique in being an institution that operates with a high level of expertise – so is the European Commission in many of the fields in which it operates. The same is the case for many EU's agencies. Yet, as regards the Commission, the Court of Justice developed standards of review to ensure that it effectively performs its Treaty-appointed functions.[60] The Court of Justice is also able to

[54] Tridimas and Xanthoulis, op. cit. *supra* note 19, at 31; Steinbach, 'All's Well that Ends Well? Crisis Policy after the German Constitutional Court's Ruling in Gauweiler', 24 *Maastricht Journal of European & Comparative Law* 1 (2017) 140, at 145.

[55] Dawson and Bobić, 'Quantitative Easing at the Court of Justice – Doing Whatever It Takes to Save the Euro: Weiss and Others', 56 *Common Market Law Review* 4 (2019), 1005, at 1022–1028.

[56] Case C-62/14 *Gauweiler*, op. cit. *supra* note 43, para 91.

[57] Case C-493/17 *Weiss*, op. cit. *supra* note 47, para 81.

[58] Dawson and Bobić, op. cit. *supra* note 55, at 1023.

[59] *Weiss II*, op. cit. *supra* note 7, paras 184, 190.

[60] Dawson and Bobić, op. cit. *supra* note 55.

order expert reports as well as question them in the hearings before it.[61] This is also a standard practice before German courts.[62]

The courts therefore do not need to become experts in the field in order to ensure that a proper peer review of decisions such as the ECB's is subject to a more detailed obligation of justification resulting in a substantive good of effectiveness.

In addition, which court, then, is in the best position to review such an assessment being made? Certainly, the Court of Justice is an institution presumed to safeguard EU-wide considerations, as opposed to a single national court.[63] Here the accountability good of publicness plays an important role. Importantly from the perspective of constitutional conflict, depending on which court we turn to, publicness might be understood as ensuring that decision-making is made in the EU or in the national interest. Indeed, the Bundesverfassungsgericht has been criticised for focusing on German fiscal and economic interests when it listed what information the ECB could have listed in its assessment in preparation for the PSPP. Yet, for matters of monetary policy, where the EU has exclusive competence, it is the common interest of the EU that should be ensured. This is another reason why the question of competences remains so prominent in this constitutional conflict.

Judicial review of monetary policy decisions is inherently not ideal: judges cannot be the ones to make complex economic assessments, as explicitly acknowledged by the Bundesverfassungsgericht.[64] Thus, another possible consequence of this litigation is that other national courts follow the German example and begin imposing their own standards and demands for justification on part of the ECB, leading to a proliferation of diverging national standards and resulting in the creation of an unrealistic burden for the ECB. This is in addition to a danger of demanding the publicness good to be delivered by the ECB in the national, rather than EU, common interest.

To remedy both these possibilities, a more substantial improvement in the accountability of the ECB may ultimately necessitate a treaty change that

61 Article 70 of the Rules of Procedure of the Court of Justice.

62 Grashof, 'The "You Know Better" Dilemma of Administrative Judges in Environmental Matters. A Note on the German Legal Context', 27 *European Energy and Environmental Law Review* (2018) 151.

63 Hence, the parochialism accusation in Marzal, 'Is the BVerfG PSPP Decision "Simply Not Comprehensible"? A Critique of the Judgment's Reasoning on Proportionality' Verfassungsblog, 9 May 2020. https://verfassungsblog.de/is-the-bverfg-pspp-decision-simply-not-comprehensible/, (last visited 16 Aug. 2022).

64 *Weiss II*, op. cit. *supra* note 7, para 173. Goldmann, 'Adjudicating Economics? Central Bank Independence and the Appropriate Standard of Judicial Review', 14 *German Law Journal* (2014) 265.

would either redefine its mandate or devise novel accountability arrangements.[65] However, as long as this does not take place, courts demanding more of the ECB in terms of assessing the redistributive effects of large-scale purchase programmes such as the PSPP does not appear to me controversial. In fact, the ECB, despite Article 130 TFEU explicitly prohibiting it from taking instructions from Member States, complied with the request of the Bundesverfassungsgericht[66] to better explain the proportionality of the PSPP. The ECB has, 'in line with the principle of sincere cooperation … decided to accommodate this request'.[67]

The lesson learned from *Gauwiler* and *Weiss* may well be that the structure of Article 5 TEU does not operate as well in the context of self-imposed mandates, where judicial review would need to be confined to accepting any and all reasons provided by the institution in question.[68] However, looking at how the Bundesverfassungsgericht introduced this change, can we really speak of a genuine pursuit of an increased level of accountability of the ECB by applying mutual respect and sincere cooperation? The next section aims to answer this question by looking at jurisdictional competition between the two courts.

## 9.4 SINCERE COOPERATION AND ACTUAL ACCOUNTABILITY OUTCOMES

> If any Member State could readily invoke the authority to decide, through its own courts, on the validity of EU acts, this could undermine the precedence of application accorded to EU law and jeopardise its uniform application. Yet if the Member States were to completely refrain from conducting any kind of ultra vires review, they would grant EU organs exclusive authority over the Treaties even in cases where the EU adopts a legal interpretation that would essentially amount to a treaty amendment or an expansion of its competences.[69]

Thus, we have before us the well-known conundrum of the European Union's constitutional setup digested in one paragraph: who has the final say on the limits of EU competence? This central and most likely eternal question of the EU's constitutional framework has important consequences

[65] For a proposal for reform carried out by a simplified revision procedure in Article 48(6) TEU, see de Boer and van't Klooster, op. cit. *supra* note 38.

[66] *Weiss II*, op. cit. *supra* note 7, para 235.

[67] www.ecb.europa.eu/pub/pdf/other/ecb.mepletter200629_Simon~ece6ead766.en.pdf, (last visited 16 Aug. 2022).

[68] Arguably this seems to be the case in Case C-62/14 *Gauweiler*, op. cit. *supra* note 43, para 60 and Case C-493/17 *Weiss*, op. cit. *supra* note 47, para 56.

[69] *Weiss II*, op. cit. *supra* note 7, para 111.

for accountability goods. Namely, both non-arbitrariness and publicness as accountability goods depend on the manner in which competence control is exercised. This constitutional conflict thus firstly tells us that meaningful limits must exist to EU competence, and its institutions can use it only in a non-arbitrary manner. Secondly, the competence control conflict also has important repercussions as to what is the common interest to be ensured through the accountability good of publicness. Translated to the context of the ECB, then, the competence conflict can ensure that when it defines its activities, it indeed stays within its Treaty-accorded role in the monetary field. In this way, the manner of exercise of its mandate will already be subject to (at least a procedural) demand of non-arbitrariness. Constitutional conflict has even more striking consequences for the purposes of the publicness good. Once a competence of conferred upon the EU, the institution exercising it must do so in the common interest of the EU. In that sense, once the judicial review takes place before a national court, it cannot restrict itself to reviewing this accountability good solely from the perspective of the national common interest.

*Ultra vires* review was first introduced in the *Maastricht* judgment of the German court, widely considered the foremother of constitutional pluralism.[70] The Bundesverfassungsgericht maintained the thesis that Member States are the 'Masters of the Treaties',[71] which are 'continuously breathing life into the Treaty'.[72] This meant that primacy of EU law only extends to acts within vires,[73] and it was the Bundesverfassungsgericht who has retained the right to control the division between intra and ultra vires. Because the principle of conferral is a shared concept of EU and national constitutional law,[74] its application is likewise shared between EU and national courts, inevitably creating conditions for a possibility of constitutional conflict.

To place an EU measure outside the borders of EU competence, one must step through a significant number of hurdles set out in the *Honeywell* decision of the Bundesverfassungsgericht.[75] The logic of these numerous steps is to maintain competence control as a task shared and coordinated with the Court of Justice. In so doing, no other court in Germany but the

70 MacCormick, 'The Maastricht-Urteil: Sovereignty Now', 1 *European Law Journal* 3 (1995), 259.

71 Cases 2 BvR 2134/92 and 2159/92 *Maastricht Treaty*, Judgment of 12 October 1993, para II.a).

72 Ibid., para II.d).2.1.

73 Kokott, 'Report on Germany' in Slaughter, Stone Sweet, and Weiler (eds.), *The European Court and National Courts, Doctrine and Jurisprudence: Legal Change in Its Social Context* (Hart Publishing, 1998), at 81.

74 Case 2 BVerfG 2/08 *Lisbon Treaty*, Judgment of 30 June 2009, para 234; *Weiss II*, op. cit. *supra* note 7, para 158.

75 Case 2 BverfG 2661/06 *Honeywell*, Order of 06 July 2010.

Bundesverfassungsgericht can conduct ultra vires review; a preliminary reference must be submitted to the Court of Justice prior to making any conclusions; and the Court of Justice has a tolerance of error in its judgment. Only after these conditions are met is the test of a 'manifest transgression' in the area 'highly significant' in the division of competences between the EU and its Member States applied.[76]

The way that these steps were applied in *Weiss II* leaves space for doubt. When is a competence highly significant in the structure of the division of competences? We know that this does not cover the substance of constitutional identity from Article 79(3) of the Basic Law, which is automatically excluded from European integration.[77] But that leaves us with little knowledge as to what highly significant is, leaving the Bundesverfassungsgericht in danger of a *laesio enormis* fallacy[78] concerning the boundaries of the German constitutional obligation to participate in the integration programme. To demand of the Bundesverfassungsgericht to more clearly define this boundary would be a welcome development.

It must also be acknowledged that the conceptual conundrum in competence control by the Court of Justice and its relationship to proportionality, as explained in the previous section, was neither explicitly raised nor contemplated by the Bundesverfassungsgericht.[79] Rather, the Bundesverfassungsgericht failed to emphasise the centrality of proportionality, and in particular its *stricto sensu* step, in its preliminary reference, therefore not engaging in a genuinely open dialogue with the Court of Justice.[80] This runs counter to its statement in *Gauweiler* that there is an obligation to 'respect judicial development of the law by the Court of Justice even when the Court of Justice adopts a view against which weighty arguments could be made'.[81] The Bundesverfassungsgericht placed great emphasis on the Court of Justice maintaining consistency with the standards concerning the ECB's mandate in *Gauweiler*[82] as well as in the Order for reference in *Weiss*.[83] And yet, the German court itself behaved entirely inconsistently: the *stricto sensu* step of the proportionality test touted as central to the review of the PSPP was only introduced in the response to the decision of the Court of Justice,

76 Ibid., paras 56, 60–61.
77 *Lisbon Treaty*, op. cit. *supra* note 74, paras 240–241.
78 Schneider, 'Gauging "Ultra-Vires": The Good Parts', 21 *German Law Journal* (2020), 968, at 976.
79 Editorial Comments, op. cit. *supra* note 9, at 971.
80 Wendel, op. cit. *supra* note 42, at 987.
81 *Gauweiler* (Judgment), op. cit. *supra* note 17, para 161.
82 Ibid., paras 180, 193, 205.
83 *Weiss* (Order), op. cit. *supra* note 52, para 79.

whereas no such expectation was hinted at in the order for preliminary reference itself, and even less so in the *Gauweiler* litigation.

Furthermore, the Bundesverfassungsgericht argued that the *stricto sensu* stage of balancing was not present in the analysis of the Court of Justice, thus warranting the application of its own proportionality test. Yet, it had not applied the *stricto sensu* stage itself either – and while it appears counter-intuitive that the ECB should do so,[84] in particular given the emphasis of the German court on the ECB's limited mandate and insufficient democratic legitimation[85] – it stated that 'it would have been incumbent for the ECB' to do so.[86] The Bundesverfassungsgericht devoted considerable attention to analysing the difference in the proportionality test developed by the Court of Justice and itself, respectively, opting unsurprisingly to apply its own standard. The German Court has in consequence been accused of parochialism,[87] and 'framing a European legal question largely in terms of German constitutional law'.[88] The Second Senate engaged in an analysis of how the test is applied in other Member States,[89] then explained to the Court of Justice its own (the latter's) proportionality test,[90] concluded it is deficient for the delimitation of competences between the EU and the national level,[91] and thence applied its own (presumably superior) proportionality test. A similar approach was subject to critique on the occasion of the Bundesverfassungsgericht's order in *Mr R*[92] when deciding to disapply the European Arrest Warrant, without submitting a preliminary reference to the Court of Justice.[93]

In the structure of constitutional pluralism, mutual respect and sincere cooperation play a central role in incrementally managing interpretative differences and ensuring the constructive nature of a possible constitutional conflict

84 Davies rightly points out that this would result in the ECB concluding that, despite its mandate to achieve price stability, it would sometimes need to abandon that aim as ultimately too costly in relation to its benefits. Davies, 'The German Constitutional Court Decides Price Stability May Not Be Worth Its Price', *European Law Blog*, 20 May 2020. <https://europeanlawblog.eu/2020/05/21/the-german-federal-supreme-court-decides-price-stability-may-not-be-worth-its-price/>, (last visited 16 Aug. 2022).

85 *Weiss II*, op. cit. *supra* note 7, para 136.

86 Ibid., para 176.

87 Marzal, op. cit. *supra* note 63.

88 Wendel, op. cit. *supra* note 42, at 993.

89 *Weiss II*, op. cit. *supra* note 7, para 125.

90 Ibid., para 126.

91 Ibid., paras 127, 133, 138.

92 Case 2 BvR 2735/14 *Mr R*. Order of 15 December 2015.

93 Nowag, 'EU Law, Constitutional Identity, and Human Dignity: A Toxic Mix? Bundesverfassungsgericht: Mr R 2 BvR 2735/14, Mr R v. Order of the Oberlandesgericht Düsseldorf, Order of the Bundesverfassungsgericht (Second Senate) of 15 December 2015, DE:BVerfG:2015:rs20151215.2bvr273514', 53 *Common Market Law Review* 5 (2016), 1441.

ensuing.[94] The way in which proportionality was introduced in *Weiss II* can hardly be referred to as a role model for this approach. Language and expressions used by constitutional courts and the Court of Justice are of importance in the way constitutional conflict and its resolution is managed, and there is a coherence in this sense among different constitutional courts in the EU.[95] The allegation of the Bundesverfassungsgericht that the judgment of the Court of Justice is 'simply not comprehensible'[96] is in that sense not the sort of language that should be employed between courts that have for so long interacted in a constructive manner, enhancing the EU's constitutional sphere. It departs from the need for mutual respect and sincere cooperation, and unnecessarily distracts from the issues that can constructively be addressed through constitutional conflict.

The advantage of constitutional pluralism has in large part been precisely addressing issues such as the competence control carried out by the Court of Justice, dynamically and incrementally developing EU's constitutional sphere and preventing outright domination of one constitutional order over the other. This has direct benefits for the goods of non-arbitrariness as well as publicness. As regards the former, constitutional conflict has the advantage of courts questioning and incrementally raising the intensity of review, and by extension, ensuring that the institution in question acts within the limits of its competence. As regards the latter, constitutional conflict has the advantage of resolving, for individual cases, the question of competence division and therefore creating precise demands as regards the common interest of the EU or the Member State in question. In that sense, declaring an action of the ECB ultra vires is an outcome for the Court of Justice as well as EU institutions to reckon with. There are constructive elements in this finding that can incrementally be resolved through the auto-correct function of constitutional pluralism.

## 9.5 CONCLUSION

When can national courts contest the findings of the Court of Justice? In other words, is it possible for the Court of Justice to make a mistake? Justice Landau, in his dissent to the *Honeywell* decision, underlined the necessity of the Court of Justice being kept in check, be it by other EU institutions or Member

94 Goldmann, 'Constitutional Pluralism as Mutually Assured Discretion: The Court of Justice, the German Federal Constitutional Court, and the ECB', 23 *Maastricht Journal of European & Comparative Law* 1 (2016), 119, at 128; Spieker, 'Framing and Managing Constitutional Identity Conflicts: How to Stabilize the Modus Vivendi between the Court of Justice and National Constitutional Courts', 57 *Common Market Law Review* 2 (2020), 361, at 381.

95 Bobić, op. cit. *supra* note 15, at 1414–1423.

96 *Weiss II*, op. cit. *supra* note 7, paras 116, 153.

States.[97] In the aftermath of the *Weiss II* decision, Justice Huber stated that there is space for improvement of the judicial review standards of the Court of Justice.[98] Legal scholarship has equally taken note of the light standard of review that the Court of Justice applies in relation to the ECB in specific.[99] Constitutional conflict in this area, it seems to me, performs an important function in delivering the accountability goods of non-arbitrariness (by specifying the limits and necessary justification for acting and the manner of such decision-making), effectiveness (by expanding the possible review of expertise decisions, expanding the pool of peer review through the use of experts in showing the correctness of decision-making), and publicness (by demanding the ECB to show how its measures are addressing an EU-wide common interest).

So while the German decision does not put into question the rule of law or basic values set out in Article 2 TEU, there are some, more permanent dangers lurking from the decision beyond its most immediate impact on the PSPP. One such danger that merits addressing is the interpretation put forward by the Bundesverfassungsgericht concerning Germany's constitutional identity in the context of risk-sharing. The Bundesverfassungsgericht's initial worry in *Gauwiler* concerned the possibility that quantitative easing may involve unforeseeable risks for national budgets beyond those directly approved by the *Bundestag*. It took into account the assurances of the Court of Justice that the OMT programme entails safeguards preventing such an outcome.[100] The same concern was raised in *Weiss*, where the Court of Justice dismissed the question about risk-sharing as hypothetical.[101] The Bundesverfassungsgericht took this to mean that the Treaties prohibit risk-sharing as such and added that this would also be contrary to Germany's constitutional identity protected by Articles 23(1) and 79(3) of the Basic Law.[102]

In that sense, identity review is a weapon of a strength incomparable to that of ultra vires review: while the latter allows for the situation to be remedied by an action of the Bundestag, the former is embedded in an unamendable characteristic of the Basic Law and without allowing any departures.[103] Translated to the language of the accountability good of publicness, a finding that an ECB measure goes against constitutional identity determines the scope of the common interest and by extension to the possible focus of any similar measure

97 *Honeywell*, op. cit. *supra* note 75, Dissenting Opinion of Justice Landau, para 99.

98 See interview with the Frankfurter Allgemeine Zeitung, <www.faz.net/aktuell/politik/inland/peter-huber-im-gespraech-das-ezb-urteil-war-zwingend-16766682.html> (last visited 16 Aug. 2022).

99 See above, n 41, 54, 55.

100 Case C-62/14 *Gauweiler*, op. cit. *supra* note 18, paras 123–126, accepted by the Bundesverfassungsgericht in *Gauweiler* (Judgment), op. cit. *supra* note 17, paras 218–219.

101 Case C-493/17 *Weiss*, op. cit. *supra* note 47, paras 165–166.

102 *Weiss II*, op. cit. *supra* note 7, paras 227–228.

103 *Gauweiler* (Judgment), op. cit. *supra* note 17, para 29.

in the future. It may well be that constitutional identity (even if at the moment offering a constructive check to the principle of conferral) as performed by courts might act as a break in the political process that might legitimately aim, at a certain point, at a reform of the existing division of competences.

The PSPP was nevertheless found to be within what the constitutional identity allows for, but the findings concerning constitutional identity have landed on fertile ground. At present, the EU's 'Next Generation EU' pandemic programme that forms part of the EU's Own Resources Decision[104] is being challenged before the Bundesverfassungsgericht by the founder of the Alternative für Deutschland (AfD) precisely on the basis of constitutional identity.[105] On 26 March 2021, the Bundesverfassungsgericht issued an unreasoned decision[106] to the Federal President to hold off signing the bill until it decides whether to grant the applicants interim relief.[107] The interim relief was not grounded, but the decision is currently pending on the merits. The central argument of the applicant revolves around the possibility that Germany becomes liable for the entire amount of the pandemic fund, effectively introducing risk-sharing into EU law. Sincere cooperation, mutual respect, as well as consistency would demand a preliminary reference to be submitted to the Court of Justice. Here, the Court of Justice would also be put in a position to abide by its own standards concerning risk-sharing, or provide new insights that were possibly beyond the interpretations provided for the OMT and PSPP. However, in the midst of these uncertainties, it may transpire that the delicate balance between the two courts is already significantly upset by the above-analysed interpretations of proportionality and jurisdiction. In such a scenario, it is possible that the constitutional conflict reaches a destructive stage that cannot be remedied by a reasonable disagreement concerning the interpretation of EMU law. This might result in a need for a more general political reckoning of the German participation in the EMU and its future development, and the Covid-19 crisis seems to have provided a direct impetus for this to take place.

[104] Council Decision (EU, Euratom) 2020/2053 of 14 December 2020 on the system of own resources of the European Union and repealing Decision 2014/335/EU, Euratom OJ L 424, 15.12.2020, pp. 1–10.

[105] More information on the initiative available here https://buendnis-buergerwille.de/verfassungsbeschwerde/, (last visited 16 Aug. 2022).

[106] 2 BvR 547/21 Decision of the Second Senate of 26 March 2021, <www.bundesverfassungsgericht.de/SharedDocs/Entscheidungen/DE/2021/03/rs20210326_2bvr054721.html>, (last visited 16 Aug. 2022).

[107] For a brief analysis of the procedural intricacies of the decision, see Repasi, 'Karlsruhe, Again: The Interim-Interim Relief of the German Constitutional Court Regarding Next Generation EU', *EU Law Live*, 29 March 2021, <https://eulawlive.com/analysis-karlsruhe-again-the-interim-interim-relief-of-the-german-constitutional-court-regarding-next-generation-eu-by-rene-repasi/>, (last visited 16 Aug. 2022).

# 10

# Adjudicating Transnational Solidarity Conflicts

## *Can Courts Ban the Destructive Potential?*

*Anuscheh Farahat*[*]

## 10.1 INTRODUCTION

This chapter focuses on transnational solidarity conflicts as a specific type of conflict in the EMU that has been aggravated by the Eurozone crisis but persists also in current debates about how to share the economic costs of both the COVID-19-pandemic and climate change. This new type of distributional conflict encompasses both quarrels about the adaptation of domestic welfare systems to EMU requirements and the distribution of costs and benefits between Member States. As EMU governance is largely executive driven and as distributive decisions in one Member State also affect other Member States, accountability for distributive decisions in the EMU gains new salience. The goal of this chapter is to understand how legal accountability and, more specifically, constitutional accountability may contribute to a constructive management of transnational solidarity conflicts. In addressing this question, the chapter will focus specifically on the accountability goods of openness and publicness, as developed in the introductory chapter.

## 10.2 TRANSNATIONAL SOLIDARITY CONFLICTS AS A CORE FEATURE AND PERIL OF THE EMU

The transformation of the EMU during and after the Eurozone crisis not only resulted in an aggravated deficit of accountability and legitimacy (1), but also provoked new types of conflicts within and between the Member States,

* The research leading to this paper has been conducted in the context of the DFG-Emmy Noether Research Group on 'Transnational Solidarity Conflicts', which is led by the author since 2017. The author wishes to thank Marius Hildebrand for research support and helpful comments on earlier versions of this paper and Lisa Kollert for additional assistance in finalising the paper.

which shall be described in this chapter as transnational solidarity conflicts (2). Transnational solidarity conflicts yield a potential for destabilising the EMU. The core question to be addressed in this chapter, therefore, is how legal, and more specifically constitutional accountability mechanisms, may contribute to mitigate the disintegrative potential of transnational solidarity conflicts in the EU (3).[1]

### 10.2.1 *Responsible Instead of Responsive Government: The Increasing Lack of Accountability and Legitimacy in the EMU*

Progressive economic integration in the EU has reinforced the legitimacy issues of European governance. Decisions taken at the supranational level increasingly affect the design of national distribution regimes or have otherwise far-reaching distributional effects for the Member States. Moreover, the EMU increases political and economic interdependencies among Euro Member States. The measures taken to rescue the common currency and counter the financial crisis have further restricted national scope for distributional policy as the political and economic costs of comprehensive welfare state regulation have become ever higher. This led to a deep legitimacy and accountability crisis: The Eurozone Member States lose the capacity and political space for implementing distributive policies, but at the same time often have to bear the consequences of decisions made by other national legislators.[2] This *problematique* is exacerbated by the fact that fiscal and economic policy recommendations on the European level can now also be enacted in the absence of majority decisions. Together these developments contribute to further political imbalance among the Member States.[3] In addition, decisions with far-reaching distributional effects within the EMU are today mostly dominated by executive bodies and thus undermine the idea of democratic-parliamentary self-legislation.[4] Even if one accepts an increasing need to

[1] The following section is based on research and thoughts that have already been presented in earlier texts (Farahat, *Transnationale Solidarität: Eine vergleichende Analyse verfassungsgerichtlicher Konfliktbearbeitung in der Eurokrise* (Mohr Siebeck, 2021) pp. 41–50 and 50–90), Farahat/Arzoz, 'Contestation and Integration in Times of Crisis: The Law and the Challenge of Austerity', in id. (eds.), *Contesting Austerity: A Socio-Legal Inquiry* (Hart, 2021), pp. 1–23, but have significantly been updated, adapted, and further developed for the purpose of this volume.

[2] Tuori/Tuori, *The Eurozone Crisis: A Constitutional Analysis* (Cambridge University Press, 2014), pp. 207f., 209ff.

[3] Menéndez, 'A European Union in Constitutional Mutation', 20 *European Law Journal* (2014), pp. 127–141, 135, 137.

[4] Enderlein, 'Das erste Opfer der Krise ist die Demokratie', 54 *Politische Vierteljahresschrift* (2013), 714–739, Wöhl, 'Machtverschiebungen vom Parlament zur Exekutive', in Hentges

allow for competing expressions of the public will,[5] parliamentary legislation by democratically elected representatives is still an irreplaceable mechanism of responsiveness in a democratic polity.[6]

In the context of the Eurozone crisis, this post-democratic *problematique* becomes even more salient, since political decision-makers have long proven to be largely ignorant to alternative ways of dealing with conflicts and negative social impacts of the measures taken.[7] This reflects a general shift from responsiveness to responsibility in democratic governance.[8] Governments and their supporting parties are increasingly compelled to act responsibly towards markets in terms of risk minimisation.[9] The yardstick for such responsibility is formed by international and supranational guidelines or standards, which have become more detailed and comprehensive, especially during the Euro crisis. The dominance of responsibility is also expressed in the rhetoric of 'no alternative', which tends to discredit any discussion of alternative response options as inadequate, inefficient, or even counterproductive.[10] In this context, responsiveness to citizens' political preferences is increasingly difficult to realise for political parties. There is a risk that open debate about alternative visions of the common good, and the appropriate measures to achieve it, is replaced by a managerial mindset of optimising governance goals through technocratic administration. Citizens in the EU Member States are thus exposed to political and economic decisions that are neither legitimised through parliamentary-democratic decision-making at the European level nor through responsive democratic procedures at the Member State level.[11] This constellation results in a new quality of conflicts about EMU governance, about the consequences of the European monetary policy for the distributive regimes of the Member States and about the democratic accountability of EMU institutions. The question therefore arises to what extent accountability

(ed.), *Krise der Demokratie. Demokratie in der Krise?* (Wochenschau Wissenschaft, 2020), pp. 92–100, 97.

5 Rosanvallon, *Democratic Legitimacy: Impartiality – Reflexivity – Proximity* (Princeton University Press, 2011), p. 243f.

6 Crouch, *Post-Democracy* (Polity Press, 2004), focusing on the aggravation of this *problematique* during the Euro zone crisis see Streeck, 'The Crises of Democratic Capitalism', in id., *How Will Capitalism End? Essays on a Failing System* (Verso, 2016), pp. 73–94.

7 Dawson, 'Opening Pandora's Box?', in id. et al. (eds.), *Beyond the Crisis: The Governance of Europe's Economic, Political and Legal Transformation* (Oxford University Press, 2015), pp. 85–93, 85, 92.

8 Mair, 'Representative versus Responsible Government', 8 *MPIfG Discussion Paper* (2009), 13ff.

9 Ibid., at p. 12.

10 On the rhetoric of the state of emergency Séville, *There Is No Alternative: Politik zwischen Demokratie und Sachzwang* (Campus, 2017), p. 271ff.

11 Tuori/Tuori, *supra* note 2, at p. 210.

mechanisms beyond parliamentary-democratic decision-making may compensate for the lack of responsiveness by enhancing openness and publicness of executive decision-making.

### 10.2.2 *Transnational Solidarity Conflicts: A New Type of Conflicts and Their Potential for Destabilising the EMU*

The Eurozone crisis has created a new dynamic of conflict that can be described as transnational solidarity conflicts. Conflicts arise not only over the extent to which the adjustment burdens caused by the common currency should be borne jointly by the members of the Eurozone but also over how social security can be secured for those population groups that do not directly benefit from freedom of movement within the EU. Today, solidarity between and within the Member States can no longer be shaped and developed independently, thereby increasingly producing conflicts between societal groups that cut across the boundaries of the national welfare state.

Transnational solidarity conflicts illustrate the unprecedented politicisation that European economic governance witnessed during the Eurozone crisis.[12] Politicisation can be understood as comprising three interrelated elements: raising awareness for a specific issue, mobilising around this specific issue, and polarising the debate about this issue.[13] The Eurozone crisis has raised public awareness of the fact that European governance has significant distributional effects between Member States and within national distributional regimes.[14] The handling of the crises has laid bare the distributional effects of monetary policy and highlighted the inextricable link between economic policy choices and monetary policy. It revealed a multiplicity of political conflicts in terms of the distribution of costs and benefits built into a highly interdependent transnational polity. With transnational solidarity conflicts flaring up, different policy preferences regarding the appropriate answer to major economic shocks have once more shown their divisive potential by splitting the European Union, yet again, into 'southern' and 'northern' blocks. The result was increasingly polarised political spaces, with new salience for and mobilisation around European issues at both the national and the supranational levels.[15]

12 See generally de Wilde/Zürn, 'Can the Politicization of European Integration be Reversed?', 50 *JCMS* (2012), 137–153.

13 Ibid., 139f.

14 See also Cramme/Hobolt, 'A European Union Under Stress', in id. (eds.), *Democratic Politics in a European Union Under Stress* (Oxford University Press, 2014), pp. 1–18, 8.

15 In a study of public debate in six Western European countries, Kriesi and Grande have shown that issues concerning the Euro have been exceptionally present in public discourse and

In the context of intensifying transnational solidarity conflicts, European issues became a pivotal point of reference and mobilisation in the construction of political identities. The consensual nature and relative sobriety of European integration were suddenly permeated by the political logic of antagonism. Measures of crisis reaction and the future of the single currency have become a central issue in national election campaigns and in the political positioning of individual parties.[16] There is a serious risk, however, that the destructive dynamic of such polarised conflicts may not stop at the level of disagreement about specific policies. Rather, when institutions face serious critique because of their decision-making, politicisation may spill over from the conflictual issue itself into the 'conflict frame',[17] that is from the policy level to the polity level. Once the political and legal infrastructure (i.e. the 'conflict frame') of a political order is perceived by a significant part of the citizenry as allowing for no alternatives to currently dominant political projects, institutions themselves might come under attack. Polarisation therefore carries a destructive threat for the political structure of the EMU and the EU as a whole.

### 10.2.3 *Constitutional Accountability as a Tool to Mitigate Adverse Effects of Transnational Solidarity Conflicts?*

In the light of intensified and potentially divisive transnational solidarity conflicts, the role of accountability of EMU institutions gains new salience. If effective accountability mechanisms are in place, it may be possible to channel the destructive potential of transnational solidarity conflicts in a way that allows not only to enhance responsiveness of EMU institutions towards the citizenry but also to prevent a spill-over of policy conflicts to the level of the polity. Against this backdrop, I will focus in this chapter on how legal accountability can contribute and in fact has contributed to mitigate the divisive potential of transnational solidarity conflicts in the EMU. The idea is that constitutional review may provide a suitable tool to articulate alternative visions of the common good that have not been taken into

have significantly increased the visibility and awareness of European economic and monetary policy. See Kriesi/Grande, 'The Europeanization of the National Political Debate', in Cramme/Hobolt (eds.), *Democratic Politics in a European Union Under Stress* (Oxford University Press, 2014), pp. 67–86.

16 See Hobolt/Wratil, 'Public Opinion and the Crisis: The Dynamics of Support for the Euro', 22 *Journal of European Public Policy* (2015), 238–256, 241f.

17 For the conceptual differentiation of conflicts and conflict frames and their interplay, see Fehmel, 'Konflikte erster und zweiter Ordnung in Europa', 42 *Leviathan* (2014), 115–136.

account in previous, crisis-driven decision-making. It may thereby contribute to enhancing publicness of an executive decision, as it allows clarifying in the first place which common goods are legitimate or ought to be considered according to the normative (constitutional) framework. Moreover, by forcing decision-makers to justify their decisions and to reveal the considerations behind a given decision, legal accountability may also enhance the openness of decisions. In the following, I will concentrate on the specific role constitutional law has played for the accountability of the EMU during and in the aftermath of the eurozone crisis considering both domestic and EU constitutional law.

Constitutional accountability merits closer inspection for at least two reasons: First, in many polities in the EMU, constitutional law serves as a major benchmark for legal accountability of political institutions and decision-makers. Second, while theoretical approaches to conflict teach us that social conflicts have the potential for destructive and disintegrative effects, they have also highlighted the potentially integrative effect of conflicts for political communities. Such integrative effects, however, presuppose mechanisms of conflict resolution that allow for the (re)articulation of a normative framework.[18] Constitutional law, as a core infrastructure for the resolution of political conflict and normative orientation in modern societies, lends itself as a natural candidate to channel social conflicts in a way that reduces their destructive tendencies to a minimum. Constitutions aim to serve as 'normative scripts'[19] for political actors, guiding and limiting political action not only in times of seeming consensus but also in times of crisis and open conflict. The core challenge for constitutionalism in times of fundamental crises is to ensure both reliable normative continuity and sufficient flexibility to adapt normative concepts to new crisis-driven societal demands.[20] It is precisely through these interpretative processes in which limits and adaptations are negotiated that constitutions may serve to productively channel social conflicts. They thereby provide a space to negotiate and ultimately determine the common goods which can legitimately or sometimes even ought to be taken into account in a political order.

[18] Pathbreaking see Simmel, 'Der Streit', in Rammstedt (ed.), *Soziologie. Untersuchungen über die Formen der Vergesellschaftung* (Suhrkamp, 1992), pp. 282–384, also Weber, *Wirtschaft und Gesellschaft* (Mohr Siebeck, 1922), p. 398, on the productive potential of conflicts, see also Fehmel, *supra* note 17, 134.

[19] Brito Vieira/Carreira da Silva, 'Getting Rights Right: Explaining Social Rights Constitutionalization in Revolutionary Portugal', 11 *ICON* (2013), 898–922.

[20] See Contiades/Fotiadou, 'The Resilient Constitution: Lessons from the Financial Crisis', in Herwig/Simoncini (eds.), *Law and the Management of Disasters: The Challenge of Resilience* (Routledge, 2017), pp. 187–207.

By the same token, individuals and social groups may integrate into a political community through discursive practices in which they – at least in their majority – accept and refer to the constitution as the relevant normative framework. Although they may interpret concrete constitutional norms in different or even divergent ways, they nonetheless refer to the same document and thereby implicitly or explicitly accept it as the dominant normative symbol of the political community.[21] In this sense, the constitution becomes indiscriminate towards the various visions of the collective self-perception. Such an understanding fits well with Claude Lefort's idea of the empty place of power in modern democracies.[22] The constitution itself symbolises this empty place if its concrete meaning remains open to reinterpretation and to differing, even diverging, meanings that are given to its provisions. 'Emptiness' in this sense does not equal arbitrariness but rather results from reiterative discursive processes in which the respective provisions are identified with different meanings by different actors.[23] It is precisely this form of emptiness through discursive and reiterated re-interpretation that allows a constitution to both channel the destructive potential of major social conflicts and provide a meaningful normative benchmark for accountability.

In light of these theoretical considerations, constitutional accountability mechanisms need to fulfil two conditions in order to allow for a productive conflict management: On a procedural level, they need to be inclusive in order to allow a variety of actors to bring their case to court and thus to construct the societal conflict as a constitutional conflict. On a substantive level, constitutional provisions need to preserve a certain emptiness in their interpretation to allow different political actors to continuously identify with constitutional provisions and make the constitution the core normative point of reference. For constitutional courts as the most authoritative interpreters of constitutional norms, this means that they should refrain from an overly saturated interpretation that injects specific economic concepts or policy choices into constitutional norms. Likewise, to guarantee that a broad variety of constitutional actors can indeed participate in the discursive and iterative process of opening and emptying the meaning of constitutional norms, constitutional courts need to make sure that the process of political will-formation and

[21] Brodocz, 'Chancen konstitutioneller Identitätsstiftung. Zur symbolischen Integration durch eine deutungsoffene Verfassung', in Vorländer (ed.), *Integration durch Verfassung* (Westdeutscher Verlag, 2002), pp. 103–120, 106.

[22] Lefort, 'La dissolution de repères et l'enjeu démocratique', in id., *Le temps présent: Écrits 1945–2005* (Belin, 2007), pp. 551–568, 560f.

[23] Brodocz, *Die symbolische Dimension der Verfassung. Ein Beitrag zur Institutionentheorie* (Westdeutscher Verlag, 2003), p. 233ff.

decision-making remains open. More specifically, this requires power asymmetries not to become too much entrenched and political decision-making not to be permanently captured and constrained by arguments of necessity or market responsibility.

If constitutional norms on EU level become a shared reference point for negotiating and managing transnational solidarity conflicts, they may contribute to enabling polity building also on EU level. At the same time, this would also enhance the conditions for improving the accountability infrastructure on the supranational level as regards to the 'publicness' dimension developed in the introductory chapter of this volume. According to this dimension, accountability serves to ensure that official action is oriented towards the common good. While the common good might be defined differently by different actors in a polity, a collectively acceptable definition of a common good may be facilitated if it echoes principles enshrined in a shared constitutional framework. Moreover, constitutional law serves as an institutionalised framework to ensure the responsiveness of political actors towards the citizenry as opposed to responsibility towards markets or private interest. Transnational solidarity conflicts, however, are governed not only by EU constitutional law but also by domestic constitutions. The following two sections of this chapter will therefore assess the role of constitutional accountability for the management of transnational solidarity conflicts in the EMU on the domestic level and on the EU level in turn.

## 10.3 LEGAL ACCOUNTABILITY BEFORE DOMESTIC COURTS

This section will analyse in how far constitutional accountability of EMU decision-makers before domestic courts during and after the eurozone crisis contributed to minimising the destructive threats of transnational solidarity conflicts in the EMU. It asks in how far domestic constitutional courts have delivered the goods identified with accountability in the introductory chapter. A specific focus will be on 'publicness' as the good seeking to ensure that political action is geared towards common, in this case constitutional goods. The core interest therefore is in how far domestic and European constitutional principles have been taken into account and in how far the requirements of procedural inclusiveness and substantive emptiness developed in the previous section of this chapter have been fulfilled. The analysis will focus on two prominent examples of domestic constitutional accountability, namely cases before the Portuguese Tribunal Constitucional (PTC) and the German Federal Constitutional Court (GFCC) representing one side of transnational solidarity conflicts, respectively.

### 10.3.1 *From Restrained to Resistive Constitutionalism: The Austerity Case Law of the Portuguese Tribunal Constitucional*

During the economic and financial crisis, the PTC emerged as a 'lone hero against austerity'.[24] In its early judgements of 2010 and 2011, however, the court adopted a restrained position towards the austerity plans of the liberal-conservative government. In its first decision on crisis measures (acórdão 399/2010), the PTC had to decide whether a tax increase in the current year and for the entire income of that year was compatible with the principle of the protection of legitimate expectations as an expression of the principle of the rule of law (Article 2 PC). The court denied a violation of the principle of the protection of legitimate expectations. It basically argued that taxpayers could not have expected that taxes would remain unchanged in the current year, given the tight budget situation resulting from the current economic and financial crisis.[25] In light of the specific weight of these budgetary constraints,[26] the court granted legislative bodies particularly large discretion.

The PTC maintained this general line in Acórdão 396/2011 declaring cuts in public service allowances and salaries at issue to be constitutional. Once again, the court resorted to the logic of the economic state of emergency and the resulting need for quick reactions and far-reaching decisions.[27] The court argued that even if the principle of equality in general requires that all citizens had to contribute equally to the public finances, this does not imply a priority of budget consolidation through tax increases over public salary cuts but leaves the choice of measures to the legislative bodies.[28] According to the court, the principle of equality only precludes arbitrary unequal treatment which imposes an unjustified and disproportionate burden on a particular societal group. On the one hand, this line of jurisprudence left the political-parliamentary process as open as possible by granting the legislator wide discretion. On the other hand, it led to the constitution almost completely taking a back seat to economic rationality and crisis exceptionalism. Rather than defining effective criteria of constitutional accountability, the court

24 Pereira Coutinho/Violante, 'Um erro histórico?', Observador, 29.03.2018. Accessed via https://observador.pt/opiniao/um-erro-historico/ (20.01.2022).

25 Acórdão N.° 399/2010, Tribunal Constitucional, para 12.1.

26 Ibid., para 12.2.

27 For the relevance of the argument of exceptionalism during the Eurozone crisis, see White, 'Emergency Europe', 63 *Political Studies* (2015), 300–318, 302ff.

28 Acórdão N.° 399/2010, Tribunal Constitucional, para 9.

emphasised that, considering the 'absolutely exceptional economic development',[29] the overriding public interest pursued with the cuts was paramount. It was 'a situation of emergency' in which the measures taken were 'absolutely necessary'.[30] Both decisions illustrate that the court did not develop any substantial standard of constitutional accountability but was rather satisfied with a procedural safeguard, namely that the legislator demonstrated that it had indeed considered alternative options before taking the respective measures.

This restrained position of the PTC changed in the second phase of its Euro-crisis jurisprudence. As of 2012, the court no longer accepted the reference to the economic crisis as a free ticket for permanently broad legislative discretion. Instead, it started interpreting the principles of equality and proportionality in a way that set a limit for long-term and structural shifts in economic burden sharing. The core instrument for this shift was the 'invention' of the principle of proportional equality in acórdão 353/2012. The question at issue was whether cancelling the 13th- and 14th-month salaries for public sector employees as foreseen under the Budget Law of 2012 was in breach of the principle of equality by placing the burden exclusively on public employees. In stark contrast to the broad discretion granted to the legislator in earlier decisions, the PTC now declared the cuts unconstitutional for violating the principle of equality in conjunction with the principle of proportionality.[31] While the court still held that a different treatment of public and private sector employees in terms of their respective burdens is permissible in times of crisis, it clarified that the extent of the unequal treatment must itself be proportionate to remain within '*limites do sacrifício*'.[32] In the eyes of the court, this was no longer the case. The new cuts hit public sector workers unilaterally so that the unequal burden sharing of the exceptional fiscal situation reached a point, where it was disproportionate regarding the constitutional principle of equality.

The principle of proportional equality structured the austerity case law of the PTC from thereon leading to a number of public pay cuts considered to

[29] Acórdão N.° 396/2011, Tribunal Constitucional, para 8.

[30] Ibid.

[31] For a critique of this crucial shift, see Pereira, 'Igualdade e proporcionalidade: um comentário às decisões do Tribunal Constitucional de Portugal sobre cortes salariais no sector público', 98 *Revista Española de Derecho Constitucional* (2013), 317–370, de Brito, 'Medida e intensidade do controlo da igualdade na jurisprudência da crise do Tribunal Constitucional', in Ribeiro/Coutinho (eds.), *O Tribunal Constitucional e a crise* (Almedina, 2014), pp. 105–121, de Brito/Coutinho, 'A "Igualdade Proporcional", novo modelo no controlo do Princípio da Igualdade?', 1 *Direito & Política* (2013), 182–191, 186ff.

[32] Acórdão N.° 353/2012, Tribunal Constitucional, para 5.

be one-sided and unconstitutional.[33] Despite some harsh political and doctrinal criticism,[34] the concept of proportional equality strengthened the benchmark for constitutional accountability. Moreover, the PTC combined this benchmark with a duty on part of the legislature to properly justify austerity measures in the light of the rights and principles enshrined in the Portuguese Constitution. Hence, domestic constitutional rights need to be 'properly' taken into account by the government and the legislature when implementing measures of crisis reaction in the EMU context.[35] It thereby combined a procedural understanding of accountability with a more 'substantiated' version of constitutional accountability. By requiring 'proportional equality', the court developed a benchmark that not only enabled a 'resilient constitutionalism'[36] by setting perceptible limits to political crisis management but also reactivated the socially progressive aspiration of the constituent moment in Portuguese constitutional law with its strong emphasis on social rights.[37] In a political constellation characterised by a strong power asymmetry between creditor and debtor countries and a dominant rhetoric of emergency and no alternatives, the adjudication of the PTC thereby allowed to effectively articulate alternative policy options in the language of constitutional law. Consequently, the political debate started to centre on the Constitution and its 'adequate' interpretation against the backdrop of a profound crisis.[38] In this sense, the accountability standard applied by the court is focused on binding political action to the common constitutional good (publicness) while at the same time leaving room to negotiate politically how this common good ought to be interpreted and realised.

At the same time, however, this line of constitutional interpretation effectively made the transnational dimension of the underlying conflicts invisible. The crucial parameters of accountability, deduced from constitutional principles of proportionality, equality, and protection of trust, framed the crisis-induced conflicts as an ideological issue between liberal, market-oriented and progressive, welfare state-oriented ideas of order and as a national redistributive

33 See Acórdão N.° 187/2013, Tribunal Constitucional; acórdão N.° 413/2014, Tribunal Constitucional; acórdão N.° 574/2014, Tribunal Constitucional.

34 For a doctrinal criticism of the concept of 'proportional equality', see Pereira, *supra* n. 31, de Brito, *supra* n. 31; de Brito/Coutinho, *supra* n. 31; for a critique of this phase of the PTC's jurisprudence more generally see de Brito, 'Putting Social Rights in Brackets?', 4 *European Journal of Social Law* (2014), 87–103, 98f., and the various contributions in Ribeiro/Coutinho (eds.), *O Tribunal Constitucional e a crise* (Almedina, 2014).

35 Acórdão 575/2014, Tribunal Constitucional, para 19f.

36 Contiades/Fotiadou, *supra* note 20.

37 Vieira/da Silva, *supra* note 19.

38 Brito Veira/Carreira da Silva/Pereira, 'Waiting for Godot? Welfare Attitudes in Portugal Before and After the Financial Crisis', 65 *Political Studies* (2017), 535–558, 539.

conflict between public servants and private sector employees. Despite strong arguments in favour of submitting the question of the compatibility of the conditionalities with the fundamental rights of the Union to the ECJ,[39] the PTC has not yet submitted any question from the crisis case law to the ECJ for a preliminary ruling. While the court thereby may have prevented an open conflict between national constitutional principles and European constitutional law, it missed the opportunity to renegotiate the social content and the social formative power of the Union's constitutional law and to concretise it in the context of the crisis.[40] Instead, the question of the mode and measure of solidarity and the distribution of any adjustment costs was nationalised and the mode of accountability remained largely deductive.

### 10.3.2 *'Lost in National Democracy?': The Aporias of the Eurozone Crisis Case Law of the German Federal Constitutional Court*

At first glance, similar considerations apply to the German Federal Constitutional Court. Like the PTC, the Bundesverfassungsgericht has set important limits to crisis management, and like the PTC, it has nationalised the crisis-induced conflict by emphasising the constitutional necessity of an autonomous choice of means at the national level. However, this type of 'nationalisation' turns out to be even more ambivalent as it harbours a strong disintegrative potential as the court largely ignores the transnational horizontal effects of its own decisions.

Already in its early decisions on the eurozone crisis measure, the GFCC insisted on the requirement of parliamentary participation in all measures with budgetary impact.[41] Building on its earlier jurisprudence in *Maastricht*[42] and *Lisbon*,[43] the court ruled that the Bundestag must always hold plenary sessions when 'essential decisions which affect the overall budgetary responsibility of the German Bundestag' are involved.[44] The court thereby blocked a delegation of decisions on crisis management to a smaller committee and insisted that the Bundestag must retain a 'continuing influence'[45] and must not be relegated to merely nodding through executive measure of

[39] See Kilpatrick, 'Are the Bailouts Immune to EU Social Challenge Because They Are Not EU Law?', 10 *EuConst* (2014), 393–421, 401.

[40] See also Violante/André, 'The Constitutional Performance of Austerity in Portugal', in Ginsburg et al. (eds.), *Constitutions in Times of Financial Crisis* (Cambridge University Press, 2019), pp. 229–260.

[41] BVerfGE 129, 124 – *EFS*; BVerfGE 130, 318 – *Rat der 9*; BVerfGE 131, 152 – *ESM/Euro-Plus-Paket*.

[42] BVerfGE 89, 155, 185 – *Maastricht*

[43] BVerfGE 123, 267, 351ff. – *Lissabon*.

[44] BVerfGE 130, 318, 356ff. – *Rat der 9*.

[45] As already in BVerfGE 129, 124, 186 – *EFS*.

crisis management.[46] In addition, the court also held that the federal government had violated its constitutional duty to provide information to the parliament[47] and stressed the need to ensure that the information forwarded to the parliament was used by the latter to allow for an open and democratic will-formation.[48] This line of reasoning reflects a mostly deductive and procedural approach to constitutional accountability. It concretises the constitutional requirements by highlighting the necessity of procedural safeguards for open parliamentary debate and will formation.

However, other parts of the court's crisis jurisprudence rather led to narrowing the space for constitutionally legitimate definitions of the common good and the measures to its realisation. In the *ESM*-ruling[49] the court build on its earlier case law in *Maastricht*, where it made Germany's participation in the monetary integration conditional to 'German conditions'[50] by linking price stability and budgetary discipline as the supreme objective of the future currency area to the principle of national democratic self-determination.[51] In the *ESM*-ruling the GFCC tightened this standard further and considered the design of the monetary union as a stability community as the 'essential basis' for Germany's participation in the EMU.[52] While the court held the concrete mechanism in this case to be constitutional, it effectively made any solidarity-based aid measures dependent not only on the approval by the Bundestag but also on the parliamentary prerogative to determine conditionalities ensuring that the overriding goal of price stability and balanced budgets is not jeopardised.[53]

Given the dominant executive mode of technocratic 'risk management'[54] during the eurozone crisis, the court can certainly be praised for protecting parliamentary budgetary rights, defending the openness and revocability of

46 BVerfGE 132, 195, 240 – *ESM/Fiskalpakt I*; BVerfGE 135, 317, 401 – *ESM/Fiskalpakt II*; BVerfGE 131, 152, 203 – *ESM/Euro-Plus-Paket* (referring on BVerfGE 129, 124, 178f.; 130, 318, 344f.); see also BVerfGE 130, 318, 344 – *Rat der 9*.

47 BVerfGE 131, 152, 215ff.; 223ff. – *ESM/Euro-Plus-Paket*.

48 BVerfGE 132, 195, 240 – *ESM/Fiskalpakt I*; BVerfGE 135, 317, 401 – *ESM/Fiskalpakt II*; BVerfGE 131, 152, 203 – *ESM/Euro-Plus-Paket* (referring on BVerfGE 129, 124, 178f.; 130, 318, 344f.); see also BVerfGE 130, 318, 344 – *Rat der 9*.

49 BVerfGE 132, 195, 240 – *ESM/Fiskalpakt I*; BVerfGE 135, 317, 401 – *ESM/Fiskalpakt II*.

50 On the problematic consequences of this 'integration on German terms', see already Joerges, 'Taking the Law Seriously: On Political Science and the Role of Law in the Process of European Integration', 2 *European Law Journal* (1996), 105–135, 114ff.

51 BVerfGE 89, 155, 202, 204 – *Maastricht*.

52 BVerfGE 132, 195, 243 – *ESM/Fiskalpakt I*; previously already in BVerfGE 89, 155, 205 – *Maastricht*; BVerfGE 97, 350, 369 – *Euro*.

53 BVerfGE 132, 195, 279ff. – *ESM/Fiskalpakt I*.

54 Chalmers, 'Crisis Reconfiguration in the European Constitutional State', in id. et al., *The End of the Eurocrats' Dream: Adjusting to European Diversity* (Cambridge University Press, 2016), pp. 266–299, 282ff.

democratic legislation against supposed crisis imperatives.[55] While this again strengthened procedural accountability under German constitutional law, the decision also contains a substantial element. The court closed the potential meanings of democracy under the Basic Law by linking it to price stability and frames possible alternatives for shaping transnational solidarity in the Eurozone (e.g. Eurobonds or a transfer union) as breaches of German constitutional law. It thereby significantly narrows the political space for negotiating a European common good. Furthermore, by linking the national principle of democracy to supranational conditionality, the court de facto contributes to depriving the legislatures in the debtor countries of precisely those political options that the court insists on securing on the national level. From a transnational perspective, it thus becomes apparent that given the power asymmetries of the consolidation regime 'more democracy' in Germany is synonymous with 'less democracy' in Greece or Portugal.[56] Rather than critically reflecting transnational power asymmetries enshrined in the crisis-ridden EMU, the court found itself entangled in an aporia of a national state-based understanding of democracy.

Unlike the PTC, however, the GFCC did not ignore the transnational dimension of the underlying conflicts entirely. In its *Outright Monetary Transactions* (OMT) and *Public Sector Purchase Programme* (PSPP) rulings,[57] it referred for the first time to the ECJ and framed the conflicts about crisis management basically as vertical conflicts about competences. The core complaint underlying both the OMT and the PSPP decision was that by buying government bonds of overly indebted eurozone Member States, the European Central Bank (ECB) is de facto violating Article 123 TFEU and thus acting ultra vires. These measures were said to imply potentially unlimited liability on the part of Germany, preventing the Bundestag from exercising its overall budgetary responsibility and thus, violating constitutional identity. In contrast to its *Maastricht* ruling the GFCC now emphasised the constitutional necessity of strengthening the democratic accountability of the ECB and limiting its independence. By referring these two cases to the ECJ, the court created an important opportunity for the transnational dimension of the conflict to be articulated in the language of European constitutional law. The GFCC's referral in OMT was celebrated by some as a 'good day for democracy in

55 This was also the overall very positive assessment in Kahl, 'Bewältigung der Staatsschuldenkrise unter Kontrolle des Bundesverfassungsgerichts: Ein Lehrstück zur horizontalen und vertikalen Gewaltenteilung', 128 *DVBl* (2013), 197–207.

56 In this sense also the criticism of Everson/Joerges, 'Who Is the Guardian for Constitutionalism After the Financial Crisis', 63 *LEQUS Paper* (2013), pp. 5–25, 17.

57 BVerfGE 134, 366 – *OMT I*; BVerfGE 142, 123 – *OMT II*; BVerfGE 154, 17 – *PSPP*.

Europe' because it revealed the legitimacy problems of the ECB's relevant decisions[58] and was said to provide an effective red line limiting technocratic crisis management.[59]

While the court in the end accepted the ECJ's assessment in OMT that the ECB has not exceeded its competences as the programme had primarily monetary policy character,[60] the controversy about how to hold the ECB accountable also for the transnational economic impact of its decisions continued in the PSPP case. Upon referral, the ECJ again argued that indirect economic policy effects do not call into question the monetary policy character of a measure and emphasised that independence of the ECB precluded a stricter proportionality review. The GFCC insisted on strictly reviewing whether the ECB had proportionally fulfilled its functions or exceeded its competences by acting disproportionately. The GFCC eventually found that the ECB had acted ultra vires.[61] It held that the 'right to democracy' under German constitutional law was violated since the ECB had neither examined nor proven that the measures foreseen in the PSPP were proportionate despite their effects on economic policy.[62] The measures taken by the ECB therefore resulted in a 'structurally significant shift of competences'[63] to the detriment of the Member States. The court also found the ECJ's decisions to 'obviously' transgress its competences as its reasoning was, in view of the GFCC, methodologically 'incomprehensible' and thus 'objectively arbitrary'.[64] On one hand, the decision by the GFCC deserves credit for laying bare the accountability problems of the executive-driven EMU governance and insisting on the centrality of parliamentary will-formation.[65] On the other hand, it also bears the risk of constitutional closure and power shift to courts rather than to the legislator. A strict proportionality review as required by the GFCC would ultimately empower constitutional courts to take a decision on

58 Murswiek, 'ECB, ECJ, Democracy, and the Federal Constitutional Court: Notes on the Federal Constitutional Court's Referral Order from 14 January 2014', 15 *German Law Journal* (2014), 147–165.

59 Petersen, 'Karlsruhe Not Only Barks, But Finally Bites – Some Remarks on the OMT Decision of the German Constitutional Court', 15 *German Law Journal* (2014), 321–327. Others were more critical, however: Wendel, 'Exceeding Judicial Competence in the Name of Democracy: The German Federal Constitutional Court's OMT Reference', 10 *European Constitutional Law Review* (2014), 263–307.

60 C-62/14, *Peter Gauweiler and Others v Deutscher Bundestag*, ECLI:EU:C:2015:400.

61 BVerfGE 154, 17, 95ff., 127ff. – *PSPP*.

62 BVerfGE 154, 17, 94 – *PSPP*.

63 BVerfGE 154, 17, 117 – *PSPP*.

64 BVerfGE 154, 17, 96, 116 – *PSPP*.

65 See also the critique by Wendel, 'Paradoxes of Ultra-Vires Review: A Critical Review of the PSPP Decision and Its Initial Reception', 21 *German Law Journal* (2020), 979–994, 989.

conflicting monetary and economic policy objectives.[66] This would not only undermine the ECB's independence but also increase the risk that particular economic and monetary policy understandings are again constitutionalised. Substantial accountability could eventually be traded for closing the democratic space for constantly (re-)negotiating the common goods in the European constitutional order.

### 10.3.3 *In Search of a European Common Good: Deductive and National Accountability in a Transnational Context*

The two constitutional courts reviewed in the previous sections largely applied a deductive approach to accountability in the EMU by applying exclusively domestic constitutional standards to transnational solidarity conflicts. In the case of the GFCC, the primary benchmark was national parliamentary sovereignty as well as fiscal stability as enshrined in the German Basic Law. In the case of the PTC, the primary benchmark were the principles of proportionality, equality and equal burden sharing as enshrined in the Portuguese Constitution. Likewise, both courts tended to 'nationalise' transnational solidarity conflicts rather than taking into account horizontal effects (in the case of Germany)[67] or supranational constitutional law (in the case of Portugal). By ignoring the European dimension of decision-making in the EMU, this line of jurisprudence decreased publicness rather than increasing it. It basically reduced the conflict to matters of domestic common goods and excluded the possibility of thinking about transnational, European common goods. To the extent that domestic constitutional courts refer to EU constitutional law, the relationship between domestic and EU constitutional law is characterised by conflict, denial of relevance or a rhetoric of deficit. What is profoundly absent is any vision of a European common good based on EU constitutional values (such as solidarity) that could inform the management of transnational solidarity conflicts and lead to EU constitutional law as a benchmark for 'publicness'. Therefore, domestic case law on transnational solidarity conflicts has at best produced integrative effects for domestic constitutional orders (inwards) but did not contribute to a further development and deepening of a European constitutional order. This is particularly remarkable, given that on a more technical regulatory level the eurozone crisis boosted further integration in the EMU.

[66] Wendel correctly emphasises the limited determinative power of the law with regard to monetary decisions. Wendel, ibid., at p. 990.

[67] For a profound critique of the PSPP-judgement in that respect, see Wendel, *supra* note 65, 993f.

The two domestic constitutional courts under review addressed transnational solidarity conflicts largely through procedural forms of accountability insisting on the need of an informed parliamentary decision and requiring the legislator to properly justify austerity measures. However, both constitutional courts have also applied some substantive aspects of accountability. The GFCC has stressed the relevance of a 'proportionality review' in the context of ECB decisions and has tried to push the ECJ to apply stricter scrutiny in this respect. However, it applied this standard only to the exercise of competences by the ECB and thereby deprived the principle out of its usual function of providing a yardstick for evaluating interferences with fundamental rights. The PTC has also applied substantive elements of accountability by developing and applying a standard of 'proportional equality' to measures of crisis reaction.

The advantage of domestic constitutional accountability regarding the achievement of integrative conflict management lies in the broad accessibility and procedural inclusiveness of accountability mechanisms. A diverse spectrum of political actors and/or individuals can challenge EMU-related decisions before domestic constitutional court. The procedural requirements are particularly low in the case of the German individual complaint (*Verfassungsbeschwerde*), but also the Portuguese system allows for a broad range of actors to challenge such decisions. Domestic constitutional accountability therefore allows to make transnational solidarity conflicts visible in the first places and channels as well as transforms them into constitutional conflicts. However, substantive emptiness of domestic constitutions remains limited during the management of transnational solidarity conflicts. While at least the GFCC kept an eye on trying to ensure openness of political will-formation in the German Bundestag, it otherwise 'closed' the meaning of several constitutional norms by upgrading economic concepts such as conditionality to constitutional principles. It thereby even enforced the 'no alternative' discourse by giving economic and political preferences the credit of constitutional value. The PTC on the other hand tried to ensure some substantial emptiness by 'opening up' the principle of equality to adapt it to new challenges and to use it as a tool to contest the EMU logic of market responsibility. At the same time, it 'closed' the Portuguese constitutions in the respective cases for interpretations that would require further austerity measures. At the very least, constitutional accountability before domestic courts has made transnational solidarity conflicts and accountability gaps more visible. It may also have partly contributed to enhancing the transparency of decision-making and increased publicness on the domestic level by positioning domestic constitutional principles as a benchmark for ensuring common goods.

## 10.4 THE UNPREPARED COURT: LIMITATIONS OF LEGAL ACCOUNTABILITY BEFORE THE ECJ

In view of the transnational conflict structure and the lack of domestic courts to take it into account, legal accountability at the supranational level seems to be a promising way to close accountability gaps in the EMU. A closer look, however, reveals that the ECJ was rather unprepared to fulfil this function and to contribute to an integrative role of European constitutional law.

The court's decisions in *Pringle*, *Gauweiler* and *Weiss* were paradigmatic of its familiar role in arbitrating vertical conflicts between the EU and its Member States. In *Pringle* the ECJ was asked to rule on the compatibility of the ESM Treaty with the no-bailout clause in Article 125 TFEU and the prohibition of the purchase of bonds under Article 123(1) TFEU. As such, the case concerned a fundamental premise of the EMU, namely that monetary policy (exclusive Union competence) and economic policy (primary competence of the Member States) can be clearly separated. At the core of the case were therefore substantial questions about fundamental constitutional principles governing the Economic and Monetary Union (EMU). In *Pringle*, the ECJ waved through the rescue mechanism so urgently needed to save the euro. It held that the ESM was an instrument that cannot be assigned to monetary but belonged to economic policy, so that the Member States did not violate the EU's order of competences when introducing the ESM on the basis of an international treaty.[68] Thus, the ECJ affirms the so-called separation thesis[69] (*Trennungsthese*), according to which economic policy and monetary policy can be accurately separated even under a common currency. The court thereby deproblematised the constitutional dimension of the ESM rather than engaging in the development of meaningful constitutional benchmarks for crisis reaction. Regarding the no-bailout clause, the court argued that the provision was intended to ensure that the state budgets 'remain subject to the logic of the market'.[70] Mutual financial assistance was therefore permissible as long as it did not threaten the overriding goal of 'maintaining the financial stability of the monetary union'.[71] In the view of the ECJ, this is ensured where the 'granting of financial assistance is tied to conditionalities that should ensure that the recipient states continue to pursue sound budgetary

[68] C-370/12, *Thomas Pringle v Government of Ireland and Others*, ECLI:EU:C:2012:756, paras 56, 58ff.

[69] On this Goldmann, 'Adjudicating Economics? Central Bank Independence and the Appropriate Standard of Judicial Review', in 15 *German Law Journal* (2014), 265–280, 269ff.

[70] C-370/12, *Thomas Pringle v Government of Ireland and Others*, *supra* note 65, para 135.

[71] Ibid.

policies'.[72] Thereby the ECJ – just like the GFCC – upgrades conditionality as a specific regulatory means to a constitutional requirement. By substantiating constitutional accountability with a particular regulatory idea, the ECJ itself contributes to the long-term closure of the political and constitutional discourse. Rather than reducing political discretion and potential interpretations of the common good in such a way, the court could have emphasised the constitutional need for political deliberation and parliamentary decision-making even in times of a financial crisis and could also have considered applying the EU Charter of Fundamental Rights whenever the act in the context of rescuing the common currency. Instead, the ECJ missed an opportunity to update a symbolic constitutional *topos* for a European constitution in times of crisis.

Compared to *Pringle*, the evaluation of the ECJ's Case Law in *Gauweiler* is more ambivalent in terms of accountability. On one hand, the court again confirmed the idea of strict separation between monetary and economic policy,[73] which allowed the court to rule the OMT program to remain within the mandate of the ECB as a purely monetary measure. On the other hand, ECJ now tried to develop more substantial benchmarks for the actions of the ECB by requiring that crisis measures are temporary limited[74] and introducing a proportionality test as a yardstick for assessing the ECB's action.[75] The concrete evaluation by the ECJ boiled essentially down to a mere rationality control and still granted the ECB broad discretion as 'monetary policy issues are usually controversial'.[76] Nevertheless, the introduction of a proportionality test in *Gauweiler* and maintained later on in *Weiss* can be understood as a cautious attempt to tie the ECB's crisis response to general constitutional topoi and to update the concrete meaning in central bank's competences in light of the recent changes in the Eurozone. It thereby introduces a light procedural standard of accountability rather than a substantial requirement. While this prevents the court from narrowing constitutional meaning to economic considerations, it also fails to grasp and address the full dimension of the accountability and legitimation problems that arise from the increasing involvement of the ECB in the political processes of macroeconomic adjustment through conditionality.

[72] Ibid., para 143, also paras 111, 121.

[73] For a critical perspective, see Goldmann, *supra* note 66, 269f., Borger, 'Outright Monetary Transactions and the Stability Mandate of the ECB', 53 *Common Market Law Review* (2016), 139–196, 149, 191.

[74] C-62/14, *Peter Gauweiler and Others v Deutscher Bundestag, supra* n. 60, para 12.

[75] Ibid., para 69.

[76] Ibid., para 75.

In contrast to the classic conflicts of competence, the ECJ proved much more hesitant to accept jurisprudence in conflicts over the legality of Union-induced crisis measures resulting from conditionalities, such as wage and pension cuts.[77] From the very beginning of the crisis, visibility of conflicts over conditionalities before the ECJ was limited for three structural reasons. First, major crisis instruments, such as the ESM, partly took place outside the European Treaties, so that it was difficult to identify contestable acts of the Union institutions. In *Mallis and Malli*, for instance, the General Court of the EU denied attribution of negotiations under the ESM to the European Commission.[78] Second, since the national authorities were left with room for manoeuvre in the implementation, even if the crisis measures were clearly traceable to the action of an EU institution, it was difficult to prove that individuals were directly affected by EU measures in the sense of Article 263(4) TFEU. In *ADEDY* the court held that the applicants were not directly affected because the contested decision of the Council of the EU left Greece with considerable room for manoeuvre in implementing the requirements.[79] Finally, national crisis response measures were only rarely implemented in the form of binding Union legal acts but were often based on Memoranda of Understanding whose legal nature and binding effect were disputed.

This latter problem also affected cases brought to the court under the preliminary reference procedure. In the first phase of the eurozone crisis, the General Court rejected a total of seven references from Portuguese and Romanian courts concerning the compatibility of conditionality-induced wage cuts in the public service with fundamental rights under the EU Fundamental Rights Charter. In all seven cases, the court argued that the referring courts had not sufficiently demonstrated the link between the wage reductions imposed by national laws and Union law.[80] Unlike in other cases, the court refrained from re-interpreting the referrals so as to establish its jurisdiction and did not ask the

77 The following argument is based on an article that I published together with Christoph Krenn (Farahat/Krenn, 'Der EuGH in der Eurokrise: Eine konflikttheoretische Perspektive', 57 *Der Staat* (2018), 357–385, 366ff.).

78 T-327/13, *Mallis and Malli v European Commission and European Central Bank (ECB)*, ECLI:EU:T:2014:909, para 39–45.

79 T-541/10, *ADEDY and others v Council of the European Union*, ECLI:EU:T:2012:626, paras 70f., 76, 78.

80 C-434/11, *Corpul Naţional al Poliţiştilor v Ministerul Administraţiei şi Internelor (MAI) and Others*, ECLI:EU:C:2011:830, para 16; C-462/11, *Victor Cozman v Teatrul Municipal Târgovişte*, ECLI:EU:C:2011:831, para 15, C-134/12, *Corpul Naţional al Poliţiştilor v Ministerul Administraţiei şi Internelor and Others*, ECLI:EU:C:2012:288, para 13; C-369/12, *Corpul Naţional al Poliţiştilor v Ministerul Administraţiei şi Internelor and Others*, ECLI:EU:C:2012:725, para 15; C-128/12, *Sindicato dos Bancários do Norte and Others v Banco Português de Negócios SA*, ECLI:EU:C:2013:149, para 12; C-264/12, *Sindicato Nacional dos Profissionais de Seguros e*

domestic courts for clarification either. The court thereby failed to provide a meaningful standard of European constitutional accountability and severely restricted access to accountability.

However, in the course of the crisis, the ECJ cautiously adapted to the new type of conflict. In *Florescu*,[81] the ECJ willingly reformulated the referred questions and held that the measures taken by the Romanian government were in fact implementing the MoU, and thus fell within the scope of application of the EU Charter of Fundamental Rights pursuant to Article 51. In *Ledra Advertising*, the Court activated the rules on the non-contractual liability of the Union. The court clarified that EU institutions were obliged to sign memoranda for the ESM only if they are compatible with Union law, including the EU Charter of Fundamental Rights and that they could otherwise be held liable under Article 268 in conjunction with Article 340 TFEU.[82] The outcome in terms of substantive accountability, however, remained rather meagre also in the case law following *Ledra Advertising*. The court readily accepted that interferences with fundamental rights were justified in the light of the imminent economic risks and raised a high bar for actually activating liability of EU institutions in this respect.[83] By resorting to the rhetoric of the economic state of emergency, the court ultimately refused to concretise a substantive fundamental rights standard. Neither did it specify what the standard would be to return to after the acute crisis phase nor did it introduce a temporal limitation of the crisis-induced interferences.

To sum up, the EU courts allowed only for limited access to constitutional accountability. In terms of accountability goods, the ECJ focused primarily on economic constitutional values but only hesitantly applied other constitutional values such as social rights and solidarity as a benchmark for substantive accountability. It thereby only rarely allowed for contestation of dominant narratives of the understanding of constitutional norms but rather joined domestic courts in upgrading specific economic concepts and political preferences (e.g. conditionality) to constitutional values. Rather European courts primarily engaged in procedural accountability by introducing requirements for justification, thus serving to ensure the effectiveness and transparency of EMU decision-making,

*Afins v Fidelidade Mundial – Companhia de Seguros SA*, ECLI:EU:C:2014:2036, para 19–21; C-665/13, *Sindicato Nacional dos Profissionais de Seguros e Afins v Via Directa – Companhia de Seguros SA*, ECLI:EU:C:2014:2327, paras 13–15.

81 C-258/14, *Eugenia Florescu and Others v Casa Judeţeană de Pensii Sibiu and Others*, ECLI:EU:C:2017:448.

82 C-8/15 P, *Ledra Advertising Ltd and Others v European Commission and European Central Bank* ECLI:EU:C:2016:701, paras 55–64.

83 See C-8/15 P, ECLI:EU:C:2016:701, para 74; equally scarce T-531/14, *Leïmonia Sotiropoulou and Others v Council of the European Union*, ECLI:EU:T:2017:297, paras 88ff.; T-107/17, *Frank Steinhoff and Others v European Central Bank*, ECLI:EU:T:2019:353, para 116.

but often also to merely rubber-stamping crisis measures. Only to a very limited extent did the ECJ ensure substantive accountability and contribute to the publicness of EMU decisions. In light of this analysis, it seems obvious that European constitutional accountability mechanisms did not yield substantial integrative effects and did not ensure meaningful accountability in the sense of concretising and re-negotiating constitutional common goods.

## 10.5 LIMITS AND PERSPECTIVES OF LEGAL ACCOUNTABILITY

Instead of a conclusion, the final section of this chapter seeks to address the limits of constitutional accountability of the EMU and to sketch out some perspectives for its future development. We have already seen that the capturing of constitutional accountability by economic policies and limited access to supranational accountability mechanisms pose significant obstacles to develop European constitutional law as a meaningful benchmark for providing publicness. However, the call for courts to play a more active and meaningful role in providing publicness as an accountability good also raises issues. As courts are typically not legitimised to take distributive decisions and likewise often not qualified to substantially review technocratic institutions, a more substantial role of courts in the EMU accountability architecture raises concerns as to the separation of powers.

As a preliminary matter, judicial review in modern societies can be seen as not only ensuring the rule of law but also contributing to democratic will-formation. The historian Pierre Rosanvallon has shown from a conflict-theoretical perspective that every majority decision excludes a part of the democratic people, while normatively the decision of the majority is supposed to represent the general will of the people and thus implicitly carries the ideal of unanimity.[84] The more pluralistic societies become, the less this implicit ideal, according to which the democratic majority also represents society as a whole, is true. It can no longer be claimed that future political decisions are already implied in the electoral decision.[85] The members of a pluralistic demos feel they belong to different social groups simultaneously so that 'the people' sort of becomes a plural of minority.[86] Consequently, parliamentary majorities do not represent the people as a whole.[87]

[84] Rosanvallon, *supra* note 5, p. 35ff.

[85] In detail on the contradiction between the fiction of unanimity and democratic pluralism with regard to the legitimacy of general elections, ibid., p. 53ff.

[86] Ibid.

[87] Ibid., pp. 7ff., 41f.

There is, therefore, an increasing need to allow for competing expressions of the public will.[88] Separation of powers could thus be best understood as an arrangement that gives institutional expression to the plurality of society and represents it in different forms. Constitutional courts lend themselves as a forum where such competing visions of the public will can not only be expressed but need to be taken into account. Using the constitution as a yardstick for accountability, constitutional courts can ensure that a currently dominant vision of the common good always needs to justify itself in the light of all other potential versions of the common good that are embodied in the constitution. In this sense, the accountability good of publicness should not be misunderstood as requiring compliance with a specific common good but rather as ensuring that the open-ended search for a common good remains the reference point of policy choices.

However, parliamentary legislation by democratically elected representatives is still an irreplaceable mechanism of responsiveness in a democratic polity. After all, the open-ended debate about and re-negotiation of the common good cannot take place before courts alone. Not only would this overburden the courts, but it would also ignore that democratic will-formation is not only an individualistic endeavour but rather requires collective processes. In light of these considerations, the primary function of future constitutional accountability mechanisms should be to foster adequate decision-making procedures and ensure sufficient space for open political will-formation and decision-making. It should help make political preferences that are often hidden behind a rhetoric of necessity visible again and challenge not only their necessity but also their compatibility with the normative script embodied in the constitution.[89] Importantly, this also implies making sure that constitutional provisions are not hijacked by political preferences or by economic concepts. In the context of the EMU in particular and the EU more generally, a core function of constitutional accountability should also be to allow for identifying and openly addressing transnational solidarity conflicts. To properly address the transnational dimension of solidarity conflicts and EMU action, both domestic and EU courts need to better reflect the impact of their decisions on other legal orders within the EMU. Only then can they together contribute to rendering European constitutional law into a meaningful normative framework for accountability.

88 Ibid., at p. 243.

89 On how the ECJ's procedural and organisational law could be 'democratised' for the Court to be able to better exercise such role, see Krenn, *The Procedural and Organisational Law of the European Court of Justice. An Incomplete Transformation* (forthcoming, Cambridge University Press, 2022) Chapter 5.

# 11

# Judicial Accountability of Financial Assistance in the Case of Eurozone Debtor Countries

*Teresa Violante*[*]

## 11.1 INTRODUCTION

This chapter investigates legal accountability of financial assistance from the perspective of borrower countries. It adopts an empirical approach taking the Portuguese case to test how accountability of the financial assistance programme, on the one hand, and of the national measures implementing conditionality, on the other, was exercised. The investigation focuses on the judicial review of austerity measures in different institutional contexts comprising the domestic constitutional court, the Court of Justice of the European Union (CJEU), and the European Court of Human Rights. It aims at assessing how far these judicial fora have delivered the accountability goods identified in the introductory chapter, particularly publicness, as the good oriented towards ensuring that public action is guided by common goods, namely that it respects the constitutional principles of equality and proportionality. These yardsticks have been specifically contemplated by the case law of the Portuguese Constitutional Court and the European Court of Human Rights.

It focuses specifically on the role of the CJEU as an accountability-rendering forum for the financial assistance programmes developed in the framework of the Eurozone crisis. On the other hand, it focuses on how far domestic constitutional adjudication can be an effective accountability tool as it was enforced to control the compatibility of economic conditionality with constitutional

* The research leading to this chapter has been developed in the framework of the DFG-Emmy Noether Research Group on 'Transnational Solidarity Conflicts'. I am thankful to the participants in the ERC Workshop on Theorising and Assessing Accountability in Post-Crisis EU Economic Governance that took place in the Hertie School, Berlin, on September 23–24, 2021, for their comments and suggestions. I am particularly grateful for the suggestions Ana Bobić and Mark Dawson have made.

yardsticks, particularly the protection of salaries and pensions, as well as general principles, such as equality in the allocation of the adjustment costs and the protection of legitimate expectations. The role of the Portuguese *Tribunal Constitucional* (PCC) as a forum for the legal accountability of austerity measures is explored in detail. The limited role of the European Court of Human Rights (ECtHR) is also addressed.

The chapter is organized into four sections, following this introduction (Section 11.1). Section 11.2 briefly outlines the normative developments of financial assistance mechanisms in the Eurozone following the Treaty of Lisbon, and the architecture of the financial assistance programme to Portugal, as well as its complex and disputed legal nature. Section 11.3 deals with the absence of judicial review of the Portuguese MoU, at both the EU and the domestic levels, and the factors that explain why such an important European Monetary Union (EMU) governance mechanism escaped judicial scrutiny. This section also identifies a prominent gap in EU case law which has only been partly addressed as late as of May 2022: the topic of knowing whether financial assistance to euro area members comes under the purview of EU law. The factors contributing to the immunization of the MoU from domestic judicial review are also explored, particularly the 'nationalization of the crisis' by the case law of the Constitutional Court. Section 11.4 deals with judicial review of national measures implementing MoU conditionality. It provides an in-depth analysis of *Associação Sindical dos Juízes* and its problematic consequences for the furtherance of inequalities between immobile public workers and the displacement of social rights and solidarity conflicts from the Luxembourg stage. At the level of domestic constitutional law, it portrays the PCC as the only judicial stage available for the accountability of financial assistance conditionality. Section 11.5 concludes and hypothesizes that more lines of tension between domestic and EU constitutionalism may emerge in the constellations related to solidarity and welfare rights.

## 11.2 THE ARCHITECTURE OF THE PORTUGUESE FINANCIAL ASSISTANCE PROGRAMME OF 2011

### 11.2.1 *Financial Assistance in the Eurozone*

The first signs of the euro area sovereign debt crisis surfaced just a few weeks after the Treaty of Lisbon entered into force. The revised EU legal framework left almost untouched the EMU, with the exception of the new Article 136 TFEU. The urgent need to equip the EU and particularly the EMU with tools to deal with a major financial crisis was overlooked.[1] There was no instrument to regulate emergency assistance to Eurozone Member States facing financial distress as the predominant paradigm affirmed that each country was fully responsible for its financial (mis)fortunes.[2]

In 2010, the first emergency mechanisms were created: the European Financial Stabilisation Mechanism (EFSM) and the European Financial Stability Facility (EFSF), the former being a 'creature of EU law',[3] established under Article 122(2) TFEU.[4] Portugal received a total of €24.3 billion from the EFSM.

Besides establishing a financial assistance mechanism applicable to all Member States; a Special Purpose Vehicle was also adopted. The European Financial Stability Facility was incorporated in Luxembourg on 7 June 2010 as a *société anonyme*, and its shareholders are the euro area Member States.[5] The EFSF has provided financial assistance to Ireland, Portugal, and Greece. It was set up as a temporary mechanism, and it does not provide further financial assistance as this task is now assigned to the European Stability Mechanism.[6]

Financial assistance under any of the mechanisms would be subject to strict conditionality: 'financial support should be contingent upon the recipient Member State fulfilling certain budgetary, financial sector, and

[1] Ruffert, 'The European Debt Crisis and European Union Law', 48 *Common Market Law Review* (2011) 1777–1806 at 1778.

[2] The only possibility of financial assistance in the framework of the EU concerned the Balance of Payments assistance, which may be granted by the EU to non-eurozone Member States under Article 143 Treaty on the Functioning of the European Union (TFEU) and Council Regulation (EC) 332/2002 of 18 February 2002 establishing a facility providing a medium-term financial assistance for Member States' balances of payments [2002] OJ L53/1.

[3] Kilpatrick, 'Are the Bailouts Immune to EU Social Challenge Because They Are Not EU Law?' 10 *European Constitutional Law Review* (2014) 398.

[4] Council Regulation (EU) 407/2010 of 11 May 2010 establishing a European financial stabilization mechanism [2010] OJ L118/1; See also Council Regulation (EU) 2015/1360 of 4 August 2015 amending Regulation (EU) No 407/2010 establishing a European financial stabilization mechanism [2015] OJ L210/1.

[5] European Financial Stability Facility Framework Agreement (as amended with effect from the Effective Date of the Amendment) between Kingdom of Belgium, Federal Republic of Germany, Republic of Estonia, Ireland, Helenic Republic, Kingdom of Spain, French Republic, Italian Republic, Republic of Cyprus, Grand Duchy of Luxembourg, Republic of Malta, Kingdom of the Netherland, Republic of Austria, Portuguese Republic, Republic of Slovenia, Slovak Republic, Republic of Finland, and European Financial Stability Facility, available at www.esm.europa.eu/content/efsf-framework-agreement (accessed 10 September 2021). (Here after EFSF).

[6] The EFSF was replaced for future assistance programmes in 2012 by the European Stability Mechanism (ESM), which was also established as an international agreement between the Eurozone states.

macroeconomic conditions'.[7] This new mode of economic governance has been qualified as 'authoritarian liberalism' for its resonance with the German experience of the late 1920s and early 1930s.[8]

### 11.2.2 *The Financial Assistance Programme to Portugal*

In April 2011, Portugal became the third Eurozone country to request financial assistance, following Greece and Ireland. The Portuguese Financial and Economic Assistance Programme (FEAP) comprised a €78 billion loan to be delivered between 2011 and 2014 provided by the International Monetary Fund (IMF), the EU, within the framework of the EFSM, and the Eurozone countries, under the EFSF. The programme incorporated three documents: the Memorandum of Economic and Financial Policies, the Technical Memorandum of Understanding, and the Memorandum on Specific Policy Conditionality (hereinafter, the MoU). The first two documents were sent as attachments to a letter of intent addressed to the IMF's executive Commission, and the third document was signed between the Portuguese Republic and the European Commission. The MoU detailed the general economic policy conditions embedded in Council Implementing Decision 2011/344/EU, of 30 May 2011, on granting EU financial assistance to Portugal.

The FEAP covered three broad lines of action to reach the 3 per cent deficit ceiling in 2013. It provided for the adoption of profound 'structural reforms' and a credible 'fiscal consolidation' strategy. As the government's report on the Adjustment Programme's execution claimed, 'these were the years of the deepest and most wide-reaching reforms in the history of [Portuguese] democracy'.[9]

The language of 'structural reforms' and 'fiscal consolidation' translates strict conditionality as a vital component of the bailout agreement. As Ioannidis notes, '[c]onditionality is the new topos of EU economic governance'.[10] To eliminate the danger of moral hazard, it 'became the basic disciplining instrument'.[11]

7 Case C-370/12 *Thomas Pringle v Government of Ireland*, ECLI:EU:C:2012:756.

8 Wilkinson, 'The Specter of Authoritarian Liberalism: Reflections on the Constitutional Crisis of the European Union', 14 *German Law Journal* (2013) 527–560; Dani, 'The EU Transformation of the Social State', in Ferri and Cortese (eds.), *The EU Social Market Economy and the Law* (Routledge, 2018) 39.

9 Governo de Portugal, Secretary of State to the Prime Minister, 'Managing the Adjustment Programme – 2011 | 2014', available at www.historico.portugal.gov.pt/media/1505374/20140829%20seapm%20gestao%20paef%20ing.pdf.

10 Ioannidis, 'EU Financial Assistance After Conditionality After "Two Pack"', 74 *Zeitschrift für ausländisches öfentliches Recht und Völkerrecht* (2014) 62.

11 Ioannidis, 'Europe's New Transformations: How the EU Economic Constitution Changed During the Eurozone Crisis', 53 *Common Market Law Review* (2016) 1240.

The bailout was negotiated between April and May 2011 by the Portuguese State with a Troika composed of the IMF, the European Central Bank, and the European Commission. The negotiations were held by a resigning government, and the EU and Eurogroup required the commitment of the main opposition parties to the MoU to ensure political consensus.[12]

### 11.2.3 *The Legal Nature of the FEAP*

The legal character of the memoranda and their conditionality has been a disputed topic. Some scholars claim that the programme had a pure proclamatory nature at the domestic level, while others argue that they are international treaties.[13] Others still recognize the hybrid nature of the programme, which combined a unilateral act (the IMF's declaration), a bilateral agreement (the framework agreement and the loan contract with the EFSF), and EU acts (on the EFSM).[14] Another strand of scholarly literature claims that, despite the mixed legal parentage of the programme, and the links with the EU legal order, the predominant pedigree relates to instruments which must be qualified as international agreements.[15]

That is not the opinion shared by Claire Kilpatrick who noted that, in the Portuguese and Irish bailouts, the 'European leg' of the memoranda prevailed as the 'pole normative position' was assigned to the 'EU sources containing the loan conditionality…, not the international sources'.[16]

[12] As noted by Pereira Coutinho, this requirement was clearly expressed in the joint declaration of 8 April 2011, stating that negotiations shall include all the opposition parties who, moreover, should confirm a new government in Parliament with the ability to fully adopt and implement the MoU. Since this declaration was made less than two months before parliamentary elections, the author argues that it can be regarded as an unlawful interference in the domestic affairs of the Portuguese State forbidden by both international law [Article 2(7) of the United Nations Charter] and EU law [Article 4(2) Treaty on European Union (Hereafter TEU)]. See Pereira Coutinho, 'Austerity on the loose in Portugal: European judicial restraint in times of crisis', 8(3) *Perspectives on Federalism* (2016) 127–128.

[13] Baptista, 'Natureza jurídica dos memorandos com o FMI e a União Europeia', 71(2) *Revista da Ordem dos Advogados* (2011) 483; Caldas and Oliveira 'A vinculatividade do Memorando de Entendimento da Troika – Em especial a disciplina orçamental', 4(4) *Revista de Direito Público e Finanças* (2011) 173–176.

[14] Pereira Coutinho, 'A natureza jurídica dos memorandos da "Troika" ano XIII', 24/25 *Themis* (2013) 147–179; Anastasia Polou, 'Financial Conditionality and Human Rights Protection: What Is the Role of the EU Charter of Fundamental Rights?', 54 *Common Market Law Review* (2017) 1002.

[15] Cisotta and Gallo, 'The Portuguese Constitutional Court Case-Law on Austerity Measures: A Reappraisal', in Kilpatrick and De Witte (eds.), *Social Rights in Crisis in the Eurozone: The Role of Fundamental Rights Challenges*, EUI WP 2014/5 85.

[16] Kilpatrick, 'Are the Bailouts Immune to EU Social Challenge Because They Are Not EU Law?', 10 *European Constitutional Law Review* (2014) 401.

Similarly, the PCC affirmed, in the first opportunity in which it was confronted with austerity policies implementing MoU conditionality, that the memoranda were legally binding. Whereas the Greek Council of State ruled out the legal value of the Greek MoU and sought to recognize its role as a political and economic plan whose implementation claimed the adoption of primary or secondary legal instruments,[17] the PCC recognized the 'binding force for the Portuguese State' of the FEAP, since it combined instruments based on both international law and EU law according to Article 8(2) of the Constitution. The international law leg was based on Article V, Section 11.3 of the IMF Agreement, whereas the EU leg was located on Article 122(2) TFEU and Council Regulation (EU) No 407/2010 of 11 May establishing the EFSM. In the words of the Court, 'These documents impose the adoption by the Portuguese State of the measures contained therein as a condition for the phased compliance with the financing contracts signed between the same entities.'[18]

## 11.3 JUDICIAL REVIEW OF THE MoU

According to Fabbrini, the intergovernmental method of governance that dominated the EMU during the Eurozone crisis led to high degree of judicial intervention by both domestic and EU courts.[19] This phenomenon can be framed as the *paradox of judicialization* in contrast to the deferential posture adopted by the US courts in economic issues. In relation to the Portuguese financial assistance programme, domestic courts were very active in the adjudication of EMU affairs. However, that does not hold true for the CJEU, which refrained from intervening in the disputes that emerged in the context of the financial assistance to Portugal.

The Portuguese MoU has never been tested in court due to what has been called a 'systemic failure in the jurisdictional system of the EU'.[20] For different reasons, the MoU escaped review by both the CJEU (1) and the PCC (2). This section reviews the circumstances underlying the immunization from judicial accountability of this important instrument of Eurocrisis governance.

[17] Markakis, *Accountability in the Economic and Monetary Union. Foundations, Policy and Governance* (OUP, 2020) 261–262.

[18] Decision 353/2012.

[19] Fabbrini, *Economic Governance in Europe. Comparative Paradoxes and Constitutional Changes* (OUP, 2016) 63 ff.

[20] Pereira Coutinho, 'The Portuguese Bailout, Social Rights and the Rule of Law', in Coli, Pacini, and Stradella (eds.), *Policy, Welfare and Financial Resources: The Impact of the Crisis on Territories* (Pisa University Press, 2017).

### 11.3.1 *EU Case Law*

Two preliminary references by Portuguese courts indirectly challenged the validity of the MoU before the CJEU but in both cases the Court held that it clearly had no jurisdiction to hear them. Previously, another preliminary reference had challenged budgetary provisions implementing austerity measures adopted in the context of an excessive deficit procedure initiated by Council Decision No 2010/288/EU of 19 January 2010.[21] The wording of the three references challenged only national law implementing pay cuts on public-sector companies and failed to establish that the impugned domestic budgetary provisions implemented EU law.[22] Significantly, the CJEU treated all three cases as analogous in spite of the different legal frameworks underlying the concerned austerity measures. Furthermore, both the *Fidelidade Mundial* and *Via Direta* cases concern Article 21(1) of the Budget Law for 2012 on the suspension of payment of holiday and Christmas bonuses or similar benefits, whose wording expressly referred to the financial assistance programme:

> For the duration of the Economic and Financial Assistance Programme (PAEF), as an exceptional measure of budgetary stability, the payment of holiday and Christmas bonuses … or any benefits relating to the 13th and/or 14th month pay to those persons referred to in Article 19(9) of [the 2011 Budget Law], as amended by Law No 48/2011 of 26 August 2011 and Law No 60-A/2011 of 30 November 2011, whose monthly remuneration is greater than EUR 1.100, shall be suspended.

The CJEU was outwardly dismissive of its jurisdiction to hear the cases alluding to the referring courts' failure to establish the link with the EU bailout terms with sufficient clarity. The poor drafting of the references can be attributed to the complexity underlying the foundational bailout and its subsequent updates.[23] However, that should have not prevented the CJEU from redrafting the questions submitted by the Portuguese courts.[24] In cases of issues of admissibility, the CJEU has developed a generous understanding according to which questions

[21] Case C-128/12 *Sindicato dos Bancários do Norte, Sindicato dos Bancários do Centro, Sindicato dos Bancários do Sul e Ilhas, Luís Miguel Rodrigues v BPN – Banco Português de Negócios SA* ECLI:EU:C:2013:149.

[22] Case C-264/12 *Sindicato Nacional dos Profissionais de Seguros e Afins v Fidelidade Mundial – Companhia de Seguros SA* ECLI:EU:C:2014:2036; Case C-665/13 *Sindicato Nacional dos Profissionais dos Seguros e Afins v Via Direta – Companhia de Seguros SA* ECLI:EU:C:2014:2327.

[23] Kilpatrick, 'On the Rule of Law and Economic Emergency: The Degradation of Basic Legal Values in Europe's Bailouts', 35(2) *Oxford Journal of Legal Studies* (2015) 325–353.

[24] Ibid Kilpatrick 349, at fn. 107 specifically; Pereira Coutinho *supra* n 20 at 81; Polou, 'Financial Assistance Conditionality and Human Rights Protection', 54 *Common Market Law Review*

submitted by national courts enjoy a 'presumption of relevance'. Questions on the interpretation of EU law referred by a national court in the factual and legislative context which that court is responsible for defining, and the accuracy of which is not a matter for the Court to determine, enjoy a presumption of relevance.[25] Only in exceptional circumstances will the Court refrain from giving a preliminary ruling providing that there is a rebuttal to the presumption.[26]

In *Escribano Vindel*,[27] a case concerning reduction in salary of a Catalonian judge, in the context of general pay cuts linked to the requirements of eliminating an excessive budget deficit, the presumption of relevance was crucial for the Court to accept jurisdiction. In this case, the only link to EU law consisted of the reiterated reference to the 'requirements of eliminating an excessive budget deficit', without any specification being put forward of the normative framework detailing the EU sources potentially involved. The contrast in the attitude of the Court of Justice between the references from the Portuguese courts and *Escribano Vindel* is startling.

The fact that the Court failed to apply the presumption of relevance might imply, as Markakis hypothesizes, that it did not regard the contested bailout measures as resulting from an EU law obligation.[28] According to this line of reasoning, the bailout terms embodied conditionality the national authorities would have to implement to access the disbursement of funds but were not legally binding. Insofar as said conditions concern areas of national competence, they would be mere recommendations. Accordingly, the EU has secondary competence to set the terms on which the financial assistance can be provided,[29] but the relevant Council decisions would not give rise to EU law obligations to transpose and implement the bailout conditions into domestic law. However, the CJEU did not come clean on this and was limited to stating that the decisions for reference did not contain any specific material showing that the national measures were intended to implement EU law.[30] Moreover,

(2017) 991–1026, at 1017–1018; Markakis, *Accountability in the Economic and Monetary Union supra* n 17 at 220 and fn. 79; Farahat, *Transnationale Solidaritätskonflite: Eine vergleichende Analyse verfassungsgerichlicher Konfliktbearbeitung in der Eurokrise* (Mohr Siebeck, 2021).

25 Case C-64/16 *Associação Sindical dos Juízes Portugueses*, Opinion of Advocate General Saugmandsgaard Øe ECLI:EU:C:2017:395 para. 28.

26 Case C-300/01 *Doris Salzmann* ECLI:EU:C:2003:283 para 29–33.

27 Case C-49/18 *Carlos Escribano Vindel* ECLI:EU:C:2019:106 para. 24–26.

28 Markakis, *Accountability in the Economic and Monetary Union supra* n 17 at 220–224.

29 Article 122(2) TFEU, which provided the legal basis for the EFSM, and not Article 136(3) TFEU, as the founding basis for the ESM.

30 Similarly, other references concerning austerity measures from countries on financial assistance were not dealt with in substance by the CJEU. See the Romanian cases: ECJ 14 December 2011, Case C-434/11 *Corpul Naţional al Poliţiştilor v Ministerul Administraţiei şi Internelor*

in later case law, as we will see below, the CJEU would eventually acknowledge that the bailout conditions form part of EU law and the Member State concerned is 'implementing Union law' within the meaning of Article 51(1) of the CFEU, at least when financial assistance is granted by the EFSM.[31]

### 11.3.2 *Ledra and Florescu*

In the following years, the Court delivered other important judgements in different settings of financial assistance that would retrospectively point to the flaws in its initial case law to decline jurisdiction in the framework of the Portuguese financial assistance programme. A first moment came when, in *Ledra*, relating to the Cyprus bailout,[32] despite rejecting the qualification of the bailout as an act of EU law act, the Court nevertheless added that EU institutions remain fully bound by EU law and the Charter when they act as agents of a distinct international organization such as the ESM.

Afterwards, in *Florescu*,[33] the Court acknowledged that a Memorandum of Understanding for Balance of payments is an act of an EU institution and could thus be referred under Article 267 TFEU for interpretation. The Court also specified that the national measure implementing MoU and a Council decision conditionality constituted an implementation of EU law and thus triggered the application of the Charter of Fundamental Rights. It has been argued that the '*Florescu* ruling serves to enhance the legal accountability of the EU institutions for their actions with respect to bailouts'.[34] However, *Florescu* related to a bailout adopted in the framework of Article 143 TFEU concerning assistance to non-euro area Member States experiencing difficulties with respect to their balance of payments. For accountability purposes, the field of financial assistance to euro area members still posed as a gap in the case law of the Court of Justice.

This gap has only partly been addressed in more recent case law of the CJEU, and in terms which raise problematic issues. This will be further addressed below.

*(MAI) and Others*; ECLI:EU:C:2011:830; Case C-134/12 *Corpul Naţional al Poliţiştilor – Biroul Executiv Central (în numele şi în interesul membrilor săi – funcţionari publici cu statut special – poliţişti din cadrul IPJ Tulcea) v Ministerul Administraţiei şi Internelor and Others* ECLI:EU:C:2012:288; Case C-369/12 *Corpul Naţional al Poliţiştilor – Biroul Executiv Central v Ministerului Administraţiei şi Internelo and Others* ELCI:EU:C:2012:725.

31 See *BPC Lux 2* below.

32 See *supra* note 25.

33 Case C-258/14 *Florescu and Others* ECLI:EU:C:2017:448.

34 Markakis and Dermine, 'Bailouts, the Legal Status of Memoranda of Understanding, and the Scope of Application of the EU Charter: Florescu', 55 *Common Market Law Review* (2018) 643.

### 11.3.3 *Constitutional Court Case Law*

As explained above, the PTC qualified the documents that integrated the financial assistance programme as legally binding and found that the MoU was 'ultimately based on Article 122(2)' TFEU, and qualified, therefore as EU law. As such, insofar as the founding documents imposed the adoption, by the Portuguese State, of conditionality, there was no discretion as to whether the domestic authorities were in fact obliged to implement the said conditions. However, the Court found that those measures afforded discretion to the State to decide on the means best able to ensure compliance with those commitments.

In Decision 353/2012, however, the judges failed to realize that the impugned measures – the total and partial suspension of the 13th and 14th monthly salary payments of public workers and pensioners – albeit absent from the initial version of the MoU, had been included in its second update. In fact, whereas the first disbursement of financial assistance is released after the signature of the MoU, further instalments are conditional on the fulfilment of the bailout conditions included in the MoU (Article 4 of Regulation (EU) 407/2010). Changes in the general economic policy conditionality are negotiated between the Commission and the beneficiary Member State. Afterwards, the Council, acting by a qualified majority on a proposal from the Commission, approves the revised adjustment programme prepared by the Member State. The disbursement of the next instalment of the loan follows the signature by the Commission and the Member State of an updated version of the MoU revised in accordance with the Council's decision (Article 3(6) and (7) of Regulation 407/2010).

The complex framework underlying the financial assistance programme added to the difficulty of the Court in handling claims involving the adjudication of complex economic issues in times of economic crisis.[35] Importantly, by failing to trace the link between the domestic impugned measures and the MoU, a document which had been qualified by the PCC as EU law, the stage was set for what would become a dominant trend of the extensive bulk of austerity case law: the 'nationalization of the crisis'[36] whereby the PTC depicted domestic measures implementing the bailout conditionality as purely domestic affairs.

35 See generally Ginsburg, Rosen and Vanberg (eds.), *Constitutions in Times of Financial Crisis* (CUP, 2019).

36 Violante and André, 'The Constitutional Performance of Austerity in Portugal', in Ginsburg, Rosen and Vanberg (eds.), *Constitutions in Times of Financial Crisis* (CUP, 2019) 254–255; Violante, 'Constitutional Adjudication as a Forum for Contesting Austerity: The Case of

The challenged austerity measures were always framed as the result of autonomous political choices between competing viable alternatives, which allowed the Court to circumvent the difficult questions concerning the relationship between EU law and the national constitution and the validity of the MoU. This nationalization strategy of the crisis immunized the austerity litigation from the reach of EU law. Had the Court acknowledged that at least some of the challenged measures were – textually – determined by the MoU, then it should have drafted a preliminary reference questioning its compatibility with EU law, namely the Charter. Such a reference[37] would be harder to dismiss by the CJEU and would have brought the challenged measures to 'their natural stage' in accordance with the transnational dimension of austerity conflicts.[38] Furthermore, it could have pushed the CJEU to face the solidarity conflicts undergirding the bailout austerity and measure the austerity against the social provisions of the CFEU. This leg of substantive accountability in relation to the public goods of social provisions of the Charter is missing not only in relation to the Portuguese financial assistance programme but generally in relation to the tension underlying social and liberal Europe.

It should be noted, however, that the nationalization of the austerity conflicts on the part of the PCC is in line with its traditional case law that had a reluctance to engage with EU law. Like other Kelsenian constitutional courts, the PCC followed the 'doctrine of isolationism'[39] for a long time, separating EU law issues from the stage of constitutional adjudication.[40] Only recently has the PCC meaningfully engaged with EU law in its decisions.[41]

Portugal', in Farahat and Arzoz (eds.), *Contesting Austerity. A Socio-Legal Inquiry* (Hart, 2021). On the nationalization of transnational solidarity conflicts by domestic constitutional courts see the chapter by Farahat in this volume, 'Adjudicating Transnational Solidarity Conflicts: Can Courts Ban the Destructive Potential'.

37 I have written on the reasons that may justify this isolationist posture of the PTC. See Violante, 'Constitutional Adjudication as a Forum for Contesting Austerity: The Case of Portugal' *supra* n. 36 183–184.

38 According to Farahat, the Eurocrisis brought about new solidarity conflicts between different political and social groups both within the Member States and between the Members States and across the border, between social groups, as interconnected conflicts. See Farahat, *Transnationale Solidaritätskonflikte. Eine vergleichende Analyse verfassungesgerichtlicher Konflikbearbeitung in der Eurokrise* (Mohr Siebeck, 2021).

39 Kustra-Rogatka, 'The Kelsenian Model of Constitutional Review in Times of European Integration – Reconsidering the Basic Features', 19 *International and Comparative Law Review* (2019) 14.

40 See further Violante, 'Constitutional Adjudication as a Forum for Contesting Austerity: The Case of Portugal', *supra* n. 36 185–186.

41 In decision 422/2020, but, in particularly, in May 2022, in Decision 382/2022. For a commentary on the latter, including its importance for the interaction between domestic constitutional law and EU law, see Violante, 'How the Data Retention Legislation Led to a

## 11.4 JUDICIAL REVIEW OF NATIONAL MEASURES IMPLEMENTING MOU CONDITIONALITY

Conditionality agreed at the level of financial assistance programmes needs to be implemented at the national level. In the sense that it is entrenched in legislation enacted in the scope of EU law, it can be challenged at the EU level, and measured against EU law standards, including the CFREU (11.4.1). However, national measures implementing conditionality can also be subject to national accountability instruments, namely review by domestic courts. In the case of the Portuguese financial assistance programme, the PCC played a pivotal role in reviewing the compatibility of several austerity measures implementing bailout conditionality (11.4.2). When domestic courts failed to provide adequate relief, litigants also turned to international courts (11.4.3).

### 11.4.1 *EU Case Law*

#### 11.4.1.1 Associação Sindical dos Juízes Portugueses[42]

As mentioned earlier, after the initial CJEU case law in relation to the Portuguese bailout, declining jurisdiction to review national measures implementing the EU bailout, and the doctrine established in *Ledra* and *Florescu*, there was a gap in the jurisprudence of the Court, concerning the field of financial assistance to euro area Member States. In *Associação Sindical dos Juízes*, the Court of Justice was finally faced with the opportunity to address this gap and confirm or reject the thesis that there was a link between domestic conditionality measures also in the context of the Eurozone and EU law.

In this case, the CJEU dealt with a reference from a Portuguese court on pay cuts that also affected judges and were adopted in the context of the excessive deficit procedure and the financial assistance programme to Portugal. Both the referring court and Advocate General H. Saugmandsgaard Øe qualified the national measure at stake as implementing EU law in the sense of Article 51 of the Charter.[43]

The case was raised in the framework of a strategic litigation plan developed by the Association of Portuguese Judges, as the complainant, in representation of

National Constitutional Crisis in Portugal', *Verfassungsblog*, 9 Juni 2022, available at https://verfassungsblog.de/how-the-data-retention-legislation-led-to-a-national-constitutional-crisis-in-portugal/ (last accessed 20 June 2022).

[42] Case C-64/16 *Associação Sindical dos Juízes Portugueses* ECLI:EU:C:2018:117.

[43] Opinion of Advocate General H. Saugmandsgaard Øe, C-64/16 *Associação Sindical dos Juízes Portugueses* ECLI:EU:C:2017:395 paras 43–53.

judges from the Court of Auditors.[44] The Association of Portuguese Judges had argued that the reductions in salaries breached the principle of judicial independence, in its double dimension of a constitutional and EU law yardstick. The judicial independence claim was raised following the Constitutional Court's assessment of the reductions in salaries that will be analysed in more detail below. The Constitutional Court's review had considered the principles of legitimate expectations and equality but not the principle of judicial independence, which justified a new wave of litigation prompted by the Association of Judges.

On a first case,[45] the Supreme Administrative Court refused to refer the dispute to the CJEU, on the basis that it did not involve EU law. To substantiate its reasoning, the Supreme Administrative Court referred to the Court of Justice's earlier case law that had declined jurisdiction to rule on preliminary references from Portuguese courts on cases concerning pay cuts adopted in the context of the assistance programme.[46] This judgment was adopted in full chambers. Three judges, however, dissented in the issue concerning the preliminary reference, in a vote drafted by Judge Medeiros de Carvalho.[47] The dissent reasoning noted, on the one hand, that the financial adjustment measures could also be construed as EU law, and, on the other, that a problem of judicial independence might also be framed under Articles 19(1) TEU and 47 of the CFEU.

The Association of Portuguese Judges was encouraged by these three dissenting votes – restricted to the issue of the preliminary reference to the Court of Justice – to pursue its litigation strategy. As it raised further challenges to the pay cuts, one of them was eventually allocated to one of the judges that had expressed his dissent on the preliminary reference issue, Judge Araújo Veloso.[48] The Association of Judges joined a legal opinion[49] authored by two EU law professors to substantiate the claim that a preliminary reference should be drafted, and the case taken to Luxembourg. This legal opinion analysed the relevance of a reference and the terms in which a question should be addressed to the Court of Justice. The wording of the question was provided

44 By questioning the reductions in salaries of judges from the Court of Auditors, the Association of Judges was able to trigger the direct jurisdiction of the Supreme Administrative Court, which is the highest instance in the administrative order.

45 Judgment of 15 October 2015, *Supremo Tribunal Administrativo*, Processo n.° 0438/14.

46 The Court referred specifically to Case C-128/18 *Dumitru-Tudor Dorobant* EU:C:2019:857.

47 The other two dissenting judges were Madeira dos Santos and Araújo Veloso. The latter would be the rapporteur and drafter of the preliminary reference that originated the famous ECJ case *Associação Sindical dos Juízes Portugueses*.

48 Judgment of 20 June 2018, *Supremo Tribunal Administrativo*, Processo n.° 067/15.

49 Silveira, Froufe, 'Parecer', in Silveira, Froufe et al., 'União de direito para além do Direito da União – As garantias de independência judicial no Acórdão Associação Sindical dos Juízes', *Julgar Online* (2018), maio, 1–46, 12–28.

and later adopted by the Supreme Administrative Court in the reference.[50] It also addressed the substance of the dispute to conclude that the pay cuts breached the principle of judicial independence enshrined in Articles 19(1), TEU, second subparagraph, and 47 CFREU.

In his opinion, Advocate General H. Saugmandsgaard Øe concluded that the principle of judicial independence, as enshrined on Article 47 CFREU, did not preclude the general salary-reduction measures adopted by Portuguese authorities to eliminate an excessive budget deficit from being applied to the members of the Portuguese Court of Auditors. He also argued that the dispute before the referring court did not involve judicial independence as such.[51]

The CJEU did not address the compatibility of judicial pay cuts with the Charter, following the case law established in *Ledra* that financial assistance MoUs entered into by EU institutions triggered the application of the Charter. Instead, in a ruling that has been qualified as 'groundbreaking', 'surprising',[52] and 'the most important judgment since *Les Verts* as regards the meaning and scope of the principle of the rule of law in the EU legal system',[53] the CJEU claimed jurisdiction on the basis of Article 19(1), TEU, second subparagraph, focusing on the role of national courts within the European judiciary and thus triggering the threshold of the requirements essential to effective judicial protection. Following a very creative line reasoning, the CJEU 'shifted the focus from the economic crisis (or Eurocrisis) to the "rule of law crisis"'.[54]

Regarding the pay cuts, the Court concluded that since the impugned measures applied to several groups of civil servants, were temporary, and aimed at the reduction of the country's excessive budget deficit, they did not impair judicial independence.

[50] This case provides a peculiar example of academic 'Euro-lawyering', a phenomenon Tommaso Pavone has described as the action of lawyers in their own countries pushing for institutional change near the domestic courts and mobilizing the courts against their own governments. They often construct 'test cases' and 'ghostwr[i]te the referrals to the ECJ that judges [a]re unable or reluctant to write themselves, supplying the European Court with opportunities to deliver pathbreaking judgments'. See Pavone, *The Ghostwriters. Lawyers and the Politics behind the Judicial Construction of Europe* (Cambridge University Press, 2022) 14–15.

[51] Pech and Kochenov, 'Respect for the Rule of Law in the Case Law of the European Court of Justice – A Casebook Overview of Key Judgments since the Portuguese Judges Case', Report n. 3, Swedish Institute for European Policy Studies, September 2021. Accessed via www.sieps.de (last accessed 30 March 2022), p. 24.

[52] Bonelli and Claes, 'Judicial Serendipity: How Portuguese Judges Came to the Rescue of the Polish Judiciary. ECJ 27 February 2018, Case C-64/16, Associação Sindical dos Juízes Portugueses', 14 *European Constitutional Law Review* (2018) 622.

[53] Pech and Platon, 'Judicial Independence Under Threat: The Court of Justice to the Rescue in the ASJP Case', 55 *Common Market Law Review* (2018) 1827.

[54] Bonelli and Claes, 'Judicial Serendipity… ' *supra* n. 53 at 623.

From the Eurocrisis perspective, particularly in the framework of the Portuguese financial assistance programme, *Associação Sindical dos Juízes Portugueses* was a disappointing ruling.[55] After having kept its doors shut to previous references concerning austerity measures adopted in the framework of the financial assistance programme, the CJEU had finally agreed to take jurisdiction on this case. Still, it maintained absolute silence as to the relationship between austerity measures and EU law and transformed an economic crisis dispute into a rule of law case. By doing so, it confirmed that the only judicial accountability forum fully available to contest financial assistance conditionality was found at the domestic level.

In fact, although the Court accepted to review the validity of the pay cuts in *Associação Sindical dos Juízes Portugueses*, its jurisdiction was determined by the universe of the workers affected by the cuts – judges from the Court of Auditors. The Court of Auditors holds jurisdiction for cases concerning EU own resources and the use of financial resources. Therefore, in the Court's view, its judges must enjoy a sufficient level of independence required under Article 19(1) TEU. The applicability of Article 47 CFEU was excluded.

The jurisdiction of the Court of Justice to review pay cuts in the context of Eurozone austerity was limited to pay cuts applicable to judges,[56] which excluded all the slashes to wages and income endured by the remaining public workers. On a first moment, the distinction could seem irrelevant since magistrates in general were subject to the same pay cuts applicable to public workers in general. However, the scrutiny of the CJEU was narrowed by the professional quality of these workers: the reductions in wages were measured solely against the principle of judicial independence as this was the single yardstick mobilized by the Court and that, indeed, triggered its jurisdiction.

The considerable distributive impact of the financial assistance programme at the national level, as well as its encroachment on core human rights provisions of the EU, were therefore overlooked. In fact, contrary to what the CJEU had stated in *Ledra*, where it affirmed the duty of EU institutions to respect the CFREU when formulating financial assistance conditionality, in *Associação Sindical dos Juízes* the Portuguese financial assistance programme does not come under the purview of the Charter and EU human rights. In fact, by adjudicating this case solely on the basis of Article 19(1) TEU, the

55 Pereira Coutinho, 'Associação Sindical dos Juízes Portugueses: judicial independence and austerity measures at the Court of Justice', 2 *Quaderni costituzionali* (2018) 511.

56 Judges from the Court of Auditors enjoy the same statute of other judges in accordance with the law.

Court inaugurated a new line of case law as this parameter had 'never served as an autonomous standard for the review of national laws'.[57] The Court distanced itself from the doctrine established in *Florescu* (which, incidentally, also concerned judges' remunerations, in the form of pensioners' rights), where it assumed jurisdiction by considering that MoU qualified as acts of EU institutions and that national implementing measures fell within the scope of Union law. That made the Charter applicable. In *Associação Sindical dos Juízes*, the CJEU dispensed the qualification of the MoU as an act of EU institution and circumvented the Charter's application. The case turned into a system scrutiny of the country's judicial structures and not, as Krajewski argues, a fundamental rights' case.[58]

As the Court partly accepted the structure designed by the Association of Portuguese Judges in its strategy to defend their salaries from austerity measures, and embraced the framing provided by the principle of judicial independence, it inescapably confirmed that its judicial forum is not fit for social conflicts.

#### 11.4.1.2 A New Distinction between Winners and Losers of European Integration

Moreover, *Associação Sindical dos Juízes* created a differentiation between immobile public workers in Portugal: on the one hand, those who come under Strasbourg's umbrella of protection (national judges); on the other hand, all the other public workers, who do not enjoy the extra accountability forum rendered by the principle of judicial independence as a trigger for the CJEU's jurisdiction to review pay cuts implemented in the framework of a financial assistance programme (which the Court had, until very recently, systematically denied the quality of Union law). Such differentiation brings to the fore a new cleavage in European and national citizenship: whereas the fault line between mobile and immobile Europeans, or between the movers (the 'Eurostars'[59]) and the stayers, had already been pinpointed in the literature,[60] a new divide emerges between national immobile citizens. On the one hand, those that

57 Krajewski, 'Associação Sindical dos Juízes Portugueses: The Court of Justice and Athena's Dilemma', 3(1) *European Papers* (2018) 402.

58 Ibid.

59 Favell, *Eurostars and Eurocities: Free Movement and Mobility in an Integrating Europe*, (Blackwell, 2008).

60 Bauböck, 'The New Cleavagge between Mobile and Immobile Europeans', in Bauböck (ed.), *Debating European Citizenship* (Springer, 2019) 125–127; Fligstein, *Euro-Clash – The EU, European Identity, and the Future of Europe* (Oxford University Press, 2008) 211–213; Dani, 'Rehabilitating Social Conflicts in European Public Law', 18 *European Law Journal* (2012) 638.

cannot resort to the protection afforded by EU law, that is, the communities that are treated as 'deserts' of EU law.[61] On the other, domestic judges, who enjoy not only the national level of protection but also the supranational guarantees, including the EU institutional machinery.

#### 11.4.1.3 A Case of Eurocrisis Strategic Litigation Turns into the Rule of Law Crisis Landmark Case

Considering *Associação Sindical dos Juízes Portugueses* under this lens, it also becomes clear that this ruling – the seminal case that inaugurated the rule of law case bulk of the Court of Justice – did not primarily concern the judicial independence of domestic legal structures. Rather, the issue frame presented by the judges' association emerged in a larger context of a litigation strategy against pay cuts in a context of financial retrenchment, where the entire public sector was affected by slashes in wages. The challenge on judicial independence is explained because the National Association of Judges was forced to raise new legal questions that had not been exhausted under previous case law to avoid preliminary dismissal of the merit of its claims near the Supreme Administrative Court. The issue frame – *do pay cuts adopted in a context of financial retrenchment breach the principle of judicial independence?* – was thereby determined by the previous constitutional case law that had accepted temporary cuts as valid under the principles of proportionality and equality. It is a case where the litigant selects an alternative frame over the prevailing one – according to which cuts would be illegal for breach of universal principles – because the latter has already been dismissed in the lower court, or, in this case, by the case law.[62] In fact, as we will see below, the Portuguese Constitutional Court had assessed said measures against the principles of proportionality and equality but not against the principle of judicial independence. There was a 'strong incentive to reframe the issue by offering an alternative dimension, or frame, on which to base the decision',[63] to maximize the chances of reaching a different decisional outcome.

Moreover, the Court of Justice's initial case law had declined jurisdiction to rule on salary-reduction measures adopted in the framework of the bailout. The reluctance of the ECJ in taking jurisdiction in austerity-related cases was

[61] This is an expression used by Pavone to refer to cases where soliciting the Court of Justice is 'either impractical or impossible'. Pavone, 'Putting European Constitutionalism in Place', 16 *European Constitutional Law Review* (2020) 689.

[62] Wedeking, 'Supreme Court Litigants and Strategic Framing', *American Journal of Political Science* (2010) 620.

[63] Ibid., 619.

salient in light of its previous case law. That is why the litigant Association of Judges, and later the referring Supreme Administrative Court, emphasized the link with EU law of the measures enforcing the salary reductions, stressing that the proceedings came within the scope of Article 47 of the Charter since the mandatory requirements for reducing the State's excessive budget deficit were imposed on the Portuguese Government by EU decisions granting, in particular, financial assistance to that Member State. The decisional outcome to base the jurisdiction of the Court solely in Article 19(1) TEU was fully unexpected. As Pech and Kochenov cogently argue,

> [T]he practical, if not far-reaching, consequence of the Court's interpretation in Portuguese Judges is that private parties, in particular judges when acting as plaintiffs, have been empowered to rely upon the second subparagraph of Article 19(1) TEU directly to challenge, in the context of domestic proceedings, national measures which can be considered to undermine the independence of any national court or tribunal which may apply or interpret EU law'.[64]

### 11.4.1.4 An 'Unforgivable Late Admission': BPC Lux 2[65]

Only in May 2022 has the CJEU come to acknowledge that the financial assistance programme to Portugal entails a link with EU law and finally addressed the mentioned accountability gap in its case law. On its ruling delivered on 5 May 2022, the court found that the Portuguese legal framework for banking resolution that came into force in 2012 was a national measure applying EU law since it represented an implementation of a MoU signed within the framework of Regulation 407/2010 establishing the EFSM. As Martinho Lucas Pires accused, this is an 'unforgivable late admission'[66] from the CJEU.

This conflict concerned the validity of a resolution measure applied by the national authority to a private bank considering the protection of the right to property afforded by Article 17 of the CFEU. To put it bluntly, petitioners claiming breach of their right to property, specifically investment funds, did not

[64] Pech and Kochenov, 'Respect for the Rule of Law in the Case Law of the European Court of Justice – A Casebook Overview of Key Judgments since the Portuguese Judges Case', Report n. 3, Swedish Institute for European Policy Studies, September 2021. Accessed via www.sieps.de (last accessed 30 March 2022). The authors claim that this line of case law has been subsequently expressly reiterated in the cases of *Miasto Łowicz and Prokurator Generalny*: Joined Cases C-558/18 and C-563/18 *Miasto Łowicz and Prokurator Generalny* EU:C:2020:234.

[65] Case C-83/20 *BPC Lux 2 Sàrl and Others* EU:C:2022:346.

[66] Lucas Pires, Op-Ed: 'Unforgivable Late Admissions: The Court of Justice Decides on Bank Resolution in *BPC Lux 2 Sàrl* (C-83/20)', *EU Law Live*, 12 May 2022, available at https://eulawlive.com/op-ed-unforgivable-late-admissions-the-court-of-justice-decides-on-bank-resolution-in-bpc-lux-2-sarl-c-83-20-by-martinho-lucas-pires/ (last visited 17 June 2022).

face an insurmountable barrier to take their case to Luxembourg. On the other hand, workers and pensioners who had seen their wages and pensions subject to cuts and freezes did not enjoy the same opportunity. This is another sign of the inequality between rights-holders enhanced by the case law of the CJEU that I mentioned previously and that points to the accountability gaps at the level of the European judicial stage with regard to financial assistance programmes.

What reasons can account for this 'late admission' of the CJEU? On the surface, one could simply think that the court was coming to terms with its jurisprudential troubled past and making amends with it. After having rejected jurisdiction in the early cases and taking the strategic shift in *Associação Sindical dos Juízes*, *BPC Lux 2* might just represent the closure of a troubled process, and be the appropriate case to build coherence with *Florescu* in which the court had already accepted that bailouts are acts of EU law. There may be something else to the story, however: the problem at stake was too important to be missed by the CJEU. In fact, the main issue of the referred questions concerned the problem of knowing whether the fact that the Portuguese applicable regime at the time of the resolution did not expressly entail the principle of 'no creditor worse off', enshrined in the Bank Recovery and Resolution Directive (BRRD),[67] entailed any violation of said directive or of the right to property enshrined in the Charter.

Bail-in powers have given rise to constitutional litigation in domestic courts and the European Court of Human Rights.[68] In *Pintar and Others v Slovenia*, the Strasbourg Court was confronted with Slovenian legislation implemented in the context of the Eurozone crisis that resulted in the bailing-in of shareholders and bondholders of banks. In the proceedings, the Slovenian Constitutional Court had already found unconstitutional breaches in the legislation, following the CJEU ruling in *Kotnik and others*.[69] The Court found that the domestic legislation governing how shareholders and bondholders bring claims for unlawful takings of property failed to provide a legal avenue to effectively challenge the lawfulness of the alleged breach of the right to property.

Moreover, there are scholarly works emerging that accuse the BRRD and the bail-in provisions of breaching the right to property of bank creditors and,

[67] Directive 2014/59/EU of the European Parliament and of the Council of 15 May 2014, establishing a framework for the recovery and resolution of credit institutions and investment firms and amending Council Directive 82/891/EEC, and Directives 2001/24/EC, 2002/47/EC, 2004/25/EC, 2005/56/EC, 2007/36/EC, 2011/35/EU, 2012/30/EU and 2013/36/EU, and Regulations (EU) No 1093/2010 and (EU) No 648/2012, of the European Parliament and of the Council).

[68] See Kern Alexander, 'Bank of Slovenia's Bail-in Powers Come Under Constitutional Scrutiny by the Strasbourg Court', *EU Law Live*, 11 October 2021 (accessed 15 August 2022).

[69] Case C-526/14 *Kotnik and others* EU:C:2016:570.

therefore, presenting a legal risk to resolution authorities in Member States. Therefore, in *BPC Lux 2*, the CJEU had every interest in taking jurisdiction and having its say on the questions referred, especially considering the possibility that the conflict may end up being adjudicated by the Portuguese Constitutional Court, in concrete review proceedings. Taking jurisdiction in this case allowed the CJEU the possibility to have the first word on the interpretation of the fundamental rights' constellation at stake, particularly from the perspective of the compatibility of the legal regime at stake and, ultimately, of the 'no creditor worse off' principle with the constitutional protection of the right to property. In fact, in the analysis of the domestic legislation, the Court was able to frame as materially providing for a solution which is substantially equivalent to the mentioned principle even though that yardstick was not expressly foreseen in the statute at the time of the bank resolution. However, to claim jurisdiction, the CJEU could not simply rely on the fact that the domestic legislation aimed at transposing the BRRD. This is where the MoU comes to the fore as the jurisdictional trigger for the CJEU.

The Portuguese legal framework on recovery and resolution of credit institutions has a mixed pedigree. It was first introduced in 2012[70] and subsequently amended, for the first time, in 2014.[71] This first amendment aimed at *partially* transposing BRRD. The 2012 piece of legislation was adopted before the Commission presented the proposal for the directive which led to the BRRD, as the Advocate General highlighted in his opinion.[72] Moreover, the 2014 act transposed part, but not all, of the BRRD. So, there was the theoretical possibility that this case could fall out of the jurisdiction of the CJEU.

The safest avenue to claim jurisdiction, however, was to lean on the fact that the original regime, dating from 2012, had been approved to implement MoU conditionality, as the Portuguese Government clarified in the proceedings. According to the MoU, since its original version, the Portuguese authorities 'amend legislation concerning credit institutions' [to] 'introduce a regime for the resolution of distressed credit institutions as a going concern under official control to promote financial stability and protect depositors'.[73]

After accepting jurisdiction in this, it was not difficult for the Court to resolve and discard the alleged breach of the right to property. In the few cases where the Court accepted jurisdiction to review austerity measures, the tension between financial stability and fundamental rights has always been resolved in

70 Decree-Law 31-A/2012, 10 February 2012.

71 Decree-Law 114-A/2014, 1 August 2014.

72 Parag. 26.

73 See Memorandum of Understanding, paragraphs 2.13 and 2.14. The MoU is available at https://ec.europa.eu/economy_finance/eu_borrower/mou/2011-05-18-mou-portugal_en.pdf.

favour of the former.[74] This creates a stronger incentive for domestic institutions to stand up as gatekeepers of 'the rights of those who do not benefit from integration and whose voice can be structurally undermined by it'.[75]

### 11.4.2 *Constitutional Adjudication*[76]

The PCC became a prominent forum for litigation concerning austerity measures at the height of the Eurozone crisis. Between 2012 and 2014, several restrictive measures, directly requested by the MoU and the bailout conditionality, were checked for their compatibility with the domestic constitutional standards. On some occasions, the PCC delivered significant blows to the Government's strategy by invalidating measures based on the principle of equality, particularly in the dimension of equality of burdens concerning the financial adjustment costs, the principle of legitimate expectations, and the principle of proportionality.[77]

It struck down further pay cuts on public workers and pensioners,[78] a new framework broadening the legal basis for firing civil servants,[79] some of the amendments to the Labor Code aimed at slashing labour costs and reducing the employees' protection against unfair dismissals,[80] and permanent cuts to pensions.[81]

Whereas in the first challenges concerning pre-bailout austerity the PCC scrutiny was self-restrained and deferential,[82] when called upon to review

74 López-Escudero, 'Judicial Protection Against Austerity Measures in the EU', in Izquierdo Sans et al. (eds.), *Fundamental Rights Challenges: Horizontal Effectiveness, Rule of Law and Margin of Appreciation* (Springer, 2021) 205.

75 Komarék, 'The Place of Constitutional Courts in the EU', 9 *European Constitutional Law Review* (2013) 449.

76 The work on this section is in part based on research that has been presented in earlier texts. See Violante, 'The Portuguese Constitutional Court and its Austerity Case Law', in Costa Pinto and Pequito (eds.), *Political Institutions and Democracy in Portugal: Assessing the Impact of the Eurocrisis in Portugal* (Cham: Springer, 2019) 121; Violante, 'The Eurozone Crisis and the Rise of the Portuguese Constitutional Court', 39 *Quaderni costituzionali* (2019) 208; Violante, 'Constitutional Adjudication as a Forum for Contesting Austerity: The Case of Portugal' *supra* n. 36.

77 For a full review of the case law, see Canotilho, Violante and Lanceiro, 'Austerity Measures Under Judicial Scrutiny: The Portuguese Constitutional Case Law', 11 *European Constitutional Law Review* (2015) 155–183, and Violante and André, 'The Constitutional Performance of Austerity in Portugal' *supra*. 36.

78 Decisions 353/2012, 187/2013, 413/2014 and 574/2014.

79 Decision 474/2013.

80 Decision 602/2013.

81 Decisions 862/2013 and 575/2014.

82 Decisions 399/2010 and 396/2011. See Teresa Violante, 'Constitutional Adjudication as a Forum for Contesting Austerity: The Case of Portugal' *supra* n. 36 175–176.

domestic measures implementing MoU conditionality the Court moved from a light level of scrutiny to a less deferential approach. On the one hand, this greater unwillingness to defer to the political branches is in line with the tendency observed in the general judicial reaction towards the Eurocrisis.[83] On the other hand, the Court justified the strengthened scrutiny with the cumulative effect of the restrictive measures, and the passage of time that created additional burdens on the domestic authorities to devise alternatives to reach fiscal stability without jeopardizing fundamental rights and the welfare system.

The primary benchmarks enforced by the PCC were the principle of 'proportional equality', in the sense that there should be an 'equal distribution of the economic burden created by austerity',[84] and the principle of legitimate expectations. Despite the detailed catalogue of welfare rights, often qualified as the longest bill of social and economic rights in a national constitution,[85] the austerity case law primarily relied on general and abstract provisions following the Court's traditional 'self-restrained', 'minimalist' and 'shy'[86] socioeconomic rights jurisprudence.

The PCC addressed austerity conflicts concerning domestic measures implementing financial assistance conditionality primarily through substantive accountability means. As the Court highlighted,[87]

> The Constitution certainly cannot remain unaware of the economic and financial reality, and in particular of a situation that can be considered to be of serious difficulty. But it has a specific normative autonomy that prevents economic or financial objectives from prevailing, without any limits, over parameters such as equality, which the Constitution defends and must enforce.

The financial impact of the decisions led to several renegotiations of the bailout programme of the MoU conditionality. The parties to the bailout agreement recognized the existence of a 'constitutional risk' to the implementation of the programme and introduced 'legal safeguards' in the MoU to mitigate 'legal risks from future potential Constitutional Court rulings'.[88]

[83] Fabbrini, *Economic Governance in Europe. Comparative Paradoxes and Constitutional Challenges* (Oxford, 2016) 100.

[84] Ribeiro, 'Judicial Activism Against Austerity in Portugal', *International Journal of Constitutional Law Blog*, Dec. 3, 2013.

[85] Magalhães, 'Explaining the Constitutionalization of Social Rights. Portuguese Hypotheses and a Cross-National Test', in Galligan and Versteeg (eds.), *Social and Political Foundations of Constitutions* (Cambridge University Press, 2013) 433.

[86] Reis Novais, *Direitos Sociais. Teoria jurídica dos direitos sociais enquanto direitos fundamentais* (Coimbra: Almedina, 2010) 374, 380.

[87] Decision 353/2012.

[88] See the revised versions of the MoU, following the seventh, eighth, and ninth updates (June and November 2013).

The introduction of the legal safeguards did not lead to a substantial change in the Court's review. On the one hand, the level of scrutiny remained intense, and the Court later struck down some of the replacement measures. On the other, the appeal to the transnational dimension of the austerity conflicts did not induce the Court to substantially engage with EU law yardsticks. If, on the surface, the judges regularly cited EU law and international law to frame the rescue package for Portugal, such references had no substantial value, and the cases were always solved against national constitutional yardsticks.

### 11.4.3 *Pensions' Cuts Case Law by the ECtHR*

Some austerity cases concerning reductions in pensions found their way to the Strasbourg court, but they failed at the admissibility stage. In *Da Conceição Mateus and Santos Januário v Portugal*[89] the Court found that the cuts in the applicants' pensions were 'clearly in the public interest within the meaning'[90] of Article 1 of Protocol 1 of the European Convention on Human Rights (ECHR) (protection of property). The Court also added that 'a wide margin of appreciation is usually allowed to the State under the Convention when it comes to general measures of economic or social policy'.[91] At a later moment, in *Silva Carvalho Rico v Portugal*,[92] the ECtHR referred to the PCC decisions of 2013 and 2014 that found the pensioners' contribution to be a proportional measure given its extraordinary and temporary nature. The Court also added that 'budgetary constraints on the implementation of social rights can be accepted as long as they are proportionate (...) and do not reduce social rights' claims to purely symbolic sums', and that the 'international recognition of the country's economic situation indicates that the present budgetary constraints constitute an imperative, which however did not reduce possessions originating in a statutory social right's claims to a level that deprives the right of its substance'.[93]

Moreover, the Court found itself incompetent to decide whether alternative measures were available, given the State's wide margin of appreciation to decide on general measures of economic and social policy.

## 11.5 CONCLUSIONS

The CJEU has provided a very limited forum for review of austerity measures adopted in a context of financial assistance to a euro area Member State. First,

89 Applications ns. 62235/12 and 57725/12, Decision on Admissibility, 8 October 2013.
90 Parag. 26.
91 Parag. 22.
92 Application n. 13341/14, Decision on the Admissibility 1 September 2015.
93 Parag. 44.

the CJEU only delivered substantial review of conditionality measures at the end of the crisis, when Portugal had already exited the bailout programme and the political pressure exerted upon the national political institutions had eased.[94] Second, the initial scope of review was limited by the type of workers affected by the specific cuts reviewed in *Associação Sindicial dos Juízes Portugueses*, where the protection offered by the CJEU was narrowed to judges. By framing the case as a rule of law crisis review – and not a Eurocrisis review – the Court narrowed its accountability-rendering stage to national judges, as special public workers, subject to a certain employment relationship which renders them a specific role in the adjudication of EU law conflicts. Third, the Court was also limited in its parameter of control. The cuts were measured against Article 19(1), subparagraph two TEU to determine if the salary-reduction measures affected the principle of judicial independence. No other constitutional goods, namely the proportionality of the reductions, social rights, or solidarity,[95] were taken into account by the Court. Fourth, in *BPC Lux 2*, a case concerning the protection of rights and interests of investors and creditors of resolved institutions, and the stability of the financial system, there was no hesitancy from the Court to accept jurisdiction, which confirms the Court's more favourable orientation towards liberal rights to the detriment of social rights.

The Court thus failed to ensure full judicial protection to austerity measures concerning salary-reductions adopted in the context of a financial assistance programme to a euro area Member State as well as in the more general framework of an excessive deficit procedure. The Portuguese bailout is exemplary of the protection offered by European law against austerity measures. Individuals and companies can be sheltered in their role as investors and judges but not as workers and pensioners.

Domestic constitutional adjudication provided the only effective avenue for full substantive accountability of MoU options: national judicial fora can provide a supplement to the missing but needed accountability in substance of the EMU institutional structure.[96] Domestic constitutional courts provided adequate fora to challenge national measures implementing the MoU in what has been called the *paradox of judicialization*, in contrast to the deferential posture adopted by the US courts in economic issues.[97]

94 The excessive deficit procedure was initiated by Council Decision 2010/288/EU of 19 January 2010 (OJ L 125, 21.5.2010), and abrogated by Council Decision (EU) 2017/1225 of 16 June 2017 (OJ L 174, 07.07.2010). Portugal had exited the financial assistance programme on 30 June 2014.

95 As Farahat stresses in her chapter to this book. Farahat, 'Adjudicating Transnational Solidarity Conflicts: Can Courts Ban the Destructive Potential'.

96 Introduction, p. 20.

97 Fabbrini, *Economic Governance in Europe. Comparative Paradoxes and Constitutional Challenges* (Oxford University Press, 2016) 63 ff.

However, since the PCC failed to scrutinize the MoU, several hurdles related to the process were not reviewed, namely aspects related to the procedure leading to the approval of the bailout – which was conducted outside the parliament and by a resigning government, the fact that it was not officially translated into Portuguese and the difficulties in accessing the updated version following each revision. These aspects, which raise serious rule of law concerns, were not reviewed and there is a full absence of procedural accountability with regard to the Portuguese programme.

Furthermore, EU institutions were not held accountable by the constitutional case law: as the conflicts were fully nationalized, the 'account-giver' was limited to the domestic institutions who were reduced to a role with limited negotiating power with the creditors which raises doubts as to the likelihood of the accountability provided through domestic judicial review in the case of borrower countries. That was not the case of the *Bundesverfassungsgericht* which, in its *PSPP*[98] ruling, was able to hold accountable not only the domestic institutions (the Bundestag and the Federal Government) but also the CJEU and the European Central Bank (ECB). The German Court, however, in its Eurocrisis case law, has always assumed the transnational dimension of the conflicts under adjudication. That fact enabled it to resort to the preliminary review mechanism when it deemed appropriate – in fact, for the first time[99] after a long history of indirect judicial dialogue between the two jurisdictions. Later, when the CJEU failed to properly hold the ECB accountable for its quantitative easing policy,[100] the German Federal Constitutional Court was able to scrutinize both institutions. To do so, it activated the ultra vires review, a tool that the court had been developing since its seminal Maastricht decision.[101] Instead of the procedural and deferential scrutiny applied by the CJEU to the ECB's statement of reasons, the German Court asked for a substantive review of the *PSPP* programme to be able to effectively check whether the ECB's actions were contained within its mandate.[102]

However, taking an austerity case to Luxembourg might prove a risky strategy for the Portuguese Court. At that time, the Court had not developed yet

98 Bundesverfassungsgericht [BVerfG] [Federal Constitutional Court], Case No. 2 BvR 859/15, (May 5, 2020), www.bundesverfassungsgericht.de/SharedDocs/Entscheidungen/EN/2020/05/rs20200505_2bvr085915en.html.

99 In the *OMT* referral decision. Bundesverfassungsgericht [BVerfG] [Federal Constitutional Court], Case No. 2 BvR 2728/13 (Jan. 14, 2014), www.bverfg.de/e/rs20160621_2bvr272813en.html.

100 Case C-493/17 *Heinrich Weiss and Others* ECLI:EU:C:2018:1000.

101 Bundesverfassungsgericht [BverfG] [Federal Constitutional Court] Oct. 12, 1993, 89 Entscheidungen Des Bundesverfassungsgerichts [BVerfGE] 155.

102 For a detailed analysis, see Violante, 'Bring Back the Politics: The PSPP Ruling in Its Institutional Context', 21 *German Law Journal* (2020) 1045–1057.

a doctrinal framework to frame the relationship between national constitutional law and EU law, particularly in cases of conflict. Whereas its German counterpart had been building a solid dogmatic frame since the *Solange* cases, and later, in relation to the link between the democratic principle and European integration, since the *Maastricht* ruling, and had at its disposal a tripartite framework to handle the relationship between the two legal orders, the Portuguese Court only in 2020 expressly dealt with the issue of primacy of EU law over national law, including constitutional law, and still in the exclusive frame of fundamental rights' issues. In some of its austerity rulings, the Court vaguely alluded to the concept of 'constitutional identity', but, to this day, ultra vires review has never been addressed nor articulated in the case law, and it is doubtful that the judges accept it as a valid tool to check power grabs by EU institutions. Ultra vires review, as enforced by the *Bundesverfassungsgericht*, implies a substantive reading of the democratic principle that makes it one of the central normative tenets of the constitutional order, but it is not replicated in the constitutional case law of other Member States.

The nationalization of the conflict by the Constitutional Court also explains why the case law was unable to substantively contest the overarching choices of the financial assistance programme implementing a regressive economic policy: not only was accountability delivered through piecemeal litigation, but there were also structural limits with regards to the effects that judicial decisions can produce at the level of economic policies, particularly in the case of Portugal, where the Constitutional Court is not equipped with decisional remedies able to address systemic and structural failures.[103]

The lessons provided by the Eurocrisis show that domestic constitutional law can provide an avenue for legal accountability of financial assistance. A future financial assistance programme would be granted in the framework of the ESM, which still has not been brought into the fabric of EU law.[104] Given its intergovernmental nature, review of conditionality would not be problematic to the PCC, as it acknowledged in relation to the nature of the Fiscal Stability Treaty.[105] Conditionality has, in the meantime, expanded its influence on other policy areas such as EU funds.[106]

[103] Roach, *Remedies for Human Rights Violations. A Two-Track Approach to Supra-National and National Law* (Cambridge University Press, 2021) 408 ff.

[104] On the process of reforming the ESM, see Markakis, 'The Reform of the European Stability Mechanism: Process, Substance, and the Pandemic', 4 *Legal Issues of Economic Integration* (2020) 350–338.

[105] Decisions 574/2015 and 575/2015.

[106] On the rise of conditionality in EU law, see Baraggia and Bonelli, 'Linking Money to Values: The New Rule of Law Conditionality Regulation and Its Constitutional Challenges', 23 *German Law Journal* (2022) 131–156.

Moreover, the Constitutional Court has been incrementally developing a doctrinal toolbox to address the relationship between domestic constitutional and EU law.[107] Although the PCC has expressly outlined the constitutional principle of friendliness towards EU integration, it has reserved the right to have the last word on the constitutional limits of the applicability of Union law on the Portuguese legal order. Should the EU standard of protection of fundamental rights fail to provide equivalent protection, in systemic terms, to the one delivered by the national Constitution, the Court may agree to review EU law or to strike down domestic legislation within the scope of EU law. Given the dominant perception of the EU judges that economic emergency and financial stability justifies the abridgement of social and economic rights, and a potential new crisis in the euro area, new lines of tension will possibly emerge in the future.

[107] Decisions 422/2020 and 382/2022.

# 12

# Human Rights Accountability in European Financial Assistance

*Anastasia Poulou*

## 12.1 INTRODUCTION

Affected by the European financial crisis that erupted in 2008, several EU Member States were dependent on financial assistance beyond the financial markets. In order to have access to financial assistance, EU Member States had to adopt structural adjustment programmes aiming inter alia at the reduction of public expenditures. As a consequence, a number of social security benefits were reduced and a great number of structural reforms were introduced, since expenditures on social security benefits and public healthcare were considered to have a strong impact on the public budget's macroeconomic balances.[1] Despite their differences, common feature of all financial assistance schemes was the combination of supranational and international legal instruments and institutions. Newly created financial assistance mechanisms, such as the European Financial Stability Facility (EFSF) and European Stability Mechanism (ESM), were created under international law and all financial assistance packages included the participation of the International Monetary Fund (IMF). This hybrid nature of European financial assistance raises the question of whether the actors involved in the award of the assistance are bound by EU human rights.

Against this background, this chapter first exposes the doubtful legitimacy of European financial assistance. Second, it analyses the Court of Justice (CJEU) case law on financial assistance conditionality from a human rights perspective, aiming to respond to the question of whether European actors were and could be bound by human rights when preparing financial assistance conditions. Third, it investigates the possibility of conceiving a

[1] For a holistic approach and assessment of the social reforms introduced to the social protection systems of states receiving financial aid after the 2008 economic crisis, see Becker and Poulou (eds.), *European Welfare State Constitutions After the Financial Crisis* (OUP, 2020).

legitimate role for courts in applying the procedural and substantive dimension of human rights accountability in times of crisis.

## 12.2 THE (NON) DELIVERY OF ACCOUNTABILITY GOODS IN THE MAKING OF EUROPEAN FINANCIAL ASSISTANCE CONDITIONALITY

During the Eurozone crisis, the constitutional balance between the different institutions had been significantly altered in a way that the delivery of the normative goods of accountability was severely hindered. Financial assistance conditionality resulted in intrusive social governance, left at the discretion of executives, and insulated from public debate and parliamentary scrutiny. The phenomenon of executive dominance side-lining the institutions of representative democracy, observed in times of crisis, was highly repeated in the Eurozone crisis experience. Decision-making was concentrated in supranational (Commission) and national (Eurogroup) executives at the European level, accompanied by the input of expert bodies (European Central Bank (ECB) and IMF). The big shift towards executive politics was reflected by the simultaneous decrease in power of both the European Parliament (EP) and national parliaments, which traditionally serve as checks on executive power.[2]

All phases of the adjustment programme-drafting were indeed lacking in transparency and democratic oversight. From the preparatory phase of negotiations, to the development of mandates and the formulation of specific measures the European Parliament was until 2013 completely marginalised.[3] On the national level, it is doubtful whether formal documents were clearly communicated to and deliberated in due time by the respective domestic parliaments.[4] Negotiations were held behind closed doors, without the presence of social partners, a deficiency explicitly criticised by the International Labour Organization (ILO).[5] In fact, the absence of prior consultation with

[2] Dawson and De Witte, 'Constitutional Balance in the EU After the Euro-Crisis', 76 *Modern Law Review* (2013) 817, 832.

[3] This observation is reaffirmed by the EP itself. See, European Parliament resolution of 13 March 2014 on employment and social aspects of the role and operations of the Troika (ECB, Commission and IMF) with regard to euro-area programme countries (2014/2007(INI)), para. 2. Generally on the EP's position in the new economic governance, see Fasone, 'European Economic Governance and Parliamentary Representation. What Place for the European Parliament?' 20 *ELJ* (2014)164.

[4] See European Parliament resolution of 13 March 2014 on the enquiry on the role and operations of the Troika (ECB, Commission and IMF) with regard to the euro-area programme countries (2013/2277(INI)), para. 30.

[5] See, ILO, 365th Report of the Committee on Freedom of Association, Case No. 2820 (Greece), Conclusions, para. 1002.

trade union organisations has been officially admitted by the Greek government and has been ascribed to the complexity of economic and political issues and the conditions under which the European support mechanism for Greece has been formulated.[6] The adoption of Regulation 472/2013 did not bring adequate change in this regard, since the rights to information and discussion awarded to the EP and the domestic parliaments do not amount to rights to participation in the decision-making process. As a result during the adjustment programme-drafting, both the EP and national parliaments were neither able to serve the good of openness, through transparent and contestable public actions, nor the good of publicness, which would encompass the consideration of different societal interests and perspectives.

The loss of democratic oversight was not only depicted in the rudimentary role of the EP and national parliaments but also in the increasing tendency towards informal governance.[7] The outcome of staff-level meetings was often decided beforehand in bilateral meetings of the most important players. Even more strikingly, national authorities seem to have received the implementation guidelines on conditions included in the Memoranda of Understanding (MoU) through simple email exchange with the Troika. Such opaqueness and informality levels exclude the transparency and consultation necessary for the genuine involvement of citizens and social partners in EU decision-making to take place. Therefore, the EP has repeatedly called for transparency in the MoU negotiations.[8] Overall, this rise of informal governance seriously affected the ability of democratic institutions to ensure the delivery of the accountability goods of openness and non-arbitrariness, since they could not apply due process guarantees in the making of financial assistance conditionality.

In sum, the institutional framework for awarding financial assistance shows profound structural shortcomings in terms of both procedural and substantive accountability. By the expansion of democratically questionable supranational decision-making, social interests were extremely marginalised and certain views, such as those of social partners, profoundly underrepresented.

6 See, ILO, 365th Report of the Committee on Freedom of Association, Case No. 2820 (Greece), Conclusions, para. 967.

7 On general patterns, see Christiansen and Neuhold, 'Informal Politics in the EU', 51 *Journal of Common Market Studies* (2013) 1196.

8 See European Parliament resolution of 12 December 2013 on constitutional problems of a multitier governance in the European Union (2012/2078(INI)), paras. 36, 72; European Parliament resolution of 13 March 2014 on the enquiry on the role and operations of the Troika (ECB, Commission, and IMF) with regard to the euro-area programme countries (2013/2277(INI)), paras. 37, 48, 66, 94, 107.

## 12.3 HUMAN RIGHTS ACCOUNTABILITY AS INSTITUTIONALISED THROUGH COURTS

Respect of human rights by decision-makers is an important factor for the delivery of accountability goods. More precisely, the accountability good of non-arbitrariness can be procedurally delivered through the adoption of procedures to 'mainstream' rights-based limitations in policy-making, that is, through impact assessments, by which officials may demonstrate that human rights have been taken into account. Substantively, human rights serve the good of non-arbitrariness, by ensuring that an adopted policy does not discriminate against a given group in society or does not infringe on the rights of individuals. Moreover, human rights endorse the delivery of the accountability good of publicness, by orientating the conduct of decision-makers towards the pursuit of a common, legitimate aim.

One of the main accountability forums able to examine decision-makers' conduct in line with the accountability goods of non-arbitrariness and publicness are courts through human rights review. First, courts are able to verify whether a rights-based impact assessment was conducted. Furthermore, through human rights review courts can make sure that a policy adopted does not result in the violation of rights of individuals. Lastly, through their proportionality review, courts ask decision-makers to demonstrate that their policies restrict rights only in pursuit of a legitimate aim and in absence of less restrictive measures.

Against this background, how did courts act as 'accountability-rendering actors' in the context of the Economic and Monetary Union (EMU)? In fact, the far-reaching reforms in fields such as social security and healthcare were in many cases experienced as violations of human rights by the respective right-holders, who sought for legal protection before national and international courts. As a result, many national constitutional courts but also the Court of Justice of the EU issued a series of rulings on the conformity of the reforms initiated during the Eurozone crisis with human rights. Hence, which was the CJEU's actual response though to the alleged human rights violations?

The Medium-Term Financial Assistance (MTFA) Facility and the European Financial Stabilisation Mechanism (EFSM) are clearly EU financial assistance mechanisms: they were established through EU Regulations on the basis of the EU Treaties and have an institutional underpinning, which entrusts major tasks to EU institutions.[9] Financial assistance conditionality is laid down in two types

[9] In detail on the institutional setting of those mechanisms, see Poulou, 'Human Rights Obligations of European Financial Assistance Mechanisms', in Becker and Poulou (eds.), *European Welfare State Constitutions after the Financial Crisis* (OUP, 2020), at p. 25.

of legal documents: on the one hand, in an MoU, and on the other hand, in Decisions of the Council of the EU. The MoU is signed by the recipient state and the European Commission. As EU institutions acting under EU law, the Commission, the ECB, and the Council of the EU should be undisputedly bound by EU fundamental rights when negotiating, drafting, and monitoring financial assistance conditionality. The question of the application of EU fundamental rights is only partly complicated when it comes to MoUs containing financial assistance conditions. This is because the character of the MoUs as binding legal agreements is disputed. If the MoUs are not binding legal documents, how could they be measured against human rights standards?

The legal status and effects of MoUs in the context of the MTFA (article 143 TFEU) were addressed by the CJEU in *Florescu*,[10] a case that originated in the context of the first financial assistance programme to Romania, following Council Decision 2009/458/EC.[11] The core terms of the Romanian bailout were laid out in Council Decision 2009/459/EC[12] and subsequently elaborated in the MoU concluded between the European Union, represented by the Commission, and Romania.[13] The applicants in the main proceedings were judges who also held teaching positions at the university, as the law permitted at that time. The contested measure at issue in the main proceedings prohibited the combining of the net pension with income from activities carried out in public institutions if the amount of the pension exceeded a certain threshold, fixed at the amount of the national gross average salary. The persons affected sought to argue that article 17 of the Charter (right to property) should be interpreted as precluding national legislation, such as that at issue in the main proceedings, which prohibited the combining of a net public-sector retirement pension with income from activities carried out in public institutions if the amount of the pension exceeded a certain threshold.

In *Florescu* the CJEU ruled that the MoU 'gives concrete form to an agreement between the EU and a Member State on an economic programme, negotiated by those parties, whereby that Member State undertakes to comply with predefined economic objectives in order to be able, subject to fulfilling that agreement, to benefit from financial assistance

[10] For a detailed analysis of the case, see Markakis and Dermine, 'Bailouts, the Legal Status of Memoranda of Understanding, and the Scope of Application of the EU Charter: Florescu', *Common Market Law Review* (2018) 643.

[11] Council Decision 2009/458/EC of 6 May 2009 granting mutual assistance to Romania [2009] OJ L150/6.

[12] Council Decision 2009/459/EC.

[13] Memorandum of Understanding between the European Community and Romania. https://ec.europa.eu/economy_finance/publications/pages/publication15409_en.pdf, last accessed on 15.08.2021.

from the EU'.[14] The Court held that the legal bases of the MoU lay in article 143 of the TFEU and Regulation 332/3002 and that it was concluded, in particular, by the European Union, represented by the Commission. Hence, the CJEU reached the conclusion that the MoU 'constitutes an act of an EU institution within the meaning of 267(b) TFEU' and may thus 'be subject to interpretation by the Court' through a preliminary ruling.[15] Furthermore, the Court added that the objectives set out in article 3(5) of Decision 2009/459, as well as those set out in the MoU, were sufficiently detailed and precise to permit the inference that the purpose of the prohibition on combining a public-sector retirement pension with income from activities carried out in public institutions, stemming from Law No 329/2009, was to implement both the MoU and that Decision and, thus, EU law, within the meaning of article 51(1) of the Charter; therefore, the Charter was applicable to the dispute in the main proceedings.[16]

Building on the outcome of *Florescu*, one can reach the conclusion that the MoUs concluded within the EU legal order, meaning in the MTFA and EFSM framework, are to be qualified as Union acts within the meaning of article 267(1)(b) of the TFEU and, thus, are amenable to a request for interpretation under article 267.[17] Moreover, the EU institutions involved in the making and conclusion of those MoUs are unavoidably bound to respect human rights, since the Charter definitely applies to EU institutions undertaking Union acts.

More difficult though is the question of whether the Charter applies in the EFSF and ESM framework. How did the CJEU respond to the question of whether the Charter is applicable in the context of European financial assistance or whether the EU institutions involved are freed from the obligation to respect the fundamental rights of the Union? The respective case law of the CJEU has to be presented separately, since it relates to different EU institutions and bodies involved in the complicated framework of European financial assistance.

### 12.3.1 *The Applicability of the Charter to the Eurogroup*

In the context of European assistance, the Eurogroup is usually entrusted with general guidelines with regard to economic policy and not with the formulation of detailed financial assistance conditions. During the eurozone crisis, it

[14] Case C-258/14 *Eugenia Florescu and Others v Casa Județeana de Pensii Sibiu and Others* [2017] EU:C:2017:448, para 34.

[15] Ibid., para 35.

[16] Ibid., para 48.

[17] For an updated analysis of article 267 TFEU, see Wahl and Prete 'The Gatekeepers of 267 TFEU: On Jurisdiction and Admissibility of References for Preliminary Rulings', *Common Market Law Review* 511 (2018).

determined the strategic choices of the economic adjustment programmes, such as the voluntary debt haircut in the case of Greece.[18] With regard to specific conditionalities though, it relied on the recommendations of the Troika. A notable exception to this rule was the case of Cyprus, in which the restructuring of the Cypriot banking sector was first decided by the Eurogroup before the Troika reached an agreement with domestic authorities.[19] The Cypriot rescue package is of particular interest, since it marks the first time that bank depositors were targeted as part of a European bailout deal. In exchange for the loans received by the ESM and the IMF, Cyprus had inter alia to wind up its second-largest bank, the Cyprus Popular Bank (also known as Laiki Bank), and to recapitalise its biggest bank, the Bank of Cyprus, at the expense of shareholders, bondholders, and depositors. In the winding up of the Cyprus Popular Bank, uninsured deposits exceeding the amount of €100,000 were completely liquidated. In the recapitalisation of the Bank of Cyprus, the depositors lost 47.5 per cent of their uninsured deposits.[20]

Given their substantial financial losses – the result of the extensive write-off of their bank deposits – uninsured depositors sought judicial protection before the courts of the EU, challenging the validity of the Eurogroup statement outlining the conditions of the bailout. Nevertheless, all their actions for annulment have been unsuccessful.[21] In fact, in the CJEU case *Mallis and Others v Commission and ECB*, the Court confirmed the orders of the General Court holding that the Eurogroup, which is an informal forum for discussion between ministers of the Member States whose currency is the euro, cannot be classified as a body, office, or agency of the EU within the meaning of article 263 of the TFEU.[22] Thus, a statement by it cannot be regarded as a measure intended

[18] Eurogroup Statement on the European Stability Mechanism with respect to Greece, Doc No 128075, 21 February 2012 <www.consilium.europa.eu/uedocs/cms_Data/docs/pressdata/en/ecofin/128075.pdf>, last accessed on 15.08.2021.

[19] See Eurogroup Statement on Cyprus, Doc No 136487, 25 March 2013 <www.consilium.europa.eu/uedocs/cms_Data/docs/pressdata/en/ecofin/136487.pdf>, last accessed on 15.08.2021.

[20] Poulou, 'The Liability of the EU in the ESM framework' Case note on Joined Cases C-8/15 P to C-10/15 P *Ledra Advertising and Others v Commission and ECB*, *Maastricht Journal of European & Comparative Law* 127 (2017), at p. 129.

[21] See Case T-327/13 *Mallis and Malli v Commission and ECB* [2014] EU:T:2014:909; Case T-328/13 *Tameio Pronoias Prosopikou Trapezis Kyprou v Commission and ECB* [2014] EU:T:2014:906; Case T-329/13 *Chatzithoma v Commission and ECB* [2014] EU:T:2014:908; Case T-330/13 *Chatziioannou v Commission and ECB* [2014] EU:T:2014:904; Case T-331/13 *Nikolaou v Commission and ECB* [2014] EU:T:2014:905. For an analysis of these cases, see Karatzia, 'Cypriot Depositors Before the Court of Justice of the European Union: Knocking on the Wrong Door?', *King's Law Journal* 175 (2015).

[22] Joined Cases C-105–109/15 P *Mallis*, para 61. See also Opinion of AG Wathelet in Joined Cases C-105–109/15 P *Mallis* [2016] EU:C:2016:294, para 65.

to produce legal effects with respect to third parties, and can, therefore, not be annulled on the basis of article 263 of the TFEU.[23] Moreover, in *Mallis* the CJEU rejected the argument that the Eurogroup is under the factual control of the Commission and the ECB, when it comes to meetings related to the ESM, and thus held that Eurogroup statements containing financial assistance conditions cannot be imputed to the EU institutions.[24]

In *Council v K. Chrysostomides & Co. and Others*, the CJEU went even further, stating that the Eurogroup is not an institution within the meaning of article 340 par. 2 TFEU, such that its actions cannot trigger the non-contractual liability of the Union.[25] This is because, according to the Court, the Eurogroup was created as an intergovernmental body, outside the institutional framework of the EU, a fact that was not slightly altered by the formalisation of the existence of the Eurogroup and the participation of the Commission and the ECB at its meetings through article 137 TFEU and Protocol No 14.[26]

Nevertheless, in view of the serious interference with the fundamental rights of individuals, which might remain without legal remedy as is illustrated by the Cypriot case, the question arises whether the Court could have decided differently, stating the Eurogroup is bound by the Charter when formulating financial assistance conditionality. The scope of the Charter is determined by article 51(1) of the EUCFR, which reads: 'The provisions of this Charter are addressed to the institutions, bodies, offices and agencies of the Union with due regard for the principle of subsidiarity.' Not being one of the seven EU institutions listed in article 13(1) of the TEU, the Eurogroup may be bound by the Charter only if it could be regarded as a body, office, or agency of the or as a configuration of the Council of the EU. As pointed out in the explanation accompanying article 51 of the EUCFR, the expression 'bodies, offices and agencies' is commonly used in the Treaties to refer to all the authorities set up by the Treaties or by secondary legislation.[27] The Eurogroup is explicitly mentioned in article 137 of the TFEU, which, with respect to its composition and the Union arrangements for its meetings, refers to Protocol No 14 annexed to the TFEU. This Protocol provides that the Eurogroup consists of the finance ministers of the euro area Member States, who 'shall meet informally … to discuss questions related to the specific responsibilities they share with regard to the single currency'. As the Court has held, this provision presents the Eurogroup as 'a forum

[23] Ibid., para 49.

[24] Ibid., para 47.

[25] Joined Cases C-597/18 P, C-598/18 P, C-603/18 P and C-604/18 P, *Council v K. Chrysostomides & Co. and Others* [2020] EU:C:2020:1028, para 90, 97.

[26] Joined Cases C-597/18 P, C-598/18 P, C-603/18 P and C-604/18 P, *Chrysostomides*, para 84, 87.

[27] Explanations relating to the Charter of Fundamental Rights [2007] OJ C303/17, 32.

for discussion, at ministerial level, between representatives the Member States whose currency is the euro', and not as a 'decision-making body'.[28]

Furthermore, the Eurogroup is not among the different configurations of the Council of the EU provided by article 16(6) of the TEU and enumerated in Annex I to the Rules of Procedure of the Council.[29] Besides not being classified as such by the TFEU, the classification of the Eurogroup as a configuration of the Council would not be in line with the different functions that each of them performs. As Advocate General Wathelet observed in his Opinion on *Mallis*, while the Eurogroup is an informal forum for discussion between euro area Member States on questions specifically related to the single currency, the Council's functions pursuant to article 16(1) of the TEU are far broader and include the exercise, in conjunction with the Parliament, of legislative power within the EU and the other decision-making powers conferred on the Council alone by the TFEU.[30]

Since it can neither be equated with a configuration of the Council nor classified as a formal decision-making body, office, or agency of the EU,[31] the Eurogroup does not fall under the scope of the Charter as defined in article 51(1) of the EUCFR. In view of the fact that, despite its informal nature, the Eurogroup very often predetermines and shapes crucial decisions in the framework of financial assistance, the conclusion that its acts cannot be assessed against the Charter is very problematic for the delivery of accountability goods. First and foremost, decisions taken under such an informal setting undermine the accountability good of openness, by depriving citizens of official information and transparent decision-making procedures. Furthermore, being left outside the scope of judicial review decisions of the Eurogroup can neither be assessed as to their non-arbitrariness nor as to their pursuit of common goals. As a result, the lack of human rights review with regard to decisions taken by the Eurogroup puts also the accountability goods of non-arbitrariness and publicness into peril.

### 12.3.2 *The Applicability of the Charter to the Commission and the ECB*

The next question relates to the case law of the CJEU with regard to the applicability of the Charter to the Commission and ECB, which as members of the Troika, had an important say in formulating and monitoring financial

28 Joined Cases C-105–109/15 P *Mallis*, para 47.

29 See Council Decision 2009/937/EU of 1 December 2009 adopting the Council's Rules of Procedure [2009] OJ L325/35.

30 See Opinion of AG Wathelet in Joined Cases C-105–109/15 P, *Mallis*, para 61.

31 Joined Cases C-105–109/15 P *Mallis*, para 61.

assistance conditionality.[32] Since Troika is a cooperation body and hence a subject that cannot be as such held accountable under international or EU law,[33] its actions have to be regarded as joint measures of EU institutions and subjects of international law (Commission, ECB, and IMF), whose commitment to human rights must be assessed separately.

The CJEU was confronted with the applicability of the Charter to the Commission and the ECB (when they negotiate and conclude the MoU) in 2016, in the seminal case *Ledra Advertising*.[34] On appeals against decisions of the General Court, which had dismissed as inadmissible actions for annulment and compensation raised after the restructuring of Cypriot banks, the CJEU clearly spelt out the obligation of EU institutions to respect human rights when formulating financial assistance conditionality. Filling the gap left on this issue in *Pringle*, the CJEU followed the Opinion of Advocate General Kokott,[35] explicitly stating that the Charter binds EU institutions in all circumstances, even when they act outside the EU legal framework.[36] In this vein, the Court clearly underlined that, in the context of the adoption of an MoU, the Commission is bound under both article 17(1) of the TEU – which confers upon it the general task of overseeing the application of EU law – and article 12(3) and (4) of the ESM Treaty – which requires it to ensure that the MoUs by the ESM are consistent with EU law – to ensure that such an MoU is consistent with the fundamental rights guaranteed by the Charter.[37]

Although article 51(1) of the EUCFR should have been mentioned, together with article 17(1) of the TEU and article 13(3) of the ESM Treaty, among the provisions that oblige the EU institutions to ensure that the MoUs are consistent with EU fundamental rights, the clear reference to the pertinence of the Charter to actions of EU institutions in the making of financial assistance conditionality constitutes a milestone for the protection of human rights in the context of post-crisis European financial assistance. *Ledra Advertising* leaves no doubt that – even if in the EFSF and ESM framework the Commission

[32] Recital 3 of the Preamble and arts 2(1)(a) and 3(1) of the EFSF Framework Agreement; article 13(3) and (7) of the ESM Treaty; article 7(1)(1) and (4)(1) of Regulation 472/2013.

[33] See also Fischer-Lescano, 'Troika in der Austerität: Rechtsbindungen der Unionsorgane beim Abschluss von Memoranda of Understanding', *Kritische Justiz* 7 (2014).

[34] For a detailed analysis of the judgement, see Dermine, 'The End of Impunity? The Legal Duties of "Borrowed" EU Institutions under the European Stability Mechanism Framework: ECJ 20 September 2016, Case C-8/15 to C-10/15, Ledra Advertising et al v European Commission and European Central Bank', *European Constitutional Law Review* 369 (2017); Poulou, note 21 above.

[35] See Opinion of AG Kokott in Case C-370/12 *Pringle* [2012] EU:C:2012:675, para 176.

[36] Joined Cases C-8–10/15 P *Ledra*, para 67.

[37] Ibid.

and the ECB act under powers conferred on them by intergovernmental agreements – their commitment to the Charter does not cease to exist.

Nevertheless, when deciding on the substance of the case, the CJEU ruled against the plaintiffs. More precisely, the Court concluded that the bail-in implemented in the Cypriot banking sector did not constitute a disproportionate and intolerable interference with the substance of the appellants' right to property, given the imminent risk of financial losses to which depositors with the two banks concerned would have been exposed, if the latter had failed. Having found no unlawful conduct on behalf of the Commission, when permitting the adoption of the bail-in, the Court dismissed the appellants' claims for compensation (articles 268 and 340 TFEU) as lacking any foundation in law.

### 12.3.3 *The Applicability of the Charter to the Council of the EU*

The Council of the EU approves financial assistance conditionality in the form of Council Decisions.[38] The CJEU was confronted early on with the assessment of Decisions of the Council containing financial assistance conditionality after actions for annulment launched under article 263 of the TFEU. More precisely, the legality of Decision 2010/320/EU was questioned, on the one hand, due to the reduction of Easter, holiday and Christmas bonuses[39] and, on the other hand, due to the increase in the retirement age and the reduction of the pensions of civil servants.[40] Council Decision 2011/57/EU was challenged on the basis of its provision improving the management of public assets,[41] introducing means-testing of family allowances[42] and limiting recruitment in the whole general government to a ratio of a maximum of one recruitment every five retirements or dismissals, without sectoral exceptions.[43]

In order for the actions for annulment to be admissible, the applicants had to prove that the regulatory acts were of direct and individual concern to them pursuant to article 263(4) of the TFEU. The Court held that the challenged provisions were indeterminate and left a margin to the Greek State as to the way they were implemented, and thus could not directly affect the applicants.[44]

38 Article 7(2) Regulation (EU) 472/2013.
39 Article 2 para 1 lit. f of Council Decision 2010/320/EU.
40 Article 2 para 2 lit. b of Council Decision 2010/320/EU.
41 Article 1 para 4 lit. k of Council Decision 2011/57/EU.
42 Article 1 para 8 lit. s of Council Decision 2011/57/EU.
43 Article 1 para 8 lit. gg of Council Decision 2011/57/EU.
44 Case T-541/10 *ADEDY and Others v Council*, paras 70 and 72–73; Case T-215/11 *ADEDY and Others v Council*, paras 81, 84, and 90.

It is only the content of the national implementing measures, which determine to what extent the applicants will suffer reductions, that might directly affect their legal situation. As a result, both actions were rejected as inadmissible.

As far as some of the contested measures are concerned, the arguments of the General Court are persuasive. Indeed, some of the provisions, such as the provision that provided for 'better management of public assets, with the aim of raising at least EUR 7 billion during the period 2011–2013'[45] and the provision on means-testing of family allowances, which stipulated 'means-testing of family allowances from January 2011 on yielding savings of at least EUR 150 million (net of the respective administrative costs)',[46] were vague and left it to the discretion of national authorities to specify the details of their implementation. As a result, the General Court convincingly held that those provisions were not of direct concern to the applicants within the meaning of article 263 para 4 TFEU.

In contrast, less convincing is the outcome in relation to other contested measures. The 'reduction of the Easter, summer and Christmas bonuses and allowances paid to civil servants with the aim of saving EUR 1,500 million for a full year (EUR 1,100 million in 2010)'[47] and the provision on 'an act that limits recruitment in the whole general government to a ratio of not more than one recruitment for five retirements or dismissals, without sectoral exceptions, and including staff transferred from public enterprises under restructuring to government entities'[48] are detailed provisions, which specified the way in which they were to be implemented by the Member State concerned. Hence, in this case, the requirement of direct and individual concern of the applicants within the meaning of article 263 para 4 TFEU should have been regarded as met.

In view of the above, it is obvious that CJEU denied the applicants' legal standing, approaching the cases on cuts in wages, pensions, and social benefits only in a procedural manner without proceeding to the assessment of their compatibility to human rights. Nevertheless and regardless of the procedural question of whether the Decisions are of direct and individual concern to individuals, pursuant to article 263(4) of the TFEU, the Council of the EU is undoubtedly included among the EU institutions which are bound by the Charter according to article 51(1) of the EUCFR read together with article 13 of the TEU. In addition, the Decisions of the Council fall under the types of

45 Article 1 para 4 lit. k of Council Decision 2011/57/EU.

46 Article 1 para 8 lit. s of Council Decision 2011/57/EU.

47 Article 2 para1 lit. f of Council Decision 2010/320/EU.

48 Article 1 para 8 lit. gg of Council Decision 2011/57/EU.

secondary legislation listed in article 288(4) of the TFEU. Thus, the Decisions of the Council adopted under the framework of European financial assistance are unilateral, legally binding acts of an EU institution and as such fall under the scope of the Charter. The fact that their content arguably reflects a negotiated agreement between different actors does not impact on their legal nature as acts of secondary EU law within the meaning of article 288 of the TFEU.[49] Against this background, it is very unfortunate to realise that individuals concerned may experience procedural hurdles when launching an action for annulment against a decision entailing lending conditions, when at the same time these decisions must be in conformity with the Charter.

Nevertheless, when, later on, the CJEU decided on the substance of financial conditions laid down in Council decisions, it held that restrictions on human rights were justified. Indeed, in case *Sotiropoulou and Others v Council*[50] the General Court dealt with an action for compensation under article 268 TFEU in respect of the loss and harm, which the applicants had allegedly sustained, as a result of the reduction of their main pensions due to the adoption of a series of Council decisions under articles 126 (9) and 136 TFEU on pension reform in Greece.[51] In support of their action, the applicants relied on two pleas in law. First, the applicants claimed that, in adopting the contested decisions, which concern inter alia the laying down of detailed measures in the social security and pension system, the Council exceeded the powers conferred by the Treaty and infringed the principles of conferral and subsidiarity as laid down in articles 4 and 5 TEU in conjunction with articles 2

[49] This point can be compared with Council Decisions concluding external EU agreements. The fact that the Council Decisions do not add anything to the agreements is no obstacle against the legal challenge of these Decisions before the Court.

[50] Case T-531/14 *Sotiropoulou and Others v Council* [2017] EU:T:2017:297.

[51] The Decisions of the Council concerned are the following: Council Decision 2010/320/EU of 10 May 2010 addressed to Greece with a view to reinforcing and deepening fiscal surveillance and giving notice to Greece to take measures for the deficit reduction judged necessary to remedy the situation of excessive deficit [2010] L145/6; Council Decision 2010/486/EU of 7 September 2010 amending Decision 2010/320/EU addressed to Greece with a view to reinforcing and deepening fiscal surveillance and giving notice to Greece to take measures for the deficit reduction judged necessary to remedy the situation of excessive deficit [2010] L241/12; Council Decision 2011/57/EU of 20 December 2010 amending Decision 2010/320/EU addressed to Greece with a view to reinforcing and deepening fiscal surveillance and giving notice to Greece to take measures for the deficit reduction judged necessary to remedy the situation of excessive deficit [2011] L26/15; Council Decision 2011/257/EU of 7 March 2011 amending Decision 2010/320/EU addressed to Greece with a view to reinforcing and deepening the fiscal surveillance and giving notice to Greece to take measures for the deficit reduction judged necessary to remedy the situation of excessive deficit [2011] L110/26; Council Decision 2011/734/EU of 12 July 2011 addressed to Greece with a view to reinforcing and deepening fiscal surveillance and giving notice to Greece to take measures for the deficit reduction

to 6 TFEU. Second, the applicants contended that the contested decisions of the Council required the introduction of drastic pension cuts that fundamentally disturbed the applicants' financial situation and resulted in the reversal of situations which they had sought in good faith. As a result, the applicants claimed that the enactment and implementation of the reductions at issue resulted in direct infringement of their right to human dignity, their right as elderly persons to lead a life of dignity and independence, and their right to social security benefits and social services providing protection in cases such as old age, laid down in articles 1, 25 and 34 CFREU, respectively.

As to the first plea in law, the General Court held that the principles of conferral and subsidiarity concern the division of responsibilities between Member States and the EU and cannot be regarded as conferred rights on individuals. Consequently, any breach of these principles is not in itself sufficient to establish the non-contractual liability of the Union.[52] In any case, the contested decisions do not infringe the principles of conferral and subsidiarity, as they were issued with a view to reinforcing and deepening the fiscal surveillance and giving notice to Greece to take measures for the deficit reduction judged necessary to remedy the situation of excessive deficit. As a result, the General Court held that the contested decisions were adopted in the context of the exercise of powers expressly conferred on the Council by article 126 (9) and article 136 TFEU.[53]

By their second plea in law, the applicants claimed that the sum of the pension cuts appears excessive and disproportionate and does not strike a fair balance between the requirements of the general interest and the protection of their fundamental rights enshrined in articles 1, 25, and 34 CFREU, namely the right to human dignity, the rights of the elderly and the entitlements to social security benefits and social services respectively. As to this complaint, the General Court held that, to the extent that the allegedly violated provisions

judged necessary to remedy the situation of excessive deficit [2011] L296/38; Council Decision 2011/791/EU of 8 November 2011 amending Decision 2011/734/EU addressed to Greece with a view to reinforcing and deepening fiscal surveillance and giving notice to Greece to take measures for the deficit reduction judged necessary to remedy the situation of excessive deficit [2011] L320/28;Council Decision 2012/211/EU of 13 March 2012 amending Decision 2011/734/EU addressed to Greece with a view to reinforcing and deepening fiscal surveillance and giving notice to Greece to take measures for the deficit reduction judged necessary to remedy the situation of excessive deficit [2012] L113/8 and Council Decision 2013/6/EU of 4 December 2012 amending Decision 2011/734/EU addressed to Greece with a view to reinforcing and deepening fiscal surveillance and giving notice to Greece to take measures for the deficit reduction judged necessary to remedy the situation of excessive deficit [2013] L4/40.

52 Case T-531/14 *Sotiropoulou and Others v Council* [2017] EU:T:2017:297, para 72.

53 Case T-531/14 *Sotiropoulou and Others v Council* [2017] EU:T:2017:297, para 73.

of the Charter constitute rules of law intended to confer rights on individuals, it must be considered whether any breach of them could substantiate the Union's liability in this case.[54] Furthermore, the Court stated that, according to settled case law, when assessing the non-contractual liability of the Union, the Court has to take into account, inter alia, the complexity of the situations to be regulated, the difficulties in the application or interpretation of the legislation and, more particularly, the margin of discretion available to the author of the act in question[55] More precisely, the decisive criterion for establishing a sufficiently serious breach of a rule of law intended to confer rights on individuals is whether there has been a manifest and grave disregard by the institution concerned of the limits of its discretion.[56] In the case at stake, the contested decisions constitute an exercise of the powers conferred on the Council by articles 126 (9) and 136 TFEU in the context of the excessive deficit procedure of an Eurozone Member State. This competence mainly involves economic policy choices for which it is justified to provide a wide margin of discretion. Hence, those provisions specify only the type of measures to be taken, which may be included in the recommendations from the Council to a Member State for the attainment of a specific objective.[57] Against this background, the General Court stated that it was necessary to assess whether the Council adopted the decisions at stake in a manifest and serious breach of the limits of its discretion.[58] As reminded by the Court, the contested decisions were issued following the conclusion of the Council that an excessive deficit exists in Greece[59] and the budgetary measures included had been extensively discussed with the Greek government and commonly agreed by the European Commission, the ECB and the IMF.[60] In light of the above, the General Court held that it was not manifestly unreasonable to envisage various cost-saving measures, including pension cuts. Therefore, in adopting the contested decisions, the Council did not exceed the limits of its wide discretion.[61]

Moreover, the Court underlined that even if the contested decisions were in fact capable of causing the alleged damage to the applicants, the rights to access social security benefits and social services are not absolute, since their exercise may be subject to restrictions justified by objectives of general interest

[54] Case T-531/14 *Sotiropoulou and Others v Council* [2017] EU:T:2017:297, para 76.

[55] Case T-531/14 *Sotiropoulou and Others v Council* [2017] EU:T:2017:297, para 77.

[56] Case T-531/14 *Sotiropoulou and Others v Council* [2017] EU:T:2017:297, para 78.

[57] Case T-531/14 *Sotiropoulou and Others v Council* [2017] EU:T:2017:297, para 81.

[58] Case T-531/14 *Sotiropoulou and Others v Council* [2017] EU:T:2017:297, para 82.

[59] Council Decision 2009/415/EC of 27 April 2009 on the existence of an excessive deficit in Greece [2009] L135/21.

[60] Case T-531/14 *Sotiropoulou and Others v Council* [2017] EU:T:2017:297, paras 83–85.

[61] Case T-531/14 *Sotiropoulou and Others v Council* [2017] EU:T:2017:297, paras 86–87.

pursued by the Union, as provided for in article 52 (1) CFREU.[62] In this vein, measures to reduce the size of pensions meet objectives of general interest, namely the ensuring of fiscal consolidation, the reduction of public expenditure, and the support of the pension system of the Member State concerned.[63] Consequently, the General Court held that these measures also met objectives of general interest pursued by the Union, namely the ensuring of budgetary discipline of Member States whose currency is the euro and the ensuring of the financial stability of the euro area.[64] In view of those objectives and the imminent risk of insolvency of the Member State concerned, the General Court came to the conclusion that the contested measures, which were specified in Greek national laws,[65] cannot be regarded as unjustified restrictions of the rights claimed by the applicants, since they do not constitute a disproportionate and intolerable interference impairing the very substance of these rights.[66] In light of the above considerations, the General Court held that the applicants did not establish that the Council had committed a serious breach of a rule of law which confers rights on individuals. Hence, in absence of one of the cumulative conditions for establishing the non-contractual liability of the Union provided for in article 340 para 2 TFEU, the action was dismissed in its entirety.[67]

### 12.3.4 *The CJEU as an 'Accountability-Rendering Actor'?*

The overview of the supranational jurisprudence shows that the CJEU held a hesitant stance towards the protection of human rights during the Eurozone crisis. First, the CJEU declined to take up the merits of cases that questioned the compatibility of crisis-driven measures with Charter-guaranteed human rights, thus shying away from the task of delivering accountability goods. More precisely, leaving conditionality measures outside the scope of human rights review, came to a detriment of the accountability good of non-arbitrariness, since decision-makers were left free to not take into account right-based

[62] Case T-531/14 *Sotiropoulou and Others v Council* [2017] EU:T:2017:297, para 88.
[63] Case T-531/14 *Sotiropoulou and Others v Council* [2017] EU:T:2017:297, para 89.
[64] Case T-531/14 *Sotiropoulou and Others v Council* [2017] EU:T:2017:297, para 89.
[65] See article 3 of law 3845/2010, article 11 of law 3863/2010, articles 12 and 44 of law 3986/2011, article 2 of law 4024/2011, article 2 of law 4024/2011, article 6 of law 4051/2012 and law 4093/2012.
[66] Case T-531/14 *Sotiropoulou and Others v Council* [2017] EU:T:2017:297, para 90. At this point, the General Court referenced the similar outcome of the case *Ledra Advertising v Commission and ECB*, in which the CJEU held that the restructuring of the Cypriot banks did not constitute an unjustified restriction of the depositors' right to property guaranteed by article 17 para 1 CFREU.
[67] Case T-531/14 *Sotiropoulou and Others v Council* [2017] EU:T:2017:297, paras 92–93.

limitations in their policy-making. Furthermore, the accountability good of publicness was left without protection, since the court did not review whether consultation existed in the making of the measures or if the policies were in line with the principle of proportionality.

Second, even during the second phase of crisis-driven case law when the CJEU finally addressed the substantive questions put to it, it did not rule in favour of the plaintiffs. The CJEU weighed their claims against the perceived need for budgetary discipline by Eurozone Member States, the precarious financial stability of the euro area and the imminent risk of insolvency of the Member State concerned, concluding that the contested measures did not comprise unjustified restrictions on human rights. As a result, the CJEU guaranteed a very low level of protection of the accountability goods of non-arbitrariness and publicness, since the protection of human rights was put under a very weak judicial review. Altogether, these decisions mean that the CJEU will not be remembered for its defence of accountability goods during the European financial crisis but rather for the judicial self-restraint that it exercised in the field.

## 12.4 THE CALL FOR A COMBINATION OF A PROCEDURAL AND SUBSTANTIVE UNDERSTANDING OF HUMAN RIGHTS ACCOUNTABILITY

The stance of the Court during the crisis reflects the general concerns about courts competing with other decision-making institutions for the ultimate say on polycentric political issues. Judges, the argument goes, are ill-suited to make decisions in matters with complex budgetary and political[68] Furthermore, courts are warned against interfering with collective policy decisions made by political fora such as parliaments, whose democratic accountability makes them better equipped to aggregate, mediate, and balance the affected interests.

The general rule of task-distribution between constitutional institutions, courts, and parliaments, applies, however, in times of proper functioning of democracy. During the current Eurozone crisis though, the constitutional balance between the different institutions had been significantly altered. As noted above, financial assistance conditionality resulted in intrusive social governance, left at the discretion of executives, and insulated from public debate and parliamentary scrutiny. Traditional *fora* of deliberation, such as parliaments, where

[68] Pieterse, 'Coming to Terms with Judicial Enforcement of Socio-Economic Rights', *South African Journal on Human Rights* (2017) 383, at p. 393.

social policies could be defended, were substantially weakened. In this context, the basic premise of democratic legitimacy, that binding collective decisions should result from procedures that allow for the effective and equal participation of the largest possible number of the actors affected, is frustrated.[69]

Under these circumstances, applying the general rule that courts should not interfere with complex choices of political bodies regarding financial assistance, would mean that the exclusion of subjects affected and the eventual violation of their human rights, would be left without any effective remedy. In a situation where the conduits of democratic participation are blocked or ineffective, courts should thus actively undertake the task to institutionalise both procedural and substantive accountability of the decision-makers.

In order to serve accountability and more precisely the good of publicness in a procedural manner, courts should review the procedural conditions under which decisions were taken, that originate from financial assistance conditionality and drastically interfere with human rights. That is, whether these decisions emerged from deliberative and inclusive procedures, which included the views of those affected.[70] Courts should particularly ask decision-makers to elaborate on how decisions were made, which social actors were consulted, and to what extent affected individuals could be heard. This role of courts should not be understood as simply a scrutiny of procedural conditions of bare majoritarianism. Through this scrutiny, courts ensure that rights of minorities and politically marginalised groups, such as the young generation, are not violated by majoritarian decision-making.

The relevance for the legal assessment of the participation or not of the affected actors is reflected in Regulation 472/2013,[71] which explicitly requires the involvement of social partners and relevant civil society organisations in the preparation of the adjustment programmes, with a view to contributing to building consensus over its content.[72] Moreover, in its decisions concerning

[69] On the understanding of legitimacy as a democratic process for the genesis of law, see Dahl, *Democracy and Its Critics* (Yale University Press, 1989) p. 106; Habermas, *Faktizität und Geltung: Beiträge zur Diskurstheorie des Rechts und des demokratischen Rechtsstaats* (Suhrkamp, 1997), at p. 321.

[70] On the democratic legitimacy of judicial review, see Ely, *Democracy and Distrust: A Theory of Judicial Review* (Harvard University Press, 1980); Dahl, *Democracy and Its critics*, ibid., at p. 188; Zurn, *Deliberative Democracy and the Institutions of Judicial Review* (Cambridge University Press, 2007), at p. 236.

[71] Regulation (EU) 472/2013 of the European Parliament and of the Council of 21 May 2013 on the strengthening of economic and budgetary surveillance of Member States in the euro area experiencing or threatened with serious difficulties with respect to their financial stability (Two-Pack Regulation), O.J. 2013, L 140/1.

[72] Article 8 of Regulation 472/2013.

pension schemes in Greece mentioned, the European Committee of Social Rights (ECSR) included the democratically questionable procedures to a factor that contributed to the violation of the Social Charter, noting that the Greek government has not discussed the pension reforms with the organisations concerned, despite the fact that they represent the interests of many of the groups most affected by the measures at issue. Thus, the ECSR ruled that, even though the controversial restrictions would under certain conditions not breach the Charter, 'due to the cumulative effect of the restrictive measures and the procedures adopted to put them into place', they do amount to a violation of the right to social security (article 12 para. 3 ESC).[73]

With regard to the institutionalisation of accountability in a substantive manner, courts should proceed to an ad hoc basis assessment of the conformity of a specific measure with the human rights affected. Nevertheless, some prominent examples illustrate the substantive red lines that could be drawn by the judiciary. For example, in Greece, a series of financial assistance conditions were especially addressed to the labour rights of the young generation, introducing differentiated treatment on the ground of age. In both the first and the second economic adjustment programmes, the Greek government assumed the responsibility to introduce sub-minima wages for groups at risk such as young people.[74] Minimum wages established by the national general collective agreement had to be reduced by 22 per cent, for youth though – namely for ages below twenty-five – wages had to be reduced by 32 per cent.[75] This differentiated treatment of young workers obviously touches upon the right to fair and just working conditions (article 31 CFREU) on the protection

[73] ECSR, Decision on the Merits, 7.12.2012, Federation of employed pensioners of Greece (IKA-ETAM) v Greece, Complaint No. 76/2012, para. 83; ECSR, Decision on the Merits, 7.12.2012, Panhellenic Federation of Public Service Pensioners (POPS) v Greece, Complaint No. 77/2012, para. 79; ECSR, Decision on the Merits, 7.12.2012, Pensioners' Union of the Athens-Piraeus Electric Railways (I.S.A.P.) v Greece, Complaint No. 78/2012, para. 79; ECSR, Decision on the Merits, 7.12.2012, Panhellenic Federation of pensioners of the Public Electricity Corporation (POS-DEI) v Greece, Complaint No. 79/2012, para. 79; ECSR, Decision on the Merits, 7.12.2012, Pensioners' Union of the Agricultural Bank of Greece (ATE) v Greece, Complaint No. 80/2012, para. 79.

[74] See European Commission, Directorate-General for Economic and Financial Affairs, The Economic Adjustment Programme for Greece, May 2010, Occasional Papers 61, p. 68. Same clause was also included in Article 2 para. 3 lit. d. Council Decision 2010/320/EU.

[75] See European Commission, Directorate-General for Economic and Financial Affairs, The Second Economic Adjustment Programme for Greece, March 2012, Occasional Papers 94, p. 147. This further 10 per cent reduction of the minimum wage of young Greek people was presented as a means to reduce the gap in the level of the minimum wage relative to peers (Portugal, Central and Southeast Europe), to help address high youth unemployment, as well as employment of individuals on the margins of the labour market, and to encourage a shift from the informal to the formal labour sector.

of young people at work (article 32 CFREU) and the rule of non-discrimination (article 21 CFREU).[76] Indicative is also the fact that the European Committee of Social Rights (ESCR) ruled in its decision 66/2011 that the differentiated reduction of the minimum wage of people under 25 constitutes a violation of article 4§1 (right to a fair remuneration) of the European Social Charter (ESC) read together with the non-discrimination clause of the Preamble to the ESC, which corresponds to articles 31 and 21 CFR. In that case, the ESCR found disproportionate discrimination against young employees, whose minimum wage was reduced below the poverty level.[77]

Moreover, drawing on the understanding of legitimacy and democracy in EU law, this chapter suggests that a democratically legitimate role of courts can be conceived, if a link between the procedural and the substantive dimension of human rights accountability is established. The basic principle is that, in order for courts' judgement in disputed financial assistance cases to be legitimised, judges should assess the observance of the procedural dimension of human rights and, depending on the outcome, calibrate the standard of review on the basis of the substantive dimension of the respective rights accordingly. More precisely, starting from the premise that the political process is, in principle, better suited for the formulation of social policies, courts should first focus on the decision-making process rather than on the content of a contested policy choice. In this vein, judges should review whether the contested measure, which allegedly represents a majority decision, has indeed been the result of a participatory and deliberative decision-making process or whether the affected individuals were excluded from the relevant procedure.

## 12.5 CONCLUSION

The overview of the supranational jurisprudence shows that the general pattern during the Eurozone crisis was that the CJEU shied away from the difficult task to overrule conditionality-driven decisions over complex social policy issues and, thus, to ensure accountability goods. In the majority of cases, the courts deferred to the legislator leaving the final say on choices regarding social policy and resource allocation to them. The application of this general rule of task-distribution between courts and parliaments relies on the assumption that

[76] The differentiated treatment of the younger generation is also incompatible with secondary EU law, like the Council Directive 2000/78/EC of 27 November 2000 establishing a general framework for equal treatment in employment and occupation, OJ L 303.

[77] ECSR, Decision on the Merits, 23.05.2012, General Federation of employees of the national electric power corporation (GENOP-DEI) and Confederation of Greek Civil Servants' Trade Unions (ADEDY) v Greece, Complaint No. 66/2011, para. 65, 68–69.

the non-neutral choices of political bodies were made after the consultation and participation of all affected individuals and vulnerable groups.

Nevertheless, it is only through taking both process and substance seriously that human rights accountability can effectively be applied and at the same time ensure a democratic role for courts. Courts should review the observance of substantive guarantees of human rights in connection with compliance with the procedural conditions inherent in a democratic legislative process. In this way, decisions on substantive political and social issues would in principle remain at the disposal of the respective political institution, which would bear the weight of defending them before the judiciary. The court would be reviewing complex policy choices, with the aim to protect human rights and ensure the delivery of accountability goods.

# 13

# Constitutive Powers and Justification

## *The Duty to Give Reasons in EU Monetary Policy*

*Joana Mendes*

### 13.1 THE MANDATE OF THE ECB AND THE LIMITS OF LAW

The withdrawal of monetary policy from the realm of democratic politics is a pillar of the 'constitution of money' in the Economic and Monetary Union (EMU).[1] A choice that appeared relatively uncontentious in the early 1990s has become the core of the ECB's legitimacy conundrum. While monetary policy was never a-political, it has until recently been perceived mostly as such, largely because of the neo-classical politico-economic premises of independence and inflation control that the Maastricht Treaty enshrined. The ECB's decisions during the EU's sovereign debt crisis were but part of an evolution of central banking that is in tension with that model.[2]

The 'whatever it takes' of 2012 was both the epitome of a crisis intervention and a first moment of a change that has had a much longer-term duration. The still-called *unconventional* monetary measures continued in place well beyond the heat of the crisis. The second and third moments signal what has been perceived as a radical change in the role of the ECB followed in 2020 and 2021. In 2020, when the Covid pandemic forced an unprecedented freeze of the economy, extraordinary fiscal and monetary stimulus, as much as vaccines, were essential ingredients to recover from economic collapse at the pace of resurgent pandemic waves. The ECB's pandemic emergency programme (PEPP) was crucial to inject the liquidity desperately needed to prevent further economic meltdown.[3] The support of economic policy – the ECB's secondary mandate – came squarely to the forefront, much beyond the

1 The 'constitution of money' is the title of Chessa, *La Costituzione della Moneta* (Jovene, 2016).
2 See, among many, Tooze, 'The Death of the Central Bank Myth', *Foreign Policy*, May 13 2020.
3 For a first analysis, see M. Goldmann, 'Borrowing Time: The ECB's Pandemic Emergency Purchase Programme', *VerfBlog*, 2020/3/27, https://verfassungsblog.de/borrowing-time/, DOI: 10.17176/20200328-002904-0.

narrow price stability that had been the purview of its monetary policy up to a decade before.[4] At the time when this emergency action arrived, the ECB was engaged in a major overhaul of its mandate through a strategic review process, which came to an end in 2021. The acute awareness of the world's fragilities, as the climate crisis compounded with a health crisis, made this discussion turn not only on monetary policy objectives in a context of deflation but also on how far the ECB should become an actor for climate protection.[5] This evolution is part of a larger phenomenon. Decarbonisation, digital transition, and inequality became part of the agendas of central banks, as, throughout the world, governments and central banks considered who has the necessary and most suitable instruments to tackle the political goals of the early twenty-first century.[6] In the case of the EU, in particular, the ECB has at crucial points stepped in to occupy a space vacated by politics.

This evolution in little less than a decade remains politically contested. Even as central banks re-focused their attention on inflation, it revealed the centrality of central banks in our systems of government. Because it occurred within the unchanged Treaty strictures, the political conflict eventually reached the courts. The judgments of the Court of Justice of the European Union (CJEU) in the cases of *Gauweiler* (2015) and *Weiss* (2019) brought to the foreground fundamental constitutional questions on the vertical allocation of competences between the EU institutions and the Member States (and hence on the very design of the EMU), on the tension between democracy and independent executives but also on the possibilities of judicial and political accountability over an ever-expanding ECB on whose controversial decisions the survival of the euro rested. The disparity between the CJEU's and the German Constitutional Court's position regarding the degree of judicial

4 See the Introductory Statement to the Press Conference by Christine Lagarde and Luis de Guindos, following the monetary policy decisions of the Governing Board of 4 June 2020 ('*In line with its mandate*, the Governing Council is *determined to ensure* the necessary degree of monetary accommodation and *a smooth transmission of monetary policy* across sectors and countries. Accordingly, we decided on *a set of monetary policy measures to support the economy* during its gradual reopening and to safeguard medium-term price stability.'), in the aftermath of the Weiss ruling of the German Federal Constitutional Court (available at www.ecb.europa.eu/press/pressconf/2020/html/ecb.is200604~b479b8cfff.en.html).

5 ECB, 'Climate Change and Monetary Policy in the Euro Area' 271 *ECB Occasional Paper Series* (2021), accessible at www.ecb.europa.eu/pub/pdf/scpops/ecb.op271~36775d43c8.en.pdf, last accessed 4 February 2022. In addition, see, inter alia, Tooze, 'Climate crisis offers way out of monetary orthodoxy' (2021), accessible at https://socialeurope.eu/climate-crisis-offers-way-out-of-monetary-orthodoxy, last accessed 3 February 2022.

6 For a critical view, King and Katz, 'Central Banks Are Risking Their Independence', *Bloomberg*, August 23rd 2021 (available at www.bloomberg.com/opinion/articles/2021-08-23/central-banks-are-risking-their-independence-mervyn-king-dan-katz).

review, in particular in the case of *Weiss*, stirred the discussion on the limits of law-based accountability. At stake was, in particular, the scope of the principle of proportionality and the justification based on the ECB's duty to give reasons. While both proportionality and reason-giving have a long-standing pedigree in EU law – with regard to the judicial review, both of legislation and of discretionary administrative action – and are formally applicable to all actions of the EU institutions, both strictures treaded on uncertain ground when applied to monetary policy measures with salient economic policy implications.

These difficulties manifestly opened fundamental questions, pertaining not only to the role of courts and of their instruments of review in relation to monetary policy, but also, and more deeply, to the role of law in the government of money. Just like other EU bodies, the ECB interprets its mandate and makes policy choices when exercising discretion. From this perspective, it presumably should be subject to control through the public law principles that have become a cornerstone of the EU's administrative rule of law.[7] But, unlike fields where judicial review is unquestioned and courts have progressively refined their techniques of control, the ECB operates in a sensitive policy field and displays a momentous power that diffusely and indirectly touches virtually every household and business (without mentioning the external aspects of its action). Due to the interaction between monetary and fiscal policy, its measures touch on the core of political decisions that in democracies are the premise of politically accountable governments and are largely outside the purview of courts (not least for reasons of standing).[8] In these conditions, can law support political accountability, irrespective of concrete instances of judicial review? While this question is posed here in relation to monetary policy and to the ECB's evolving role, it has a broader relevance. How law operates in relation to executive bodies should not be limited to its judicial enforcement, not least because of the political stakes involved in the interpretation of the law when it comes to the delimitation of competences in the EU legal order.

This chapter addresses this question by analysing the functions of the duty to give reasons in relation to the powers of the ECB. It starts by characterising the ECB's powers as a specific instance of constitutive powers. Constitutive powers are not a prerogative of the ECB, but given its *potentia* as holder of the modes of money creation and the constitutional design of the EMU, they raise particular concerns regarding the legality of its actions (Section 13.2).

7 Making that argument in relation to the US Federal Reserve, see Conti-Brown, Listokin, and Parrillo, 'Towards and Administrative Law of Central Banking', 38 *Yale Journal on Regulation* 1 (2021), at p. 4.

8 Noting the same in relation to the Federal Reserve, *idem*.

The constitutive character of the ECB's powers explains the conundrum of the degree of judicial review over matters involving monetary policy. The judicial clash in *Weiss* on the role of courts in relation to the actions of the ECB shows that both full and limited review are, for different reasons, untenable or, at least, the CJEU and the FCC judgments confirm the limited role of courts in ascertaining the law in matters of monetary policy, irrespective of the degree of judicial review they chose to apply (Section 13.3). The existence of constitutive powers and, in particular, the specific circumstances that turned the constitutive powers of the ECB into a virtually intractable constitutional challenge postulate a shift in understanding the role of law in relation to the action of executive bodies. The legal and constitutional scope of the duty to give reasons in EU law will demonstrate that law can and must operate in the absence (or irrespective) of judicial review (Section 13.4). In particular, this perspective shows that the duty to give reasons, in its legal and constitutional vein, can support political accountability of the ECB's actions, substantively and not only procedurally. The chapter concludes by situating the limited relevance of the path proposed here to the democratisation of the government of money in the EU (Section 13.5).

## 13.2 THE ECB'S DISTINCT CONSTITUTIVE POWERS

### 13.2.1 *The Constitutional Question and What Lies Beneath*

The debate on the legality of quantitative easing (QE) was mostly motivated by the economic implications of this type of instruments. There lies the dividing line between considering the QE ECB programmes as still being part of its monetary policy mandate or, on the contrary, falling under the realm of economic policy, in relation to which the ECB has only a supporting role.[9] The vertical allocation of powers defined in the Treaty turned a political-economic discussion over the characteristics of monetary policy programmes into a fundamental constitutional question with profound consequences. Far from being only a matter of legality, the delimitation of competences squarely put the finger on the structural flaws of the EMU (specifically on the lack of a fiscal union), as well as on the limits of the model of central bank independence, the degree of which is inversely proportional to the scope of central bank mandates.[10]

[9] See Case C-62/14 *Gauweiler* EU:C:2015:400 and Case C-493/17, Weiss, EU:C:2018:1000.

[10] See, inter alia, Leaman, *The Bundesbank Myth: Towards a Critique of Central Bank Independence* (Palgrave Macmillan, 2001).

The democratic implications of the interplay between monetary policy and fiscal (economic) policy – the first assigned to a supranational independent institution double-removed from democratic politics, the second, to Member States' governments – make the delimitation of the ECB's competence a particularly pressing constitutional question. The EMU constitutional framework combined with the politico-economic significance of quantitative easing as a mode of money creation makes this a fundamental political issue where the boundaries of democratic politics are at stake.

But lurking beneath the discussion on the limits of the ECB's mandate is also the broader question of the role of law in structuring and controlling the powers of executive bodies which are either independent or placed at arms-length from democratic politics. The interplay between law and administration in contemporary polities is perhaps less dramatic than the pressing questions facing the ECB, and the spectacular clash between two high courts over the boundaries of monetary policy and on how to review them. Yet, it is equally significant to understand, first, whether key public law assumptions hold in policy areas where administrative institutions shape today's societies and, second, to devise solutions for the flaws of current institutional designs and for suitable judicial and political accountability.

### 13.2.2 A *Functional Analysis of the ECB's Powers*

Setting for now aside the constitutional and political specificities of monetary policy and of the ECB's institutional setting, its powers have the following functional characteristics in common with other executive bodies: first, its mandate (whether narrowly or broadly interpreted) requires it to act in situations of uncertainty, reacting to the information that it collects and analyses, with a view to defining the best course of action on the basis of prognostic assessments that only the ECB/ECSB is both technically and legally competent to undertake; second, its decisions involve arbitrating between competing interests (that the conflicting objectives within its mandate mobilise), as well as assessing the effectiveness of the public action that, while taken by other institutions, can impact on the goals of its measures;[11] third, its mandate is delimited and concretised by resorting to open-textured norms whose meaning depends on the interpretation of evaluative and goal-oriented terms, and varies according both to the specific contexts in which the ECB needs to act and to the prevailing (even if contentious) perceptions of what the scope and

[11] In the case of monetary policy, these other institutions are national governments conducting fiscal policies and the agencies competent in related policy fields.

direction of its actions should be; and fourth, the long-term effects of its decisions will be fundamental for its credibility.

These characteristics give the ECB constitutive powers.[12] Constitutive powers entail a circular and reflexive process between law application and law creation: legal norms define the mandates of executive and administrative bodies, but the meaning of those norms is determined through the action of those bodies; at the same time, the public interests that those bodies are meant to protect only come to bear through that very same action. Constitutive powers do not exist without the legal norms which executive and administrative bodies interpret and which allow them to exercise discretion. Yet, two factors, in particular, blur the distinction between interpretation and discretion in these instances and, therefore, break down the boundaries between law creation and law application. First, the executive or administrative body produces or catalyses the knowledge that is needed to interpret the norm. The intricate relationship between, on the one hand, the concepts that the legal norm uses to delimit the administrative and, on the other, the complex facts that the norm regulates,[13] makes the interpretation of the norm depend on the specification of technical terms and, hence, on the factual assessments that the administrative body was set up to make. It is the technical competence of the executive or administrative body that justifies the legal competence that it is given, within the constraints of a mandate that is both constitutionally and politically conditioned. Second, the attribution of meaning presupposes an understanding of the concrete aims of executive action and of how a particular factual situation may challenge those aims. Defining the meaning of the norm (e.g. price stability) is intertwined with shared normative understandings on what the role of that body should be in reaction to socio-economic and political realities and perceived needs of public action (e.g. what in each period price stability entails and how it can be articulated with other public policy objectives). Such definition of meaning has two intertwined effects. It generates and stabilises normative expectations (e.g. defining what is price stability sets the terms of what will be considered legally compliant measures). It gives existence to the public interests that delimit the legal mandate and that justify the existence of the administrative institution, and of its powers

[12] They were outlined in Mendes, 'Constitutive Powers of Executive Bodies: A Functional Analysis of the Single Resolution Board', 84 *The Modern Law Review* 6 (2021), 1330–1359, which also defines constitutive powers as characterised in this paragraph.

[13] Sand, 'Hybrid Law – Law in a Global Society of Differentiation and Change', in Calliess, Fischer-Lescano, Wielsch and Zumbansen (eds.), *Soziologische Jurisprudenz. Festschrift für Gunther Teubner zum 65. Geburtstag* (Berlin: De Gruyter, 2009) 871–886, at 879–880, noting that 'law and politics become increasingly dependent on the semantics of the specialised areas they regulate' (at 886).

and instruments of action (e.g. price stability is also the public interest that the ECB needs to protect and achieve). Given their indeterminacy, these public interests only come into being retrospectively, through administrative action (e.g. price stability only becomes tangible through the action of the ECB). Ultimately, by acting, the administrative institution construes the legal norms that also ground what they may lawfully do.

Constitutive powers are not a prerogative of the ECB. These can arise in the conditions set out above, which apply to other administrative entities with rather different institutional characteristics and constitutional constraints.[14] They acquire, however, a specific dimension in the case of the ECB, as will be seen in more detail below, and shed light on the difficulties of judicial review. They are also relevant for the discussion over the distinction between the *existence* and the *exercise* of a competence, which stemmed from the contrasting *Weiss* judgments of the CJEU and of Germany's Federal Constitutional Court (FCC) on proportionality. In fact, this controversy brought to light the constitutive nature of the ECB's powers. One of the many points of criticism directed against the FCC judgment in *Weiss* was that it applied wrongly the principle of proportionality, not only because of its self-referential way of approaching proportionality and of a misplaced degree of judicial review but also because, according to the Treaty, a proportionality assessment of competences only pertains to their exercise, not to their existence.[15] That is indeed what stems from Article 5(4) TEU, but – as others have also pointed out – the mandate of the ECB is such that can be delimited only through its action, that is, through the exercise of competence.[16] Its constitutive powers mean that it construes the legal norms that also ground what it may lawfully do. The distinction between the *existence* and the *exercise* of a competence then breaks down.

### 13.2.3 *The Blurred Boundaries of Legality*

It follows from the above that the ECB is deciding on the scope of its mandate and, hence, it *is deciding* on its own competences. The FCC was, therefore, accurate in its diagnosis.[17] But it pointed at the wrong causes. The ECB's

[14] As demonstrated in Mendes, *supra*, note 12.

[15] See, among others, Wendel, 'Paradoxes of Ultra-Vires Review: A Critical Review of the PSPP Decision and Its Initial Reception', 21 *German Law Journal* 5 (2020), 979–994.

[16] Borger, 'Outright Monetary Transactions and the Stability Mandate of the ECB: *Gauweiler*', 53 *Common Market Law Review* 1 (2016), 139–196. See also Bóbic in this volume.

[17] Albeit not autonomously, contrary to what the FCC claimed: German Federal Constitution Court (FCC) BverfG, Judgment of the Second Senate of 5 May 2020–2 BvR 859/15, para 134 and 136.

actions are jurisgenerative not for lack of suitable judicial review of its actions (though there is certainly room to criticise the CJEU in this regard).[18] They are jurisgenerative because of the functional nature of their powers in the conditions in which they must be exercised.[19] For this reason, the existence of constitutive powers is not a pathology that must be corrected. But that does not mean that it is unproblematic.

Constitutive powers denote a fundamental tension within the very structure of constitutional democracies, which attribute to law a quality which it cannot have (or that it can only imperfectly achieve) in the circumstances in which central banks (and other administrative institutions) act: the ability to contain and constrain substantively the future-oriented powers of administrative entities acting in conditions of technical and political complexity and uncertainty. As the characterisation of constitutive powers indicates, this does not mean that law is meaningless. As mentioned, these public powers can only exist because the law provides for their existence: constitutive powers presuppose the very legal norms whose meaning executive bodies get to define. But, in a fundamental way, law does not have the capacity to contain and constrain their exercise as the rule of law strictures prescribe. For the same reason, but from a different perspective, also the role that economists attribute to rules in the debate between rules-based and discretionary monetary policy – in which the former is linked to the defence of a narrow mandate of independent central banks and the latter is held to be incompatible with this model role of central banking – is misguiding. And, yet, the characterisation of the ECB's mandate along the model of a rules-based monetary policy continues to underpin the ECB's constitutional status of independence.

None of the above means, however, that legal substantive strictures are irrelevant to ascertain whether the ECB (or other bodies whose powers have the same functional characteristics) has acted within or outside its mandate. If constitutive powers only exist because legal norms can lawfully authorise their holders to act, legal norms must, to some extent at least, structure the way in which meaning will be given.[20] The concept of

[18] See below.

[19] Insofar as the conditions for the emergence of constitutive powers are linked to their functional nature, they raise similar problems to those elicited by de-politisation through knowledge-based institutions (M. Bartl, 'Internal Market Rationality, Private Law and the Direction of the Union: Resuscitating the Market as the Object of the Political', 21 *European Law Journal* 5 (2015), 572–598), and to the EU's purposive competences (G. Davies, 'Democracy and Legitimacy in the Shadow of Purposive Competence', 21 *European Law Journal* 1 (2015), 2–22). I am grateful to Mark Dawson for raising this point.

[20] In this sense, they are constituted powers (see, further, Mendes, note 12 above).

constitutive powers points, rather, to the concrete nature of the law that governs administrative and executive actions in the areas where they emerge. This law varies according to normative understandings of problem definition and on adequate responses generated in institutional settings where abiding by legal norms merges with the need to ensure the social acceptance of the interpretations and solutions that the administration adopts.[21] Without those normative understandings, which the administrative bodies translate into legal forms, legal norms would be inoperative. So, as much as a specific conception of the relationship between monetary and fiscal policy has underpinned the current Treaty framework and the norms that delimit the mandate of the ECB, also a different understanding of that relationship has enabled the ECB to claim – and the CJEU to ascertain – that its quantitative easing programmes are within its mandate of price stability. That such understandings are contested is something that the *Weiss* saga (as much as the *Gauweiler* judgments before) has clearly revealed to the legal world. But, in the specific circumstances in which it acted, that contestation did not prevent the ECB from acting according to the normative understandings that formed in its institutional environment in relation to the meaning and scope of monetary policy. It is noteworthy that this process is deeper and more complex from the often too easy criticism of competence creep. As much as constitutive powers may lead to expansive interpretations of the scope of an entity's mandate – as was the case with the ECB – they can be constitutive in exactly the opposite sense.[22] As I will explain next, the empowerment of the ECB does not necessarily follow from its constitutive powers.

### 13.2.4 A *Distinct Instance of Constitutive Powers*

Constitutive powers point to a relationship between law and administrative power that is different from accepted conceptions on the role of law in liberal democratic polities (a direction that requires further inquiry as to its legal and normative implications). Characterising the powers of the ECB as an instance of constitutive powers arguably helps approach in a more accurate way the question of the legality of its action. Yet, this proposed angle of analysis must not overshadow what is distinctive about the ECB's powers and their evolution.

[21] This specific confluence is noted in Rosanvallon, *La legitimité démocratique. Impartialité, reflexivité, proximité* (Paris: Seuil, 2008), 19–20.

[22] That is the case of the SRB, as argued in Mendes, note 12 above.

The ECB has the ability to control the means of money creation and to influence fundamentally the fiscal policy decisions of elected governments (as any central bank, given the interrelation between monetary and fiscal policy). This immense political power (in the sense of *potentia*) sets it apart from other administrative institutions. Compounded with constitutive powers, this trait manifestly makes it an excessively powerful institution and can only be constitutionally justified – if at all – if those powers can be subject to suitable forms of control. Its *potentia* allowed it to engage in an expansion of its mandate unimaginable when the ECB was set up in 1992.[23] In the political-economic context of the 2010s and in the very first years of the 2020s, the constitutive nature of its powers meant an unparalleled expansion of its monetary policy mandate, following an interpretation of its role, which at first it took on hesitantly, in the midst of the sovereign debt crisis (with the political support of national governments sitting in the Council), and is in the process of consolidating as a settled way of approaching its mandate. This is not the place to retell this story.[24] It is, however, important to underline, that the empowerment that the ECB has witnessed in the last decade is not a necessary consequence of the existence of constitutive powers.

That empowerment was only possible because of a complex combination of different economic and political circumstances that, while part of a broader change in central banking, raise specific constitutional and political difficulties in the EMU.[25] The very assessment of the legality or illegality of the ECB's quantitative easing programmes – whether they are still in the realm of monetary policy (whether legitimately or illegitimately) or, on the contrary, make illegal (and illegitimate) inroads into economic policy – is politically loaded (as the political curricula of some of the plaintiffs in *Gauweiler* and *Weiss* clearly show). Claiming, for instance, that – while the ECB's QE programmes were justified in the aftermath of the sovereign debt crisis and, hence, could be legally upheld as such – as soon as conditions of normality would be reached, the ECB needed to retreat to the narrow monetary policy mandate that it had pursued prior to the crisis, lest it being in breach of the Treaty, is entering a political battlefield. Here, legality is but one factor in a politico-economic (and also geo-strategic) discussion that touches on the very terms in which the EMU could be created in 1992.

23 On the distinction between *potentia* and *potestas*, see Loughlin, *Foundations of Public Law* (Oxford: Oxford University Press, 2010), 164–171.

24 See, inter alia, Borger, *The Currency of Solidarity: Constitutional Transformation During the Euro Crisis* (Cambridge: Cambridge University Press, 2020).

25 See, further, Tooze, *supra*, note 2.

That was the battlefield that the CJEU entered – almost inadvertently, it seems – with its *Weiss* judgment of 2019.[26] The legal dispute over the ECB's mandate reflects the fundamental mismatch between the 'new ECB' and the political-economic premises that underlie the Treaty's EMU rules.[27] Albeit not always explicitly, this is the background of the different conceptions of the ECB's normative role within the EMU, and of the boundaries of monetary policy, part of the ongoing debate that heated up considerably after the FCC's *Weiss* judgment in May 2020. The terms of the relationship between the two limbs of the ECB's mandate – the extent to which they are in tension, what the meaning and extent of 'support' may be and, hence, the degree of permissible economic intervention – depends largely on which political economy theory one advocates and on how the very design of the ECB mandate meant endorsing a specific political-economic conception of monetary policy (monetarism) and the rejection of another (Keynesianism). That, in turn, impacts on the ECB's independence and how it can be justified (or not) as democratically legitimate.[28] This background and the combination of constitutive powers and the political power (*potentia*) of the ECB account for much of the difficulties in finding a suitable degree of judicial review of the ECB's monetary policy, beyond the principled arguments that can be drawn from its technical expertise and its institutionally safeguarded independence.

## 13.3 THE DEGREE OF JUDICIAL REVIEW OF MONETARY POLICY: A VIRTUALLY UNRESOLVABLE CONUNDRUM?

Monetary policy is an area where few would expect judicial review, or at least that judicial review could have an impactful role. It touches on core aspects of how a society is organised, not least because it conditions how constitutionally protected public goods and fundamental rights can be delivered. Yet, the impact of monetary policy measures is 'generalised and indirect', which,

26 The judgment shows little if any awareness of the fundamental difference between *Gauweiler* – adjudicating measure announced in the height of a crisis as an emergency solution – and *Weiss* – whose object is a quantitative easing measure adopted in circumstances of normality.

27 The term 'new ECB' is taken from Beukers, 'The New ECB and its Relationship with the Member States of the Euro Area: Between Central Bank Independence and Central Bank Intervention', 50 *Common Market Law Review* (2013), 1579–1620.

28 See, among others, Chessa, *La Costituzione della Moneta* (Jovene, 2016) (showing how the ECB mandate meant casting away Keynesianism as a political-economic paradigm); de Boer and van't Klooster, 'The ECB, the Courts, and the Issue of Democratic Legitimacy after Weiss', 57 *Common Market Law Review* 6 (2020), 1693–1710; M. Dani et al., 'It's the Political Economy…! A Moment of Truth for the Eurozone and the EU', 19 *ICON* 1 (2021), 309–327.

in principle, precludes individual standing;[29] in addition, their institutional setting – entrusted to an independent central bank vertically detached from economic policies of Member States, and subject to very limited accountability by the EU and national parliaments – arguably makes direct litigation by institutional actors unlikely. In an article analysing the role of administrative law in relation to the US Federal Reserve, the authors noted the 'rarity of Fed litigation' and rightly pointed out that this is also a 'testament to the Fed's nearly unique power and autonomy'.[30]

However, like any other area where public authority is exercised, with the limited exception of *actes de gouvernement*, the possibility of judicial review is a tenet of the rule of law. In the EU, its significance is deeper. The structural principle of attributed competences makes the possibility of judicial review for the respect of the boundaries of the institutions' competences (ultra vires), in particular, a cornerstone of the whole EU construction. Of course, *how* that review is conducted matters to define the extent to which the Court will be having a say on how law can be deployed to delimit the powers that law conveys. In the case of monetary policy, behind the law stands not only the relative scope of action of Member States and of the EU institutions (the ECB and the Council coordinating economic policy) but also the tenability of the economists' rules-bound-view on monetary policy that underpins the mandate of the independent ECB. Such a view presumes that the ECB's monetary policy be kept strictly bound by economically defined yardsticks, poured into legal norms.[31]

### 13.3.1 *Neither Intrusion nor Deference: The Legal Implications of Full and of Limited Review in* Weiss

On the intensity of judicial review over the ECB's actions, the two courts' rulings on *Weiss* could possibly not be further apart (a disparity that the judgments in *Gauweiler* had already anticipated).[32] Like other aspects of the judicial dispute,

[29] Conti-Brown, *supra*, note 7 at p. 5, with reference to the US Federal Reserve.

[30] Idem, ibidem.

[31] According to the monetarist paradigm, the narrow legal mandate of the independent ECB confines it to price stability and makes this solution compatible with democratic legitimacy (which stems from the Treaty rules that delimit its authorisation to act); should there be the need for policing the boundaries of that mandate, another independent institution is there to make sure that rules are abided by, without interference from democratic politics.

[32] Cf. Gauweiler, *supra*, note 9 and German Federal Constitution Court (FCC) BverfG, Judgment of the Second Senate of 21 June 2016 – 2 BvR 2728/13. On the degree of judicial review, see, among others, Goldmann, 'Adjudicating Economics? Central Bank Independence and the Appropriate Standard of Judicial Review', 15 *German Law Journal* 265 (2014).

these differences have been extensively noted in the literature.[33] I take them up here again only to the extent necessary to illustrate the conundrum of judicial review in these matters; that will also point out the weaknesses of the critique addressed to the FCC's position and of the praise that the CJEU's judgment got.

The FCC applied what most commentators considered to be a too-stringent gauge incompatible with the discretion that a central bank must have in monetary policy. It did so by drawing on the principle of proportionality and by requiring that its third limb (proportionality *stricto sensu*) be applied to ascertain whether the limits of the ECB's monetary policy mandate had been breached.[34] In this way, on the one hand, the FCC took the consequences from the premises of the monetarist paradigm that the EMU rules enshrined, as it insisted that the ECB's narrow mandate be upheld as a matter of law and of democratic legitimacy.[35] On the other, it departed from that paradigm, because it demanded that the 'economic and social policy effects' of the ECB's measures, including the impact that 'a programme for the purchase of government bonds has on, for example, public debt, personal savings, pension and retirement schemes, real estate prices and the keeping afloat of economically unviable companies' be weighed 'against the monetary policy objective that the programme aims to achieve and is capable of achieving'.[36] Having found that the ECB had not proceeded in this way, it required that it conduct a proportionality assessment and demonstrate that the economic effects of its measures were not disproportionate. This outcome resulted in a difficult compromise between exercising full judicial review, which the FCC held necessary, and, at the same time, giving sufficient leeway to the scope of monetary policy decisions.[37] (Dis)proportionate to what exactly is something

[33] See, among many others, de Boer and van't Klooster, *supra*, note 28 above, 1710–1721. The different degrees of judicial review applied by both courts stem from the different premises of their reasoning regarding the delimitation of the ECB's mandate and its institutional position (the CJEU emphasised its independence, the FCC its diminished democratic legitimacy).

[34] FCC, Weiss, para 165, 173, 176 and 179. On why this is doctrinally problematic, see Feichtner, 'The German Constitutional Court's PSPP Judgment: Impediment and Impetus for the Democratization of Europe', 21 *German Law Journal* 5 (2020), 1097–1098; Marzal, 'Is the BVerfG PSPP Decision "Simply Not Comprehensible"', *VerfBlog* (2020), https://verfassungsblog.de/is-the-bverfg-pspp-decision-simply-not-comprehensible/; M. Wendel 'Paradoxes of 'Ultra-Vires Review: A Critical Review of the PSPP Decision and Its Initial Reception' 21 *German Law Journal* 5 (2020), 979–994.

[35] For a critique on how the defence of legality became a matter of democracy and can be an obstruction to democracy, see Feichtner, idem.

[36] FCC, Weiss, para 139. On how this departs from the monetarist paradigm, see de Boer and van't Klooster, *supra*, note 28, at p. 1717.

[37] FCC, Weiss, para 235. The ECB would act as a result of the German constitutional organs exercising their duty of monitoring the decisions of the Eurosystem, through their oversight of the Bundesbank participation therein (para 232 and 233).

that was not immediately clear (even if the judgment gave some hints in this regard).[38] The ECB needed in any event to '[identify], [weigh] and [balance] against one another' the monetary policy objective of its programme and its economic policy effects.[39] In the plentiful commentary that ensued after May 2020, very few agreed with the FCC's contention that full judicial review was due. Most pointed out that such a degree of review constrains the ECB to a specific way of acting and limits unduly the discretion that the Treaty gives it. The principle of proportionality, applied as the FCC requires, postulates a clear identification of the conflicting positions that must be weighed, something that is not possible in monetary policy.[40]

Be that as it may, the 'elephant in the room', when the discretion of the ECB is invoked in relation to the limits to judicial review, is what the ECB's discretion implies. Weighing different monetary policy alternatives in view of their economic policy effects is *not* a process that can be delimited by legal norms that identify the public interests to be protected or that specify thresholds of protection. It is a policy-making process where what price stability is and what it requires is defined at each point by the ECB itself (in coordination with political actors) and where various alternatives are open-ended. The lack of a concrete conflict prevents a balancing process that the full application of proportionality requires.[41] This argument has deeper consequences. The presumption that the legal norms could operate in this field and limit public authority as they do in other areas of public law does not hold. Or, put differently, to assume that the Treaty norms can constrain the policy process that the ECB must undertake – that is, that monetary policy can be rules-based as the monetarist paradigm presumes – necessarily restricts the ECB's scope of action in circumstances different from those that the Treaty framework envisaged. Indeed, proportionality is much more than a legal principle structuring the way to reach an outcome lawfully. How the FCC applied it presumes

38 The interests voiced in the procedure by the litigants and the experts heard (see de Boer and van't Klooster, n 27 above, 1720) sought to preserve the political-economic model that the Treaty enshrines. Preservation of the status quo means also maintaining the powers imbalances that it crystalises (see Feichtner, *supra*, note 34 above, at p. 1094).

39 FCC, Weiss, para 165.

40 Egidy, 'Proportionality and Procedure of Monetary Policy', 19 *International Journal of Constitutional Law* 1 (2021), 292–293, arguing (rightly) that the technique applied in fundamental rights' protection to identify disproportionate limitations can hardly be applied to force the consideration of alternative measures concerning competing public interests that are difficult to pin down. Pointing also to a misapplication of fundamental rights jurisprudence to matters of monetary and economic policy, Feichtner, *supra*, note 34, 1097.

41 Feichtner, idem, ibid., showing the difficulties in applying a proportionality test to determine the scope of the ECB's competences; and Egidy, *supra* note 40, 293. Egidy sees nevertheless the scope for the application of proportionality to monetary policy (294–296).

that it is both possible and legally needed to hold on to the limits that the monetarist paradigm of monetary policy determines and that are specified in the Treaty.[42]

From the opposite perspective to the one the FCC endorsed – that is, for those who defend that courts should not have a role in matters of monetary policy – the very existence of judicial review 'qualifies as bold judicial law-making' of the type that exceeds the boundaries of the judiciary function.[43] The fact that the CJEU is confronted with the need to adjudicate on such matters justifies *the* deferential approach to the ECB's exercise of discretion that the Court endorsed. Commentators were almost unanimous in this regard.[44] The two arguments invoked are, in the case of the ECB, overlapping and circular: the legal and technical competence of the ECB and its independence, which the Court must respect. The comparative advantage of the ECB's expertise is obviously uncontested. But this is a weak argument if not accompanied by a specification of what is special about monetary policy that prevents a more intense judicial review, for lack of expertise, which is possible in other areas where the Court also lacks expertise (where the correct interpretation of the law requires the Court to define, for example, if what financial stability requires in conditions of uncertainty falls within the mandate of the EU financial agencies or of its Single Resolution Board).[45] Independence and the way the Court had already delimited the boundaries of the ECB's mandate (by reference to the objectives and to the tools of monetary policy, in *Pringle* and *Gauweiler*) come to the rescue. Judicial review is necessarily limited because it cannot impinge on the Treaty-protected independence of the ECB; furthermore, as the Court had also already established in *Gauweiler* and in *Pringle*, foreseeable indirect economic effects of monetary policy do not affect the classification of a measure as monetary. The Treaty norms and the Court's case law, therefore, settle the issue of the degree of judicial review: deferential review limited to verifying whether manifest errors of assessment were committed (or, more specifically, *the* deference that the Court applied) is the only possible way of controlling the legality of the ECB's action. That is consonant with the need to preserve the space of manoeuvre that the ECB

42 See, further, Dani et al. *supra* note 28.

43 Mayer, 'The Ultra Vires Ruling: Deconstructing the German Federal Constitutional Court's PSPP Decision of 5 May 2020', 16 *European Constitutional Law Review* (2020), 733–769, at p. 752, noting that 'this … is a step which the Federal Constitutional Court was never prepared to take in relation to the Bundesbank. There is no case of judicial review of Bundesbank action'.

44 See, however, Dani et al. *supra*, note 28.

45 On those specificities, in relation to the difficulties of applying the principle of proportionality, see Egidy, *supra*, note 40.

must have to adapt its instruments to varying circumstances.[46] In this reading, the Court suitably attuned the application of proportionality to how it can operate in an area of limited judicial review, in accordance with its standard of review in instances of discretion.[47] The Court was, therefore, right in holding that 'nothing more can be required of the European System of Central Banks (ESCB) apart from that it use its economic expertise and the necessary technical means at its disposal to carry out that analysis with all care and accuracy'.[48]

This position, however, fails to acknowledge that the way the CJEU reviewed the ECB's programmes, in light of its discretion means de facto a blanket authorisation to the ECB that only gives legal anchoring to its *potentia*. The lack of clarity of what are the interests that must be put in proportion in a proportionality assessment does not only taint the third limb of proportionality that the FCC wrongly applied to an exercise of a competence and that the CJEU rightly omitted from its judgment.[49] It turns proportionality into a 'free-standing ground of review' that obfuscates what the Court is doing when applying this principle. 'Free-standing ground of review' – a term coined by Kosta – allows the Court to invoke the principle without actually conducting a proportionality assessment, because it does not balance conflicting interests.[50] That was the critique of the FCC to the CJEU's *Weiss* judgment, when pointing out the difficulty in identifying which opposing interests the CJEU had considered and weighed.[51] More than applying low-intensity review, the judgment meant an outright deferral to the economic expertise of the ECB.[52] In fact, what the CJEU allowed for was what the FCC had already critiqued in its *Gauweiler* judgment in 2016: it enabled the ECB to 'decide autonomously upon the scope of [its] competences'.[53] That much is confirmed by the assumption that when the ECB acts in controversial monetary policy it must only deploy with care and accuracy its *expertise*, which either is implicitly considered to be neutral to the political consequences of its measures, or, at least, necessarily incorporates their economic consequences (however classified).[54] Combined with the judicial interpretation of the delimitation of monetary policy, the result is that it is

46 CJEU, Weiss, para 63.

47 CJEU, Weiss, para 73, 78 and 81 [cite commentaries].

48 CJEU, Weiss, para 91 (already in Gauweiler, para 75).

49 But see, above, text accompanying note 16.

50 Kosta, 'The Principle of Proportionality in EU Law: An Interest-Based Taxonomy', in Mendes (ed.), *EU Executive Discretion and the Limits of Law* (OUP, 2019) 198, 213–219, arguing that this was what happened in *Gauweiler* (idem, 215–218).

51 FCC, Weiss, 132.

52 As argued in Dani et al., *supra*, note 28, at p. 319.

53 FCC, Weiss, para 134, citing its *Gauweiler* judgment of 21 June 2016, para 136.

54 CJEU, Weiss, para 91.

virtually impossible to judicially prevent possible abuses of law by the ECB.[55] Ultimately, we are before an instance of judicial abdication.[56]

### 13.3.2 *Beyond the Semblance of Judicial Review*

When applied to monetary policy, both full and limited reviews have difficulties that ultimately make them untenable. The judgment showed, thereby, the weaknesses of judicial accountability in this field. In very different ways, both degrees of review amounted only to a semblance of judicial review (as much as this critique appears counter-intuitive when applied to the FCC's judgment).[57] At the risk of oversimplifying the intricacies of both judgments, their result in terms of a court's ability to control the action of a central bank is comparable. They both acted as if their arguments and tools of review could constrain the actions of the ECB to patterns of legality that, at the end, are defined by the ECB itself, given its constitutive powers.

The CJEU sanctioned the 'whatever it takes' famously pronounced by Draghi in 2012. It had done so in *Gauweiler* and took the same position, in very different circumstances – and less comprehensibly – in *Weiss*, when the programme under scrutiny was not a response to an emergency. The FCC, in turn, ultimately took a decision that, as mentioned above, was, at best, an awkward compromise between stringent review and needed leeway of executive action.[58] The way out was merely procedural. The *Bundesbank* was prohibited from partaking in the PSPP, unless within three months, the ECB Governing Council would adopt 'a new decision that demonstrates in a comprehensible and substantiated manner that the monetary policy objectives pursued by the ECB are not disproportionate to the economic and fiscal policy effects resulting from the programme'.[59] This result contrasted starkly with the FCC's spectacular clash with the CJEU and with its harsh critique of the latter's judgment. Indeed, most commentators, writing and speaking in the immediate aftermath of the judgment, did not expect *any* substantial impact of the *Weiss* judgment on the ECB's monetary policy.[60] The reasons invoked were mostly of constitutional nature: the ECB is outside of the FCC's jurisdiction and the intricate way – if

55 In this sense, FCC, Weiss, para 137. But see the criteria that the CJEU set for the legality of monetary policy instruments, in particular in relation to the prohibition of monetary financing (Article 123 TFEU).

56 Violante, 'Bring Back the Politics: The PSPP Ruling in Its Institutional Context', 21 *German Law Journal* 5 (2020), 2053.

57 See, further, Dani et al., *supra*, note 28, 318–321.

58 See note 36 above.

59 FCC, Weiss, para 235.

60 On this same note, Feichtner, *supra*, note 34, at p. 1091.

not flawed, as most argued – through which the FCC arrived at its conclusion could not, for legal and political reasons, have a bearing on the ECB.[61]

But there was another critique to the judgment's outcome: what the FCC required could easily be met. By collecting information that was even in the public domain, the ECB could satisfy the FCC's demand for proportionality. It only needed to channel that information institutionally to the German government and parliament and all would be settled. Why then risk a constitutional crisis at the worst possible moment?[62] Both in institutional and in academic circles, the outcome of the judgment was seen as simply entailing the transmission of information. As soon as the judicial storm would pass, no far-reaching consequences to the actions of the ECB would be longer visible. That was, in fact, what happened.[63] What was, in substance, a major disagreement (with potentially immense constitutional consequences) on the way that a reviewing court should mobilise proportionality as an instrument of either full or limited review had no bearing in legal and policy terms. The result, in short, was a clear failure of substantive accountability through judicial control. This conclusion, in turn, also means that the association between full review with substantial accountability, on the one hand, and limited review with procedural accountability, on the other, hides more than it reveals.[64]

[61] The institutional reactions to the judgment buttressed this position (e.g. ECB, 'ECB takes note of German Federal Constitutional Court ruling and remains fully committed to its mandate', 5 May 2020, available at www.ecb.europa.eu/press/pr/date/2020/html/ecb.pr200505~00a09107a9.en.html; more exceptionally, CJEU, 'Press release following the judgment of the German Constitutional Court of 5 May 2020' 8 May 2020, available at https://curia.europa.eu/jcms/upload/docs/application/pdf/2020-05/cp200058en.pdf).

[62] The worst moment referred both to the PEPP, whose legality was controversial but all recognised to be essential to face the economic consequences of the pandemic, and to the bad signal that the FCC was giving to the EU's constitutional outliers, Hungary and Poland (see, among others, Sarmiento, 'An Infringement Action Against Germany After Its Constitutional Court's Ruling in Weiss? The Long Term and the Short Term', EULawLive, https://eulawlive.com/op-ed-an-infringement-action-against-germany-after-its-constitutional-courts-ruling-in-weiss-the-long-term-and-the-short-term-by-daniel-sarmiento/; Biernat, 'How Far Is It from Warsaw to Luxembourg and Karlsruhe: The Impact of the PSPP Judgment on Poland', 21 *German Law Journal* (2020), 1104–1115).

[63] See 'Account of the monetary policy meeting of the Governing Council of the European Central Bank held in Frankfurt am Main on Wednesday and Thursday, 3–4 June 2020', under 'Monetary policy stance and policy considerations' (at www.ecb.europa.eu/press/accounts/2020/html/ecb.mg200625~fd97330d5f.en.html); 'Weidmann sieht Forderungen des Verfassungsgerichts als erfüllt an', Frankfurter Allgemeine Zeitung, 3 August 2020 (at www.faz.net/aktuell/finanzen/jens-weidmann-verfassungsgerichtsurteil-zur-ezb-erfuellt-16887907.html).

[64] For a proposal of how process-based judicial review should bridge the procedural-substantive divide and become 'justification-enhancing', see Gerstenberg, 'The Uncertain Structure of Process Review in the EU: Beyond the Debate on the CJEU's Weiss Ruling and the German Federal Constitutional Court's PSPP Ruling', *Just Cogens* 3 (2021), 279–301.

Few noted the significance of its judgment laid elsewhere: the FCC had disclosed the deeper constitutional difficulties that the ECB's action raised for the construction of the EMU.[65] In terms of accountability, the judgment's immediate outcome was significant, even if admittedly not consequential (at least in the short-term) for the conduct of monetary policy: the FCC had referred the question back to the political institutions.[66] So, even if both judgments had shown, in opposing ways, that neither full review nor limited review may be suitable means to control monetary policy, each pointed in a very different direction. While the CJEU empowered the ECB, the FCC stressed the importance of vertical checks by politically accountable institutions.

One question, however, remained unanswered. If the courts have, at the end, little to say in monetary policy matters – either because of the way they interpret the substantive mandates or because of the unsuitability of the tools that can deploy to contain legally the executive action of central banks – can law have a role in structuring and limiting the action of ECB? The answer is positive, but it is far from being straightforward. One must search for legal strictures that must be present irrespective of judicially generated or judicially enforced duties.

## 13.4 THE DUTY TO GIVE REASONS

### 13.4.1 *Reasons in Weiss*

The FCC censored both a 'lack of balancing and [a] lack of stating the reasons' by the ECB.[67] The German government and the German parliament had failed, as a result, to take suitable measures against the ECB's Governing Council. They had 'neither assessed nor substantiated' whether the PSPP was compliant with EU law.[68] If the problem was one of proportionality, it was compounded with insufficient documentation and communication of the balancing act that the ECB needs to undertake between the monetary and the economic policy consequences of its actions. In addition to stressing the importance of political accountability in matters of monetary policy, the FCC had also pointed to the relevance of the duty to give reasons. But beneath the fury of criticism it received, these strengths of the judgment were mostly ignored.

65 Dani et al., *supra*, note 28.
66 On the second point, Violante, *supra*, note 56, at p. 1053, pointing out the role of national constitutional courts.
67 FCC, Weiss, para 176 and 177.
68 FCC, Weiss, para 116.

It is hardly surprising that the relevance of the duty to give reasons went largely unnoticed. While in EU law it is a constitutional requirement applicable to all legal acts of the institutions, it is often dismissed as a routine practice without significant legal consequences or much noteworthy controversy. It is often invoked in judicial litigation, but hardly ever leads to pronouncements of breach capable of leading to the annulation of the legal act. That is largely due to the balanced approach to the duty of reason-giving that the EU Courts have developed and refined over the decades.[69] According to the formula that the Court also cited in *Weiss*, the statement of reasons

> must show clearly and unequivocally the reasoning of the author of the measure in question, so as to enable *the persons concerned* to ascertain the reasons for the measure and to enable *the Court* to exercise its power of review, [but] it is not required to go into every relevant point of fact and law.[70]

In this way, the Court 'proceduralises rationality' and attunes its demands to each litigious situation, considering the need of effective judicial protection in each case.[71] Accordingly, the EU Courts consistently emphasise that the specific requirements of the duty to give reasons depend on the circumstances of each legal act, in particular, on the substance and wording of the measure, the nature of the reasons given, the interests that the persons directly and individually concerned may have in obtaining explanations, the context of the measure, and 'the whole body of rules governing the matter in question'.[72] This flexibility built into the duty allows the Courts to modulate their degree of review of compliance with this duty and to avoid the slippery step of turning the review of a procedural requirement into a review of the substantive legality of the act.[73] It also allows them to adapt a duty that applies indistinctly to all the legal acts of the institutions to their legal effects, for example, by distinguishing the scope of the duty to state reasons of an individual measure and of a measure intended to have general application.[74] All this mirrors the function

69 On this, see further, Mendes, 'The Foundations of the Duty to Give Reasons and a Normative Reconstruction', in E. Fisher, J. King and A. Young (eds.), *The Foundations and Future of Public Law* (OUP, 2020), 299–321, 308–109. The analysis that follows has been developed first in this piece, from where the materials cited are taken.

70 CJEU, Weiss, para 31, emphasis added.

71 The term is from Mashaw, *Reasoned Administration and Democratic Legitimacy. How Administrative Law Supports Democratic Government* (CUP, 2018), at p. 117.

72 CJEU, Weiss, para 33, which does not include the specification of all these parameters but follows this same line (for those, see, among many, Case C-15/10, *Etimine v Secretary of State for Work and Pensions*, EU:C:2011:504, para 114, or Case T-122/15, *Landeskreditbank v ECB*, EU:T:2017:337 para 124).

73 P. Craig, *EU Administrative Law*, 3rd ed. (OUP, 2018), 318–320.

74 As reflected in CJEU, Weiss, para 32.

that the duty to give reasons has in judicial proceedings. It operates as a norm of control, which, as the case law indicates, is instrumental for two purposes: to enable *the persons concerned* to ascertain the reasons for the measure and to enable *the Court* to exercise its power of review.[75]

### 13.4.2 *Reasons and Integration: Constitutional Foundations*

In EU law, however, this duty has a deeper constitutional foundation, which gives it a different political significance and generates different legal implications from those that the case law normally expresses. The general duty to give reasons was meant also to enable 'Member States and (…) all interested nationals [to ascertain] the circumstances in which the [institutions have] applied the Treaty'.[76] While related to the need to afford legal protection to persons concerned (eventually through judicial review), this function was distinct from this strictly protective dimension of the duty to give reasons. It was justified because of the limited (attributed) competences of the supranational institutions whose powers had the capacity to constrain the sovereignty of the Member States.

More deeply, in the case of the ECSC, the requirement that the Community ought to 'publish the reasons for its actions' was enshrined in a provision where the *functions* of the Community were outlined (Article 5 ECSC Treaty) and then specified as a legal duty of the High Authority (Article 15 ECSC Treaty). A systematic interpretation of Article 5 ECSC shows that there was an intrinsic link between the transparency that ought to derive from a statement of reasons and the action of the Community's institutions, in particular of the High Authority at its core.[77] That the whole Community needed to be a 'glass house' was one of the foundational blocks of the integration process.[78] It was a means of ensuring the acceptance and cooperation of the natural and legal persons subject to the authority of the High Authority and, crucially of the Member States. Politically, without persuading through reasons, the Community would fail. Legally, if the acts of the High Authority needed to be the expression of the objectives of integration set in Article 3 ECSC (binding on the institutions), the statement of reasons was the means

[75] Note 70 above.

[76] Case 24/62, *Germany v Commission* :EU:C:1963:14, 69; Joined Cases 36, 37, 38–59 and 40/59, *Präsident et al. v High Authority*, EU:C:1960:36 439. What is stated in this paragraph is analysed in detail in Mendes, *supra*, note 68, pp. 309–313.

[77] Mendes, *supra*, note 69, pp. 311–312.

[78] Reuter, *La Communauté Européenne du Charbon et de l'Acier* (LGDJ, 1953) 76, cited in Mendes, idem, ibidem.

to enable a judgment on whether that legal bound was respected. Importantly, those passing that judgment were 'the Member States and (...) all interested nationals' who could thus ascertain 'the circumstances in which the [institutions have] applied the Treaty'.[79]

The political and legal significance of this public understanding (still visible in institutional litigation over the correct use of a legal basis) was overshadowed by how the Court developed the duty to give reasons as a norm of control (suitable for purposes of judicial review of legal acts involving discretion).[80] Nevertheless, the duty to give reasons was constitutionally, first and above all, 'a guarantee against arbitrary action, by enabling *the public to understand and investigate the actions of the executive invested with important powers*'.[81] Its purpose was, hence, to ensure substantive accountability, that is, to demonstrate how the choices made by the institutions 'plausibly aimed for and achieved non-arbitrary results'.[82] Importantly, it should ensure the ability of the public to pass that judgment. Of course, this referred to the knowledgeable public, who could have standing before the court (and, possibly, political weight within their Member States). But, nevertheless, the public understanding that the statement of reasons ought to facilitate would allow the High Authority to avert the 'hostility of certain milieus[,] [those who] had expressed an accusation all the more formidable as obscure of "technocracy", evoking the intervention of tenebrous powers, which in the modern political mythology have replaced the ancient gods'.[83] Not least, the political accountability that the duty served could – and should – be exerted by the parliamentary assembly, which at the time was, nevertheless, a rather weak institution.

This constitutional understanding of the duty to give reasons must be revived for today's EU, given that the scope of duty to give reasons was broadened by the Lisbon Treaty, the same Treaty that introduced modifications intended to establish a 'more institutionally solid, democratic and citizen-oriented foundation' of the Union.[84] Such revival is particularly needed in the instances

79 See note 75 above.

80 Mendes, *supra*, note 69, pp. 313–314.

81 Joined Cases 36, 37, 38–59 and 40–59, *Präsident et al. v High Authority*, Opinion AG Lagrange, at 451(emphasis added), cited and analysed in Mendes, idem, ibidem.

82 Dawson and Maricut-Akbik, in this book (text after fn 83).

83 Reuter, *La Communauté Européenne du Charbon et de L'Acier* (LGDJ, 1953), p. 52 (cited in Mendes, 'The Foundations of the Duty to Give Reasons and a Normative Reconstruction', in Fisher, King and Young (eds.), *The Foundations and Future of Public Law* (OUP, 2020), at p. 314).

84 Craig, *The Lisbon Treaty. Law, Politics and Treaty Reform* (OUP, 2010), pp. 71–77 and 247. The cited expression is from Calliess and Rüffert, *EUV/AEUV: das Verfassungsrecht der Europäischen Union mit Europäischer Grundrechtecharta* (München: Beck, 5th ed, 2016), Article 296, pt 4.

in which its executive bodies can have constitutive powers, as is the case of the ECB. Justification, as a guarantee of substantive accountability, must then reflect the balancing of competing interests involved in decision-making and show how different groups and interests are advantaged and disadvantaged by a non-arbitrary decision.[85] That is a necessary component of generation of the public interests that the decision embodies, in relation to the legal framework in which it is embedded. It is, in other words, a necessary part of the exercise of constitutive powers and must be controllable as such. However, it is, arguably, not the task of the court reviewing the legality of judicially contested measures to enforce this constitutional dimension of the duty to give reasons. That must be primarily realised by the deciding body and by its political overseers.

### 13.4.3 *Reasons as a Norm of Conduct*

The constitutional foundation and function of the duty to give reasons means that, beyond the judicially suitable way in which the EU Courts review compliance with this duty, a statement of reasons must enable a public understanding of how public action of the EU institutions is contributing to achieve the objectives of EU integration, as interpreted at each point in accordance with the political priorities set by the competent bodies. From the same perspective, compliance with the duty to give reasons must enable a judgment of the compromise achieved between competing public interests, of the choices made by the decision-maker when defining a specific course of action, established in articulation with (and, hence, constituting) the legally defined purposes. Although this resonates strongly with a proportionality assessment (not surprisingly the duty to give reasons and proportionality often operate in tandem), it is not the same as proportionality. Showing the compromises achieved between competing public interests may be made through a proportionality assessment or not; per se, it does require that the balancing be conducted in the specific terms that the principle of proportionality mandates (in the EU legal order, or in the legal order of any of its Member States).

From this perspective, the statement of reasons is not primarily a means 'to enable *the persons concerned* to ascertain the reasons for the measure and to enable *the Court* to exercise its power of review', as it is in the hand of courts, where it must be applied with care to avoid turning a procedural requirement into a substantive review of the adequacy of the reasons given.[86] It does not

85 Dawson and Maricut-Akbik, in this book (paragraph after fn 82).

86 See note 71 above. That care is a constant note in the case law and reflected also in Weiss, para 30 to 33.

function as a norm of control, but as a norm of conduct: it is part of the process of normative concretisation inherent in decision-making and, as such, it provides the decision-maker with criteria of action, among others (economic models and parameters, efficacy, political convenience, non-binding international standards).[87] While being externally binding, it functions as a self-regulatory measure for the deciding body, an instrument to facilitate a substantiated judgment of the conditions, criteria and implications of the acts it adopts, in articulation with the purposes of legal action as defined in the enabling norms. It is also an essential part of its institutional duty of cooperation that the deciding institutions owe to those that, in a democratic polity, must hold them to account: they must make such process explicit to facilitate the action of their political overseers.[88] As such, the duty to give reasons, understood in this way, places a specific demand to decision-makers when at stake is the adoption of potentially or knowingly controversial measures, such as the quantitative easing programmes of the ECB. Compliance with the duty to give reasons must allow the political institutions to contest, where needed, measures of a controversial nature, that is, it is an essential condition of accountability and it must facilitate it. In the case of the monetary policy measures adopted by the ECB, controversial or not, the constitutional duty to give reasons requires the ECB to show, in its decision-making process, to the Member States and to the European Parliament (as well as to national parliaments, insofar as the economic policy of the Member States is implicated) how the public interests it needs to balance are being concretised, how it reconciles the conflicts among them, in view of the priorities they set in given economic circumstances, and the substantive implications of such balancing and priorities. Taking this position, however, requires a straightforward admission of the unavoidable political dimension of the technical competence of the ECB, which is still only hesitantly recognised – despite the evolution of the past decade – in particular by the EU institutions and by the Member States. It requires admitting that the ECB has constitutive powers that allow it to construe its own mandate and to give meaning to price stability, by mobilising its expertise.

As I argued elsewhere, with reference to the work of Jerry Mashaw, as a norm of conduct the duty to give reasons must reflect a decision-making process that makes legal acts 'a plausible instance of rational collective action', in

[87] On this distinction and definition, see Rodriguez de Santiago, *Metodología del Derecho Administrativo. Reglas de racionalidad para la adopción y el control de la decision administrativa* (Marcial Pons, 2016), pp. 24–25.

[88] Article 13(2) TEU ('The institutions shall practice mutual sincere cooperation') read in coordination with Article 10(1) and (2) TEU arguably give textual support to a legal duty as proposed in the text.

relation to the substantive yardsticks that the applicable norms define.[89] It also establishes a suitable threshold to allow a meaningful political control. The independent ECB is not exempted from this dimension of the duty to give reasons that flow from the Treaty framework, as ascertained by the origins of the duty to give reasons and extrapolated to a Union purportedly based on democracy. The fact that this dimension of the duty to give reasons has not been concretised through judicial actions does not make it less relevant in EU law. It is a *legal duty*, which must be enforced as such by the EU institutions that may hold the ECB *politically* accountable. Being too bound by the Treaties, the European Council, the Council and the European Parliament – the EU's representative institutions (Article 10(2) TEU) – must develop mechanisms that ensure that the constitutional dimension of the duty to give reasons comes to bear in EU's institutional practice, for the sake of the public understanding that this duty was initially intended to convey, albeit, of course, in the very different institutional environment of the EU. It is, arguably, this legal *and* political path that must be developed to ensure that the ECB is subject to substantive accountability, that the 'normative goods' of non-arbitrariness can actually be achieved, and that its actions can actually be 'probed and contested' (in the sense of 'substantive openness' that Dawson and Maricut-Akbik suggest in the introduction to this book).[90] While the incentives need to induce such a change must not necessarily come from judicial review, clearly the CJEU has also an institutional responsibility in this regard.

At this point, it is pertinent to return to its monetary policy judgments. Referring to the contested nature of the ECB programmes it assessed (the OMT and the PSPP), the CJEU was right to assert both in *Gauweiler* and in *Weiss* that 'the fact that a reasoned analysis is disputed does not, in itself, suffice to establish a manifest error of assessment on the part of the ESCB'.[91] This makes sense from the perspective of a court that adopts a standard of limited review to protect the discretion of the ECB. But it was wrong – straightforwardly wrong, given the political and legal implications of the expansion of the ECB's mandate – to assert, in the same paragraph, that 'nothing more can be required of the ESCB apart from that it use its economic expertise and the necessary technical means at its disposal to carry out that analysis with

[89] Mashaw, 'Public Reason and Administrative Legitimacy' in Bell, Elliot, Varuhas and Murray (eds.), *Public Law Adjudication in Common Law Systems. Process and Substance* (Hart, 2016), pp. 11–22, at 17. See too Mashaw, *supra*, note 71, pp. 158–159, arguing that political reasons ought to be given by administrators in connection to both statutorily defined criteria of judgment and other legal sources of public values (such as the Constitution).

[90] I borrow 'normative goods' from them.

[91] Gauweiler, para 75 and Weiss, para 91.

all care and accuracy'.[92] This passage both reveals and confirms that limited review was, in this case, a hands-off approach with unlimited deference to the ECB's economic expertise (a judicial version of sorts of 'whatever it takes'). As the analysis on the duty to give reasons indicates, in *legal* terms, there is much more to expect from the ECB, even if the role of courts in reviewing monetary policy measures is limited. In a legal system grounded on law – a law that purportedly must have democratic origins or endorsement – law must have a structuring role in the exercise of public authority, even when the nature of the policy field limits considerably the possibilities of control being exerted through courts. Even if courts cannot enforce certain dimensions of the law, they must not dismiss them.

## 13.5 NOT A FIX TO THE EMU CONSTITUTIONAL CHALLENGES

The reconstruction of the duty to give reasons proposed here draws both on its origins in EU law and on the constitutional framework in which it is now inserted. It shows that the duty to give reasons has an action-guiding role that must facilitate public understanding of how executive action is shaping the public interests that EU executive bodies are mandated to pursue. This is a function of the duty that has been hitherto neglected in EU law and that is particularly pertinent in instances in which the EU executive bodies exercise constitutive powers, as the ECB does. Understood as a norm of conduct, the duty to give reasons defines thresholds of justification different from those required by the Court when applying it as a norm of control in instances where discretion is exercised. The justification that EU law requires from its institutions is primarily a function of the political accountability that also the ECB must be subject to, its independence notwithstanding. This reconstruction shows that law has a life beyond justiciability, to paraphrase an expression of a former EU Ombudsman referring to good administration.[93] It provides yet another 'fix' to the conundrum that the ECB poses since it became a 'runaway institution' that can de facto define the limits of its own mandate.[94]

[92] Idem, ibidem.

[93] Characterised as having 'a life beyond legality' ('Legality and good administration: is there a difference?', Speech by the European Ombudsman, Nikiforos Diamandouros, at the Sixth Seminar of National Ombudsmen of EU Member States and Candidate Countries on 'Rethinking Good Administration in the European Union', Strasbourg, France, 15 October 2007, available at www.ombudsman.europa.eu/en/speech/en/370).

[94] I owe the expression 'runaway institution' to my colleague Anna-Lena Högenauer.

This chapter indicates a way to delimit the role of law in structuring the exercise of executive powers that goes beyond the role that the Courts can have in relation to monetary policy matters. Whether it is possible to devise a degree of judicial review, that runs neither the risk of doing too much, nor of doing too little, is a question that is most likely to occupy lawyers for a long time to come. No matter the outcome of this debate, its contribution to the democratic legitimacy conundrum of the ECB is likely to be very limited, if any.[95] Constraining the ECB back into the substantive limits that the Treaty enshrines means pining it down to a political-economic programme that, while politically and technically contested today, remains de jure outside the realm of democratic contestation. Admitting that the ECB can continue acting as it has in the past decade without a Treaty change is to perpetuate zombie rules and the power imbalances that they enshrine, at the expense of leaving the determination of such rules to processes consonant with democratic constitutionalism.[96]

From this perspective, also the path proposed in this chapter cannot be a fix to the constitutional challenges that the EMU poses. The reconstruction of the duty to give reasons presented here can only provide a limited contribution to improve its political accountability, for which law can and must contribute. With the meaning proposed here, accountability through the duty to give reasons carries a 'promise of control' because it enhances the possibilities of parliamentary scrutiny and political contestation over the changed role of the ECB and the new interpretations of the law that enable it. It does not carry a 'promise of democracy'.[97] Yet, it is clear that the ECB's accountability must not be understood as a voluntary exercise.[98] Independence does not shelter the ECB from a duty to give reasons that in EU law is more far-reaching than usually assumed. If judicial review must in principle be confined to the procedural vein of the duty to give reasons, the historical reconstruction of this duty's rationale shows that, outside of the court, the duty must be understood as a substantive *legal* stricture that ought to enable political control over the decisions of the ECB, its independence notwithstanding. Justification that permits contestation does not mean that the ECB must follow the views of its political controllers, even if it presumes that the ECB be responsive to the political implications of their decisions.[99] Admittedly, this is a difficult line

[95] On this conundrum and arguing that judicial review is not a suitable way of accountability from a perspective of democracy, see de Boer and van't Klooster, *supra*, note 28, pp. 1693–1710.

[96] Dani et al., *supra*, note 28.

[97] On these terms, see the Dawson and Maricut-Akbik in this book.

[98] As it is largely understood, see also Dawson and Maricut-Akbik in this book.

[99] See, in this sense, Dawson and Maricut-Akbik (text at fn 34).

to draw. Yet, the analysis above shows that, in what concerns the duty to give reasons, there is no legal necessity to the limited procedural accountability of the ECB.[100] On the contrary, that status quo currently results from the limited understanding of the scope of the duty to give reasons that judicial review conveys and, presumably, is shared in institutional practice. The constitutional dimension of the duty to give reasons highlighted here, if developed institutionally, may secure public-interest-based executive action understood in substantive terms, even if independence places clear limits to the ability of political accountability to induce substantive policy changes.

But, if the analysis in this chapter changes nothing to the premise that remains at the core of the EMU – monetary policy must be withdrawn from the realm of democratic politics – the characterisation of the ECB's powers as constitutive shows more than just how the law can operate in monetary policy beyond judicial review. It points to the democratic stakes of the decisions that are adopted in this policy field, to the inevitable political character of the ECB's monetary policy, and hence, to the constitutional difficulties of keeping it in the hands of an institution as strongly independent as the ECB.

100 Specifically in what concerns the duty to give reasons, the finding that procedural accountability dominates in matters of monetary policy currently holds (Dawson and Maricut-Akbik in this book).

# Index

www.ingramcontent.com/pod-product-compliance
Lightning Source LLC
LaVergne TN
LVHW091525200926
848483LV00002B/307
* 9 7 8 1 0 0 9 2 2 8 8 3 1 *